Paul Among Jews

Paul Among Jews

A Study of the Meaning and Significance of Paul's Inaugural Sermon in the Synagogue of Antioch in Pisidia (Acts 13:16–41) for His Missionary Work among the Jews

WENXI ZHANG

WIPF & STOCK · Eugene, Oregon

PAUL AMONG JEWS
A Study of the Meaning and Significance of Paul's Inaugural Sermon in the Synagogue of Antioch in Pisidia (Acts 13:16–41) for His Missionary Work among the Jews

Copyright © 2011 Wenxi Zhang. All rights reserved. Except for brief quotations in critical publications or reviews, no part of this book may be reproduced in any manner without prior written permission from the publisher. Write: Permissions, Wipf and Stock Publishers, 199 W. 8th Ave., Suite 3, Eugene, OR 97401.

Wipf & Stock
An Imprint of Wipf and Stock Publishers
199 W. 8th Ave., Suite 3
Eugene, OR 97401
www.wipfandstock.com

ISBN 13: 978-1-61097-295-6

Manufactured in the U.S.A.

All scripture quotations, unless otherwise indicated, are taken from the Holy Bible, New International Version®, NIV®. Copyright ©1973, 1978, 1984 by Biblica, Inc.™ Used by permission of Zondervan. All rights reserved worldwide.

Contents

Abbreviations vii
Preface xi

1. A History of Research 1
2. The Literary Function of Jesus' Inaugural Sermon (Luke 4:16–30) 34
3. The Literary Function of Peter's Inaugural Sermon (Acts 2:14–40) 65
4. Paul's Inaugural Sermon to the Jews in Antioch of Pisidia in Acts 13:16–41 110
5. The Significance of Paul's Inaugural Sermon for Understanding His Ministry to Israel 152
6. Conclusion 191

Bibliography 203
Scripture Index 225
Subject/Name Index 243

List of Abbreviations

AB	Anchor Bible
ACFEB	Association catholique française pour l'étude de la Bible
ACNT	Augsburg Commentary on the New Testament
AnBib	Analecta biblica
ANTC	Abingdon New Testament Commentaries
ANTJ	Arbeiten zum Neuen Testament und Judentum
BAFCS	The Book of Acts in Its First Century Setting
BAR	*Biblical Archaeologist Reader*
BBB	Bonner Biblische Beiträge
BBR	*Bulletin for Biblical Research*
BETL	Bibliotheca Ephemeridum theologicarum Lovaniensium
Bib	*Biblica*
BSac	*Bibliotheca Sacra*
BTB	*Biblical Theological Bulletin*
BWA(N)T	Beiträge zur Wissenschaft vom Alten und Neuen Testament
BZNW	Beihefte zur Zeitschrift für die neutestamentliche Wissenschaft
CahRB	*Cahiers de la Revue biblique*
CBQ	*Catholic Biblical Quarterly*
ConNT	Coniectanea neotestamentica
CTM	*Currents in Theology and Mission*
EBib	Études bibliques
ETL	*Ephemerides theologicae Lovanienses*

ExpTim	*Expository Times*
FB	Forschung zur Bibel
FilolNT	*Fiologia neotestamentaria*
FRLANT	Forschungen zur Religion und Literatur des Alten und Neuen Testaments
HTR	*Harvard Theological Review*
ICC	International Critical Commentary
Int	*Interpretation*
JBL	*Journal of Biblical Literature*
JETS	*Journal of the Evangelical Theological Society*
JSNT	*Journal for the Study of the New Testament*
JSNTSup	Journal for the Study of the New Testament Supplement Series
JSOT	Journal for the Study of the Old Testament
JSOTSup	Journal for the Study of the Old Testament Supplement Series
JTS	*Journal of Theological Studies*
KEK	Kritisch-exegetischer Kommentar über das Neue Testament (Meyer-Kommentar)
LD	Lectio Divina
May	*Mayéutica*
Neot	*Neotestamentica*
NICNT	New International Commentary on the New Testament
NJBC	R. E. Brown et al. (eds.), *New Jerome Biblical Commentary*
NovT	*Novum Testamentum*
NTG	New Testament Guides
NTS	*New Testament Studies*
NTT	New Testament Theology
PD	Parole de Dieu
RB	*Revue biblique*

RTP	*Revue de théologie et de philosophie*
SacPag	Sacra Pagina
SBB	Stuttgarter biblische Beiträge
SBLBSNA	SBL, Biblical Scholarship in North America
SBLDS	SBL Dissertation Series
SBLMS	Society of Biblical Literature Monograph Series
SBLSP	*Society of Biblical Literature Seminar Papers*
SBLSymS	SBL Symposium Series
ScrB	*Scripture Bulletin*
Sem	*Semitica*
SJLA	Studies in Judaism in Late Antiquity
SNTSMS	Society for New Testament Studies Monograph Series
StANT	Studien zum Alten und Neuen Testament
TDNT	G. Kittel and G. Friedrich (eds.), *Theological Dictionary of the New Testament*
TS	*Theological Studies*
TynBul	*Tyndale Bulletin*
TynNTC	Tyndale New Testament Commentaries
VTSup	Vetus Testamentum Supplements
WBC	Word Biblical Commentary
WUNT	Wissenschaftliche Untersuchungen zum Neuen Testament
ZNW	*Zeitschrift für die Neutestamentliche Wissenschaft*

Preface

My special interest in Paul and his speeches in the Acts of the Apostles began in the spring semester of 2007 during a doctoral seminar on Acts with Dr. Frank Matera at the Catholic University of America. On the one hand, I was deeply interested in Paul's speeches in Acts. On the other hand, I was fascinated by the complicated relationship between Paul and his fellow Jews in Acts.

I found that there had been much research done either on Paul's speeches in Acts or on his dealing with Jews. But there has not yet been a thorough and comprehensive narrative analysis of Paul's inaugural speech in Antioch of Pisidia (Acts 13:16–41) in relation to Paul's mission to the Jews in Acts. How does this speech unify Paul's missionary work among the Jews as a whole? How does this speech function as a model speech that Paul delivers to the Jews? How does this inaugural speech relate to Paul's missionary work among the Jews in Acts?

Many authors have been profoundly influenced by the so-called two-period theory. The first period is the proclamation of the good news to the Jews (Acts 2–13); the second period is the proclamation to the Gentiles (Acts 14–17). Therefore, the speech of Paul to the Jews in Antioch of Pisidia is the last call to the Jews. The end of the speech marks the end of Paul's missionary work to the Jews and the turning point of Paul's mission from the Jews to the Gentiles. I think this view should be explored further.

This book examines the meaning and significance of Paul's inaugural sermon at Antioch of Pisidia in order to understand its literary function in Paul's ministry among Jews according to the Acts of the Apostles.

In chapter 1, I provide a history of research of the speeches in Acts in general and Paul's inaugural speech in particular (Acts 13:16–41). I conclude that, since this is Paul's inaugural sermon, a study of the literary function of Jesus' and Peter's inaugural sermons may shed some light on the literary function of Paul's inaugural sermon.

In chapter 2, I study the literary function of Jesus' inaugural sermon at Nazareth (Luke 4:16–30), and in chapter 3, I analyze Peter's inaugural sermon at Pentecost (Acts 2:14–40). I conclude that both sermons have a parallel literary function in the narrative of Luke-Acts and are significant for understanding the ministries of Jesus and Peter in Luke-Acts.

In chapter 4, I examine Paul's inaugural sermon, noting that the full content of his preaching is reserved for his inaugural sermon. In this sermon, he argues from the Scriptures that God fulfilled his promise to David by raising Jesus from the dead.

In chapter 5, I investigate, from a narrative critical point of view, the literary function of Paul's inaugural sermon in relation to the narration of his ministry to Israel in Acts.

In chapter 6, I draw two conclusions from my study of Paul's inaugural sermon. First, Paul's inaugural sermon has a significant literary function for understanding his ministry to Israel in Acts; namely, this sermon functions as the model for how Paul regularly preaches to Jews in Acts. Thus, it unifies the different narratives of Paul's ministry among Jews in Acts. Second, through this inaugural sermon and its related narrative, Luke demonstrates that Paul is a missionary to both Jews and Gentiles in the Acts of the Apostles.

Now that I have finished my study in the US, I want to acknowledge the help and support that I have received from so many people and several institutions.

First and foremost, I own much to Rev. Larry Lewis, MM, the coordinator of Chinese Seminary Teachers and Formators Project, who generously offered me scholarships to finish my MA and PhD degrees in the United States. He always showed his understandings, support, and encouragement to me. I cannot thank him enough for his kindness.

This year is the centennial anniversary of the Maryknoll Society (1911–2011) and the twentieth anniversary of the Chinese Seminary Teachers and Formators Project (1991–2011). I send my warmhearted congratulations, sincere thanks, and best wishes to the Maryknoll Society and to Fr. Larry Lewis for their wonderful ministries in the whole world. In the past twenty years, the Maryknoll Society has helped more than 100 Chinese priests, Sisters, and lay persons study in the US and now working in different diocese and congregations all over China. The Maryknoll Society has already created history for the Church in China. I also give thanks to Ms. Anli Lin, Fr. Larry's assistant, and to Sr.

Janet Carroll, the former director of U.S China Catholic Bureau, for their kindness and support to me.

I offer heartfelt thanks to my director, Dr. Frank Matera, who has been the most helpful person for me from the beginning of my research to the completion of this dissertation. My thanks are beyond words for his scholarly guidance, instructive criticism, challenging remarks, and very generous availability. His way of doing research in balance, sober judgment, and clarity has influenced my way of doing research. I also owe much to my readers, Professor Francis Gignac, SJ and Professor John Paul Heil, who were very generous with their time and gave me helpful suggestions and encouragements.

Studying at CUA was challenging, but it was enjoyable as well. I do feel blessed to have had the chance to study at CUA with the internationally well respected and deeply committed scholars on the faculty. I owe a debt of gratitude to all my professors who encouraged me and helped me in many ways. It is because of their encouragement and kind support that I finished my study. My special thanks is extended to Professors Joseph Fitzmyer, SJ, Francis Moloney, SDB, Alexander Di Lella, OFM, and Raymond Collins.

I also owe a debt of gratitude for the Theological College community in Washington DC, the faculty, the student priests, and especially the two rectors: Fr. Thomas Hurst, SS, and Fr. Melvin Blanchette, SS. They were very kind to me and gave me supports in all aspects that I could concentrate on my writing. I was so blessed to live in this love-filled community, which I called home in the US; I held them dearly in my heart.

I am very grateful to Fr. Robert Maloney, CM, for his proof reading of my manuscript. He very patiently read and corrected and smoothed out my English, and offered many helpful suggestions. Fr. Philip Brown, SS, also helped me in this regard. I gave him thanks for his help as well.

To the community of Our Lady of China Pastoral Mission, the Chinese communities in Philadelphia, Atlanta, San Diego, and in the west coast, I am thankful for their constant support, concern, and care while I was studying at CUA. Although I worked alone on my studies, I never really felt alone. Their love for the Church in China always reminded me to prepare myself to better serve the Church in China. I was so blessed to know these communities and my experiences with them enriched my life as a priest.

Finally, I wish to thank all the priest friends and Sisters of my home diocese of Zhao-Xian, especially my two bishops: Bishop Raymond Wang Chonglin and Bishop Joseph Jiang Mingyuan, who encouraged me immensely on my studies and my priesthood. My heart is full of deep gratitude for their constant trust in me, their encouragement, and support. To my beloved father Paul Zhang Guangyin and mother Martha Bai Yingxu, who first taught me to love the Word, which I treasure so dearly. They all returned back home to heaven, yet their example of faithfulness and service always inspires me in my life. To the memories of my two bishops and my parents, I dedicate this volume.

Wenxi Zhang
Hebei Catholic Major Seminary
Shijiazhuang, Hebei Province, China

1

A History of Research

INTRODUCTION

IN THIS FIRST CHAPTER, I will review how scholars have dealt with Paul's speech to the Jews in the synagogue of Antioch in Pisidia (Acts 13:16-41). In the first part of this chapter I will provide a general survey of historical and critical research on Acts; in the second part, I will provide a brief survey of historical and critical research and some general studies of the speeches in Acts; in the third part, I will provide a history of research of Paul's speech; in the fourth part, I will draw a conclusion and explain how I intend to study this speech.

I. A GENERAL STUDY OF HISTORICAL AND CRITICAL RESEARCH OF ACTS

Before the end of the eighteenth century, the traditional view was that Acts was a history of all the apostles and the early Church, written by Luke, Paul's traveling companion who followed Paul and witnessed all of the events recorded in Acts, which he wrote down faithfully. This traditional view was called into question towards the end of the eighteenth century. As Hugo Grotius (1583-1645) and John Lightfoot (1602-75) observed, Acts was far from narrating the history of all the apostles as its title implied, since its author focused mainly on Peter and Paul.[1]

William Paley (1743-1805) studied critically the Paul of Acts and the Paul of the Pauline epistles. By comparing the two, he sought to

---

1. W. Ward Gasque, *A History of the Interpretation of the Acts of the Apostles* (Peabody, MA: Hendrickson, 1989) 12-20. Gasque's original quotations are from Hugo Grotius, "Annotationes in Acta Apostolorum," in *Annotationes in Novum Testamentum*, vol. 2 (Paris, 1622) and John Lightfoot, *A Commentary upon the Acts of the Apostles* (London, 1645).

ascertain the historicity of the events narrated in the two documents. According to W. Ward Gasque, Paley pointed out the problem of the agreements and divergencies of Acts and the Pauline epistles. The divergencies show the independence of the two, and the agreements show the substantial reliability of Acts.[2]

Scholars also recognized that the account of Peter and Paul was not complete in Acts, for the author of Acts is silent about many things that we learn from the Pauline epistles.[3] For example, Acts fails to mention Paul's withdrawal to "Arabia" (Gal 1:17b).[4] Eugen A. Schwanbeck suggested that a possible explanation for this phenomenon is that the author of Acts was unwilling or unable to present further information about the two apostles and the early Church community. This explanation of the unwillingness of the author to present the complete life of Paul and Peter led to the development of tendency criticism, whereas theories about the inability of Luke to narrate the complete lives of the two apostles led to source criticism.[5]

A. Tendency Criticism

If Luke, the author of Acts, was unwilling to narrate some of the stories of other apostles in the early Church, then he deliberately omitted something that he must have known, and he must have made a selection of the material available to him. What reasons led him to make this selection? Can the readers of Acts discern the underlying purpose of the author that guided him in his selection and organization of his materials? What aim, what 'tendency,' was he pursuing?

According to Gasque, the modern critical study of Acts began with these tendency criticism questions.[6] There are many scholars that are worth mentioning. I focus on the so-called Tübingen School, whose founder was Ferdinand C. Baur (1792-1860). Through his followers

---

2. Gasque, ibid., 20. Gasque's original quotation is from William Paley, *Horae Paulinae: or the Truth of the Scripture History of St. Paul evinced by a comparison of the Epistles which bear his name with the Acts of the Apostles and with one another* (London, 1790).

3. Ernst Haenchen, *The Acts of the Apostles: A Commentary* (Philadelphia: Westminster, 1971) 14-15.

4. Joseph A. Fitzmyer, *Paul and His Theology: A Brief Sketch* (2nd ed.; Englewood Cliffs, NJ: Prentice Hall, 1989) 3-6.

5. Haenchen, *Act*, 15. Haenchen's orginal quotations are from Eugen A. Schwanbeck, *Über die Quellen der Schriften des Lukas* (Darmstadt: Leske, 1847) 74.

6. Gasque, *A History of the Interpretation of the Acts of the Apostles*, 21.

he became the dominating influence in German NT research until nearly the end of the nineteenth century.[7] His basic thesis was that early Christianity was marked by severe conflicts between two groups that represented two different concepts of Christianity: a Jewish (Petrine) Christian party and a Gentile (Pauline) Christian party. Acts was an attempt to reconcile these two hostile parties. The vital question of the apostolic and subapostolic age was the issue of the legitimacy of the mission to the Gentiles. A positive contribution of tendency criticism was the recognition of the importance of the question of the purpose of Acts. It also recognized that Paul was the main character of Acts. Yet its weakness is also obvious, for "it makes an unwarranted simplification of history, rigidly differentiating 'Gentile Christianity' from 'Jewish Christianity,' and turns a problem of the initial stages into the driving force behind an epoch which had long since been moved by other questions and forces."[8]

According to Ernst Haenchen, Johannes Weiss's 1897 work, *Absicht und literarischer Charakter der Apostelgeschichte*, gives the impression of being a latecomer to 'tendency criticism.' He thought that Acts attempted to make an apology for the Christian belief before the Gentiles in the face of Jewish indictment, an apology that demonstrates how it has come about that Christianity has taken over and fulfilled the worldwide mission of Judaism. Christianity is born of Judaism, and its teaching has fulfilled Jewish hopes. Accordingly it replaces Judaism proper.[9]

B. Source Criticism

For tendency criticism the reason for the fragmentary character of Acts was the unwillingness of the author to say more. Another possibility was his inability to say more. This could have been occasioned by the incompleteness of his sources. In fact, if we read the prologue of the Gospel of Luke carefully, we can discern that the author did not claim to be an eyewitness. The presence and use of other sources is evident from the variety and unevenness of the style and from contradictions within the narrations. Three separate accounts of Paul's conversion (9:1–19; 22:3–16; 26:2–18) and two of Peter's vision (10:9–16; 11:5–17) suggest

---

7. Ibid., 26–27.
8. Haenchen, *Acts*, 17.
9. Ibid., 23–24.

that there are multiple sources behind Acts. The author compiled Acts from already assembled written sources. These sources can be identified as Petrine and Pauline sources, or sources from different communities such as Jerusalem, Antioch, and Ephesus, as well as a travel diary.[10]

C. Form Criticism

Hermann Gunkel was the first to draw attention to the smaller units and their types in the field of Christian literary history. His predecessors had been accustomed to think in terms of great source documents, e.g., the Yahwist and the Elohist in the OT sources.[11] In 1923, Martin Dibelius applied this 'form–critical' method to the study of Acts.[12] He shows that Luke draws upon a great number of synoptic gospel sources in writing his Gospel. Yet we cannot presume that Luke used similar sources in writing Acts. This shows how problematic the presumption is that Luke used the same working method in writing Acts as he did in writing his Gospel. Luke is the first to write an account of the early church's growth. In the composition of Acts, Luke did not have a great amount of source material, and he was not able to follow any predecessor that we know of who had already offered a prototype for this literary form.

According to Dibelius, there are no substantial, coherent sources behind Acts, but rather a number of smaller units, which he calls "legends," "tales," or "anecdotes."[13] This shows that a large amount of Acts was written by the author himself. This includes the speeches. They are intended to bear witness to the gospel. This is especially true of apostles' missionary speeches, which probably correspond to Christian preaching about the year 90; "So does one preach—and so should one preach!"[14] The apologetic speeches are intended to prepare the early Christians to use these ideas in their self-defense in a court setting. Paul's Miletus address shows the portrait of the apostles Luke wished to present. It is also an admonition to the whole Church.

10. Ibid., 24–28.
11. Ibid., 35.
12. Martin Dibelius, "Stilkritsches zur Apostelgeschichte," in *Aufsätze zur Apostelgeschichte* (ed. Heinrich Greeven; Göttingen vandenhoeck & Reprecht, 1968) 9–28. See also Martin Dibelius, "Style Criticism of the Book of Acts," in *The Book of Acts: Form, Style, and Theology* (ed. K. C. Hanson; Minneapolis: Fortress, 2004) 32–48.
13. Dibelius, "Stilkritsches zur Apostelgeschichte," 28.
14. Dibelius, *Book of Acts*, 67.

II. A Survey of Historical and Critical Research on the Speeches of Acts and Some General Studies on the Speeches in Acts

Before the age of the historical-critical study of Acts at the end of the eighteenth century, the traditional view was that Acts was written by Luke, Paul's traveling companion. He followed Paul and witnessed all the events and heard Paul's sermons. Then he faithfully wrote about the history of all the apostles and the history of the early Church. With regard to the critical study of the speeches in Acts, Johann G. Eichhorn was probably the first scholar to publish the idea that the speeches in Acts were Luke's creation. He studied the content and the style of the speeches in Acts, and he concluded that the speeches are of one and the same author.[15] Wilhelm M. L. de Wette argued that there were some written sources for the speeches.[16] Thus it is probable that Luke did not freely compose the letters and the speeches in Acts, especially if he used some written sources.

Matthias Schneckenburger thought that the speeches were Luke's own compositions. The speeches were intended to give examples of early Christian preaching and to defend the veracity of the early Christian proclamation of Jesus as the savior of Gentiles and Jews.[17] He wrote in reference to Paul's speech in Antioch of Pisidia (Acts 13:16–41):

> Es scheint, daß der Verfasser durch Voranstellung der antiochenischen sie als Muster der paulinischen Lehre auf seiner Reise überhaupt zu betrachten gibt. Oder wird man wohl für diese Rede auf der ersten Missionsreise genauere Quellen statuiren wollen, die dem Lucas zugekommen seien, als für später gehaltene Vorträge? Allerdings ist die Wahrscheinlichkeit eines Spezialberichts . . . zu behaupten; ob dieser aber ein authen-

---

15. Marion L. Soards, *The Speeches in Acts: Their Content, Context, and Concerns* (Louisville, KY: Westminster/John Knox Press, 1994) 2. Johann G. Eichhorn (*Einleitung in das Neue Testament* [2 vols.; Leipzig: Weidmann, 1810]) writes "Die Reden selbst, ob sie gleich verschiedenen Personen in den Mund gelegt worden, folgen einem und demselben Typus, tragen einerlei Character, brauchen einerlei Beweisart, und haben unter sich so viel gemein, daß sie sich dadurch als Reden eines und desselben Schriftstellers erproben (2. 38)."

16. Ibid. See also Wilhelm M. L. de Wette, *Lehrbuch der historisch-kritischen Einleitung in die kanonischen Bücher des Neuen Testaments* (6th rev. ed.; Berlin: Georg Reimer, 1860) 250.

17. Soards, *Speeches in Acts*, 3. See also Matthias Schneckenburger, *Über den Zweck der Apostelgeschichte: Zugleich eine Ergänzung der neueren Commentare* (Bern: C. Fischer, 1841) 127–51.

> tischer war, von den Missionsären selbst ausgegangen, [ist] sehr zweifelhaft und unwahrscheinlich... Nehmen wir mithin diese Rede als ein Muster der paulinischen Lehrweise: so springt von selbst ihre große Verwandtschaft mit den Reden des ersten Theils in die Augen; sie ist nur ein Widerhall der Vorträge des Petrus und Stephanus... Vergegenwärtigen wir uns die sonst bekannte Lehrweise des Paulus, so können wir nicht umhin, es auffallend zu finden...[18]

Schneckenburger regards this speech as a model of Pauline sermons. According to Soards, the consensus of German critical scholarship around the turn of the twentieth century was summarized by Adolf Jülicher who maintained that the speeches in Acts are the free composition of the author.[19]

Current study of the speeches in Acts focuses on the speeches in relation to Greco-Roman historiography. In their study of Luke's speeches in Acts, scholars have constantly referred to the well-known statement of Thucydides (1.22.1):

> With reference to the speeches in this history, some were delivered before the war began, others while it was going on; it was hard to record the exact words spoken, both in cases where I was myself present, and where I used the reports of others. But I have used language in accordance with what I thought the speakers in each case would have been most likely to say, adhering as closely as possible to the general sense of what was actually spoken.[20]

Although there are different interpretations of this statement, most scholars understand that Thucydides did not record the speeches verbatim but presented the general sense of what had been delivered. For Henry J. Cadbury it is obvious that the ancient writers and their readers regarded the speeches more as editorial and dramatic comment than as the historical account of what the speaker actually said.[21] He continues that historians might comment on events and their significance, providing insight into their context, historic situation, the character of the

---

18. Ibid., 129–30.

19. Soards, *Speeches in Acts*, 5. cf. Adolf Jülicher, *Einleitung in das Neue Testament* (Grundriss der Theologischen Wissenschaften 3/1; 5th/6th eds.; Tübingen: J. C. B. Mohr, 1913) 404–5.

20. Thomas F. Glasson, "The Speeches in Acts and Thucydides," *ExpT* 76 (1964/65) 165.

21. Henry J. Cadbury, *The Making of Luke-Acts* (London: SPCK, 1958) 185.

speakers, and their thought world. Neither the form of direct quotation nor the appropriateness of the words to the speaker and his occasion proves that the writer had any actual knowledge of what was said in the speeches. Even an historian such as Thucydides probably relied more on his dramatic imagination and sense of fitness than on knowledge, oral memory, or written sources. It is likely that the author of Acts followed this literary convention to compose the speeches in Acts.[22]

After Cadbury's work came the ground-breaking work of Dibelius. Although he did not publish a commentary on Acts, his two essays, "Paul on the Areopagus" and "The Speeches in Acts and Ancient Historiography" have significantly influenced German exegesis and criticism of the speeches in Acts. He has largely set the agenda for subsequent studies. Dibelius surveyed the speeches of the ancient historians, and he concluded that the historical writing that contains speeches in ancient times followed certain conventions. To the writer of the speeches, it was not important to establish what speech was actually made; rather, it was more important to introduce speeches into the structure in a way that would be relevant to his purpose. Even if he can remember, discover, or read the actual speech, the author would not feel obliged to make use of it.[23] The purpose of inserting speeches was to provide insight (1) "into the total situation" through different angles; (2) "into the meaning of the historical moment;" (3) "into the character of the speaker;" (4) "into general ideas that would help to explain the whole situation;" and (5) "to further the action" of the narration.[24]

Through a careful comparative study of ancient historiography and the speeches in Acts, Dibelius concludes that there is one striking parallel in Acts: at vital turning points in the history of the early Christian community Luke inserted speeches that do not necessarily fit the historical occasion but have an obvious literary function in Acts as a whole. All of these speeches appear at significant points and bear the imprint of the author's mind. He has inserted them into his narrative, or rather into the narrative provided by his source. In doing so, he has followed the tradition of ancient historical writing.[25] The speeches in Acts serve the theological purpose of the author by illuminating the significance of the events.

22. Ibid., 184–93.
23. Martin Dibelius, *The Book of Acts: Form, Style, and Theology* (ed. K. C. Hanson; Minneapolis: Fortress, 2004) 53.
24. Ibid., 50.
25. Ibid., 73.

On the one hand, Luke follows the literary technique of ancient historiography by freely composing all the speeches to serve his purpose of writing. On the other hand, he is primarily a preacher and only secondarily a historian. He actually invented a new form of speech, the missionary sermon, in the writing of history. This new form, the missionary speech, is uniform in form and content, inasmuch as the speaker preaches the gospel and calls for conversion. He also thinks that the missionary speeches have their value as sources "because they undoubtedly derived from sermons remembered by the community from a long time ago."[26] Perhaps the main point inherited by most of the subsequent scholars was that the speeches in Acts were Luke's own composition. From this point a remarkable amount of tradition-historical analysis of the speeches has been done in order to find what traditions and models were used by Luke in the process of writing the speeches in Acts.[27] Soards writes: "But the consistent concern of these studies with questions of tradition history has caused the analysis of the speeches to fall into exclusive or fragmented, and thus reductionistic categories—literary, historiographic, or theological—for assessing 'the meaning to be attributed to the speeches in the work as a whole.'"[28]

After reviewing the history of the comparative studies of the speeches in Acts and ancient historiography, Soards tries to understand more fully the character of the speeches in Acts. To do this he compares the speeches of Acts with three distinguished bodies of literature: Greco-Roman historiography, selected portions of the LXX, and selected pieces of literature from Hellenistic Judaism.

By his comparative study of the speeches in Acts and ancient historiography Soards successfully repudiates each of Eckhard Plümacher's six points.[29] Plümacher had built on the studies of Dibelius and Ulrich

---

26. Ibid., 82.

27. Soards, *Speeches in Acts*, 9. It does not mean that all scholars agree that the speeches in Acts are of Luke's composition. W. Ward Gasque ("The Speeches of Acts: Dibelius Reconsidered," in *New Dimensions in New Testament Study* [ed. R. N. Longenecker and M. C. Tenney; Grand Rapids: Zondervan, 1974] 232–50) vigorously defended the historical authenticity of the speeches in Acts. Stanley E. Porter ("Thucydides 1. 22.1 and Speeches in Acts: Is There a Thucydidean View?" *NovT* 32, [1990], 121–42, here 142) also suggests that Thucydides intends us to accept the veracity and accuracy of his reports of the speeches in the history.

28. Ibid.

29. Eckhard Plümacher, "Lukas als griechischer Historiker," *PWSup* 14 (1974)

Wilckens, and he advanced the investigation of the speeches in relation to ancient historiography. After a careful scrutiny of Plümacher's six points, Soards writes that Plümacher's meticulously articulated case is not fully persuasive, although one cannot deny some relationship between the speeches of Acts and Hellenistic historiography. Thus he concludes that there is a clear relationship between the form and style of speeches in Hellenistic historiography and the form and style of the speeches in Acts. Nevertheless, the contents of the speeches in Acts are quite distinct from the contents of the speeches in Hellenistic historiography.[30]

Soards thinks that there is a relationship between the speeches in the LXX and in Acts. The speeches of Acts function like the "great speeches" of the Deuteronomistic History, i.e., they unify the large account in which they occur by means of repetition. Furthermore, the pointed recapitulation of history in 2 Esdras 19 shows sufficient parallels in form, style, and content to suggest that Ezra's prayer may have provided inspiration for elements of certain speeches in Acts. Despite these similarities, there is a difference between the two. There is an apologetic tone in almost all of the speeches in Acts, yet there is no apologetic dimension to the Septuagint speeches.[31] Soards concludes in this way:

> In form and rhetoric one can see that the speeches in Acts are often parallel to speeches in Greco-Roman historiography. In content, however, the speeches of Acts are more like portions of the Septuagint than comparable to Greco-Roman historiographical addresses. Yet, in their purpose—that is, in the use of Greco-Roman historiographical forms in religious compositions for the basic instruction of adherents of a particular religious

---

235–64. The six points are: (1) the speeches in Acts are similar to those in Greco-Roman historiography in that they are loosely connected with the context; (2) the speeches in Acts follow the function of the speeches in Historiography, in which they are compelling forces for the subsequent events; (3) like other ancient speeches, Luke brings speeches to an end by reporting either that the speaker said much more that is not recorded or how the speech was interrupted; (4) in Acts 5:36–37, the speech starts with an introduction of historical examples, which is common to the historiographical speeches; (5) Hellenistic historiography tended to imitate the style and ambience of the classical period of Greek; similarly, speeches in Acts tend to a Septuagintal style and flavor; (6) there is a common archaizing characteristics in Acts and in the historiographical speeches. See also E. Plümacher, *Lukas als hellenistischer Schriftsteller: Studien zur Apostelgeschichte* (SUNT 9; Göttingen: Vandenhoeck & Ruprecht, 1972).

30. Soards, *Speeches in Acts*, 143.
31. Ibid., 156–57.

> conviction—the speeches in Acts are most like the work of the fragmentary writings of Hellenistic Jewish historians.
>
> Nevertheless, in sheer repetitiveness the speeches in Acts stand apart. One can say that the most distinctive feature of the speeches is repetition—of forms and of content.[32]

One of the most distinctive features of the speeches in Acts is repetition. Ever since Johann G. Eichhorn in the nineteenth century, the character of repetition of the speeches in Acts had been pointed out.[33] Scholars have found out that there are five to nine formal elements within the missionary speeches. There is a repeated general pattern in this type of speech. Haenchen, Eduard Schweizer, Wilckens, Hans Conzelmann, and others have recognized similar repeated elements in the missionary speeches. By following the list of commonly occurring elements of Schweizer, Fitzmyer gives his modified list of the repeated elements.[34]

There are different explanations why there is such a repetitive character to the speeches in Acts. Charles H. Dodd thinks that some of the speeches, especially the early speeches attributed to Peter, are from a common source. He identifies this as a source from "the Aramaic-speaking Church at Jerusalem . . . substantially earlier than the period at which the book was written."[35] The first four speeches of Peter are similar. They are not what Peter said on this or that occasion "but the *kerygma* of the Church at Jerusalem at an early period."[36] Dibelius thinks that the repetitive character of the speeches reflects the way of preaching typical of Luke's own days. Yet Wilckens believes that the speeches to Jews were Luke's construction intended to express his own theology, and the speeches to Gentiles were composed by following the traditional pattern of 1 Thess 1:9-10 and Heb 5:11-6:2. In the third edition of his work Wilckens maintains that

---

32. Ibid., 160–61.

33. Ibid., 2. See also Eichhorn, *Einleitung in das Neue Testament*, 36–43.

34. Joseph A. Fitzmyer, *The Acts of the Apostles: A New Translation with Introduction and Commentary* (AB 31; New York: Doubleday, 1998) 107. He concludes that there are nine uniform elements in missionary and evangelizing speeches: (1) direct address (adapted to situation); (2) appeal for attention; (3) misunderstanding of listeners; (4) quotations of OT introducing body of speech; (5) christological kerygma; (6) proof from OT about kerygma; (7) reply to problem posed by misunderstanding; (8) call for repentance; proclamation of salvation; (9) focus of message on audience.

35. Charles H. Dodd, *The Apostolic Preaching and its Development* (New York: Harper & Brothers Publishers, 1962) 20.

36. Ibid., 21.

Luke knew the Deuteronomistic tradition and brought its pattern into Acts, above all in Stephen's speech, and developed this pattern further in composing the missionary speeches to Jews.[37]

Fitzmyer insightfully writes: "Either Dodd or Dibelius may be right, but there is really no way to be certain about the provenience of such common and persistent elements in the speeches of Acts."[38] It is true that we cannot regard the speeches in Acts as merely *creatio ex nihilo* on Luke's part; there must be some stories or legends about the possible preaching of Peter and Paul in pre-Lukan tradition. The character of repetition seems to argue for a final redactor of the speeches. Therefore, the speeches are ultimately Lukan composition. In these speeches Luke introduces his own theological and missionary aims.[39]

Having observed the highly repetitive character of the speeches in Acts, Soards takes a new direction for understanding their literary role and purpose. His thesis is that "the speeches are a crucial factor in the coherence of Acts account" and "they achieve the unification of the otherwise diverse and incoherent elements comprised by Acts. Through the regular introduction of formally repetitive speeches Luke unified his narrative; and, more important, he united the image of an otherwise personally, ethnically, and geographically diverse early Christianity." [40]

III. HISTORY OF RESEARCH: PAUL'S SPEECH IN ANTIOCH OF PISIDIA (ACTS 13:16-41)

A. Martin Dibelius

Dibelius studied the missionary speeches or sermons in Acts 2, 3, 5, 10, and 13. He pointed out some stereotyped repetition of the same outline. Regularly there is an introduction to show the situation at the moment. It is followed by the kerygma of Jesus' life, passion, and resurrection. Then the disciples bear witness to Jesus' resurrection, and there is a proof text from the OT. The speech concludes with a call to repentance. There is a

---

37. Ulrich Wilckens, *Die Missionsreden der Apostelgeschichte: Form- und traditionsgeschichtliche Untersuchungen* (3rd. ed., WMANT 5; Neukirchen-Vluyn: Neukirchener Verlag, 1974) 203.

38. Fitzmyer, *Acts*, 106.

39. Ibid., 106–7.

40. Soards, *Speeches in Acts*, 12.

uniform form and content to these missionary speeches. He concluded that this type of speech has nothing to do with historiography, for the author of these speeches is primarily concerned to preach the gospel. The content of these speeches is to give a compressed form of gospel preaching. It is to be supported by proof texts from the OT, and the audiences are exhorted to repent. The main purpose of these speeches, then, is to preach and to teach.[41] In the last analysis the author of these speeches is not a historian but a preacher.[42]

The "form" of these speeches, according to Dibelius, seems to have been the customary form of preaching in the author's time, about 90 C.E. "This is how the gospel is preached and ought to be preached."[43] The customary form should be considered as a type common to all Christians. He thinks that the repetition of some old-fashioned phrases in the kerygma—such as "servant or child of God" in 3:13 and "a man attested to you by God" in 2:22—may speak for a dependence on older texts or some written materials. Yet it is hard to be sure. He remarks further that the missionary speeches with their repetitions have their value as sources because they undoubtedly derived from sermons remembered by the community from long ago.[44]

With regard to Paul's speech in Acts 13:16–41, Dibelius makes the following observations: 13:16–22 is a survey of the history of Israel; 13:23–25 is the kerygma of Jesus' life, passion, and resurrection; 13:31 is the witness of the disciples, and 13:38–41 is an exhortation to repentance. The speech follows the fundamental scheme of the missionary sermon. However, he finds that there is a new element in Paul's missionary sermon to the Jews in this passage (13:16–41). The first section of the survey of Israel's history in 13:16–22 has no connection with the missionary sermon. He further affirms that it has no connection with the content of this sermon as a whole. Any Jewish speaker could have spoken this history of Israel. Compared with other missionary speeches, we can see that the first section of the

---

41. Dibelius, *Book of Acts*, 67–68.

42. Ibid., 80.

43. Ibid., 67. "And if no distinction is made in Acts between Jewish and Gentile listeners and between Peter and Paul as speakers, we can assume that the scheme of preaching indicated was not calculated simply for specific audiences. Luke would not ascribe this type of sermon to Peter and to Paul indiscriminately and let it be made both in the centurion's house and in the synagogue if he had not considered it as a type common to all Christians."

44. Ibid., 82.

speeches starts with a link to the situation (2:14–16; 3:12; 5:29; 10:34–35). It provides the beginning of a sermon preached in a synagogue. Yet this apparently irrelevant opening is connected with the situation after all, and the presentation of the history of Israel is intended to awaken the memory of instructions in the synagogue.[45]

It is expected that Paul gave a sermon to the Jews in a synagogue location. But Dibelius asks why a speech would be reported in Athens, since Athens is only one of the stations of Paul's journey. Why is there no sermon reported at Philippi or at Corinth? The missionary Paul must have spoken at each of these three cities; Luke could therefore choose freely from one of the cities to have Paul deliver a speech. Certainly Luke did not choose Athens for historical or biographical reasons, for he reports that Paul's speech in Athens was not a success. Athens symbolizes the center of the intellectual life of Greece. Paul has penetrated into the center of the ancient Gentile world and brought the good news to them. That is why Luke makes Athens the scene of the single example of a sermon to the Gentiles preached by Paul.[46] Luke wrote this speech in Acts 17 as an example of a typical sermon to Gentiles and gave it the setting of Athens.[47] Unfortunately, he did not recognize that the speech that Paul preached to the Jews in Antioch of Pisidia of Acts 13:16–41 is the only complete speech that Paul ever delivered in a synagogue location. As we shall see, Luke may have written this speech in Acts 13 as an example of a typical sermon to the Jews.

B. Ulrich Wilckens

Wilckens builds his studies on the foundation of Dibelius. Yet he thinks that Luke is more creative than Dibelius suggested. Dibelius thinks that the old-fashioned repetitious kerygmatic phrases may have come from an older tradition. Undoubtedly the missionary speeches represent the missionary sermons that the audiences remembered from long before. Wilckens wants to demonstrate that the missionary sermons do not depend on a scheme of preaching from Luke's own time. Rather, they are entirely the inventions of Luke for his own theological purposes. His conclusion is, "Die Apostelreden der Acta aber sind in hervorra-

---

45. Ibid., 66–69.
46. Ibid., 58.
47. Ibid., 125.

gendem Sinne Summarien dieser seiner theologischen Konzeption; sie sind nicht als Zeugnisse alter oder gar ältester urchristlicher Theologie, sondern lukanischer Theologie des ausgehenden ersten Jahrhunderts zu werten."[48]

Wilckens studied the six missionary sermons to the Jews (2:14–39; 3:12–26; 4:9–12; 5:30–32; 10:34–43; 13:16–41). In comparing the six sermons, he found that all of them followed the same schematic plan. The parallel characteristics are particularly clear in the sermons of 2:14–39, 3:12–26, and 13:16–41. The scheme of the sermons follows the six elements that we have discussed before. He thinks that each sermon is closely connected with the narrative context and thus concludes that "die zu behandelnden Predigten sind alle ausnahemslos gut in den jeweiligen Erzählungszusammenhang eingefügt, auf ihn bezogen und von ihm her auch im einzelnen geprägt. Nähte oder Risse werden nirgends sichtbar."[49]

Wilckens disagrees with Dibelius's view that the missionary sermons reflected an older tradition which could be found in 1 Cor 15:3–8. He tries to show that in the missionary sermons to the Jews there is nothing that resembles the preaching in 1 Corinthians 15. He tries to demonstrate that the contents of the missionary sermons are Lukan composition. There were no older sources for the speeches as there were for the John the Baptist tradition and for the suffering, death, resurrection, and glorification of Jesus. They all manifest a Lukan point of view. They all reflect Luke's theology.

Jacques Dupont presents a penetrating criticism of Wilckens's view.[50] He first gives a presentation of Wilcken's book and in the fourth part he discusses the use of the christological titles in Acts. He studies the titles "Christ," "servant of God," "the holy and righteous One," "Lord," "Ruler and Savior," and "Son of God." He concludes that Luke uses archaic materials in writing Acts.[51]

Wilckens thinks that there are two stages in the apostolic witnesses of the salvation that Jesus brings to us. The first is the period of proclaiming salvation to the Jews, which is narrated in Acts 2–13, and the second

---

48. Wilckens, *Die Missionsreden der Apostelgeschichte*, 186.

49. Ibid., 71.

50. Jacques Dupont, "Les Discours Missionnaires des Actes des Apôtres : d'après un ouvrage récent ," in *Etudes sur les Actes des Apôtres* (Paris: Cerf, 1967) 133–55.

51. Ibid., 145–55.

period is the proclamation of the good news to the Gentiles, which is found in Acts 14-17. These sermons are all adapted to the situation.[52]

With regard to the missionary sermon in 13:16-41, Wilckens thinks that the first section of the speech in 13:16-23 is salvation history. This section has a connection with the situation of this synagogue sermon. It is appropriate to narrate the history of Israel in a synagogue location. He writes, "Und die Predigt in 13 hat den charakteristischen Skopos: die umgreifende heilsgeschichtliche Plannmäßigkeit des ganuen Geschehenszusammenhangers vom Beginn der Heilsgeschichte in der Erwählung der Väter bis hin zur gegenwärtigen Situation der drehenden Verwerfung Israels."[53] The promise to David has been fulfilled in the resurrection of Jesus. The theme of promise and fulfillment is in this speech. He concludes, "Die Predigten der Apostel erscheinen so als typische Beispiele apostolischer Verkündigung in der jeweiligen Situation."[54]

Based on Wilckens's two-period theory (chaps. 2-13, preaching to the Jews; chaps. 14-17, preaching to the Gentiles) of the proclamation of the salvation, he thinks that the sermon Paul delivers to the Jews in the synagogue of Antioch in Pisidia is the turning point of the whole narration of Acts. This sermon is the last call to the Jews, for they have rejected the Word of God and now Paul and Barnabas are going to the Gentiles to preach to them, and they shall listen. Therefore, the sermon in Acts 13 serves as a turning point in proclaiming the offer of salvation from the Jews to the Gentiles.[55]

---

52. Wilckens, *Die Missionsreden der Apostelgeschichte*, 72-100. He writes, "Die Kirchengeschichte wird in zwei Phasen dargestellt, die entsprechend dem göttlichen Heilsplan aufeinander folgen: die Phase der Verkündigung unter den Juden und die Phase der Heidenmission. Die Unterschiede zwischen diesen beiden Phases kommen auch in der verschiedenen Form der Predigaten c 2-13 einerseits und c 14 und 17 andererseits zu theologischem Ausdruck (p.99)."

53. Ibid., 55.

54. Ibid. "Diese Predigt in der Synagoge ist der letzte Bußruf an die Juden. Da diese das Wort Gottes aber verstoßen, wird es von nun an ganz und endgültig den Heiden verkündigt (13:46), die es im Gegensatz zu den Juden annehmen (13:48)."

55. Wilckens (*Missionsreden*, 70-71) writes about the sermon that "sie fügt sich nicht nur gut in den Erzählungszusammenhang ein, sondern bildet selbst sogar den entscheidenden Mittelpunkt des berichteten Geschehens."

C. Marcel Dumais

Dumais studies the missionary language or the manner in which Christian meaning is communicated and argues that the speech in Acts 13 is a homiletic *midrash* of the *pesher* type based on Nathan's promise to David in 2 Samuel 7. The homily takes the verb "I shall raise up" and other allusions in the LXX version of Nathan's prophecy that God would raise up a seed of David as a hidden reference to the resurrection.[56] Dumais acknowledges that this proposition is not entirely new. Jan W. Doeve had pointed out earlier that the passage in 2 Sam 7:12b–14a forms the background of the speaker's entire argument of the coming up out of Egypt, of the Judges, of Saul, and here too we find the promise of the seed of David, who will have a kingdom for ever. Furthermore, it is said of this king that Yhwh will be a Father to him, and he shall be a Son to Yhwh.[57]

Dale Goldsmith recognizes that the discovery of a P 2 Sam 7:10b–14a at Qumran in the 1950s has raised the question of the nature of the influence of 2 Samuel 7 in an acute way: Was there a consciously developed tradition of interpretation of the Nathan oracle in terms of the resurrected Christ in early Christian missionary work to the Jews?[58] He studies the parallel words of Acts 13 and 2 Samuel 7 and concludes that "there seems to be sufficient connection between the ideas and wording of II Sam 7:11–16 and Acts 13 to suggest the possibility of an early Christian *pesher* tradition related to the Nathan oracle."[59]

Dumais presents a detailed study of the thesis that Acts 13 is a midrash pesher on 2 Samuel 7. He tries to combine the question of hermeneutics with the question of the interpretation of the text.[60] Since he seeks to approach the text through these two points of views, he tries to exegete the speech and illustrate that Acts 13 is how the Christian message was communicated to the Jews in the early church. He fundamentally follows that three-part structure of the speech. Yet he de-

---

56. Marcel Dumais, *Le Langage de l'évangélisation: L'Annonce Missionaire en milieu juif (Actes 13, 16–41)* (Tournai/Paris: Desclée; Montréal: Bellarmin, 1976) 87–98.

57. Jan W. Doeve, *Jewish Hermeneutics in the Synoptic Gospels and Acts* (Assen: Van Gorcum, 1953) 172.

58. Dale Goldsmith, "Acts 13, 33–37: A Pesher on II Samuel 7," *JBL* 87 (1968), 321–24, here 321.

59. Ibid., 322. See also Jan W. Bowker, "Speeches in Acts: A Study in Proem and Yelammedenu Form," *NTS* 14 (1967) 96–111.

60. Dumais, *Langage de l'évangélisation*, 35.

lineates the speech essentially into two major parts and a conclusion. Part I (13:16b–25) is the time of the ancestors in the past. It is the time of promise. Part II (13:26–37) is the time of the present. It is the time of fulfillment of the promise in the Part I. The conclusion (13:38–41) is a call for repentance, that is, to believe in the name of Jesus and be justified.[61] He thinks that the contents of speech in vv. 17–22 reflect the literary scheme of the creed of Israel.[62] By recalling the heart of the creed of Israel, the speech concludes with the fulfillment of the promises in the resurrection of Jesus. He picks up some *mots vedette* in Parts I and II and sees the promise and fulfillment scheme in the speech. He also notices the importance of the OT citations and illusions. Then, working from the verbal and thematic links, he concludes that the speech is a midrash of the P 2 Samuel 7.[63]

D. Robert F. O'Toole

O'Toole intends to study Luke's portrayal of Jesus' resurrection as revealed by the literary and thematic unity of Acts 13:13–52, for he thinks that Jesus' resurrection in Acts often fades into the background of other concerns in Acts.[64]

First, O'Toole tries to establish the literary unity of Acts 13:13–52. He argues that Luke uses certain terms like λόγος ("word"), ἀκούειν ("to hear"), and σωτηρία ("salvation") to unify the speech into a literary unity in Acts 13:13–52.[65] Second, there is also a thematic unity. The major theme is the theme of Jesus' resurrection. In Acts 13:33 the word ἀναστήσας refers to Jesus' resurrection, which has fulfilled the promise. This promise in Acts 13:32–33 refers to a general view of salvation brought by Jesus whom the Father raised from the dead. This salvation includes Jesus' resurrection and the resurrection of all who believe in him (13:30–37), the forgiveness of sins (13:38), justification (13:38–39), and eternal life (13:46, 48). He concludes that the literary and thematic unity of Acts 13:13–52 indicates what Luke emphasizes is Jesus' resurrection.[66]

61. Ibid., 59–60.
62. Ibid., 131–56.
63. Ibid., 90–114.
64. Robert F. O'Toole, "Christ's Resurrection in Acts 13, 13–52," *Bib* 60 (1979) 361–72, here 361.
65. Ibid., 362–63.
66. Ibid., 364–72.

E. Christie A. Joachim Pillai

Pillai has written two volumes on this speech. In his first volume he bases his investigation on the proposition that "it would seem that the meaning of a speech and the question of its historicity are two factors so closely interrelated and mutually illustrative that an unbiased investigation should not exclude either one or the other."[67] In this study he then follows methodologically all the successive stages of exegetical inquiry: historical background, textual criticism, literary criticism, historical criticism, and a final conclusion. He uses the historical-critical method to approach the text.

Pillai traces the development of the literary model of the speech in Acts 13. He sums up the process of development of the Christian message in the following way: (1) OT Scriptures as the Word of God; (2) historical Jesus—his words deeds as source of tradition, then apostolic tradition; (3) witnesses in Jerusalem; (4) the *kerygma* proclamation of the facts of salvation, especially outside Jerusalem.[68]

According to Pillai, the speech in Acts 13 follows this pattern: the word of exhortation (13:17–22), the word of John the Baptist (13:24, 25), the *kerygma* proper of the word of salvation (13:26b–31a), the Jerusalem witness (13:31b), the arguments from Scripture (13:33–37), the apostolic *didache (teaching)* (13:38, 39), the eschatological *paraenesis* (13:40, 41). Therefore, he concludes that with great editorial skill Luke puts together these pieces of traditional material used by Paul, with the help of 13:23 and 32, which are Pauline to the core, being centered on the theme of "promise and fulfillment." Thus Luke gives us a "pattern of Pauline teaching" about the middle of the first century. It is a work of both tradition and composition, both historical and redactional.[69]

In his second volume, Pillai focuses on the apostolic interpretation of the history in light of the speech in Antioch of Pisidia. He divides the speech into five units:

(1) The history of the chosen people (13:17–23)

(2) The history of John (13:24–25)

(3) The history of Jesus (13:26b–31a)

---

67. Christie A. Joachim Pillai, *Early Missionary Preaching: A Study of Luke's Report in Acts 13* (Hicksville, NY: Exposition, 1979) 5.

68. Ibid., 52–62, here 61.

69. Ibid., 120–21.

(4) The history of the disciples (13:31b-37)

(5) The history of the listeners (13:38-41).[70]

The speech has a three fold dimension of time: "past," "present," and "future." The first two units belong to the "past of preparation," the third and fourth units belong to the "present of fulfillment," and the fifth unit is the "future of appropriation" and the "consummation of the New Israel in Christ."[71] This speech is an outline of "revelational history."[72] The past of preparation is described in the history of Israel in 13:17-22, in which it shows God's election, liberation, and promise. It is followed by the witness of the final prophet, John the Baptist, before the messianic event in 13:24-25. "The second board of the diptych runs parallel to the first, implying the themes of typology and fulfillment. The prophetic role of the chosen people is fulfilled in the history of Jesus—the elected One who is liberated according to the promise from the pangs of death by resurrection; the disciples' story is introduced as the first and initial witness to the messianic event."[73]

The whole picture of the redemptive history is presented as a call to faith in Jesus—the central person of universal history, for he sets us free, as promised. Thus the new Israel is constituted in Jesus. This speech demonstrates that the whole process of sacred history is a continuous account of all the major redemptive events from the past to the disciples of Jesus and all future believers of Jesus.[74]

F. Mattäus F. J. Buss

Buss's study follows the studies of this speech by Otto Glombitza.[75] Yet he studies the text of the speech more closely. Buss uses the redaction-criticism method and focuses on the study of the styles and themes of this speech. He tries to demonstrate how and in what manner the whole speech in Antioch of Pisidia is an integrated literary and thematic unity

---

70. Christie A. Joachim Pillai, *Apostolic Interpretation of History: A Commentary on Acts 13:16-41* (Hicksville, NY: Exposition, 1980) 3.

71. Ibid., 4.

72. Ibid., 105.

73. Ibid.

74. Ibid., 106.

75. Otto Glombitza, "AKTA XIII. 15-41: Anylyse einer lukanischen Predigt vor Juden," in *NTS* 5 (1959) 306-17.

by its editor, Luke. Furthermore, he shows how this speech reveals the redaction and theology of Luke.[76]

Buss states that he uses redaction criticism to study this speech (unserer Studie bleibt redaktionsgeschichtlich ausgerichtet).[77] He disagrees with Dibelius's saying that the first section in 13:16-23 does not have a connection with the missionary speech nor does it have a connection with the content of the speech. This section, according to Buss, has a close relationship with the speech. Acts 13:17-20a is close to the Deuteronomistic creed in Deut 26:5-9.[78] In 13:24-26 John the Baptist is regarded as the last prophet in the OT who witnesses to the savior, Jesus, whom 13:23 introduces. He thinks the theology and style of 13:26 bear the imprint of Luke. It shows his literary creativity.[79] He writes that 13:27-31 is the development of "the word of salvation" in 13:26. The Jerusalem event shows strong Lukan language style.[80] Jesus' resurrection is a salvation event, and it has fulfilled the promise made to David. Thus Luke uses the OT to prove the promise of David, which is fulfilled in Jesus' resurrection to his Jewish audiences. The salvation of God now extends to all people, Jews and Gentiles alike.

The most distinctive aspect of Buss's study is his structure of the speech. He divides the speech into five parts: I. Apg 13,16b-23: Die heilsgeschichtliche Hinführung zum Thema der Predigt vom Heil in Jesus Christus; II. Apg 13, 24-26: Johannes d. T. im Rahmen der Heilsbotschaft; III. Apg 13, 27-31: Das Passion- und Auferweckungskerygma; IV. Die Auferweckung Jesu im Zeugnis des AT nach Apg 13, 32-37; V. Der Redeabschluß (Apg 13, 38-41). Through the study of the speech he concludes that Luke presents us with a programmatic understanding of salvation history. In this history, the history of Israel, the Jesus event, and current salvation have been made one. Through the resurrection of Jesus, God has brought us the fulfillment of the promise in the OT.[81] In conclusion, he writes:

76. Matthäus F. J. Buss, *Die Missionspredigt des Apostels Paulus im Pisidischen Antiochien:Analyse von Apg 13, 16-41 im Hinblick auf die literarische und thematische Einheit der Paulusrede* (FB 38; Stuttgart: Katholisches Bibelwerk, 1980) 17-18.

77. Ibid., 17.

78. Ibid., 8-9.

79. Ibid., 64.

80. Ibid., "Die Darstellung des jerusalemitischen Geschehens ist stark geprägt von *lukanishem Sprachstil* und ist gleichzeitig reich an *Verweisen und Anspielungen auf das AT*," 80.

81. Ibid., 142-45.

Zusammenfassend läßt sich sagen, daß die verbindenden Schlüsselbegriffe der Pauluspredigt nicht nur die formale, sondern auch die innere Einheit der Rede und damit auch der Heilsgeschichte begründen. Im Rückblick auf das AT (vv. 16a–22) sieht der Verfasser der antiochenischen Rede die typologische Bedeutung der Geschehnisse, sieht, wie die Begriffe Verheißung, Heil und (Auf-)Erweckung–Erhöhung aufeinander bezogen sind und sich immer stärker mit Wirklichkeit füllen, wie alles Handeln Gottes an seinem Volk und dann an dessen Führern sich schließlich auf die (Auf-)Erweckung der einen Rettergestalt, Jesus, sich hinordnet (vv. 23. 32. 33), der wiederum allen das Heil schenkt (vv. 38f). Durch ihn erben alle, die an ihn glauben, das ewige Leben (vv. 40. 46. 48). So erfüllt sich die tiefste Hoffnung Israels (vgl. auch Lk 10, 25; 18,18), die größte Sehnsucht der Menschen.[82]

G. John J. Kilgallen

Kilgallen argues that Acts 13:38–39 is the goal of Paul's speech in Antioch of Pisidia. In the context of Paul being asked to say a word of exhortation to the crowds, Acts 13:38–39 speaks of forgiveness of sins and justification. These two verses are a fitting response to the synagogue leaders' request and the personal needs of the Jewish audience. So the context into which Paul's words are situated suggests that 13:38–39 are the final goal of the speech. In the text of the speech, the particle οὖν ("therefore") in 13:38 seems to suggest that 13:38–39 is the climax of Paul's speech. In light of the request of the synagogue leaders, the verb καταγγέλλεται ("it has been preached") also points to the same direction.[83]

Kilgallen also notices the dynamic development of the time from past to present. The past is recalled so as to reach to the present of the audience. It is the past that generates the present. There is a temporal driving force in the speech. Consequently, the resurrection is the fulfillment of the promise made to the fathers. Yet this past event must be brought forward to the present. Therefore, Kilgallen concludes that the past serves the present, the salvation that Jesus' resurrected life brings, that is, the forgiveness of sins and justification by believing in Jesus in 13:38–39.[84]

---

82. Ibid., 146.

83. John J. Kilgallen, "Acts 13, 38–39: Culmination of Paul's Speech in Pisidia," *Bib* 69 (1988) 480–506, here 481–83.

84. Ibid., 486.

H. Danielle Ellul

Ellul studies the speech in Antioch of Pisidia in a synchronic way. She pays close attention to the text and its rhetoric and narrative techniques. She follows the traditional structure of the speech in three sections, according to the three apostrophes in 13:16, 26, and 38. It is clear that these marks are techniques intended to call the attention of the audiences either to the importance of the speech or to show new development in the thoughts of the speech. The three apostrophes divide the text into three parts in three successive moments.[85]

In the first part (13:16–25), Paul addresses the "people of Israel" and "God-fearers" and deals with the time of the past, the time of their ancestors. In the second part (13:26–37), he addresses his audiences as "children of the family of Abraham" and "those who fear God." Yet the main change is that he places himself in the contemporary time together with those audiences, for it is "to us this word of salvation has been sent." In the third section (13: 38–41) he simply addresses the audiences as "my brothers." He does not specify the audiences as "people of Israel" or "children of the family of Abraham." He leaves aside all the historical dimensions. This disregard of the historical dimension opens the present to the future, for whoever believes in him is justified (ἐν τούτῳ πᾶς ὁ πιστεύων δικαιοῦται). There is no distinction between the Jews and the Gentiles; there is only a distinction between believers in the resurrected Lord and nonbelievers.[86]

In these three successive moments from the past to the present, and to the future, there are three creeds. The first section presents the OT creed that God is the Creator (13:17b–23) and John the Baptist is disqualified as Messiah (13:24–25). The second presents the NT creed that is Jesus' crucifixion and resurrection (13:26–31) and David is disqualified as Messiah (13:32–37). The third presents the Pauline creed that God conquers sin (13:38–39) and consequently the Law has lost its salvific function forever and there is a danger for Israel to be disqualified as God's people (13:40–41).[87]

---

85. Danielle Ellul, "Antioche de Pisidie: Une Prédication . . . trois Credos? (Actes 13,13–43)," *FilolNT* 5 (1992) 3–14, here 3.
86. Ibid.
87. Ibid., 6–14.

I. DAVID A. DESILVA

DeSilva acknowledges that the sermon in Antioch stands at the important turning point in Acts, for the mission of the church begun in the first half has now reached a new stage—a proclamation of the good news to the Gentiles.[88]

First, Desilva thinks that the opening summary of the history of Israel in Acts 13:17-22 has a close connection with the contents of the missionary sermon, for this underscores the connection between God's initiative in Israel's history and his initiative in the present fulfillment of the Davidic, messianic promise.[89] This historical exordium assures that continuity of the present work of God with the history of God's mighty acts on behalf of Israel. Second, the theme of promise and fulfillment is the golden thread that connects the promise to David, fulfilled in the raising of Jesus from among David's seed. Third, Luke does not simply demonstrate the reality of Jesus' resurrection; he shows the consequences of the resurrection and the continued work of the incorruptible One (13:32-41). Fourth, he interprets the word ἔργον ("work") as the incorporation of the Gentiles through the promised risen Messiah, the "light to the Gentiles" (Isa 49:6; Acts 13:47; 26:23). This work has been prepared (Luke 2:32; Acts 1:8; 2:21) and is now fulfilled in the risen Lord. In him the future hope of Israel and the blessings of the Gentiles are assured. Fifth, through this speech Luke tries to accomplish the turning point of the mission, the Jews' rejection and the acceptance of the Gentiles of Paul's proclamation.[90]

J. Huub van de Sandt

De Sandt's studies focus on the three quotations in Acts 13:32-52. First, he studies the original contexts of these quotations (Ps 2:7b; Isa 55:3c; Hab 1:5; and Isa 49:6b) in the LXX. Then he concludes that the quotation in Acts 13:32-52 is a reflection of Luke's LXX interpretation.[91]

---

88. David A. deSilva, "Paul's Sermon in Antioch of Pisidia," *BiblSac* 151 (1994) 32-49, here 32.

89. Ibid., 38.

90. Ibid., 48-49.

91. Huub van de Sandt, "The Quotations in Acts 13: 32-52 as a Reflection of Luke's LXX Interpretation," *Bib* 75 (1994) 26-58.

The quotation of Ps 2:7b in Acts 13:33b is taken verbatim from the LXX and serves as the scriptural proof text of Jesus' resurrection. The original context is the vain rebellion against God's anointed one. There is an agreement between Psalm 2 and Acts 13:27–33, for each presents the action of human beings as opposed to the action of God.[92]

The quotation of Isa 55:3c, "I will renew with you the everlasting covenant, the benefits (blessings) assured to David," in Acts 13:34b, "I will give you the benefits (blessings) assured to David," shows that the resurrection of Jesus is the blessings assured to David. In Acts 13:34a, "And that he raised him from the dead never to return to corruption," implies that Jesus' resurrection is the fulfillment of the prophecy on the "blessings of David." In Luke's view, the passage of the imperishable blessings of David in Isa 55:3c of the LXX is fulfilled in Jesus' resurrection to eternal life. In order to prove this, Luke inserts 13:35–37 and a further quotation from Ps 16:10, "You will not suffer your holy one to see corruption." Luke uses Acts 13:38–39 to explain further the "blessings of David," that is; forgiveness of sins and justification. By writing "*To you* forgiveness of sins is being proclaimed," in 13:38, Luke wants to underscore that the "blessings of David" are offered to the audiences. "Forgiveness of sins" is in agreement with Isa 55: 7d, "and he shall find mercy, for he (the Lord) shall abundantly forgive your sins." De Sandt further explains that Luke probably understands the purpose of the effective prophetic word in Isa 55: 11 in the perspective of Isa 45:23–25, where justification is found. This justification is applied to "everyone who believes" since, in Isa 45:23–25, the Gentile nations are addressed.[93]

With regard to the quotation of Hab 1:1–11 in Acts 13:41, de Sandt shows the original context of the quotation is the announcement of a work that people will never believe (ἔργον ὃ οὐ μὴ πιστεύσητε). God will astonish the ungodly oppressors and all who are suffering injustice. God announces his verdict in Hab 1:5, "Look over the nations and see, and be utterly amazed! For a work is being done in your days that you would not have believed, were it told." In Acts 13:41, Luke interpolates the word ἔργον ("work") into his conclusion. The repetition of the word "work" has been purposely inserted in the same verse (13:41). In Acts the singular ἔργον ("work") is found in 5:38; 13:2; 14:26; 15:38, and into each case this word indicates the mission to the Gentiles. Luke's

---

92. Ibid., 31–32.
93. Ibid., 33–42.

duplication of this term in the Habakkuk quotation is to stress the same aspect: the amazement about God's work has to do with the mission to the Gentiles.⁹⁴

K. Marion L. Soards

Soards bases his thesis about this speech in Acts on the pioneering studies of Dibelius and Noth. Dibelius writes that the tradition of the historical writings teaches us that the interpreters of the historical speeches must first ask, "What is the function of the speeches in the whole work."⁹⁵ There is a parallel with the speeches in Acts. That is, at vital points in the history of the community Luke has inserted speeches to function in the whole of Acts.⁹⁶ Therefore it is important to interpret these speeches in Acts as a whole rather than interpret each speech on its own. Soards's investigation tries to comprehend the literary role of the speeches in Acts. Consequently, he studies the part the speeches play in the work as a whole.⁹⁷

Noth recognized that the specific repeated elements of the great speeches in Deuteronomy unify the presentation of the whole premonarchical period of Israel's history.⁹⁸ Soards's thesis is that the speeches in Acts are highly repetitive and they serve the function of unification, the crucial factor in the coherence of the whole Acts account.⁹⁹

Under these two guiding principles, Soards studies Paul's speech at Antioch of Pisidia (Acts13:16b–41, 46–47). He divides the speech into two major sections (13:16b–25; 13:26–37), followed by a conclusion (13:38–41), and after further developments there is an epilogue (13:46–47). He analyzes this speech and states that there are four themes

---

94. Ibid., 42–50.
95. Dibelius, *Book of Acts*, 53.
96. Ibid., 75.
97. Soards, *Speeches in Acts*, 13. He further comments, "One should not deny the value of the detailed study of individual speeches or of clusters of speeches, but one should recognize that simply treating the speeches in this manner turns the Acts account into a series of episodes. If Acts is viewed in this way, it is indeed a peculiar narrative."
98. Martin Noth, *The Deuteronomistic History* (trans. of *Überlieferungsgeschichtliche Studien* [2nd ed.; Tübingen: Niemeyer, 1957] JSOTSup 15; Sheffield: JSOT Press, 1981) 1–110.
99. Soards, *Speeches in Acts*, 12.

in it. Soards does not give any order to these themes. Here I give an order to them for the sake of clarity.

The first theme is God's authority. He writes that in 13:17–23 God is clearly the dominant figure in the history of Israel, whereas other characters come and go. It is God who "chose" (ἐξελέξατο) our ancestors. It is God who "exalted" (ὕψωσεν) the people. It is God rather than Moses who "led" the Israelites "out of" (ἐξήγαγεν) Egypt. Each point of the story from the wildness to David emphasizes God's power and authority.[100]

The second theme is the fulfillment of the plan of God. In 13:23, "From this man's descendants God, according to his promise, has brought to Israel a savior, Jesus." This indicates that God works in relation to a plan and that God is the one who possesses the power to fulfill the plan. Furthermore, the second major section of the speech (13:26–37) focuses on Jesus, his death and resurrection. But in the interpretation of the significance of Jesus' events, God is still the overarching figure whose divine purposes were fulfilled through Jesus. Despite the injustice of Jesus' death, the speech regards the cross as the fulfillment of Scripture rather than as a scandal; thus it is clear that Jesus' death happened according to God's plan. The LXX quotations of Ps 2:7, Isa 55:3, and Ps 15:10 are not about David, for according to the plan of God he died (13:36), but about Jesus, who sees no corruption.[101]

The third theme is witness. In the speech, after a narration of the history of Israel and the coming of the savior Jesus, John the Baptist witnesses to the veracity of the declaration that Jesus is the savior whom God promised to Israel. John the Baptist announces that he is not the promised savior that Israel expected but that a greater one is coming after him. John the Baptist is in the line of the history of Israel and bears witness that Jesus is the savior. In 13:31, it says, "And for many days he appeared to those who had come up with him from Galilee to Jerusalem. These are now his witnesses before the people." The disciples are the witnesses who proclaim Jesus' gospel to the people. They bear witness to Jesus' resurrection. This statement once again emphasizes the familiar "witness" theme (1:8) of Acts.[102]

---

100. Ibid., 82.
101. Ibid., 83–87.
102. Ibid., 83–85.

The fourth theme is the universal dimension of the Christian proclamation. The phrase "the believer" (ὁ πιστεύων) in 13:39, "echoes 10:43 and recalls the universalistic scope of the citation from Joel in 2:17."[103] In 13:47, it says, "I have made you a light to the Gentiles, that you may be an instrument of salvation to the ends of the earth," citing the LXX of Isa 49:6 in an abbreviated form. This verse presents a similar statement to Acts 1:8 and 26:23b. The last of these statements points to the universal dimensions of the Christian proclamation. It is clear that God's will is at work directing the actions of the apostles to all the peoples, Jews and Gentiles.[104]

Soards concludes that there are some fundamental theological issues in all the speeches of Acts. They are divine authority, Jesus, the fulfillment of God's plan, and the theme of witness.[105]

The speeches in Acts tell of a transcendent but active God who relates to humans in order to bring to fruition God's divine will. The speeches declare that God's plan has been and is being brought to realization in Jesus Christ. Yet God's plan exists and is in operation prior to Jesus and after his exaltation. The plan continues to be realized by divine necessity in the obedient witness of the apostles and other members of the early Christian community. Thus, the decisive activity of God in relation to Jesus Christ inaugurated the ongoing testimony to God's saving work. In the whole book of Acts one encounters the theme of Spirit-empowered witness from the beginning (1:8) to the end (28:23) and all along the way. The role of the speeches in Acts is to tell the stories of the witness—of their articulation, acceptance, or rejection—and to do so in such a way that through repetition the unified witness is emphasized in the whole of Acts.[106]

L. Josef Pichler

Pichler's work is a historical research in methodology. The main title suggests the issue of his study is a theological one: the reception of Paul in Acts. He tries to deal with the possibility of the reception of Pauline theology in Acts from a literary point of view. The subtitle specifies

103. Ibid., 87.
104. Ibid., 88.
105. Ibid., 182–200.
106. Ibid., 199.

the subject of the study; Paul's inaugural sermon in the synagogue at Antioch of Pisidia, because he thinks that the inaugural speech of Paul in Acts carries the programmatic characteristics. It is clear that the reception of Paul in Acts is closely related to the description of Paul by Luke in Acts.[107]

The question of the reception and description of Paul in Acts 13:16–52 focuses on the theme of Luke's understandings of Paul. In approaching this theme, he writes that we do not need to point out the common elements or differences between Paul's self-understanding and Luke's presentation of Paul, but we must ask the reason why sometimes there are similar and at other times different presentations between Paul's self-understanding in his letters and Luke's understandings of Paul in Acts.[108]

Pichler thinks it is important to know the Lukan community in order to understand the motives of the reception of Paul in Acts. He maintains that there were mainly two theological problems in the Lukan community. The first was whether the Jewish law was still valid for the community. This was a real test in apostolic times (cf. Galatians 2 and Acts 15). The second problem was the abrupt painful break between the apostolic time and the post-apostolic time. Therefore, it was important to build this continuity between these two periods, and it is important to find an authoritative figure in this postapostolic period.[109]

Luke tries to show that Paul's preaching is apostolic. Paul does not fit the criteria to be an apostle according to Acts 1:21. Yet after the death of Jesus, Paul's preaching is true to the Gospels. Paul can be the example and model of a fervent missionary and an obedient servant of the word of God in the Christian life.[110] Luke tries to show that "*die paulinische Predigt ist apostolische Predigt, und die apostolische Predigt ist selbstverständlich paulinische Predigt.*"[111]

Luke draws a parallel between the work of Jesus and Paul (Luke 22:47–23:25 with Acts 21:27–26:32; Luke 2:32, 34b with Acts 9:15; Luke 4:16–30 with Acts 13:14–52; Luke 9:51 with Acts 19:21). This parallel be-

---

107. Josef Pichler, *Paulusrezeption in der Apostelgeschichte: Untersuchungen zur Rede im pisidischen Antiochien* (Innsbruck: Tyrolia-Verlag, 1997) 11.

108. Ibid.

109. Ibid., 316–17.

110. Ibid., 320.

111. Ibid., 321.

tween Jesus and Paul shows the continuity of Paul's preaching and work after Jesus. It also shows that Jesus is the only leader of the church community.[112] Paul is only a follower of Jesus; he is a trustworthy preacher of the gospel of Jesus. This gives authority to Paul's preaching. Pichler quotes Robert L. Brawley, "A Hellenistic audience would have found parallels between Jesus and the protagonists in Acts clues to the true successors of the founder and to the legitimate tradition."[113]

There is also a parallel between Peter and Paul. Paul's inaugural speech at Antioch of Pisidia is parallel to Peter's speech in Acts 2:14–41. As Jesus' inaugural speech in Luke 4:16–30, these two speeches present the program of their preaching. The program is the development from the mission to the Jews to a mission to the Gentiles. In Acts 10, Peter is described as the prototype to preach the gospel to the Gentiles. Here Paul is in harmony with Peter. Therefore "die Pragmatik des gemeinsamen Schemas der Missionsreden läuft auf einen gemeindlichen Konsens hinaus, der die Lehre in gleicher Weise betrifft wie die gläubige Praxis."[114]

Pichler concludes:

> Lukas kennt zwar zentrale Anliegen der paulinischen Theologie und bringt diese auch als theologisch unverzichtbare Positionen in sein Werk ein, doch er rezipiert sie nicht, weil sie paulinisch sind, sondern ausschließlich deswegen, weil durch sie der Sinninhalt des Evangeliums erst endgültig offenbar wird. Paulus ist für Lukas wichtig in seiner Heilverkündigung und als christliches Vorbild.[115]

He continues,

> "Paulus ist also nicht der begnadete Theologe und Kirchenlehrer, sondern er ist für die lukanische Gemeinde der vorbildhafte Missionar, das *Leitbild* und der *Mystagoge*."[116]

---

112. Ibid., 344.
113. Robert L. Brawley, *Luke-Acts and the Jews: Conflict, Apology, and Conciliation* (SBLMS 33; Atlanta: Scholars Press, 1987) 66.
114. Pichler, *Paulusrezeption in der Apostelgeschichte*, 358.
115. Ibid.
116. Ibid., 359.

M. Michel Quesnel

Quesnel studies the three speeches given by Paul in Acts 13:16b–41, 17:22b–31, and 20:18b–35. First he studies the three speeches in a synoptic way. He finds that the first two speeches show that Paul is partially successful. Yet in the third one, Paul apparently fails, for his own people do not accept him. Quesnel's question: Is there any figure that is parallel to Paul? He first notes that Peter is parallel to Paul, as is apparent from the two inaugural speeches by Peter in Acts 2:14b–35 and Paul in Acts 13:16b–41. But in the second part of the Acts, the differences between Peter and Paul are more numerous than the similarities.

With regard to Paul's farewell speech in Miletus, Quesnel notices a parallel between this speech and Jesus' words in Luke 22:15–20. Paul's life shows a parallel with Jesus' life. He writes, "Comme Jésus également, Paul est de plus en plus seul à mesure qu'il avance vers ce qui pourrait être appelé sa Passion, bien qu'elle se termine de façon non sanglante, et même par un quasi acquittement."[117]

N. N. Esaú García

García states that Paul's speech from Antioch of Pisidia inaugurates the evangelization of Asia Minor. The text represents an important fact of the missionary teaching of the ancient Church, resulting in the most important event in our faith: the resurrection as a mystery of salvation. Furthermore, it is interesting to go to the heart of the preaching in the missionary activity of the early Church. It is an announcement that reflects an internal dynamism within a community that makes one respond in a concrete way to the christological announcement of Paul.[118]

García concludes that the speech in Pisidia is the core of the evangelization realized by the missionaries in Antioch. Before transmitting the Christian message, Paul presents a prelude to the great salvific events realized by God for his people. With this historical recollection, Paul reminds the audience that God is permanently present in the history of the people of Israel. Furthermore, he reiterates that the message of salva-

---

117. Michel Quesnel, "Paul Prédicateur dans les Actes des Apôtres," *NTS* 47 (2001) 469–81, here 480.

118. N. Esaú García, "El Discurso de Antioquía de Pisidia en los Hechos de los Apóstoles," *May* 33 (2007) 109–69, here 109.

tion is universal. God shows his salvific action to all through his Son Jesus Christ. Everyone who believes in Jesus Christ can be justified.[119]

The use of *midrash* that establishes lines of analogy with other texts of the Scriptures offers new dimensions for interpreting the argument of the speech. In the context of the announcement about the resurrection, it is essential to relate the messianic "crucified Jesus Savior" and the "resurrected Jesus" who, by his resurrection, is constituted universal mediator.[120]

The resurrection of Jesus is presented as the realization of the Davidic promise. The whole speech reflects a fundamental intention: to recognize that God has promised, for the good of his people, a coming that is certain and lasting beyond the dynasty of David; the tradition has understood this promise in a messianic and eschatological sense.[121]

The evangelist expresses, through the speech in the Jewish synagogue, some fundamental elements in Pauline theology: the whole history of salvation is expressed through the fulfillment of Jesus as Messiah. Because of this, he is not only considered David's descendant; he is also the Word of salvation for all people. With his death and resurrection all the promises are fulfilled and accomplished. Because of God's faithfulness to his promises, he will fulfill all that was promised to his people. This salvific fulfillment is expressed through the justification and the forgiveness of sins for everyone who believes in his Son, Jesus Christ.[122]

In light of these parallels, we can consider the speech in Antioch of Pisidia as an outline of Pauline catechetical theology and as the overture to a catechesis about the risen Jesus Christ.[123]

IV. CONCLUSION

Having reviewed the research of this speech, it is clear that some significant studies have been done on this speech. The studies of Dibelius and Wilckens have laid the foundation for the study of the missionary speeches in Acts. Both of them confirm that these speeches are composed by Luke and consequently express Lukan theology. Dibelius thinks that

---

119. Ibid., 169.
120. Ibid.
121. Ibid.
122. Ibid.
123. Ibid.

the first section does not really connect with the content of the speech. His undertaking has stimulated several studies of the inner literary and thematic unity of this speech. Buss and Pillai show the internal unity of this speech by highlighting the editorial skill of Luke.

For almost all the authors the central theme is the promise and fulfillment. Some recognize that there is a continuity from the past promise to the current fulfillment and pointing further to all who believe in the name of Jesus. They will have forgiveness of sin and justification. Some focus on Jesus' resurrection as the climax of the speech, and some highlight the effects of Jesus' resurrection, i.e., forgiveness of sin and justification.

Some approach the speech in relation to other speeches. They try to compare this speech either with other Pauline speeches in Acts or with other speeches by other speakers in Acts and in Luke. They find some parallels and similar theological views. The speeches in Acts unify different narratives in Acts.

Although there are different approaches to study this speech, nearly all scholars agree that Paul's speech to the Jews in Synagogue in Acts 13:16-41 is a speech composed by Luke. It is a Lukan composition telling what Paul would have said had he addressed to the Jews in Synagogues. It expresses Lukan theology regarding Paul's preaching and mission to the Jews.

There have been a number of studies in recent years, but there has not yet been a thorough and comprehensive narrative analysis of the speech in Antioch of Pisidia in relation to Paul's mission to the Jews in Acts. How does this speech unify Paul's missionary work among the Jews as a whole? How does this speech function as a model speech that Paul delivers to the Jews? How does this inaugural speech relate to Paul's missionary work among the Jews in Acts? Many authors have been profoundly influenced by the so-called two-period theory. The first period is the proclamation of the good news to the Jews (Acts 2-13); the second period is the proclamation to the Gentiles (Acts 14-17). Therefore, according to Wilckens, the speech of Paul to the Jews in Antioch of Pisidia is the last call to the Jews. The end of the speech marks the end of Paul's missionary work to the Jews and the turning point of Paul's mission from the Jews to the Gentiles. I think this view should be explored further.

Since it is an inaugural speech, in the second chapter I will study Jesus' (Luke 4:16-30) and Peter's (Acts 2:14-40) inaugural speeches to determine the literary function of these inaugural speeches in the two-part work of Luke. In the third chapter I will study this speech in detail and present an exegesis of it. In the fourth chapter, I will study how Acts portrays Paul's mission among the Jews in Acts. Finally, I will present my conclusion of the meaning and significance of Paul's inaugural sermon in the synagogue of Antioch in Pisidia (Acts 13:16–41) for his missionary work among the Jews in the Acts of the Apostles.

2

The Literary Function of Jesus' Inaugural Sermon

(Luke 4:16–30)

INTRODUCTION

PAUL'S SERMON TO THE Jews in Antioch of Pisidia (Acts 13:16–41) is his inaugural sermon. Besides this sermon, there are two inaugural sermons in Luke-Acts. They are Jesus' sermon in the synagogue of Nazareth (Luke 4:16–30) and Peter's sermon at Pentecost (Acts 2:14–40).

I will study the literary function of these two inaugural sermons with a view to determining the literary function of Paul's sermon in Acts 13:16–41. In order to do this, in this chapter I will study how Jesus' sermon in the synagogue functions in the Gospel of Luke and Acts. Then in the next chapter, I will study how Peter's speech functions in Acts. After studying these two inaugural sermons, I will draw a conclusion at the end of Chapter Three as to how these two sermons function in the Gospel of Luke and in Acts.

In order to gain some insight to Jesus' inaugural sermon, I will focus on the text and provide an exegesis of it. After the exegesis, I will study its literary function in Luke-Acts. In the first part of this chapter, I will focus on the literary context and the structure of the sermon; then I will offer a detailed exegesis of it. In the second part, I will study the literary function of this sermon in Jesus' ministry and in Luke-Acts as a whole. Finally, I will draw a brief conclusion based on my exegesis.

I. JESUS' INAUGURAL SERMON IN THE SYNAGOGUE OF NAZARETH (LUKE 4:16-30)

A. The Literary Context

It is widely recognized that Luke uses geography to structure and advance his narrative in Luke-Acts.[1] Luke sets Jerusalem at the center of his story. In the Gospel, the narrative begins in Jerusalem, and the whole narrative moves toward Jerusalem. In Acts, the mission of the apostles starts in Jerusalem, and it moves to the ends of the earth (Acts 1:8).

After the infancy narrative, Luke presents the preparation for Jesus' public ministry (3:1-4:13). The preparation includes John the Baptist's witness about the coming Messiah (3:15-17), Jesus' baptism as the Son of God (3:21-22), Jesus' genealogy (3:23-37), and his temptation (4:1-13). After this, Luke narrates Jesus' public ministry in Galilee and the surrounding areas (4:14-9:50). Next he narrates Jesus' journey to Jerusalem (9:51-19:27). Finally, Jesus arrives in Jerusalem. Luke then presents Jesus' ministry in Jerusalem (19:28-21:38), his passion, his death (22:1-23:56a), and his resurrection (23:56b-24:53).[2]

The immediate context for Jesus' teaching in the synagogue of Nazareth (4:16-30) is the preparation for Jesus' public ministry (3:21-4:13). Jesus' baptism and temptation are separated by his genealogy. These three episodes are linked together by his identification as the "Son of God" (3:22, 38; 4:3, 9) and the manifestation of "the Holy Spirit" (3:22; 4:1).[3]

Only Luke stresses that Jesus "was praying" at his baptism (3:21). This reveals the intimate relation between Jesus' prayer and his baptism. "In Luke-Acts times of prayer and worship are frequently the occasions for divine revelations to characters in the story."[4] During Jesus' deep communion with God in prayer, God sends the Holy Spirit to anoint him and

---

1. Luke T. Johnson, *The Gospel of Luke* (SacPag 3; Collegeville, MN: Liturgical Press, 1991) 14.

2. Joseph A. Fitzmyer, *The Gospel According to Luke I-IX: Introduction, Translation, and Notes* (AB 28; New York: Doubleday, 1981) 135-42.

3. Franklin S. Spencer, *The Gospel of Luke and Acts of the Apostles* (Nashville, TN: Abingdon, 2008) 116.

4. Robert C. Tannehill, *The Narrative Unity of Luke-Acts: A Literary Interpretation* (2 vols.; Philadelphia: Fortress, 1986) 1. 56. He writes, "This is true of Zechariah (Luke 1:9-11), Anna (2:37-38), Cornelius (Acts 10:2-6), Peter (10:9-16), Paul (Acts 9:11-12; 22:17-21), and the prophets and teachers of the church in Antioch (13:2). This is true also of Jesus."

to affirm his status as God's beloved Son (3:22). François Bovon notes that after Jesus' baptism (βαπτισθέντος) he continues to pray (προσευχομένου). "Prayer becomes the appropriate human response to God."[5]

The announcement from heaven (3:22) echoes God's appointment of both a powerful Messiah (Psalm 2) and a "gentle servant of justice" (Isa 42:1-4).[6] The descent of the Spirit upon Jesus "is a preparation for the ministry, the 'beginning' of which is noted in the immediately following context (v. 23)."[7] The coming of the Spirit upon Jesus has a narrative function; "it initiates a sequence of events."[8] Jesus is not only filled with the Holy Spirit, he is also led by the Holy Spirit into the desert (4:1). After resisting the temptations of Satan, Jesus returns to Galilee in the power of the Spirit. In his inaugural sermon, he announces that "the Spirit of the Lord is upon me," and he states his public mission (4:18). Robert Tannehill writes that except for Jesus' genealogy (3:23-38), the Holy Spirit is connected with each of the narrative episodes between 3:22 to 4:18 "and is directly related to Jesus' mission."[9]

After presenting Jesus as God's beloved son, Luke informs us of Jesus' age, origin, and genealogy (3:23-38). "The establishment of one's identity, status, or legitimacy in a post or office (as priest or king) often demanded the recording of ancestry."[10] In the Hellenistic biographies, the purpose of genealogies is to "establish the basis for the divine *dynamis* (power) at work in the hero or sage."[11] Immediately after the pronouncement of Jesus' divine sonship at his baptism, the genealogy "resists any tendencies to deny or downplay Jesus' humanity."[12] Jesus was thought to be the son of Joseph (3:23). Luke traces Jesus' ancestry to Adam and ultimately to God. William Kurz writes, "This view 'from below' seems intended to complement, not contradict, his earlier more theological explanation of Jesus' divine sonship, a view 'from above.'"[13]

---

5. François Bovon, *Luke 1: A Commentary on the Gospel of Luke 1:1-9:50* (Hermeneia; trans. Christine M. Thomas; Minneapolis: Fortress, 2002) 128.

6. Spencer, *Luke and Acts*, 117.

7. Fitzmyer, *Luke I-IX*, 481.

8. Tannehill, *Narrative Unity of Luke-Acts: Luke*, 57.

9. Ibid.

10. Fitzmyer, *Luke I-IX*, 490.

11. Johnson, *Luke*, 72.

12. Spencer, *Luke and Acts*, 117.

13. William S. Kurz, *Reading Luke-Acts: Dynamics of Biblical Narratives* (Louisville:

The baptism and genealogy (3:21–38) should be read together when addressing the question of Jesus' identity. Jesus is the Son of God, and his origin is from God (3:38). At the same time, he is rooted in human history, for he is also a son of Adam. The genealogy "gives Jesus' position within the ancestral subdivision of God's people as well as his temporal relationship to the people's history."[14] The genealogy also demonstrates the whole course of salvation history. Jesus is the climax of salvation history. The line of humanity has reached its "definitive fulfillment in Jesus." Consequently, "God's people is in the eschatological age of the Spirit's outpouring."[15] This new age of Jesus "is seen as related to the course of history stemming not only from Israel but from humanity and ultimately from God himself. God's purpose in creating humanity in the beginning is seen to reach a new stage in the *archē* of the period of Jesus itself."[16] Bovon recognizes that Jesus' genealogy has a literary function. It lies between his baptism as the Son of God and his temptation as the Son of God. The genealogy presents Jesus in human history as truly human, thereby making the temptations of the Son of God real.[17]

The temptation or testing of Jesus in the desert is the last of the preparatory episodes introducing Jesus' public ministry (4:1–13). The three temptations are related to the question of the nature of Jesus' mission as the Son of God. The three temptations represent false understandings of Jesus' mission. Jesus' responses to them present him as the Son of God who is "obedient to his Father's will and refusing to be seduced into using his power or authority as Son for any reason other than that for which he has been sent."[18] Compared with Israel of old, which asked for signs from God, Jesus refuses to ask for signs from God and the royal authority befitting a Son. He is the Son who follows the path of service and obedience to the Father.[19] These tests of Jesus "symbolize the seduction in the hostility, opposition, and rejection which confronted him constantly

---

Westminster/John Knox, 1993) 48.

14. William S. Kurz, "Luke 3:23–38 and Greco-Roman and Biblical Genealogies," in *Luke-Acts: New Perspectives from the Society of Biblical Literature Seminar* (ed. Charles H. Talbert; New York: Crossroad, 1983) 169–87, here 175.

15. Ibid.

16. Fitzmyer, *Luke I–IX*, 498.

17. Bovon, *Luke 1*, 137.

18. Fitzmyer, *Luke I–IX*, 510.

19. Bovon, *Luke 1*, 146.

throughout his ministry."[20] Jesus overcomes these temptations through God's word and is the more powerful one. Satan departs from him for a time (4:13). Satan will return to test Jesus in the passion narrative.

Luke starts with a summary of Jesus' Galilean ministry in 4:14–15. This summary functions as a bridge. On the one hand, it concludes the preparation of Jesus' ministry. Now Jesus is "armed with the power of the Holy Spirit" and returns to Galilee. He is fully prepared by the power of the Holy Spirit. The Spirit inaugurates the period of Jesus. On the other hand, this scene gives a preview of the forthcoming Galilean ministry of Jesus. It focuses on two elements. The first is Jesus' teaching in the synagogues. The second is the universal appeal of his teaching. The news of him spreads throughout the whole region, and he is praised by all (4:15). Yet this is just a preview. The readers are still waiting for Jesus' teaching.

Luke 4:16–30 is probably a reworking of Mark 6:1–6.[21] In 4:16, 22, and 24, Luke seems to have used part of Mark's account to compose this pericope. Mark 6:1–6 is an account of Jesus' visit to the synagogue in his hometown of Nazareth. But Luke "has deliberately placed this incident at the very outset of the ministry of Jesus."[22] The episode of Jesus' rejection at Nazareth, then, is the occasion for the inaugural sermon that Jesus gives in the synagogue of Nazareth.

The immediate context after the passage (4:16–30) is Jesus' teaching and healing in the synagogue of Capernaum (4:31–37). Luke then narrates the healing of Simon's mother-in-law (4:38–39) and other healings (4:40–41). Jesus then departs from Capernaum to preach in other places (4:42–44). His Galilean ministry continues until 9:50, after which he journeys to Jerusalem. After delivering his inaugural speech, Jesus then begins his ministry. I will explain the relationship between Jesus' inaugural sermon and his ministry after my exegesis of the passage (4:16–30).

B. The Structure of the Sermon

Luke 4:16–30 is a distinct literary unit. "The unit is enclosed in an inclusion."[23] In v. 16 Jesus comes to Nazareth (ἦλθεν εἰς Ναζαρά), and in

---

20. Fitzmyer, *Luke I–IX*, 510.

21. Ibid., 527; Bovon, *Luke 1*, 150.

22. Graham N. Stanton, *The Gospels and Jesus* (Oxford: Oxford University Press, 1989) 91.

23. Charles H. Talbert, *Reading Luke: A Literary and Theological Commentary on the Third Gospel* (rev. ed.; Macon, GA: Smyth & Helwys, 2002) 57.

v. 30 he passes through their midst and goes away (αὐτὸς δὲ διελθὼν διὰ μέσου αὐτῶν ἐπορεύετο). In this pericope, there are several interactions between Jesus and his audience. After entering the synagogue, he stands up and reads the Scripture passage from the book of the Prophet Isaiah. This creates an expectation on the part of the audience. He then sits down to interpret the passage, which arouses surprise in his audience. In response to the reaction of the audience, Jesus speaks again, using proverbs and the stories of the prophets Elijah and Elisha. The audience responds negatively, and Jesus leaves Nazareth.[24] There is a development, then, in the responses between Jesus and his audience.

Most commentators recognize the chiastic or concentric structure of vv. 16b–20.[25] Some commentators divide this pericope into two parts according to its contents: Jesus' programmatic announcement of his ministry (vv. 16–22) and the rejection of Jesus by his compatriots (vv. 23–30). With some modifications, I follow the structure of Ulrich Busse, Bart J. Koet, and David L. Tiede. The structure of the passage is as follows:[26]

1. Jesus comes to Nazareth, his hometown (v. 16ab)

2. Phase I: Jesus reads the Scripture and the audience responds (vv. 16c–20)

   a. Jesus reads the Scripture (vv. 16c–20a)

      A   He stands up to read (v. 16c)
      B   The book of Isaiah is given to him (v. 17a)
      C   He opens the book (v. 17b)
      D   He reads the text of the prophet (vv. 18–19)
      C′ He closes the book (v. 20a)
      B′ He gives it back to the attendant (v. 20b)
      A′ He sits down (v. 20c)

   b. The audience responds with expectation (v. 20d)

---

24. Bart J. Koet, "Today This Scripture Has Been Fulfilled in Your Ears: Jesus' Explanation of Scripture in Luke 4, 16–30," in *Five Studies on Interpretation of Scripture in Luke-Acts* (Studiorum Novi Testamenti Auxilia XIV; Leuven: Leuven University Press, 1989) 24–55, here 28–29.

25. David L. Tiede, *Prophecy and History in Luke-Acts* (Philadelphia: Fortress, 1980) 35; see also Talbert, *Reading Luke*, 27–28.

26. Ulrich Busse, *Das Nazareth-Manifest Jesu: Eine Einführung in das lukanische Jesusbild nach Lk 4, 16–30* (SBS 91; Stuttgart: Katholisches Bibelwerk, 1977) 49.

3. Phase II: Jesus interprets the text of the Scripture and the audience responds (vv. 21–22)

    a. Jesus interprets the Isaiah text (v. 21)

    b. The audience responds with surprise (v. 22)

4. Phase III: Jesus responds to the audience's response and they further respond with rage (vv. 23–29)

    a. Jesus speaks to the audience (vv. 23–27)

        1) Jesus reveals the thoughts of the audience (v. 23)
        2) Jesus announces that a prophet is not accepted in his hometown (v. 24)
        3) Jesus recounts the stories of the prophets Elijah (vv. 25–26) and Elisha (v. 27)

    b. The audience responds with rage (vv. 28–29)

5. Jesus leaves Nazareth and goes on his way (v. 30)

C. A Detailed Exegesis

In preparation of his ministry, Jesus is empowered by the Holy Spirit as the Son of God. He is identified as God's only Son, the Messiah anointed to carry out God's mission in this world. With a summary of Jesus' ministry in Galilee, Luke connects this episode with what he narrated before about Jesus' empowerment by the Holy Spirit in 4:14, and he previews Jesus' ministry of teaching in synagogues and the responses of praise to his teaching in 4:15. Luke sets Jesus' first public teaching ministry in his hometown of Nazareth.

1. Jesus Comes to His Hometown Nazareth (v. 16ab)

Nazareth has a special significance for Luke. He repeatedly mentions that Nazareth is Jesus' hometown (1:24; 2:4, 39, 51; Acts 10:38).[27] It is the place where Jesus grew up, as is apparent from the verbs τρέφω, ἀνατρέφω, which refer not only to raising a child but to the period of childhood that Jesus spent at home, during which he was nourished, raised, and educated.[28] Although Luke narrates that Jesus has already taught in synagogues (v. 15), he reserves the first account of Jesus' preaching for

---

27. Johnson, *Luke*, 78.
28. Bovon, *Luke 1*, 152.

Nazareth. Since Luke uses a geographical scheme for the preaching of Jesus throughout Luke-Acts, it is appropriate to locate his inaugural sermon in Nazareth, where he grew up.[29] The mention of Nazareth as the place where Jesus grew up prepares the way for the saying in v. 24, "No prophet is acceptable in his hometown (ἐν τῇ πατρίδι αὐτοῦ)."

As was his custom (κατὰ τὸ εἰωθὸς αὐτῷ), Jesus goes to the synagogue on the Sabbath. In the Synoptic Gospels, only Luke emphasizes that Jesus goes to the synagogue habitually. Like his parents, Jesus is presented as a pious Jew with a good upbringing who attends the synagogue service regularly and preaches there (4:15, 31, 33, 44; 6:6; 13:10).[30] In Acts, the apostles and early Jerusalem Christians continue to go to the temple (2:46; 3:1; 4:1; 5:12, 42; 21:26). Moreover, the synagogue is the place where the apostles, especially Paul and his companions, preach the gospel (Acts 13:5, 14; 14:1; 17:10; 18:4, 26; 19:8). In Acts 17:2 the phrase, "as was his custom," is also used in regard to Paul. As was his custom (κατὰ δὲ τὸ εἰωθὸς τῷ Παύλῳ), Paul enters the synagogue and discusses the Scripture with the people for three Sabbaths. The beginning of the pericope, then, presents the synagogue as the setting of Jesus' teaching in Nazareth on a Sabbath.

2. Phase I: Jesus Reads the Scripture and the Audience Responds (vv. 16c–20)

In the first phase, Jesus reads from the book of Isaiah and the audience responds with expectation.

A. Jesus Reads the Scripture (vv. 16c–20a)

The literary structure of these verses is clear. "[T]he passage sustains highly detailed assessments of its construction, perhaps providing one of the more convincing New Testament examples of chiastic literary structure."[31] The chiastic structure is as follows:

    A He stands up to read (v. 16c)

    B The Book of Isaiah is given to him (v. 17a)

    C He opens the book (v. 17b)

    D He reads the text of the Isa 61:1–2 and 58:6 (vv. 18–19)

---

29. Robert C. Tannehill, *The Shape of Luke's Story: Essays on Luke-Acts* (Eugene, OR: Wipf & Stock, 2005) 21.
30. Johnson, *Luke*, 78.
31. Tiede, *Prophecy and History in Luke-Acts*, 35.

C′ He closes the book (v. 20a)

B′ He gives it back to the attendant (v. 20b)

A′ He sits down (v. 20c)

The first segment, from A to C, leads up to the text of the book of Isaiah that Jesus reads. The second segment, from C′ to A′, leads out of the text of Isaiah. The two segments have strikingly repetitive procedural details.[32] In this slow motion of the drama, the focus is on Jesus reading from the book of Isaiah (D). "This produces a pattern of ring-composition with the quotation from Isaiah situated as a pivotal point of utmost importance in the center."[33] The text of Isaiah is Jesus' solemn announcement.

The series of actions—Jesus' standing up to read, sitting down after the reading, beginning to speak, and the presence and help of the synagogue attendant—show that Luke is describing a synagogue service on the Sabbath.[34] In the synagogue setting, Jesus is invited by the leader of the assembly "to read and expound a Scripture text as happened to Paul and Barnabas at Antioch in Pisidia (Acts 13:15)."[35] This is part of the synagogue service in first-century Palestine.[36] Luke mentions the prophetic text from Isaiah only briefly. He is more interested in the fulfillment of the text in Jesus' ministry.[37]

> Luke narrates that Jesus finds (εὗρεν) the text of Isaiah. It is doubtful that there was a fixed reading of the book of Isaiah in the first-century synagogue service in Palestine. In any case, it is Luke who chooses this text of Isaiah to express his understanding of Jesus' ministry as the God-sent messianic prophet and in

---

32. Ibid.

33. H. J. B. Combrink, "The Structure and Significance of Luke 4:16–30," *NEOT* 7 (1973) 24–48, here 31.

34. Busse, *Das Nazareth-Manifest Jesu*, 107–12.

35. Fitzmyer, *Luke I–IX*, 531.

36. Paul Billerbeck ("Ein Synagogengottesdienst in Jesu Tagen," *ZNW* 55 [1965] 143–61) has made a detailed study of the synagogue service in first-century Palestine. The process of the services is as follows. First, the service begins with prayers. It includes singing of a psalm, recitation of the Shema (Deut 6:4–9; 11:13–21), and prayers of Tephilah and the Shemoneh Esreh (the eighteen blessings). Second, the center of the service is the reading from Torah and a section from the Prophets (see Acts 13:15). Third, a sermon is given to expound the Scripture readings. Finally, the service ends with a blessing by the chief leader of the synagogue and the priestly blessing of Num 6:24–26. See Fitzmyer, *Luke I–IX*, 531; Bovon, *Luke 1*, 153.

37. Fitzmyer, *Luke I–IX*, 531.

his account it is Jesus himself who "deliberately sought out the passage."³⁸

The quotation in 4:18-19 is a conflation of two texts from LXX Isa 58:6d and Isa 61:1a, b, d, 2a.

πνεῦμα κυρίου ἐπ' ἐμέ οὗ εἵνεκεν ἔχρισέν με εὐαγγελίσασθαι πτωχοῖς ἀπέσταλκέν μέ (ἰάσασθαι τοὺς συντετριμμένους τῇ καρδίᾳ), κηρύξαι αἰχμαλώτοις ἄφεσιν καὶ τυφλοῖς ἀνάβλεψιν καλέσαι ἐνιαυτὸν κυρίου δεκτὸν (καὶ ἡμέραν ἀνταποδόσεως παρακαλέσαι πάντας τοὺς πενθοῦντας) (LXX Isa 61: 1-2).

πνεῦμα κυρίου ἐπ' ἐμέ, οὗ εἵνεκεν ἔχρισέν με εὐαγγελίσασθαι πτωχοῖς, ἀπέσταλκέν με, κηρύξαι αἰχμαλώτοις ἄφεσιν καὶ τυφλοῖς ἀνάβλεψιν, ἀποστεῖλαι τεθραυσμένους ἐν ἀφέσει, κηρύξαι ἐνιαυτὸν κυρίου δεκτόν (Luke 4:18-19).

(οὐχὶ τοιαύτην νηστείαν ἐγὼ ἐξελεξάμην, λέγει κύριος, ἀλλὰ λῦε πάντα σύνδεσμον ἀδικίας, διάλυε στραγγαλιὰς βιαίων συναλλαγμάτων), ἀπόστελλε τεθραυσμένους ἐν ἀφέσει (καὶ πᾶσαν συγγραφὴν ἄδικον διάσπα) (LXX Isa 58: 6).

Two phrases are omitted from the Lukan quotation: the first is Isa 61:1c, "to heal the brokenhearted" (ἰάσασθαι τοὺς συντετριμμένους τῇ καρδίᾳ), which one would expect to follow after "to bring glad tidings to the poor" in Luke 4:18. The second is the phrase "the day of vengeance of our God" (Isa 61:2b, καὶ ἡμέραν ἀνταποδόσεως παρακαλέσαι πάντας τοὺς πενθοῦντας), which one would expect to find in Luke 4:19. One phrase is added in a modified form in the quotation: the phrase "set free the oppressed" (ἀπόστελλε τεθραυσμένους ἐν ἀφέσει) is changed to "to set free the oppressed" (ἀποστεῖλαι τεθραυσμένους ἐν ἀφέσει) and added at the end of Luke 4:18. Luke's quotation basically is conformed with the Greek text of the LXX, except that the verb καλέσαι ("to call for") in Isa 61:2a is changed to κηρύξαι ("to preach") in Luke 4:19.

The omission of the phrase "to heal the brokenhearted" in Isa 61:1c is "of little consequence."³⁹ "Luke generally conserves space in citations."⁴⁰ But if this phrase "to heal the brokenhearted" had been

---

38. Ibid., 532.

39. Ibid. Traugott Holtz (*Untersuchungen über die alttestamentliche Zitate bei Lukas* [Berlin: Academie Verlag, 1968] 40) suggests that ἰάομαι pertains only to the case of physical healing for Luke. It is possible that the phrase "to heal the brokenhearted" was absent in Luke's copy of the LXX.

40. Bovon, *Luke 1*, 153. Édouard Delebecque (*Évangile de Luc: Texte Traduit et*

retained, this would have given a basis for the saying, "Physician, heal yourself," in Luke 4:23. Luke does narrate Jesus' healing ministry. The omission of the phrase "the day of vengeance of our God" (Isa 61:2b) in Luke 4:19 is probably deliberate in order to stress the grace of God rather than the negative aspects of God's judgment.[41] The texts of Isa 61:1–2a and 58:6 are "combined by a midrashic technique which resembles the later rabbinic hermeneutical rule, the *gezerah shavah*."[42] This is a technique by which verses that have one or more words in common can be compared with each other in order to "elucidate each other."[43] The word ἄφεσις ("release") is the common word in the texts of Isa 58:6 and 61:1–2a.

The quotation in Luke 4:18–19 has its own structure. There are two units: (1) the Spirit of the Lord is upon me because the Lord has anointed me; (2) the Lord has sent me (a) to preach good news to the poor, (b) to proclaim release to the captives and (c) recovery of sight to the blind, (d) to send the downtrodden away released, (e) and to proclaim the Lord's acceptable year.[44] The sentence, "the coming of the Spirit of the Lord upon me because he has anointed me," in unit 1 is "in a position of great emphasis."[45] In unit 2, the main verb ἀπέσταλκεν is explained by four infinitives that form a chiastic construction.[46]

Annoté [Paris: Belles Lettres, 1976] 23) thinks that Luke is citing from memory and consequently misses that phrase.

41. Stanton, *Gospels and Jesus*, 92. See also Joachim Jeremias, *Jesus' Promise to the Nations* (trans. S. H. Hooke; London: SCM Press, 1958) 38.

42. Koet, "Today This Scripture," 29.

43. Ibid. Jean Koenig (*L'Herméneutique Analogique du Judaïsme Antique d'après les Témoins Textuels d'Isaïe* [VTSup 33; Leiden, Brill, 1982] 50) claims that this hermeneutical rule of comparing the common word or words has even been used for translations from Hebrew to the LXX. It has existed for a long time.

44. There is a dispute with regard to the punctuation in v. 18. Some put a stop after πτωχοῖς. Grammatically, the infinitive form εὐαγγελίσασθαι is dependent on the verb ἔχρισεν. In the punctuation of UBSGNT 4th edition and Nestle-Aland 27th edition, the infinitive εὐαγγελίσασθαι is grammatically dependent on the verb ἔχρισεν. I agree with the punctuation of Fitzmyer (*Luke I–IX*, 525), Bovon (*Luke 1*, 149), Johnson (*Luke*, 77), Tannehill (*Narrative Unity of Luke-Acts: Luke*, 62). I put a stop after ἔχρισεν με so that grammatically εὐαγγελίσασθαι is dependent on ἀπέσταλκεν. I. Howard Marshall (*The Gospel of Luke: A Commentary on the Greek Text* [NIGTC; Grand Rapids: Eerdmans, 1978]183) writes that this punctuation "agrees with that of the MT and LXX, and fits in with Luke's interpretation of the quotation in 4:43; it is to be preferred."

45. Combrink, "The Structure and Significance of Luke 4:16–30," 31.

46. Ibid., 29.

Tannehill pays special attention to the repeated words and grammatical forms. The object "me" (ἐμέ, με) appears three times. Later, "release" (ἄφεσις) occurs twice, and there is a series of four infinitives that depend on the verb ἀπέσταλκεν ("he sent"), three of which (εὐαγγελίσασθαι, κηρύξαι, κηρύξαι) refer to preaching.[47] The whole quotation emphasizes that the Holy Spirit has anointed Jesus and sent him to proclaim the good news of deliverance (release) to the poor. Tannehill concludes:

> These repetitions mark rhythmic phrases which correspond to short poetic lines, for the repetitions indicate that something which has already been said is being picked up and repeated but also enriched and expanded through new expression. Thus there is a pulsating series of overlapping phrases which poetically develop a single thought.[48]

Isaiah 61:1-2 belongs to a hymn of Isa 61:1-11. The original purpose of the passage is to explain the mission of the prophet. After the prophet's mission, there will be a period of favor and deliverance for Zion.[49] The message of deliverance parallels the coming of the Jubilee year (Lev 25:8-17), when debts are cancelled and slaves set free. "It is a picture of forgiveness and spiritual liberation."[50] Luke uses this passage to describe Jesus' mission and the arrival of the period of God's favor in Jesus. The present time is like the message of consolation that the Prophet Isaiah preached. "In fact, the totality of the deliverance that Isaiah described is now put into motion with Jesus' coming."[51]

The phrase "the Spirit of the Lord is upon me" recalls the coming of the Holy Spirit at Jesus' baptism in Luke 3:22. The anointing of Jesus

---

47. Tannehill, *Narrative Unity of Luke-Acts: Luke*, 61. In fact, one of the four infinitives (ἀποστεῖλαι) is related to the main verb ἀπέσταλκεν.

48. Ibid., 62.

49. James A. Sanders, "From Isaiah 61 to Luke 4," in *Christianity, Judaism, and other Greco-Roman Cults: Studies for Morton Smith at Sixty* (SJLA 12; ed. Jacob Neusner; Leiden: Brill, 1975) 1. 75-106. Koet ("Today This Scripture," 31-34) thinks that the context of Isaiah 61 is the prophetic call and mission and a message of joy and consolation for Zion. Yet the text from Isaiah 58 is a prophetic warning against the rich who worship God with fasting but do not take care of the poor among them. The allusion of the Jubilee year pleasing to God is also a call to conversion for the rich. Koet's basic view is that this is a call to repentance for the rich among the audience. I do not agree with this.

50. Darrell L. Bock, *Luke 1:1-9:50* (ECNT 3A; Grand Rapids, MI: Baker Books, 1994) 406.

51. Ibid.

is interpreted as God's anointing of Jesus with the Holy Spirit to which Acts 10:38 will refer. "The Spirit of the Lord" signals God's special action (Judg 3:10; 11:19; 1 Sam 10:5–13). The Spirit had been promised to the messianic king (Isa 11:1–2). The verb "anointing" is linked with "preaching and hearing." "It designates an interior enlightening to know God's word and a strengthening to follow it."[52]

Is Jesus' anointing to be understood as a messianic or prophetic anointing? Fitzmyer understands it as the anointing of the eschatological prophet. He writes that "this passage certainly contains no reference to a Davidic dynasty or a royal function of Jesus."[53] Tannehill thinks that this interpretation would isolate the text from the preceding references to Jesus as the Davidic Messiah and "Son of God," a title associated with Messiah in Luke-Acts.[54] John Nolland sees both a prophetic and messianic anointing here.[55] Luke Timothy Johnson thinks that this passage explains what kind of Messiah Jesus will be. The anointing shows that Jesus is "a *prophetic* Messiah." The Spirit anointed Jesus to be the herald of good news. Later, the Spirit will be "poured out" on Jesus' followers at Pentecost.[56]

In Luke 4:16–30, Luke uses the prophetic text of Isaiah to depict the nature of Jesus' ministry. He compares Jesus' ministry to the min-

---

52. Carroll Stuhlmueller, "Deutero-Isaiah and Trito-Isaiah," in *NJBC* (ed. Raymond E. Brown, Joseph A. Fitzmyer, and Roland E. Murphy; Englewood Cliffs, NJ: Prentice Hall, 1990) 346.

53. Fitzmyer, *Luke I–IX*, 529. Fitzmyer (*The One Who is to Come* [Grand Rapids, MI: Eerdemans, 2007] 144) notes that the anointing is a prophetic anointing and falls in line with the use in the OT and the Qumran texts of משׁיח for prophets. He demonstrates that the use of משׁיח for prophets in Qumran literature is clear (pp. 99–101). John Meier ("From Elijah-like Prophet to Royal Davidic Messiah," in *Jesus: A Colloquium in the Holy Land* [ed. Doris Donnelly; New York: Continuum, 2001] 145–83, here 46) writes "[T]he massive amount of the Gospel record dedicated to Jesus' miracle working, his itinerant prophetic ministry, his eschatological message, and even his narrative parables, which belong more to the prophetic than to the sapiential mode of speaking, argues that the Elijah-like eschatological prophet is probably the best single model for the historical Jesus."

54. Tannehill, *Narrative Unity of Luke-Acts: Luke*, 63.

55. John Nolland, *Luke 1–9:20* (WBC 35A; Dallas, TX: Word Books, 1989) 196. On the one hand, Nolland thinks the natural sense in the Isaianic context is prophetic. On the other hand, he notes that Luke juxtaposes Χριστός with Ἰησοῦν ὃν ἔχρισας in Acts 4:26–27, and in the baptism account "son" (Luke 3:22). He concludes that the anointing has some messianic content.

56. Johnson, *Luke*, 81.

istries of Elijah and Elisha. This presentation of Jesus as the prophet is significant for this passage and Jesus' ministry. "In fact, it is likely that the audience in the synagogue saw nothing more here than a prophetic eschatological claim."[57] This passage is set in the contexts of Jesus' infancy (1:5–2:52), baptism (3:21–22), healings (4:38–41), and preaching of the kingdom of God (4:43–44). These passages focus on Jesus as the anointed Son of God (2:32, 35; 3:22; 4:41) and preacher of the kingdom (4:43–44).[58] Tiede writes that it is "risky or at least futile" to attempt to decide the exact nature of anointing, whether it is royal or prophetic in this passage.[59] David Ravens notices that there is "a much closer connection between the roles of Χριστός and prophet" in Luke-Acts than in other NT writings.[60] Darrell Bock writes that the citation of Isaiah 61 seems to signal "the dawning of the new eschatological age" for the first-century audience. Jesus himself proclaims that he is the one who brings salvation to this new age. He has been anointed to a special task to preach the good news to the poor. This is further spelled out by the four infinitive phrases.[61]

The verb "to preach good news" (εὐαγγελίσασθαι) summarizes Jesus' mission as the "prophetic spokesperson or representative of God." "This verb is thematic in Luke-Acts for the prophetic message."[62]

Luke lists four groups of people as the object of Jesus' mission.[63] The first is the "poor" (πτωχοῖς). This foreshadows Luke's emphasis on this social class.[64] The poor are not only the "economically and socially poor." They are those who are in prison, the blind, and the oppressed (4:18). They also include those who are hungry, weeping, hated, persecuted,

---

57. Bock, *Luke 1:1–9:50*, 406.

58. Tannehill, *Narrative of Luke-Acts: Luke*, 63. See also Bock, *Luke 1:1–9:50*, 407.

59. Tiede, *Prophecy and History in Luke-Acts*, 46.

60. David Ravens, *Luke and the Restoration of Israel* (ed. Stanley E. Porter; JSNTSup 119; Sheffield: Sheffield Academic Press, 1995) 124.

61. Bock, *Luke 1:1–9:50*, 407.

62. Johnson, *Luke*, 79.

63. Samuel J. Roth (*The Blind, the Lame, and the Poor: Character Types in Luke-Acts* [ed. Stanley E. Porter; JSNTSup 144; Sheffield: Academic Press, 1997] 162) claims that the poor, the captive, the blind and the oppressed in Luke 4:18–19 function as "character types destined for divine rescue, that is, rescue by God or by God's agent." They are the promised recipients of Jesus' salvation. The widows and the lepers and the blind later in the text are those who are poor as well.

64. Fitzmyer, *Luke I–IX*, 532.

and rejected (6:20b–22). They are those who are physically disabled, the cripples, lepers, and the deaf. "The poor" is not only used literally, it is also used metaphorically.[65] The poor "represent generically the neglected mass of humanity."[66] It is the poor who need the salvation that Jesus brings. Consequently, they respond most "directly and honestly" to Jesus' message of the good news. Their material or spiritual deprivation often "translates into spiritual sensitivity, humility, and responsiveness to God's message of hope" in Jesus.[67] The poor in Luke-Acts symbolize the "acceptance of Jesus, the prophet announcing the new message of God's salvation."[68]

Jesus' mission of proclaiming the good news to the poor is the theme of Jesus' whole ministry which is further developed in the rest of 4:18. He is sent to release captives, to restore sight to the blind, to give the oppressed relief, and to proclaim a year acceptable to the Lord. These concepts have a literal and a metaphorical meaning. On the one hand, the captives can refer to debtors imprisoned for poverty, the oppressed, and those who are overwhelmed with troubles. On the other hand, they are those "whom Satan holds in bondage because of sin, disease, or demon possession."[69] The image of release is release from captivity and includes release from sin and spiritual captivity in Luke (Luke 1:77; 7:47; 24:47; Acts 2:38; 5:31; 10:43; 13:38; 26:18).[70]

"To restore sight to the blind" has a literal and metaphorical sense in Luke. On the one hand, the blind are those who are physically unable to see. On the other hand, they are those who are spiritually in darkness and in need of God's divine enlightenment. "Sight and light are used metaphorically for perceiving revelation and sharing in salvation. In this sense, Jesus, as well as Paul, has been sent to 'to open their eyes so that

---

65. Johnson, *Luke*, 79.

66. Fitzmyer, *Luke I–IX*, 250–51. Jack D. Kingsbury (*Conflict in Luke: Jesus, Authorities, Disciples* [Minneapolis: Fortress, 1991] 45) writes, "The term 'poor' in Luke's story is global in scope, encompassing many sorts of persons who are outcast, disabled, or needy, to wit: the economically disadvantaged, the hungry, those who weep, the persecuted, the blind, the lame, the deaf, the crippled, those who are lepers, and even those suffering death."

67. Bock, *Luke 1:1–9:50*, 408.

68. Fitzmyer, *Luke I–IX*, 251.

69. Kingsbury, *Conflict in Luke*, 45. See also Roth, *The Blind, the Lame, and the Poor*, 97–101.

70. Bock, *Luke 1:1–9:50*, 408.

they may turn from darkness to light and from the power of Satan to God' (Acts 26:18; cf. also Luke 1:78-79; 2:30-32; Acts 26:23)."[71]

Jesus announces the coming of the Lord's year of favor—a Jubilee Year.[72] It is a time of release since, in the Jubilee Year, family property is returned to its original owners and imprisoned debtors are set free. A Jubilee Year is also called a "year of release" (Lev 25:10). The heart of the Jubilee Year is the cancellation of debts or the notion of release.[73] This is designed to give the poor a new start. There is salvation for the poor in their release from debts. The Jubilee Year of God's favor described in the text of Isaiah is now announced by Jesus. This is the time of God's kingdom which Jesus inaugurates.[74] "Jesus' assertion, then, is that he is the Messiah through whom God proffers salvation to Israel."[75]

B. THE AUDIENCE RESPONDS WITH EXPECTATION (V. 20D)

After reading the Scripture passage, Jesus returns the scroll to the synagogue attendant and sits down. The synagogue assembly gazes attentively at Jesus. Luke writes ἦσαν ἀτενίζοντες αὐτῷ ("they were fixing their eyes on him") to describe the reaction of the assembly. The verb ἀτενίζω occurs frequently in Luke-Acts (Luke 22:56; Acts 1:10; 3:4, 12; 6:15; 7:55; 10:4; 11:6; 13:9; 14:9; 23:1). "In most instances it expresses a steadfast gaze of esteem and trust—the nuance intended here."[76] It is part of the assembly's initial reaction of surprise, admiration, and consequently expectation. They are expecting Jesus to interpret the passage.

---

71. Tannehill, *Luke* (ANTC; Nashville, TN: Abingdon, 1996) 92.

72. W. Grundmann, ("δεκτός," *TDNT*, 2. 59) interprets δεκτός messianically. The word δεκτός refers to the acceptable time chosen by Yahweh. It is the messianic age. This time is the time of salvation of God's divine presence (Isa 49:8; 58:6). Jesus announces the coming of this messianic age (Luke 4:18). According to Luke, the messianic age arrives when Jesus comes to the world. It is in Jesus that the promised messianic age is fulfilled.

73. R. Bultmann ("ἀφίημι," *TDNT*, 1. 510-11) notes that the noun form ἄφεσις in Isa 58:6; 61:1 means "eschatological liberation." In the NT, ἄφεσις almost always means forgiveness of sins (Mark 1:4; Matt 26:28; Luke 1:77; 24:47; Acts 2:28; 5:31; 10:43; 13:38; 26:18; Col 1:18; Heb 10:18). "Even where ἄφεσις is meant in the sense of 'liberation' (twice in Lk. 4:18 quoting Is. 61:1 and 58:6), this at least includes the thought of forgiveness."

74. Tannehill, *Luke*, 93; See also Fitzmyer, *Luke I-IX*, 533.

75. Kingsbury, *Conflict in Luke*, 45.

76. Fitzmyer, *Luke I-IX*, 533.

3. Phase II: Jesus Interprets the Text of the Scripture and the Audience Responds (vv. 21-22)

A. JESUS INTERPRETS THE PROPHECIES OF ISAIAH (V. 21)

After reading the passage from Isaiah 61, Jesus sits down and says to the audience, "Today this Scripture passage is fulfilled in your hearing." This sentence summarizes Jesus' interpretation of the reading. The adverb σήμερον ("today") is placed before the verb πεπλήρωται ("it is fulfilled"). This is to highlight the significance of σήμερον. It is "a key term in Luke's theology and stresses that the opportunity for salvation is this very moment."[77] It is not only the time when Jesus brought salvation, it is the time of salvation for the contemporary church of Luke's day.

The adverb σήμερον is immediately followed by the verb πεπλήρωται, "it is fulfilled." The perfect tense is "almost equivalent to a present tense."[78] It means that on this very day, this Scripture passage of Isaiah is fulfilled in their hearing. Jesus fulfills this prophecy and has "brought the realization of these promises." He has brought the start of a new age.[79] Whereas Mark announces the fulfillment of time (Mark 1:4-15), Luke proclaims that the "fulfillment of the Scriptures simultaneously includes the fulfillment of time."[80] Consequently, Jesus invites all who hear the gospel to accept him and the salvation he has announced.

B. THE AUDIENCE RESPONDS WITH SURPRISE (V. 22)

Luke uses three expressions to describe the audience's response: ἐμαρτύρουν, ἐθαύμασον, and ἔλεγον· οὐχὶ υἱός ἐστιν Ἰωσὴφ οὗτος. The difficulty in interpreting the verbs in v. 22 is related to the sharp change of Jesus' attitude in v. 23. Many attempts have been made to explain this

---

77. Bock, *Luke 1:1–9:50*, 413. Luke uses it ten times in his gospel (2:11; 5:26; 12:28; 13:32-33; 19:5, 9; 22:34, 61; 23:43) and nine times in Acts. Hans Conzelmann (*Theology of St. Luke* [trans. Geoffrey Buswell; Philadelphia, PA: Fortress, 1982] 36) writes, "Luke sees salvation already as a thing in the past. The time of salvation has come about in history, as a period of time which, although it determines the present, is now over and finished."

78. Marshall, *Gospel of Luke*, 185.

79. Koet, "Today This Scripture," 24-55, here 37. Koet studies the verbs πληρόω, πίμπλημι τελειόω and their compounds and concludes that these verbs are used in three ways: (a) "to indicate the end of a certain period ; (b) to describe the realization of certain prophecies or obligations from the Scriptures or on the basis of the Scripture; and (c) to clarify a certain state of mind, especially the fullness of Spirit" (p. 36).

80. Bovon, *Luke 1*, 154.

change. From a linguistic point of view, Joachim Jeremias understands ἐμαρτύρουν αὐτῷ in a hostile way (as a dative of disadvantage), and he translates it as "they witnessed against him." Jeremias points out that ἐθαύμασον means both admiring surprise and opposition to what is strange. He thinks that Jesus purposely leaves out the day of vengeance after proclaiming the favorable year of the Lord. This leads to the hostility of the audience, and "they protested with one voice and were furious because he only speaks about God's year of mercy without mentioning the Messianic vengeance and consequently they express the scornful question, 'Is not this the son of Joseph?'"[81] Most commentators, however, take this verse as a positive response of the audiences.[82]

The question "Is not this the son of Joseph?" shows their common understanding of the identity of Jesus. It points to his family relationship and to his ties with his hometown.[83] They are pleasantly surprised that such gracious words come from Jesus, a native of Nazareth, and show their admiration of him. The response that Jesus is Joseph's son from Nazareth should be interpreted with v. 23, "which refers to what Jesus should do in his hometown."[84] Since he has just preached the passage

---

81. Joachim Jeremias, *Jesus' Promise to the Nations* (trans. S. H. Hooke; Naperville, IL: Alec R. Allenson, 1958) 44–46. See also Hugh Anderson, "Broadening Horizons: The Rejection at Nazareth Pericope of Luke 4:16-30 in Light of Recent Critical Trends," *Int* 18 (1964) 259-75, here 266-67. Fearghus Fearghail ("Rejection in Nazareth: LK 4:22," *ZNW* 75 [1984] 60-72, here 72) interprets this verse as the audience's rejection of Jesus' preaching from the beginning. He translates it, "And they all witnessed to him, but were astonished at the words of grace (i.e. salvation) that came from his mouth, and (i.e. for) they said 'Is not this Joseph's son?'"

82. Koet, ("Today This Scripture," 40) writes that μαρτυρέω, θαυμάζω, and λόγοι τῆς χάριτος all show a positive appraisal of Jesus' interpretation. "This positive reaction reflects the manner in which the people reacted to Jesus earlier (Luke 4, 14–15; cf. 4, 32–36). One can conclude that in 4, 22 the listeners in Nazareth react to Jesus' explanation with surprise full of admiration." Manfred Korn ("Jesu Antrittspredigt in Nazareth als Programm des lukanischen Doppelwerks," in *Die Geschichte Jesu in Veränderter Zeit: Studien zur Bleibenden Bedeutung Jesu im Lukanishen Doppelwerk* [Tübingen: Mohr, 1993] 56-85, here 81) writes "Wir kommen zu dem Ergebnis, daß alles dafür spricht, Lk 4,22 nicht im negativen Sinn zu interpretieren." John C. Poirier ("Jesus as an Elijianic Figure in Luke 4:16-30," *CBQ* 71 [2009] 349-63, here 352) writes that "the people of Nazareth implicitly *accept* Jesus by asking him to heal his hometown folk."

83. Albert Vanhoye, "L'Intérêt de Luc pour la Prophétie en Lc 1,76; 4, 16-30 et 22,60-65," in *The Four Gospels 1992: Festschrift Frans Neirynck* (ed. F. Van Segbroeck et al; BETL 100; Leuven : Leuven University Press, 1992) 1529-48, here 1539.

84. Tannehill, *Luke*, 93; Vanhoye ("L'Intérêt de Luc," 1540) writes, "Entre la question du v. 22, comprise dans le contexte propre à Luc, et la phrase de Jésus, il n'y a pas

of Isaiah and proclaimed its fulfillment in himself, he should, according to the Mediterranean culture, give preference to his own hometown of Nazareth.[85] He should show in-group loyalty to his compatriots. They expect to benefit from Jesus' ministry.

4. Phase III: Jesus Responds to the Audience's Response, and They Respond with Rage (vv. 23-29)

A. JESUS SPEAKS TO THE AUDIENCE (VV. 23-27)

1) Jesus Reveals the Thoughts of the Audience (v. 23)

Jesus' response shows that he knows the inner thoughts of the people (Luke 5:22; 6:8; 7:39-40; 9:47; 11:17). He says, "Certainly you will quote this proverb to me, 'physician, heal yourself!'" This proverb means that a physician should first take care of his own family, neighbors, and hometown people.[86] The word σεαυτόν ("yourself") in the proverb refers to ἐν τῇ πατρίδι σου ("in your hometown"). In plain language, they demand, "Do here in your hometown the things we have heard you did in Capernaum." Through this proverb and their subsequent demand of Jesus, he reveals the true response of his compatriots.

This proverb and the demand show Jesus' compatriots' jealousy of Capernaum. It shows their possessive mentality.[87] Their demand that Jesus do here what he has done in Capernaum may express their anger at Jesus for not showing in-group loyalty to his compatriots, whom he should have benefited first. Instead of bringing benefit to his compatriots, Jesus has brought benefits to their rival, Capernaum. They think

---

la moindre incohérence. Il y a seulement progression, de l'implicite à l'explicite (le καί initial du v. 23 indique un rapport de continuité). Jésus lit dans les cœurs et dévoile les implications secrètes de la question exprimée: elle recouvre une attitude possessive."

85. Bruce J. Malina, *Windows on the World of Jesus: Time Travel to Ancient Judea* (Louisville, KY: Westerminster John Knox, 1993) 47-70.

86. S. J. Noorda, "'Cure Yourself Doctor!' (Luke 4,23). Classical Parallels to an Alleged Saying of Jesus," in *Logia: Les Paroles de Jésus: The Saying of Jesus* (ed. Joël Delobel; BETL 59; Louvain: Louvain University Press, 1982) 459-67, here 463. He writes, "We may describe it in the following way: One must not refuse to do to one's relatives the favours which one does to others, or, one must not benefit others, while refusing the same benefits to one's relatives. Also this topos is well attested in the classical tradition."

87. Vanhoye ("L'Intérêt de Luc," 1539) interprets the proverb as a possessive orientation. It means, "Tu es l'un de nous. Tu nous appartiens. Tes dons extraordinaires, tu dois les mettre à notre service."

that he has betrayed his loyalty to them. The proverb and the request also imply their cynicism and incredibility. If you are the prophet who has fulfilled the promise in the Prophet Isaiah, show us a sign. Show your compatriots the signs that you have shown to others. By referring to Capernaum here, Luke contrasts Nazareth with Capernaum in the narrative.[88]

2) Jesus Announces the Unacceptability of a Prophet in His Hometown (v. 24)

Instead of acceding to the request of his compatriots, Jesus says, "No prophet is acceptable in his own hometown." By saying this, "Jesus identifies himself as a prophet."[89] The word "prophet" functions as a connective to what precedes in v. 17 (the prophet Isaiah) and to what follows in v. 27 (the prophet Elisha). The use of "prophet" is possibly "an implicit contrast" and "corrective" to the pronouncement of the congregation that Jesus is the son of Joseph from Nazareth (2:4).[90] Jesus is not only a native of Nazareth, he is also a prophet. A prophet comes back to his hometown and proclaims the good news of salvation and the Jubilee Year. His compatriots' skepticism fails to recognize God's offer in Jesus, a native of Nazareth. Because of their lack of faith in Jesus, he will not perform signs to satisfy them. Jesus' refusal to perform what his compatriots asked leads them to reject him.

The verbal adjective δεκτός in 4:19 basically means "pleasing" or "acceptable." So κηρύξαι ἐνιαυτὸν κυρίου δεκτόν means to proclaim an acceptable year of the Lord. It is a year that the Lord shows his favor or salvation. Jesus the Prophet who proclaims the year acceptable to the Lord is not accepted by his compatriots.[91] "It is proverbial that a great man is often regarded with suspicion and even rejection among his own people."[92]

---

88. Jeffrey S. Siker, "'First to the Gentiles': A Literary Analysis of Luke 4:16–30," *JBL* 111 (1992) 73–90, here 81.

89. Fitzmyer, *Luke I–IX,* 537. See also Vanhoye, "L'Intérêt," 1536–37.

90. Siker, "First to the Gentiles," 82.

91. J. Bajard ("La Structure de la Péricope de Nazareth en Lc IV, 16–30," *ETL* 45 [1969] 165–71, here 170) thinks that δεκτός carries the same meaning in 4:24. In responding to the request of his compatriots for favoritism, Jesus quotes this proverb to say that a prophet does not exist to bring the benefit to only his compatriots.

92. Marshall, *Gospel of Luke,* 188.

Jesus' words that "no prophet is acceptable in his hometown" introduce the theme of rejection against the prophets in Luke-Acts. His rejection was prophesized by Simeon (2:34). This prophecy is beginning to be fulfilled. Jesus' words about the rejection of a prophet in his hometown are fulfilled immediately in 4:28. Many commentators attempt to explain the sharp change of the mood of Jesus' compatriots from v. 22 to v. 28, from a positive to a hostile mood.

Fitzmyer thinks that Luke 4:16–30 is a conflation of two stories: on the one hand, the story of Jesus' bringing fulfillment of the prophecy in the prophet Isaiah, which ends with a success note in v. 22; on the other hand, the story of rejection of Jesus and his message in his hometown, which ends with Jesus' departing from Nazareth and bringing salvation elsewhere.[93] Although there is a tension between these two stories, they show that Jesus' offer of salvation encounters both success and rejection.

"Jesus, who takes the role of prophet during his ministry, is governed by the purpose of God and the precedent of scriptural prophets."[94] Here Jesus provides the examples of Elijah and Elisha to prove that no matter what a prophet does, he is not accepted in his hometown. Because his compatriots have rejected him, he will bring salvation elsewhere. Human rejection cannot hinder God's salvation through Jesus.

3) Jesus Alludes to the Stories of the Prophets Elijah (vv. 25–26) and Elisha (v. 27)

The phrase ἐν τῇ πατρίδι αὐτοῦ at the end of v. 24 responds to the request of Jesus' compatriots ἐν τῇ πατρίδι σου (v. 23). The word πατρίς means fatherland, hometown, native country. It continues the theme of the native land in vv. 25–27 with the phrase ἐν τῷ Ἰσραήλ. It is clear that there is a contrast in locality between Israel and non-Israel. There is also a contrast between "many widows" (πολλαὶ χῆραι) in Israel with only one widow beyond Israel; "many lepers" (πολλοὶ λεπροί) in Israel with only one leper beyond Israel.[95]

---

93. Fitzmyer, *Acts*, 528.
94. Tannehill, *Luke*, 93–94.
95. We can see the contrast clearly by putting the verses in the following way: In Elijah's time, during a famine over all the land, there were *many widows in Israel*, Elijah was sent to none of them except to *a widow at Zarephath in Sidon*; similarly, in the time of Elisha the prophet, there were *many lepers in Israel*, none of them was cleansed except *Naaman the Syrian*.

Here Jesus uses the example of two great OT prophets to explain that his mission is beyond the constraints of his hometown. In his time, Elijah was a prophet in Israel. In his native country Israel, there were many widows who needed help because of the drought, yet Elijah was sent only to a widow in Sidon, which is beyond the boundary of Israel. It was there that he saved the widow and her son. Similarly, there were many lepers in Israel during the time of Elisha, yet none of them was cleaned except the leper Naaman the Syrian, a Gentile. The common characteristic of the two prophets is that both brought benefits to non-Israelites. The contrast in v. 23 is between Jesus' hometown of Nazareth and his new residence at Capernaum. The contrast in vv. 25–27 is between the prophets' home country Israel and the foreign lands of Syria and Phoenicia.

By using the examples of Elijah and Elisha, Jesus warns his compatriots. In the history of Israel, prophets were rejected by the people of Israel. Therefore, they brought salvation to non-Israelites. The people from their native country (ἐν τῷ Ἰσραήλ) did not receive salvation. In Stephen's speech, he reveals that the people of Israel repeatedly rejected the prophets (Acts 7:1–53). In an analogous way Jesus, who is from Nazareth, proclaims the fulfillment of God's salvation through the prophecy of Isaiah and meets skepticism and incredulity in his hometown. He will bring salvation to people other than his compatriots. His compatriots will not receive salvation from him because of their rejection of him.

B. The Audience Respond with Rage (vv. 28–29)

After hearing Jesus' response, his compatriots reverse their initial positive response to him in v. 22. They reject him and his message.[96] This rejection foreshadows Jesus' rejection and crucifixion (23:26) and the fate of his followers.

To sum up, because of the skepticism of his compatriots, "Jesus intimates that God's gift will be offered to others, as happened in the days of Elijah and Elisha (4:23–27). Incensed by this, his compatriots seek to kill him (4:28–30). This pattern of a gracious offer of salvation,

---

96. From a source-critical point of view, Fitzmyer (*Luke I-IX*, 527–28) thinks that this passage is conflated, since its plot is not smooth. It is a conflation of a fulfillment story, ending on the note of Jesus' success in vv. 20–22, and the rejection story in vv. 23–30.

that is refused and then offered to others is repeated in the lives of the Spirit-filled figures that dominate Acts: Peter, John, Stephen, and Paul."[97] Although there is no extension of salvation to the Gentiles in the period of Jesus' ministry, this extension will be carried out by his disciples. "This foreshadows the gentile mission in Acts."[98]

5. Jesus Leaves Nazareth and Goes on His Way (v. 30)

Although Jesus' compatriots try to push him off the cliff, he passes through them and continues on his way. In v. 31 Jesus goes to Capernaum, and there he brings salvation. Jesus follows the examples of Elijah and Elisha to bring salvation to people other than his compatriots. God's salvation cannot be hindered because of human rejection. Jesus completes his mission according to God's plan. No one else can control his ministry.

The rejection of Jesus in his hometown confirms that he is a prophet. Like the prophets Elijah and Elisha, Jesus is not accepted in his hometown. He sets out a way that begins in Nazareth and leads to Jerusalem, the city of destiny for prophets. From there, his disciples will continue to proceed on the way to Antioch, Asia Minor, Greece, and Rome, the end of the world.[99]

To summarize, Luke 4:16-30 is the beginning of Jesus' ministry. In Nazareth he delivers his inaugural sermon and proclaims that he is fulfilling the prophecy of Isaiah by preaching the good news to the poor and proclaiming an acceptable year of the Lord. His compatriots are surprised and seem to react positively at first. Jesus, however, reveals their true response, and they show their skepticism toward him and his message. Their lack of faith leads Jesus to cite the proverb, "No prophet is accepted in his hometown." He further uses the examples of two prophets to demonstrate that salvation was given to people other

---

97. Frank J. Matera, *New Testament Theology: Exploring Diversity and Unity* (Louisville, KY: Westminster John Knox, 2007) 56.

98. Tannehill, *Narrative of Luke-Acts: Luke*, 71. See the list of Christopher J. Schreck, "The Nazareth Pericope: Luke 4:16-30 in Recent Study," in *L'Evangile de Luc: The Gospel of Luke* (ed. Frans Neirynck; BETL 32; Leuven: Leuven University Press, 1989) 399-471, here 443-49. Poirier ("Jesus as an Elijianic Figure in Luke 4:16-30," 362-63) claims that the crowd at Nazareth originally welcomed Jesus and probably wanted to experience Jesus' benefit among them. Yet Jesus implicitly compared them with the apostatized public of Elijah and Elisha's day. He thinks that his compatriots are like those Israelites of Elijah and Elisha's day, who rejected the prophets. Jesus' compatriots do not have faith in Jesus and reject him and his message.

99. Ibid. See also Fitzmyer, *Luke I-IX*, 539.

than their compatriots because they rejected it. This irritates his compatriots. Consequently, they reject him. Jesus, however, follows God's plan by continuing on his way in order to bring good news to all who accept his salvation.

II. THE LITERARY FUNCTION OF JESUS' SERMON TO HIS MINISTRY IN THE GOSPEL OF LUKE AND ACTS

It is widely held that Luke 4:16–30 is "programmatic for Luke-Acts."[100] Luke places this pericope at the very outset of Jesus' public ministry to announce Jesus' mission. This shows that it is "especially significant for an understanding of his work as a whole."[101] But how does this pericope function as programmatic for Luke-Acts? To answer this question, I will focus on its literary function in Luke-Acts.

A. Jesus' Inaugural Sermon Functions as a Model Sermon that He Delivers to the Jews

In Luke 4:14–15, Luke gives a summary of Jesus' Galilean ministry by narrating that he taught in the synagogues. But there is no specific indication of the content of Jesus' message as there is in Mark 1:14–15. The narrative creates an expectation among its readers who want to know the content of his teaching. In response to this, Luke presents a model of Jesus' teaching in the synagogue of Nazareth in 4:16–30.[102] This sermon, then, serves as "an illustration of his ministry."[103]

After Jesus' teaching in the synagogue of Nazareth, he goes to Capernaum to teach the people on the Sabbath (4:31). People are amazed at his teaching (4:22, 32). Similarly, Jesus teaches the crowds from Simon's boat (5:3). Pharisees and teachers of the law come from every village of Galilee and Judea, and from Jerusalem, to hear the teaching of Jesus (5:17). Jesus continues to teach in synagogues on the Sabbath

---

100. Frans Neirynck, "Luke 4, 16–30 and the Unity of Luke-Acts," 357. See also Korn, "Jesu Antrittspredigt in Nazareth als Programm des lukanischen Doppelwerks," 56–85; Koet, " Today This Scripture," 24; J. Kodell, "Luke's Gospel in Nutshell (Lk 4:16–30)," *BTB* 13 (1983) 16–18.

101. Jacques Dupont, "The Salvation of the Gentiles and the Theological Significance of Acts," in *The Salvation of the Gentiles* (trans. John R. Keating; New York/Ramsey/Toronto: Paulist, 1979) 11–33, here 21.

102. Bock, *Luke 1:1–9:50*, 394.

103. Marshall, *Gospel of Luke*, 177.

58   PAUL AMONG JEWS

(6:6; 13:10). Luke, however, does not give the content of Jesus' teaching. He does not need to specify what Jesus teaches since Jesus' inaugural sermon exemplifies his normal teaching to the Jews in synagogues on the Sabbath. Jesus must go to other cities to proclaim the good news that he is commissioned to preach according to 4:18–19. Wherever Jesus goes, he preaches the same good news.[104]

B. Jesus' Inaugural Sermon Announces the Main Themes in Luke-Acts

Luke uses this inaugural sermon to prepare the main themes that he is going to explore in the Gospel of Luke and in Acts. This sermon "functions as a guide to the reader in understanding the following story of Jesus' ministry."[105] There are different ways to summarize these themes. I will focus on the following ones.

1. The Theme of the Holy Spirit

During Jesus' preparation for his mission, he is empowered by the Spirit. The Spirit is the driving force of his mission. It is the Spirit that initiates his mission.[106] Jesus' whole ministry is initiated and empowered by the Spirit. The Spirit is "the inaugurator of Jesus' public ministry."[107]

At the end of the Gospel the risen Lord sends the Spirit to his disciples (Luke 24:49). In Acts 2:33, Luke narrates that it is through the exalted Lord that he sends the Spirit upon the Christian community. "The repeated references to the Spirit in Luke 4 establish a relation between the opening of the Gospel and the opening of Acts. In the Gospel God's Spirit is active at the birth of Jesus and as Jesus embarks on his ministry 'full of the Spirit.' In Acts, at the 'birth' of the Christian community, God's Spirit is bestowed by Jesus. "[108]

---

104. Tannehill, *Narrative Unity of Luke-Acts: Luke*, 85.

105. Ibid., 62.

106. Stanton, *Gospel and Jesus*, 91–92. He notes that during Jesus' baptism, the Holy Spirit descends upon him and empowers him. The Holy Spirit connects Jesus' baptism with his inaugural sermon. Jesus returns to Galilee in the power of the Spirit (4:14) because he has been anointed with God's Spirit (4:18) in baptism. From Luke's point of view, Jesus, the one who was born of the Spirit (1:35) is "full of the Spirit."

107. Joseph A. Fitzmyer, "The Role of the Spirit in Luke-Acts," in *The Unity of Luke-Acts* (ed. J. Verheyden; BETL 142; Leuven: Leuven University Press, 1999) 165–83, here 172.

108. Stanton, *Gospel and Jesus*, 92. See also Fitzmyer (*Luke I–IX*, 227–31, here 230) who writes that "the Spirit poured out on Pentecost inaugurates a new age." It is clear that "the role of the Spirit as initiator was important for the inception both of Jesus' life

2. The Theme of Jesus' Identity as a Messianic Prophet

Jesus is depicted as a prophet in Luke 4.[109] He announces that "no prophet is acceptable in his own country." He also compares his ministry with the ministries of the prophets Elijah and Elisha. He is "the messianic prophet sent by God."[110] He is recognized as "a great prophet" (7:16), "one of the prophets of old" (9:8, 19). He is "a prophet mighty in deed and word in the eyes of God and all the people" (24:19). Jesus describes himself as a prophet (13:33).

Luke regards Jesus as the prophet like Moses promised in Deut 18:15–18. In the transfiguration, Moses and Elijah talk with Jesus about the "departure" that he will accomplish in Jerusalem. The disciples are called to "listen to him" (9:35). The role of prophet is explicitly applied to Jesus in Peter's speech (Acts 3:22–23) and Stephen's speech (Acts 7:37). Jesus is also depicted in the role of Elijah (Luke 7:16 see 1 Kgs 17:23). He heals people outside of Nazareth just as Elijah healed people outside of Israel (Luke 4:25–27 versus 1 Kgs 17:8–16). Jesus is the prophet like Moses, the eschatological prophet who is the mouthpiece of God (Exod 4:15–16), "uttering with authority God's words to human beings" (Luke 4:32, 43; 5:1; Acts 10:36).[111]

3. The Theme of Proclaiming the Good News

As a prophet, Jesus is sent to proclaim good news to the poor. Luke uses the verb εὐαγγελίζομαι, "to proclaim good news," to describe Jesus' mission. This verb is a characteristically Lukan verb.[112] "The proclamation of 'good news' is the purpose of Jesus' ministry (Luke 4:43)."[113] In 4:43–44,

---

and his ministry; but now it has become the initiator of a new era of salvation-history, when the Spirit becomes God's presence to his people anew."

109. Robert L. Brawley, "The Identity of Jesus in Luke 4:16–30 and the Program of Luke-Acts," in *Luke-Acts and the Jews: Conflict, Apology, and Conciliation* (SBLMS 33; Atlanta, GA: Scholars Press, 1987) 6–27, here 21. He writes, "Luke 4 climaxes with the identity of Jesus as a prophet. This is certainly a programmatic theme for Luke-Acts."

110. François Bovon, *Luke the Theologian: Fifty-five Years of Research (1950–2005)* (2nd rev. ed.; Waco, TX: Baylor University Press, 2006) 202. Luke T. Johnson (*Luke*, 81) claims that Luke 4:18 explains what kind of Messiah Jesus is. He is a prophetic Messiah.

111. Fitzmyer, *Luke I–IX*, 213–15.

112. Matera, *New Testament Theology*, 70 n. 22. He writes that this verb appears only once in Matthew and not at all in Mark. He notes that this verb appears ten times in Luke and fifteen times in Acts.

113. Ibid., 69.

Luke uses three verbs (εὐαγγελίσασθαι, ἀπεστάλην, and κηρύσσων) to summarize Jesus' ministry. These verbs correspond to the text of Isaiah in 4:18-19 that the anointed one is sent (ἀπέσταλκεν) to proclaim the good news (εὐαγγελίσασθαι) and to preach (κηρύξαι) a year of acceptable to the Lord. They emphasize Jesus' ministry of proclaiming the good news.[114] In 8:1 and 20:1, the verb εὐαγγελίζομαι is employed to summarize Jesus' activities.

The content of Jesus' good news is the kingdom of God (4:43).[115] The twelve disciples do the same, according to 9:6. They do what Jesus did. In the forty days of Jesus' appearances and instructions of his disciples, he instructs them about the kingdom of God. In Acts Jesus' followers continue to proclaim the kingdom of God and the good news of Jesus Christ (Acts 8:12; 14:22; 19:8; 20:25; 28:23, 31).

4. The Theme of the Character of Jesus' Ministry

Luke makes it clear that Jesus is sent to proclaim the good news of the kingdom of God. His inaugural sermon implicitly explains the content of the kingdom of God. To proclaim the good news of the kingdom of God is to announce and bring about a "reversal of fortunes in favor of the poor and disposed."[116] This inaugural sermon is the summary of Jesus' ministry in the rest of Luke. Jesus' ministry fulfills what he proclaims in his inaugural sermon. "His healings and exorcisms release those whom Satan oppresses and holds captive (4:31–37; 13:10–17). His table fellowship with sinners (5:29–30; 15:1–2) and his authoritative declaration that their sins have been forgiven (7:48) indicate that in his ministry God is offering Israel a year of divine favor, a jubilee that remits sin, the most serious of all debts."[117]

In the sermon on the plain, Jesus proclaims a reversal of fortunes: Blessed are the poor, the hungry, the weeping, and the persecuted. Through Jesus, salvation will be given to them. He comes to call sinners

---

114. John J. Kilgallen ("Provocation in Luke 4, 23–24," *Bib* 70 [1989] 511–16, here 516) writes, "It is the work of the Isaian figure, anointed to preach and announce, to call to repentance, to offer freedom and hope, to teach, that is the perennially powerful work of Jesus—a work of that teaching word which is life-giving."

115. Agustín Del Agua, "The Lucan Narrative of the 'Evangelization of the Kingdom of God': A Contribution to the Unity of Luke-Acts," in *The Unity of Luke-Acts* (ed. J. Verheyden; BETL 142; Leuven: Leuven University Press, 1999) 639–61.

116. Matera, *New Testament Theology*, 70.

117. Ibid.

in order to grant them salvation. He brings salvation to a poor widow (7:11–17) by raising her dead son; he cleanses a leper (5:12–16) and ten other lepers, including one Samaritan who comes back to give thanks to Jesus (17:11–19); he calls Levi, a tax collector (5:27–32) and stays with Zacchaeus (19:1–10); he heals the blind beggar (19:35–43); he cures a woman who has been crippled for eighteen years (13:10–17); he also heals a centurion's slave (7:1–10). These acts show that Jesus is the one who brings salvation to those who most need God.

5. The Theme of Release or Forgiveness of Sins

In the quotation from Isaiah, Luke uses the rule of *gezerah shavah*. He combines two texts (Isaiah 58 and 61) that use the word ἄφεσις ("release or deliverance"). Jesus comes as the eschatological Messiah to bring remission of debts in a year of God's favor. He brings release to the poor.

Jesus' healings and exorcism bring release to the people who are sick or possessed by Satan. Since various sorts of physical and mental disorders are understood to be caused by the bondage of Satan. Jesus' healings break the bonds of Satan and bring release to those who are sick or possessed by demons (Luke 13:10–17; 8:26–39).

In a year of God's favor, debtors are released. Their debts are cancelled. In an analogical sense, Jesus comes to bring forgiveness of sins. The word ἄφεσις is often associated with the word ἁμαρτιῶν. The use of ἄφεσις with ἁμαρτιῶν "comes from the Jewish religious use of the word 'debt' in the sense of sin."[118] Jesus forgives sins (5:20), for he has the authority to forgive sins (5:24). He has table fellowship with tax collectors and sinners (5:30), for his mission is to call sinners (5:32). Jesus comes to seek the lost, to call sinners to repentence (15:10, 32; 19:10).

After his resurrection, Jesus commissions his disciples to preach forgiveness of sins in his name to all nations (24:47). His disciples do as he told them and preach repentance for the forgiveness of sins in his name in Acts (2:38; 5:31; 10:43; 13:38; 26:18). According to Luke, Jesus' work of saving is summed up as bringing release to human beings from their debts, that is, their sins.[119] His disciples are called to preach this release from the debt of sin that Jesus has brought to all.

---

118. Fitzmyer, *Luke I–IX*, 223.
119. Ibid., 224–25; see also Tannehill, *Narrative Unity of Luke-Acts: Luke*, 103–9.

6. The Theme of Prophecy and Fulfillment

Jesus announces, "Today, this Scripture passage is fulfilled in your hearing" (v. 21). He regards his ministry as the fulfillment of the prophecy of Isaiah. The theme of prophecy and fulfillment has a programmatic character in Luke-Acts. For Luke, the OT is "a book of prophecies and sacred history, but it is also a divine message that permits interpretation of the present time and comprehension of the person of Christ."[120] "Luke hears the Scripture like a prophetic voice that announces the coming, death, and resurrection of the Messiah."[121] Jesus' ministry is to fulfill the prophecy of Isaiah; that is, to bring a reversal of fortunes to those who are poor, blind, captive, and oppressed.

His public ministry fulfills this prophecy of Isaiah. Luke 7:22 shows that Jesus has fulfilled the prophecy in 4:18-19. This theme of prophecy and fulfillment continues as Jesus goes to Jerusalem. He goes to Jerusalem to fulfill everything written by the prophets about the Son of Man (18:31). The Scripture passage must be fulfilled which states that Jesus was counted among the wicked. He realizes that what is written about him will be fulfilled in Jerusalem (22:37). Thus after his resurrection, he teaches his disciples that everything written about him in the whole of Scripture had to be fulfilled and that the Messiah had to suffer and rise from the dead on the third day (24:44, 46).[122] This theme continues to guide the development of Acts. The objective of the OT texts in Acts is "to present the person and the work of Jesus as the fulfillment of the promise made by God to 'our ancestors' (cf. Acts 3, 12-26; 7, 2-53, etc.) and formulated throughout the OT tradition."[123]

7. The Theme of Rejection and Mission to the Gentiles

Jesus announces that no prophet is acceptable in his home country. He cites the ministry of two OT prophets, and he is rejected by his compatriots in Nazareth. By this rejection, Luke confirms Jesus' identity as a

---

120. Bovon, *Luke the Theologian*, 116.

121. Ibid., 117-18.

122. J. A. Sanders ("Isaiah in Luke," in *Luke and Scripture: The Function of Sacred Tradition in Luke-Acts* [ed. Craig A. Evans and James A. Sanders; Minneapolis: Fortress, 1993] 14-25, here 15) writes that it is clear that early Christians searched the OT Scripture texts midrashically and tried to understand why the Messiah suffered the fate of a criminal and was crucified after his resurrection.

123. Del Agua, "The Lucan Narrative of the 'Evangelization of the Kingdom of God,'" 641-42.

true prophet. The passage of Isaiah in 4:18–19 depicts Jesus' prophetic activity. Consequently, the people of Nazareth expect to benefit from Jesus. He explains his ministry further in 4:23–27 by the examples of the prophets Elijah and Elisha. In the Scriptures, Elisha and especially Elijah are characterized as "zealots for the maintenance and restoration of God's covenant with Israel."[124] Their mission was to urge the Israelites to repent and to rebuild their covenant relationship with God. Jesus' compatriots realize that they are not going to receive special treatment. They are called to repent instead. Consequently, they become furious and reject Jesus.[125]

The rejection Jesus' teaching continues throughout the Gospel. His teaching angers the scribes and the Pharisees (6:11), and he regards "this generation" as "fickle" (7:31–35), "faithless and perverse" (9:41). The section of Jesus' journey to Jerusalem "heightens the reader's appreciation of the conflict between Jesus and Israel by exposing the contrasting points of view espoused by Jesus on the one hand and the crowd and its religious leaders on the other."[126] Finally, these conflicts lead to Jesus' suffering and death in Jerusalem. This theme of rejection continues in Acts. Jesus' disciples and followers continue to preach, calling their audience to repent and believe in Jesus' name. Consequently, they are rejected, persecuted, martyred. Yet some people do repent and believe in Jesus. Thus Israel is divided. Jesus' disciples and followers form the reestablished Israel.

Jesus uses the two examples of the prophets to show a deeper significance. The contrast between Israel and a Syrian or a Phoenician shows the antithesis between Israel and the Gentiles.[127] Although Gentile conversion is not a problem during Jesus' ministry, "the status of the gentile converts among the elect that remains at issue in Luke's community."[128] Luke traces this problem to the savior of the restored Israel. Jesus continues God's divine plan as foreseen in Elijah and Elisha who bring God's salvation to the non-Israelites.[129]

124. Koet, "Today This Scripture," 54.
125. Ibid.
126. Frank J. Matera, "Jesus' Journey to Jerusalem (Luke 9:51–19:46): A Conflict with Israel," *JSNT* 51 (1993) 57–77, here 74.
127. Dupont, *The Salvation of the Gentiles*, 22
128. Tiede, *Prophecy and History in Luke-Acts*, 50.
129. Jean-Noël Aletti ("Jésus àNazareth (Lc 4, 16–30): Prophétie Écriture et

Although Jesus does not preach to the Gentiles during his ministry, he heals a centurion's slave, and he applauds the centurion's strong faith (7:1-10). He also heals the Gerasene demoniac (8:26-39). He teaches the parable of the Good Samaritan (11:29-37), and he praises the Samaritan leper because he comes back to give thanks. Later, in Acts, preaching the good news to Gentiles becomes an issue, and it is discussed at the Jerusalem council (Acts 15). In Acts, Luke deals with the issue of accepting Gentiles to the new reestablished Israel, showing that the church is still faithful to Moses and the prophets. Jesus' inaugural sermon anticipates the church's inclusion of Gentiles in Acts.

III. CONCLUSION

In conclusion, we can see that Jesus' inaugural sermon has a significant literary function. It presents a model of Jesus' sermons to the Jews in their synagogues. It defines Jesus' mission as the messianic prophet who has been sent to preach the good news of release and deliverance to the poor. Luke places this episode at the very outset of Jesus' public ministry in order to communicate the major themes he will explore in his double work. Thus, it functions as an interpretative text for understanding Luke's Gospel and Acts. The rest of the Lukan story should be read in light of this scene.

Typologie," in *A Cause de L'Évangile: Études sur les Synoptiques et les Actes* [LD 123; Paris: Cerf, 1985] 431-51, here 449) writes, "Quant à l'Église, elle est allée annoncer l'Évangile aux païens, mais elle n'aurait pu le faire sans l'autorité d'une parole inouïe celle de Jésus même seul capable de montrer comment pareille annonce était en parfaite continuité avec le plan divin de salut. Lc 4, 16-30 a précisément pour fonction de présenter l'acte fondateur de cette exégèse."

3

The Literary Function of Peter's Inaugural Sermon

(Acts 2:14–40)

INTRODUCTION

Peter's sermon at Pentecost is not his first sermon in Acts. Yet it is his first recorded missionary sermon preached to Jews in Acts. It inaugurates a series of missionary speeches. Peter delivers this sermon to Jews, in Jerusalem, from all the nations (2:5). In this sermon, Peter announces the coming of a new age at the outpouring of the Spirit at Pentecost. God has made Jesus of Nazareth Lord and Messiah. He calls them to repent and be baptized in the name of Jesus Christ for the forgiveness of sins and to receive the gift of the Spirit.

My purpose in studying Peter's sermon to the Jews in Acts 2:14–40 is to determine its literary function in Acts in order to prepare a context to understand how inaugural sermons work in Acts in general, especially Paul's inaugural sermon in Acts 13:16–41. There are three parts in this chapter. In the first part, I will study this sermon, its literary context, and its structure, and I will provide an exegesis of this text. In the second part, I will study the literary function of this sermon. In the third part, I will draw a conclusion based on the similarity between the literary context and function of the inaugural sermons of Jesus and Peter.

I. PETER'S INAUGURAL SERMON TO THE JEWS IN JERUSALEM AT PENTECOST (ACTS 2:14–40)

A. Literary Context of the Sermon in Acts 2:14–40

Peter's inaugural sermon is in a section that deals with the origin of the new community (1:1–26) and its mission of bearing witness in Jerusalem (2:1–8:4). The Jerusalem community will experience trials (4:1–22; 5:17–42), persecutions, and martyrdom (7:54–8:4). These persecutions, however, will only cause the scattered Christians to go to Judea and Samaria to preach the Word (8:5–40). The Word thus will be preached to Jews and Gentiles. Finally, the issue of Gentile Christians will be settled at the Jerusalem Council (9:1–15:35). Peter will start his mission in Jerusalem (1:15–26) and complete it there (15:7–12).

After Peter completes his work, Paul will become the main character in the second half of Acts (13:1–28:31). After Paul is called by the risen Lord, he will bear witness to Christ's resurrection. He will bring the Word of God to Asia Minor (13:1–14:28). He will then continue his universal mission to Israelites and Gentiles (15:36–22:21). Finally, as a prisoner, he will carry the name of the Lord to Rome and bear witness about the hope of Israel to kings and Israelites (22:22–28:31).[1]

1. The Remote Literary Context

I will focus on the study of the literary context of Acts 2:14–40 in the context of the Christian community in Jerusalem after Jesus' resurrection (Luke 24; Acts 1:1–8:4). Jerusalem is Jesus' destiny (Luke 9:51), where he suffers, dies, and rises from the dead. It is also the place where he appears to his disciples to instruct and commission them to be his witnesses (Luke 24:1–49). Finally, he ascends into heaven and sends forth the Spirit upon his followers in Jerusalem.[2]

After his resurrection, the risen Lord meets two of his disciples on the way to Emmaus and interprets (διερμήνευσεν) for them the things that refer to him in the Scriptures (Luke 24:26–27). For Luke, Jesus is the center of Scripture. Jesus combines instruction with meal fellowship

---

1. Joseph A. Fitzmyer, *The Acts of the Apostles: A New Translation with Introduction and Commentary* (AB 31; New York: Doubleday, 1998) 120–23.

2. I regard the Gospel of Luke and Acts as written by one author, commonly known as Luke. Therefore, I include Luke 24 as part of the literary context of Acts 2:14–40 since all these events happen in Jerusalem.

(24:30). This meal fellowship is an occasion to reveal the purpose of God in Jesus' destiny.³ His disciples' eyes are opened as he opens (διανοίγω "explains") for them the meaning of the Scriptures (Luke 24:32), and they begin to understand the hidden meaning of Scripture.

Jesus again appears to his disciples in Jerusalem. He instructs them and commissions them to be his witnesses (Luke 24:36–48). They could not understand Jesus' passion predictions while he was with them (9:22, 44; 17:25; 18:31–33; 22:37). Now he opens their minds to understand the Scriptures.⁴ Everything written about him in Scripture must be fulfilled. Jesus helps his disciples to review what has happened in him. Jesus' passion, death, and resurrection have fulfilled what was written in the Scriptures about him as the Messiah. It is faith in Jesus' resurrection that opens the disciples' minds and hearts to understand the Scriptures. Jesus commissions them and previews their mission. They will proclaim the forgiveness of sins to all the nations in his name and bear witness to his ministry and resurrection (Acts 1:21–22).

Luke's presentation of Jesus' instructions to his disciples follows this outline: first, it narrates the circumstances (24:5, 18, 38); second, it narrates Jesus' ministry (24:19); third, it issues a call to bear witness to Jesus' resurrection (24:48); fourth, it issues a call to repent for the forgiveness of sins (24:47) and preach his name to all the nations.⁵

Luke links the beginning of Acts (1:1–12) with the end of his Gospel (Luke 24:44–53). He summarizes the message of the Gospel in Acts 1:1–2. He links Acts 1:3 with Jesus' resurrection appearances, instructions, and commission in Luke 24. He specifies that for forty days Jesus appeared and instructed his disciples (Acts 1:3). Forty is a conventional biblical period (1 Kgs 19:8; Exod 24:18; 34:28). Luke emphasizes that it is over a considerable period of time, not just one day that Jesus instructs

---

3. Tannehill, *Narrative Unity of Luke-Acts: Luke*, 290–91; Richard J. Dillon (*From Eye-Witnesses to Ministers of the Word: Tradition and Composition in Luke 24* [Rome: Biblical Institute, 1978] 107) affirms that in Luke's mind Jesus, as the master, breaks bread with his disciples to show that the master shares his mission and destiny with his disciples.

4. Dillon (ibid., 169) writes that Jesus' self-disclosure through the interpretation of Scripture becomes a mandated "ministry of the word" for his disciples. Therefore, Jesus' Easter instruction to his disciples becomes the crucial foundation of their witness.

5. Jacques Dupont ("La Portée Christologique de L'Évangélisation des Nations," in *Nouvelles Études sur Les Actes des Apôtres* [LD 118; Paris: Cerf, 1984] 37–57, here 42–43) writes, "Nous avons tâché de montrer ailleurs que la triple présentation du message pascal en Lc 24 suit déjàle schéma des discours missionaires des Actes."

his disciples (24:1, 13, 28, 36, 50). This long period of time assures that the disciples are fully instructed by the risen Lord and qualified to be his witnesses (Acts 1:21).[6] Luke also uses this interval of time to prepare for the coming of the "fifty days" of Pentecost.

Luke sums up the contents of Jesus' instruction to his disciples as "the kingdom of God."[7] This was the teaching of Jesus during his earthly ministry (Luke 4:43). It now connects "the contents of Jesus' earthly teaching to that about which the disciples will instruct others to the very end of Acts (cf. 8:12; 14:22; 19:8; 20:25; 28:23, 31)."[8] Accordingly, Jesus' preaching of the kingdom of God in Acts 1:3 and Paul's preaching of the kingdom of God in Acts 28:31 form "an *inclusion*, a thematic unity."[9]

After instructing his disciples, Jesus commands them to stay in Jerusalem to wait for the promise of the Father. They will be clothed with power from on high (Luke 24:49) and baptized with the Spirit (Acts 1:5). After receiving power from the Spirit, they will be Jesus' witnesses in Jerusalem, throughout Judea and Samaria, and to the ends of the earth (1:8).

The place of Jerusalem is emphasized. It is the place of Jesus' crucifixion, resurrection, post-resurrection appearances, instructions, and ascension. It is also the place where his disciples will receive the power of the Spirit and the starting point of their mission. Therefore, Jerusalem represents the continuity between Jesus' mission and his disciples' mis-

---

6. Charles H. Talbert (*Reading Acts: A Literary and Theological Commentary on the Acts of the Apostles* [New York: Crossroad, 1997] 23–24) notes that Jesus' forty-day instruction to his disciples functions theologically in two ways. First, the forty-day instruction guarantees that the disciples are fully instructed and prepared to be his witnesses. Second, the period of forty days limits the legitimate post-resurrection instruction to forty days to avoid the claims of secret teachings of Jesus.

7. Fitzmyer (*Luke I–IX*, 155) says that in the OT "kingdom of God" means "Yahweh's kingship" or "Yahweh's kingdom." It expresses "an eschatological hope for a period when God's salvation would be realized, when his dominion over the minds and lives of human beings would be accomplished, and they would be withdrawn from subjection to danger, evil, and sin." In the NT, the kingdom of God is understood in the Christ-event. God's kingship comes in Jesus' person and works (Luke 11:20). "The kingdom of God enters history in Jesus' ministry, passion, death, and resurrection. As the Christ and the risen Lord, he is the Father's special anointed agent for the preaching and establishment of this dominion henceforth among human beings."

8. Ben Witherington III, *The Acts of the Apostles: A Socio-Rhetorical Commentary* (Grand Rapids, MI: Eerdmans, 1998) 109.

9. Richard I. Pervo, *Acts: A Commentary* (Hermeneia; Minneapolis: Fortress, 2009) 38. He further writes that Luke tries to show that Paul will continue to teach in Rome the contents of Jesus' teaching to his disciples in Jerusalem. See also Fitzmyer, *Acts*, 203.

sion. From Jerusalem, Jesus' disciples are commanded to bear witness to his resurrection to all the nations.

For forty days, Jesus instructs his disciples in the Scriptures through the Holy Spirit (1:2). This is the first time that "Holy Spirit" appears in Acts. "Luke thus emphasizes the significance of the Spirit right from the very beginning of Acts."[10] It appears fifty-six times thereafter.[11] The Spirit is the driving force in Acts (9:31). Jesus prepares his disciples with "the power from on high" (Luke 24:49), that is, the Spirit (Acts 1:4–5). Luke uses two images to express the power of the Spirit coming upon the disciples. They will be clothed with the Spirit and baptized by the Spirit. The heavenly Father will send his promise to cloth them, to strengthen and protect them, and to remain with them. The image of being baptized with the Spirit is thought of as analogous to the water in which a convert is immersed.[12] Luke uses various images to talk about the experience of the Spirit.[13]

Jesus identifies the Spirit as the Father's promise (Luke 24:49; Acts 1:4).[14] He connects the Spirit with OT prophecy and prepares us for what follows in Acts 2:16–22. The outpouring of the Spirit at Pentecost is related to the prophecy of Joel 3:1–5. Luke implies a relation of the Spirit to Yhwh God, who is Jesus' Father. It is explained in Acts 2:33 that Jesus, "having been exalted to the right of God, received from the Father the promised Spirit and poured it out." In Luke's gospel, the Spirit is active in the infancy narrative. John the Baptist proclaims a baptism with the Spirit (Luke 3:16). Jesus' whole ministry is initiated and guided by the Spirit (Luke 3:22; 4:1, 14; 4:18). A special relationship between the risen Lord and the Spirit is formed. When Jesus is no longer physically present after his ascension, the

---

10. Fitzmyer, *Acts*, 193.

11. Fitzmyer (ibid., 196) lists the 57 occurrences of the "Spirit" in Acts. They are: Acts 1:2, 5, 8, 16; 2:4, 17, 18, 33, 38; 4:8, 25, 31; 5:3, 9, 32; 6:5; 7:51, 55; 8:15, 17–19, 29, 39; 9:17, 31; 10:19, 38, 44, 45, 47; 11:12, 15, 16, 24, 28; 13:2, 4, 9, 52; 15:8, 28; 16:6, 7; 19:2, 6; 20:23, 28; 21:4, 11; 28:25.

12. C. K. Barrett, *A Critical and Exegetical Commentary on the Acts of the Apostles* (ICC; 2 Vols.; New York: T & T Clark, 1994) 1.74.

13. Talbert, *Reading Acts*, 25. Talbert (p. 26) lists different ways that Luke describes the same experiential reality of the Holy Spirit. These expressions include receiving, being with, and being baptized with the Holy Spirit, etc.

14. Tannehill (*Narrative Unity of Luke-Acts: Acts*, 12) suggests that Jesus' words in Luke 11:13 identify the Spirit as a gift promised from the Father. This verse follows the prayer in which disciples are taught to address God as Father and a parabolic saying about a father's gifts to his son.

Spirit becomes the substitute for the risen Lord himself. Christ is present in the Father's promise, which is poured out at Pentecost.[15]

The promise of baptism with the Spirit in v. 5 will come "in a few days." It carries a timeline. This causes the disciples to inquire, "Lord, are you at this time going to restore the kingdom of God?"[16] Jesus' reply in vv. 7–8 changes the focus of their question. His disciples should not focus on the timing of the coming of the kingdom of God, for they will be empowered by the Spirit to become his witnesses to the whole world.

It is important to bear witness to Jesus' resurrection, for it is a significant part of fulfilling God's plan, which includes the preaching about Jesus' resurrection to all the nations. Because the Jews in Jerusalem rejected him, they still do not recognize that the one whom they have rejected is the Messiah. Jesus' disciples have understood the Scriptures with regard to his resurrection. They must now proclaim that the one they denied has been raised from the dead. He is the Messiah promised by the prophets.[17] They are called to bear witness to his resurrection not only in Jerusalem but to all the nations, to the ends of the earth (Luke 24:47; Acts 1:8).

In order to fulfill their mission, the disciples will receive the power (δύναμις) of the Spirit. The word δύναμις appears ten times in Acts. It means mighty deeds (2:22; 8:13; 19:11), or the power that causes them (3:12; 4:7; 10:38), or the power that causes the apostles and Stephen to speak boldly or work mighty deeds (4:33; 6:8).[18] It shows that the disciples will be empowered by the Spirit, the divine agency in Acts.[19] The imagery that Jesus' followers will be "clothed with power from on high" (Luke 24:49) is particularly fitting. They will receive the Spirit from the exalted Christ, the mantle of prophecy, to bear witness to his resurrection and to work signs and wonders in his name.[20]

---

15. Fitzmyer, *Luke I–IX*, 228–30.
16. Witherington, *Acts*, 109–10.
17. Tannehill, *Narrative Unity of Luke-Acts: Luke*, 294–95.
18. Pervo, *Acts*, 42–43; see also Walter Grundmann, "δύναμαι," *TDNT*, 2. 284–317.
19. Barrett, *Acts of the Apostles*, 1. 79.
20. Johnson (*Luke*, 406) recognizes the prophetic role of Moses and Elijah in the Gospel. In Jesus' transfiguration, Moses and Elijah were "in glory" and talked about Jesus' exodus (departure) in Jerusalem. Moses and Elijah transmit their spirits to their successors. Joshua inherits the spirit of Moses (Deut 34:9). When Elijah ascends into heaven, he leaves his prophetic "mantle" for his successor Elisha to wear (2 Kgs 2:14). Pervo (*Acts*, 45–46 n. 43) recognizes the similarities between the ascensions of Elijah

Before the coming of the Spirit, Luke narrates for a second time Jesus' ascension (Luke 24:51; Acts 1:9). Commentators have tried to reconcile these two accounts.[21] In Acts 1:2, Luke refers to Jesus' ascension, even though he has already narrated Jesus' ascension in Luke 24:51. "Ancient historians were less fastidious in such matters of overlap than are some contemporary scholars."[22] The ascension brings the Gospel to an appropriate end. Jesus has finished his earthly ministry. At the same time, it opens a new age for his followers.[23] "The ascension thus functions as the end of the Period of Jesus; once the risen Christ has taken his leave, the Period of the Church under Stress begins."[24] Fitzmyer divides salvation history in the following three fold way:

(a) Period of Israel: the period of law and the prophets (Luke 1:5–3:1)

(b) Period of Jesus: the period of Jesus' ministry, death, and exaltation (Luke 3:3–24:51)

(c) Period of the Church: the period of the spread of the word of God (Luke 24:52–Acts 1:3–28:31)[25]

With his ascension, Jesus' earthly ministry has come to an end. His followers will not see him in a visible way any more, but they will expe-

---

and Jesus: (a) the use of ἀναλαμβάνω in 2 Kgs 2: 9, 10 and Acts 1:2, 11, 22; (b) the phrase εἰς τὸν οὐρανόν in 2 Kgs 2:1, 10, four times in Acts 1:10–11; and (c) the specific reference to the followers as they are watching the ascension in 2 Kgs 2:10, 12; and Acts 1:9–10.

21. Hans Conzelmann, *The Theology of St. Luke* (trans. Geoffrey Buswell; Philadelphia: Fortress, 1982) 203 n. 4; Barrett, *Acts of the Apostles*, 1. 82.

22. Johnson, *Luke*, 404.

23. Pervo, *Acts*, 45; Conzelmann (*Theology of St. Luke*, 16–17) divides salvation history into three periods: (1) the period of Israel; (2) the period of Jesus' ministry; (3) the period of *ecclesia pressa* "church under stress." John H. Sieber ("The Spirit as the 'Promise of My Father' in Luke 24:49," in *Sin, Salvation, and the Spirit: Commemorating the Fiftieth Year of the Liturgical Press* [ed., Daniel Durken; Collegeville, MN: Liturgical Press, 1979] 271–78, here 272) follows the division of three periods of salvation history. There is an intermediate or interim period between Jesus' public ministry and the period of the church. This interim period is narrated from Luke 23:50 to Acts 1:26. It is about the resurrection accounts, the post-resurrection instructions of Jesus to his disciples, and his ascension.

24. Fitzmyer, *Acts*, 194. He writes ("The Ascension of Christ and Pentecost," *TS* 45 [1984] 409–40, here 424) "[W]e can see that his 'ascension' is nothing more than *the* appearance from glory in which Christ took his final leave from the community of his followers-his last visible leave-taking from the assembled followers. "

25. Fitzmyer, *Luke I–IX*, 185.

rience his power through his Spirit. Thus Christians live in the period between Jesus' departure and parousia.

Jesus' followers return to Jerusalem (Acts 1:12). The eleven apostles devote themselves to prayer (1:13–14). The community prepares itself in prayer for the coming of the Spirit. Prayer is the appropriate preparation to be empowered by the Spirit. This group of one hundred and twenty people will be the nucleus of the early Christian community. They will be the restored Israel.[26]

The post that Judas left must be filled, since there must be twelve apostles (Luke 6:13). At the last supper, Jesus says to the Twelve, "I confer on you a kingdom just as my Father has conferred on me that you may eat and drink at my table in my kingdom and sit upon thrones as judges of the twelve tribes of Israel" (Luke 22:29–30). Luke anticipates Jesus' enthronement. He also anticipates that Jesus' twelve apstles will "rule over the restored house of Israel."[27] Jesus promises the Twelve that they "will thus become the leaders of reconstituted Israel, the people of God."[28] For Luke, "It is important that the number twelve in connection with the twelve tribes is associated with his conception of Israel" (Acts 26:6–7).[29]

The purpose of restoring the twelve apostles is to prepare them to be witnesses to Jesus' resurrection at Pentecost. As the new leaders of the twelve tribes, the Twelve are reconstituted so they can bear witness to Jesus' resurrection to the whole house of Israel that will be represented in Jerusalem at Pentecost (Acts 2:36).[30]

26. Talbert (*Reading Acts*, 30) writes, "[T]he one hundred and twenty disciples, symbolizing the restored Israel (Acts 15:16), are of sufficient size to require a council of leaders for themselves."

27. Craig A. Evans, "The Twelve Thrones of Israel: Scripture and Politics in Luke 22:24–30," in *Luke and Scripture: The Function of Sacred Tradition in Luke-Acts* (ed. Craig A. Evans and James A. Sanders; Minneapolis: Fortress, 1993) 154–70, here 170. He interprets Luke 22:24–30 against the background of Dan 7:9–27 and Ps 122:3–5. Both texts contribute to the general idea of Israel's restoration and the judgment of the nations. There is a hope of the restoration of the twelve tribes. They will judge the nations. See also Jacob Jervell, "The Twelve on Israel's Thrones: Luke's Understanding of the Apostolate," in *Luke and the People of God: A New Look at Luke-Acts* (Minneapolis: Augsburg, 1972) 75–112.

28. Fitzmyer, *Acts*, 220.

29. Jervell, "The Twelve on Israel's Thrones," 86.

30. Fitzmyer (*Acts*, 221) holds that despite the death of the Messiah, God still continues to address the twelve tribes of Israel through the twelve disciples of Jesus. To prepare the stage for the proclamation at Pentecost, the Twelve had to be reconstituted. See also Tannehill, *Narrative Unity of Luke-Acts: Luke*, 22; Jervell, "The Twelve on Israel's

The Twelve are witnesses to Jesus' whole ministry, from the baptism of John, which marks the beginning of his ministry (Luke 3:23; 16:16; Acts 1:5; 10:37; 11:16; 13:24-25; 18:25; 19:3-4) to his ascension, which marks its end. During Jesus' ministry, he has taught his disciples, especially on the journey from Galilee to Jerusalem (Luke 9:51-19:27).

Only Luke narrates the forty-day post-resurrection period of Jesus' instructions to his apostles. This is a period of "transition and preparation" for the apostles.[31] "The main purpose in creating this period of time was to provide an opportunity for the risen Lord to give further teachings to his disciples."[32] Through Jesus' instruction, the disciples understand the Scriptures (Luke 24:26-27, 32, 44-45). Peter expounds the replacement of Judas in light of the Scriptures. He sees that everything happens according to OT prophecy, God's plan (Acts 1:16, 21). By replacing Judas, the Church reestablishes the Twelve and prepares them to face the whole house of Israel at Pentecost. Yet they need to wait for the coming of the Spirit (Luke 24:49; Acts 1:8). They wait in prayer.

2. The Immediate Literary Context

The descent of the Spirit at Pentecost in Acts 2:1-13 is the immediate context of Peter's sermon in Acts 2:14-40. There are two parts to Acts 2:1-13: part one depicts the coming of the Spirit (vv. 1-4), and part two narrates the effect of the coming of the Spirit and the responses of the audience (vv. 5-13). I follow Pervo's analysis of this passage.[33] In part one, vv. 1-4 form a single sentence focused on the word πάντες ("all"): all were gathered together (v. 1) and all were filled with the Spirit (v. 4). Verses 3-4 are parallel in structure. In vv. 1-4, Luke uses the verbs συμπληρόω, πληρόω, and πίμπλημι to emphasize that all the assembly is filled with the Spirit. The wind, sound, and the tongues as of fire describe the experience of the Spirit descending upon the whole assembly. As the result of being filled with the Spirit, the assembly begins to speak in other tongues.

The Pentecost event is introduced with ἐν τῷ συμπληροῦσθαι τὴν ἡμέραν τῆς πεντηκοστῆς ("when the time for Pentecost was fulfilled"). This phrase recalls ἐν τῷ συμπληροῦσθαι τὰς ἡμέρας τῆς ἀναλήμψεως

Thrones," 94; idem, *The Theology of the Acts of the Apostles* (Cambridge: Cambridge University Press, 1996) 79-82.

31. I borrow the term from Tannehill (*Narrative Unity of Luke-Acts: Acts*, 9-25).
32. Sieber, "The Spirit as the 'Promise of My Father' in Luke 24:49," 272.
33. Pervo, *Acts*, 59.

αὐτοῦ ("when the days of his being taken up were fulfilled") in Luke 9:51. "In both cases the fulfillment of a time is emphasized because the days in question bring the fulfillment of prophecy."[34] The coming of Pentecost is the fulfillment of the coming of the Spirit that Jesus promised his disciples (Luke 24:49; Acts 1: 4, 5, 8). "Luke sees this day as important in salvation history, speaking of it as coming to full number, i.e., coming to fulfillment, just as he saw the beginning of the Travel Account in the story of Jesus' ministry (Luke 9:51)."[35] This is the time of fulfillment. Jesus' disciples are empowered by the Spirit and begin to bear witness to him.

The descent of the Spirit comes with wind, fire, and noise. These symbols have a rich meaning. According to *The Book of Jubilees* 6:17–21 (ca. 150 B.C.E), the feast of Pentecost (in Hebrew the Feast of Weeks) celebrates the gift of receiving the Torah by Moses at Mount Sinai. The fire and noise allude to the description of a theophany at Sinai (Exod 19:16, 18–19).[36] In Israel's salvation history, the Sinai covenant establishes the relationship between God and the Israelites. They received the gift of the Torah. At Pentecost, they renew this covenantal relationship.

---

34. Tannehill, *Narrative Unity of Luke-Acts: Acts*, 26. Luke 9:51 refers to the fulfillment of the prophecies of Jesus' passion in Jerusalem in Luke 9:22, 31, 44. Jesus is going to Jerusalem to fulfill his mission. Luke 9:51 is the solemn start of the journey.

35. Fitzmyer, *Acts*, 237.

36. It is widely recognized that these symbols allude to the Sinai event in Exodus 19. See Pervo, *Acts*, 61. Luke T. Johnson (*The Acts of the Apostles* [SacPag 5; Collegeville, MN: Liturgical Press, 1992] 46) lists three reasons why the description of Pentecost is related to the event of receiving the Torah from God at Mount Sinai. He writes that (1) nowhere is the same cluster of symbols found all together except in the LXX description of Sinai (Exod 19:16), with its repeated emphasis on the noise, and the "descending of God upon it in fire" (Exod 19:18); (2) the development of this symbolism by Philo Judaeus (*On the Decalogue* 33), who connects the giving of the Torah of God to the communion of speech by flame; (3) Luke consistently uses the Moses typology for the story of Jesus. Jacques Dupont ("The First Christian Pentecost," in *The Salvation of the Gentiles* [trans. John R. Keating; New York: Paulist, 1979] 35–59, here 38–39) finds several vocabulary allusions in Acts 2 to Exodus 19–20. Fitzmyer (*Acts*, 234) concludes, "Even if these allusions are not unambiguous, they at least associate the Lucan account of the giving of the Spirit to the Exodus account of the giving of the Torah on Sinai." Robert L. Brawley (*Text to Text Pours Forth Speech: Voices of Scripture in Luke-Acts* [Bloomington: Indiana University Press, 1995] 76–77) notes that fire has three metaphorical meanings in antiquity: divine presence, judgment, and purification. He thinks that fire at Pentecost fulfills the promise in Luke 3:16; the connotations of purification and judgment refer to future eschatological realizations (Acts 3:23; 17:31).

Luke uses the Feast of Pentecost to narrate the giving of the gift of the Spirit. The Twelve and the early Christians receive the gift of the Spirit.[37] All these symbols confirm that "all were filled with the Holy Spirit" (v. 4).[38] This is their baptism in the Spirit (Luke 3:16). They are empowered by the Spirit, the power from on high (Luke 24:49; Acts 1:2). As a result of their empowerment, they speak in other languages, as the Spirit enabled them (v. 4). The Spirit is the source and initiator of divine prophecy in the apostles.[39]

Pentecost is the next great pilgrim feast after Passover. This is the occasion when, after Jesus' crucifixion at Passover, Jerusalem is filled with Jews from all over the world.[40] Luke introduces the theme of universality at the Pentecost event.

Part two (vv. 5–13) begins in v. 5 with a brief introduction of the Jews in Jerusalem. They are from every nation under heaven. They are Jews from many nations (vv. 9–11a). But they hear, in their own languages, the mighty deeds of God (v. 11b).

They are confused (συνεχύθη), bewildered (ἐξίσταντο), and amazed (ἐθαύμασον). All were bewildered and perplexed (ἐξίσταντο δὲ πάντες καὶ διηπόρουν). Two points are emphasized. First, the Jews in Jerusalem represent all Jews. Second, they are all confused, perplexed at the sign of tongues enabled by the coming of the Spirit upon the whole assembly.

The Jews from the long list of nations represent Israel in its wholeness, including the diaspora. "Just as the Twelve represent the nucleus of the people that is being restored, so does this audience represent all the

---

37. Johnson (*Acts*, 45) regards the Pentecost event as spiritual transformation of the disciples. The real event is the empowerment of the disciples by the Spirit. If we compare this event with other resurrection narratives in the NT (John 20:22–23; 1 Cor 15:45), "[W]e can even say that Luke's Pentecost story is a rendering of the primordial Christian experience of the resurrection."

38. Barrett (*Acts of the Apostles*, 1. 114) notes that fire is sometimes said to rest on the heads of rabbis as they studied or disputed about the Torah. It is a symbol of God's divine enlightenment or guidance. I think the early Christians could have understood that these symbols signified the presence of the Spirit at Pentecost. The Hebrew word רוּחַ and its Greek equivalent πνεῦμα can mean "wind" or "spirit." God's Spirit comes as wind blows. It appears in a physical form like tongues of fire. The Spirit comes upon Jesus also in the physical form of a dove (Luke 3:22).

39. Darrell L. Bock (*Acts* [BECNT; Grand Rapids, MI: Baker, 2007] 98) recognizes the connection between being filled with the Spirit and prophesying. Some examples are Elizabeth (Luke 1:41), Zachariah (1:67), Peter (Acts 2:17–40; 4:8, 31), and Paul (13: 9).

40. Barrett, *Acts of the Apostles*, 1. 112.

lands to which the Jews had been dispersed."[41] Peter's sermon to the Jews emphasizes that he wants to address the whole house of Israel (2:36). Luke shows that Peter's sermon is essential for all the Jews. It signifies that from the very beginning the mission initiated by the Spirit is universal. Because the mission is universal, a language sign is needed. Both the universal nature of the audience and the language sign are "indications of an effort to emphasize the intended scope of mission."[42]

The Jews at Pentecost have heard the mighty deeds of God (v. 11). Yet Luke does not present the detailed contents of the utterance of the assembly. The audience cannot understand the meaning of this event. They asked, "What does this mean?" Some say, "They have just had too much new wine." The question and the misunderstanding create a tension and need to be explained. The reader is expecting an explanation of this event.

B. The Structure of Peter's Sermon

There are two delimitations of Peter's sermon at Pentecost. Some think that the sermon ends at v. 36. Verses 37–41 are the responses to Peter's sermon.[43] Most commentators think this sermon ends at either v. 40 (Pervo, Soards), or v. 41 (Haenchen, Jervell).[44] I judge that the sermon ends at v. 40. This sermon includes Peter's direct address to the Jews at Pentecost. It is interrupted by a question from the audience "what are we do to do, brothers?" Peter then responds to the question and call to repentance and promise of salvation. He ends his response to the question at v. 40 ("Be saved from this corrupt generation"). The verb σώθητε in v. 40 corresponds to σωθήσεται in v. 21. The sermon ends with a call to conversion.

Peter addresses his audience three times (vv. 14, 22, and 29). In v. 37, they address Peter and the other apostles as "brothers." The addresses in vv. 22 and 29 form one unit, focusing on David's prophecy as fulfilled

---

41. Johnson, *Acts*, 47.

42. Tannehill, *Narrative Unity of Luke-Acts: Acts*, 27.

43. Gerd Lüdemann, *The Acts of the Apostles: What Really Happened in the Earliest Days of the Church* (Amherst, NY: Prometheus Books, 2005) 51–55. Johnson (*Acts*, 48–56) delimits the sermon to 2:14–36, while 2:37–42 is the portrait of a restored people. Fitzmyer (*Acts*, 249, 264–67) ends the speech at v. 36, while vv. 37–41 is a reaction to Peter's discourse.

44. Pervo, *Acts*, 75; Soards, *Speeches in Acts*, 32; Haenchen, *Acts*, 176–77; Jacob Jervell, *Die Apostelgeschichte* (KEK; Göttingen: Vandenhoeck & Ruprecht, 1998) 140–41.

in Jesus. There are three main sections. In 2:14–21, Peter focuses on the narrative circumstances of Pentecost. He refutes the misunderstanding of the audience with regard to the coming of the Spirit and interprets it as the fulfillment of the Prophet Joel. In 2:22–36, Peter develops his christological argument from Scripture that Jesus is the Messiah (v. 36). In 2:37–40, in response to a question from the audience, Peter calls for repentance and promises salvation through the name of Jesus the Lord. He concludes the sermon with a brief summary and final exhortation in v. 40. I outline the structure of Peter's inaugural missionary sermon at Pentecost in Acts 2:14–40 in the following way:[45]

1. Peter refutes the misunderstanding of the audience and presents the significance of the Pentecost event from the Prophet Joel (vv. 14–21)
    a. Opening address to the audience (v. 14)
    b. Correction of the misunderstanding and presentation of the thesis of fulfillment (vv. 15–16)
    c. Citation of the Prophet Joel (vv. 17–21)
2. Christological argument: Jesus is the promised Messiah (vv. 22–36)
    a. Christological Kerygma: God raises Jesus from the dead (vv. 22–24)
    b. Scripture proof citation (vv. 25–28)
    c. Interpretation of the previous scriptural citation (vv. 29–31)
    d. Christological Kerygma: Jesus' resurrection, exaltation, and the coming of the Spirit at Pentecost (vv. 32–33)
    e. Proof from Scripture (vv. 34–35)
    f. Christological Kerygma: God has made Jesus Lord and Messiah (v. 36)
3. Call to repentance and promise of salvation (vv. 37–40)
    a. The audience is moved and ask for advice (v. 37)
    b. Peter's responses (vv. 38–39)

45. Having consulted the analysis of Pervo (*Acts*, 75), Soards (*Speeches in Acts*, 32), and Schweizer ("Concerning the Speeches in Acts," 208), I have structured the sermon this way.

1) Repent and be baptized in the name of Jesus Christ (v. 38a)

   2) Receive the promise of the Lord: the gift of the Spirit (vv. 38b-39)

  c. Summary and final exhortation (v. 40)

C. Detailed Exegesis of Acts 2:14-40

1. Peter Refutes the Misunderstanding of the Audience and Presents the Significance of the Pentecost Event from the Prophet Joel (vv. 14-21)

After the reconstitution of the Twelve (1:15-26), the first thing Luke narrates is the coming of the Spirit at Pentecost (2:1-13). The descent of the Spirit upon the disciples and the early Christian community fulfills Jesus' promise (Luke 24:49; Acts 1:4, 5, 8). They receive the Spirit (2:3). They are empowered and begin to speak in different tongues. The Pentecost event arouses confusion, bewilderment, and ironic remarks. Luke uses Peter's sermon to explain the significance of the Pentecost event.

A. Opening Address to the Audience (v. 14)

As the spokesman of the reconstituted Twelve (1:26), Peter delivers his first missionary sermon to Jews. This is a solemn proclamation. He stands up (σταθείς) and thus takes the stance of a Greek orator for a public speech (5:20; 11:13; 17:22; 25:18; 27:21). He raises his voice and addresses the whole assembly. The phrase ἐπῆρεν τὴν φωνὴν αὐτοῦ may be borrowed from the LXX (Judg 2:4; 9:7; 21:2; Ruth 1:9, 14; 2 Sam 13:36).[46] The verb ἀπεφθέγξατο appears in Acts 2:4. They are filled with the Spirit and begin to speak in different tongues, as the Spirit enabled them to proclaim (ἀποφθέγγεσθαι). After receiving power from the Spirit, Peter fulfills what the risen Lord has commissioned his disciples to do: to be his witnesses first in Jerusalem (1:8).

The audiences that Peter addresses are Judeans and all those who are sojourning in Jerusalem for the feast. The verb κατοικοῦντες ("dwelling") "suggests that they were Jews from the diaspora who had returned, out of religious motivation, to live in the city of Jerusalem."[47] There are

---

46. Haenchen, *Acts*, 178; Fitzmyer, *Acts*, 251.

47. Frank Matera, "Responsibility for the Death of Jesus according to the Acts of the Apostles," *JSNT* 39 (1990) 77-93, here 79.

Jerusalemites and devout Jews.⁴⁸ They represent all the Israelites in Judea and diaspora, the whole house of Israel (2:36). The universality (πάντες) of the audience is emphasized.

Peter calls for his audience's attention and says, "Let this be known to you."⁴⁹ This expression forms an *inclusio* with "Let the whole house of Israel know" in v. 36.⁵⁰ Before, Jesus' disciples could not understand Jesus' suffering, death, and resurrection as the fulfillment of Scripture. With the instruction of the risen Lord, they have understood that Jesus is the fulfillment of Scripture (Luke 24:49). They have gone through a transition from ignorance to understanding. Now Peter bears witness to what he has learned from the risen Lord.

B. Correction of the Misunderstanding and Presentation of the Thesis of Fulfillment (vv. 15–16)

Peter relates his sermon to what has just occurred (2:1–13). He refutes the mockery, "They have had too much new wine." This mockery seems related to the miracle of tongues: too much wine has made the apostles drunk; this is why they are speaking in tongues. It is also possible that this mockery relates to the background of the Pentecost of New Wine.⁵¹ In any case, Peter refutes the accusation. He says that these people are not drunk, for it is only nine o'clock in the morning. It is too early to be drunk.

The Pentecost event has been foretold by the Prophet Joel. Luke introduces the citation from LXX Joel 3:1–5a.

---

48. Bruce J. Malina & John J. Pilch (*Social-Science Commentary on the Book of Acts* [Minneapolis: Fortress, 2008] 29) claim that the Greek word Ἰουδαῖοι means the inhabitants of the region of Judea. It should be translated as Judeans. This is a generic term that embraces all persons of Israelite origin resident among various non-Israelite majority populations.

49. The exact expression γνωστὸν ἔστω is a Lukan favorite. It appears in Acts 2:14; 4:10; 13:38; and 28:28. It usually introduces something significant to the Jews in Peter and Paul's speeches. Luke uses this expression to reveal something new in salvation history with regard to Jesus, which the Jews should have known.

50. Pervo, *Acts*, 76.

51. Fitzmyer (*Acts*, 235) mentions that there are three Pentecosts: the Pentecost of New Grain; the Pentecost of New Wine; and the Pentecost of New Oil. Luke may have known these Pentecost Feasts. At the Pentecost of New Wine, people could drink too much wine. See also Y. Yadin, *The Temple Scroll 2* (Jerusalem: Israel Exploration Society, 1983) 78–96.

c. Citation of the Prophet Joel (vv. 17–21)

The citation in Acts 2:17–21 is from LXX Joel 3:1–5a. Except for a few additions and changes, the text of Acts is close to that of the LXX.

LXX Joel 3:1 καὶ ἔσται μετὰ ταῦτα καὶ ἐκχεῶ ἀπὸ τοῦ πνεύματός μου ἐπὶ πᾶσαν σάρκα καὶ προφητεύσουσιν οἱ υἱοὶ ὑμῶν καὶ αἱ θυγατέρες ὑμῶν καὶ οἱ πρεσβύτεροι ὑμῶν <u>ἐνύπνια</u> ἐνυπνιασθήσονται καὶ οἱ νεανίσκοι ὑμῶν ὁράσεις ὄψονται 2 καὶ ἐπὶ τοὺς δούλους καὶ ἐπὶ τὰς δούλας ἐν ταῖς ἡμέραις ἐκείναις ἐκχεῶ ἀπὸ τοῦ πνεύματός μου 3 καὶ δώσω τέρατα ἐν τῷ οὐρανῷ καὶ ἐπὶ τῆς γῆς αἷμα καὶ πῦρ καὶ ἀτμίδα καπνοῦ 4 ὁ ἥλιος μεταστραφήσεται εἰς σκότος καὶ ἡ σελήνη εἰς αἷμα πρὶν ἐλθεῖν ἡμέραν κυρίου τὴν μεγάλην καὶ ἐπιφανῆ 5 καὶ ἔσται πᾶς ὃς ἂν ἐπικαλέσηται τὸ ὄνομα κυρίου σωθήσεται.	Acts 2:17 καὶ ἔσται <u>ἐν ταῖς ἐσχάταις ἡμέραις (λέγει ὁ θεός)</u> ἐκχεῶ ἀπὸ τοῦ πνεύματός μου ἐπὶ πᾶσαν σάρκα, καὶ προφητεύσουσιν οἱ υἱοὶ ὑμῶν καὶ αἱ θυγατέρες ὑμῶν καὶ οἱ νεανίσκοι ὑμῶν ὁράσεις ὄψονται καὶ οἱ πρεσβύτεροι ὑμῶν ἐνυπνίοις ἐνυπνιασθήσονται· 18 καί γε ἐπὶ τοὺς δούλους <u>μου</u> καὶ ἐπὶ τὰς δούλας μου ἐν ταῖς ἡμέραις ἐκείναις ἐκχεῶ ἀπὸ τοῦ πνεύματός μου, <u>καὶ προφητεύσουσιν.</u> 19 καὶ δώσω τέρατα ἐν τῷ οὐρανῷ ἄνω καὶ σημεῖα ἐπὶ τῆς γῆς κάτω, αἷμα καὶ πῦρ καὶ ἀτμίδα καπνοῦ. 20 ὁ ἥλιος μεταστραφήσεται εἰς σκότος καὶ ἡ σελήνη εἰς αἷμα, πρὶν ἐλθεῖν ἡμέραν κυρίου τὴν μεγάλην καὶ ἐπιφανῆ. 21 καὶ ἔσται πᾶς ὃς ἂν ἐπικαλέσηται τὸ ὄνομα κυρίου σωθήσεται.

In v. 17, the phrase "after this" (μετὰ ταῦτα) is presented in B 076 (C pc) sa mss. This is to conform to LXX Joel 3:1a. It is more likely to change the original form of Acts 2:17 back to the form of LXX Joel 3:1a. Therefore, I judge ἐν ταῖς ἐσχάταις ἡμέραις to be original. There is one change of wording at the beginning of Acts 2:17. Luke changes "after this" (μετὰ ταῦτα) to "in the last days" (ἐν ταῖς ἐσχάταις ἡμέραις).

After the phrase "in the last days," most manuscripts have λέγει ὁ θεός, while the Western text reads λέγει ὁ κύριος (D E latt; Ir lat). George D. Kilpatrick thinks that "in general the tendency may have been to change κυριοσ to θεοσ as κυριοσ is ambiguous and may mean God or Christ, but θεοσ like Ιησουσ or Χριστοσ is not."⁵² It is possible that ὁ θεός is changed by later scribes from ambiguous ὁ κύριος. However, "no evidence that such a tendency as Kilpatrick suggests operated in the case of codex Bezae."⁵³ Because of the overwhelming external evidences of the presence of λέγει ὁ θεός, I judge this is the original. In fact, there is no significant difference in meaning here. Luke adds "God declares" (λέγει ὁ θεός) after "in the last days."

There is a transposition in v. 17. The sentence, "Your young men shall see visions" is transposed before "your old men shall dream dreams." The accusative case ἐνύπνια is changed to dative case ἐνυπνίοις.

In v. 18, there are three additions, γε is put between καί and ἐπί. The possessive pronoun μου is added after "upon my servants" (ἐπὶ τοὺς δούλους) and after "upon my handmaids" (ἐπὶ τὰς δούλας). The main addition is "and they shall prophecy" (καὶ προφητεύσουσιν) at the end of v. 18. This sentence is not in the Western tradition. It seems that the Western text keeps close to the LXX Joel 3:1-5a text in quoting it.

In v. 19, there are three additions. The word "above" (ἄνω) is added after "in the heaven" (ἐν τῷ οὐρανῷ) and the word "below" (κάτω) after "on the earth" (ἐπὶ τῆς γῆς). The main addition is that the word "signs" (σημεῖα), which is added before ἐπὶ τῆς γῆς. There are no changes in the 27th edition of Nestle-Aland in vv. 20-21. There are only some insignificant changes in ℵ D gig r with regard to these two verses. There are no omissions in the citation from the LXX Joel 3:1-5a.

These changes and additions express Lukan theology. The addition "God declares" in v. 17 can be seen as part of the introductory formula of the prophecy. It claims God's authority for the prophecy. The prophecy has divine origin. The change from "after this" to "in the last days" is significant for Luke. "After this" means some indefinite time in the future (the prophecy will happen). But Luke sees the coming of the Spirit as inaugurating "the last days of the Lord." He gives the prophecy an eschatological interpretation. Thus, through the outpouring of the Spirit, a new period of God's salvation arrives. It is the start of the period of the *eschaton*. It is a period guided by the Spirit.

---

52. George D. Kilpatrick, "An Eclectic Study of the Text of Acts," in *Biblical and Patristic Studies in Memory of Robert Pierce Casey* (ed. J. Neville Birdsall and Robert W. Thomson; Freiberg: Herder, 1963) 65-66.

53. Bruce M. Metzger, *A Textual Commentary on the Greek New Testament* (2nd ed.; Stuttgart: German Bible Society, 1994) 256.

There are two parts in Acts 2:17–21. Part 1 includes vv. 17–18; part 2 includes vv. 19–20 and a conclusion in v. 21. In part 1, the main verb is ἐκχεῶ, and the preposition is ἐπί. Its structure is as follows:

A. ἐκχεῶ ἀπὸ τοῦ πνεύματός μου

  B. ἐπὶ πᾶσαν σάρκα,

      C. καὶ προφητεύσουσιν οἱ υἱοὶ ὑμῶν καὶ αἱ θυγατέρες ὑμῶν

      καὶ οἱ νεανίσκοι ὑμῶν ὁράσεις ὄψονται

      καὶ οἱ πρεσβύτεροι ὑμῶν ἐνυπνίοις ἐνυπνιασθήσονται

  B'. καί γε ἐπὶ τοὺς δούλους μου καὶ ἐπὶ τὰς δούλας μου ἐν

  ταῖς ἡμέραις ἐκείναις

A'. ἐκχεῶ ἀπὸ τοῦ πνεύματός μου, καὶ προφητεύσουσιν.

There is a distinct structure in vv. 17–18. God will pour out his Spirit upon all flesh (B), male and female, young and old (C). As a result of this outpouring of God's Spirit, your sons and daughters shall prophesy; your young men shall see visions, and your old shall dream dreams. In the original context of Joel, "all flesh" refers to all the people of Judah.[54] This prophecy is for your sons and daughters, young and old men. God says, "I will pour out my Spirit upon my servants and my handmaids in those days." In Joel, these male and female slaves are part of all flesh upon whom God will pour out his Spirit. For Luke, in these last days, these are God's servants and handmaids. They are the newly reestablished Israel, represented by Jesus' apostles.

At the end of v. 18, the phrase "I will pour out my Spirit" is repeated (A'). This corresponds to the same phrase in v. 17 (A). The effect of God's pouring out his Spirit is that "they will prophesy" (προφητεύσουσιν). This phrase is added by Luke to emphasize that the prophetic proclamation is the gift of the Spirit. At Pentecost, Luke explains that through the outpouring of the Spirit these Galileans speak in other tongues (prophesy) about the mighty deeds of God (v. 11).

"Seeing visions" and "dreaming dreams" are in synonymous parallelism.[55] Vision and dream are "specifically prophetic modes" in the

---

54. Fitzmyer, *Acts*, 252.
55. Barrett, *Acts of the Apostles*, 137.

OT.⁵⁶ Visions play a significant role for the prophetic characters in Acts (7:31; 55–56; 9:3–10, 12; 10:3, 17, 19; 11:5; 16:9–10; 18:9; 27:23).⁵⁷

Part 2 includes vv. 19–20. In this part, Luke adds "above," "signs," and "below." The main verb is δώσω. The objects of δώσω are "portents" (τέρατα) in the heavens and "signs" (σημεῖα) on the earth. The portents above are described as "the sun turned to darkness, the moon to blood." The signs below are described as "blood, fire, and cloud of smoke." In the prophecy of Joel, these portents and signs will happen before the coming of the great and splendid day of the Lord. These are "intended as an apocalyptic warning."⁵⁸ Pentecost signifies the coming of the last days of the Lord. By adding the word "signs" before "on the earth," Luke focuses on the signs on the earth, which is related to the phenomenon at Pentecost.⁵⁹ In his sermon, Luke will narrate the signs that Jesus has done and the signs that his apostles will perform in their ministries in Acts

Luke concludes his citation from Joel in v. 21. The original context of v. 21 in Joel is the coming of the day of the Lord. The MT reads וְהַנּוֹרָא יוֹם יְהוָה הַגָּדוֹל ("the great and fearful day of the Lord").⁶⁰ The day of the Lord is the day of salvation for his people and judgment for his enemies. Before the day of the Lord, everyone who calls on the name of the Lord will be saved. The name of the Lord (κυρίου) in Joel means the name of Yahweh. For Luke, the coming of the Spirit inaugurates the last days of the Lord. The church is in a new period. In this period, everyone who calls on the name of Jesus, the risen Lord, will be saved. Verse 21 recalls the univer-

---

56. Johnson (*Acts*, 49) writes that vision is a vehicle of prophecy in LXX Num 24:4; 16; 1 Sam 3:1; 2 Sam 7:17; Ps 89:19; Hos 12:10; Mic 3:6; Obad 1:1; Nah 1:1; Hab 2:2–3; Zech 10:2; Isa 1:1; 13:1; 19:1; Jer 14:14; Lam 2:9; Ezek 1:1; 8:3; 40:2; Dan 4:20; 8:1. He notices that dream is "a regular if ambiguous mode of prophecy" (Gen 37:5; 41:8; Deut 13:1–5; 1 Sam 28:15; Zech 10:2; Jer 28:25–32, 36; Dan 1:17; 2:1; 4:2).

57. Ibid.

58. Fitzmyer, *Acts*, 253. Barrett (*Acts of the Apostles*, 137) writes, "Signs are being done on earth in these last days; but (except so far as they may be included in the wind and fire of the day) portents in heaven have not appeared. Joel lists them freely, and Luke as freely takes them over. It is clear that he wanted the words with which he concludes his quotation in v. 21, but he could if he wished have omitted the intervening clauses."

59. Pervo (*Acts*, 80) writes, "In any event, the reader of Acts is invited to admire 'signs on earth' but is not encouraged to investigate cosmological phenomenon."

60. The LXX has "ἡμέραν κυρίου τὴν μεγάλην καὶ ἐπιφανῆ." It is possible that ἐπιφανῆ is a misinterpretation of הַנּוֹרָא. This verb is from ירא (to fear) not from ראה (to see). See Fitzmyer, *Acts*, 253; Barrett, *Acts of the Apostles*, 138.

sal theme in v. 17. God will pour out his Spirit upon all flesh. All who call upon the name of the Lord will be saved. This verse functions as a bridge to conclude the citation from Joel and prepares for the proclamation that Jesus is Lord and Messiah (v. 36).

The citation of LXX Joel 3:1–5a serves to explain the meaning and significance of the narrative of Pentecost in Acts 2:1–13. The coming of the Spirit and the sign of tongues fulfill the prophecy of Joel. The outpouring of the Spirit marks the arrival of the last days. It is through the gift of the Spirit that these Galileans proclaim God's mighty deeds in tongues. The Spirit empowers them to be prophets, and they will prophesy. During these last days, many signs and wonders will happen before the coming day of the Lord. Before this day, everyone who calls on the name of Lord will be saved. Thus Pentecost marks the dawn of "the last days." Luke uses this citation from Joel to interpret Pentecost, and the citation "is understood as a divine promise that is realized progressively, but only partially, in Acts as a whole."[61] "The last days are a chain of occurrences, a historical process, ending with the parousia."[62]

2. Christological Argument: Jesus is Lord and Messiah (vv. 22–36)

In this section (vv. 22–36), Luke argues from Scripture that Jesus is Lord and Messiah. He first proclaims the kerygma about Jesus of Nazareth, whom God raised from the dead (vv. 22–24). He quotes David's Psalm (Ps 16:8–11) that God's holy one will not see corruption (vv. 25–28). He argues that this passage does not apply to David, since he died, was buried, and his tomb is still in their midst (v. 29). Rather, being a prophet, David foresaw and spoke of the resurrection of the Messiah, one of his descendants. God raised Jesus from the dead and exalted him at the right hand of God. This exalted Jesus receives the promise of the Spirit from the Father and pours it upon believers at Pentecost. Therefore, God has made Jesus both Lord and Messiah. The crowd, therefore, should call upon the name of the risen Lord and be saved.

---

61. Tannehill, *Narrative Unity of Luke-Acts: Acts*, 30.

62. Jacob Jervell, *The Theology of the Acts of the Apostles* (Cambridge: Cambridge University Press, 1996) 108.

A. Christological Kerygma: God Raises Jesus from the Dead (vv. 22–24)

Peter starts to fulfill the promise of the Prophet Joel: they shall prophesy (vv. 17–18). He addresses his audience as "fellow Israelites." The name "Israel" is given by Yahweh to Jacob, a patriarch of God's people (Gen 32:29). This salutation prepares for Peter's climatic proclamation to "all the house of Israel" that Jesus is Lord and Messiah.

"Jesus the Nazorean" is the person that Peter proclaims. The name "Jesus" is emphasized by its prominent place at the beginning of the sentence (v. 22). Christian preaching begins with the name of Jesus. He is referred to as a "man" (ἄνδρα), to whom later pronouns refer: τοῦτον (v. 23), ὅν (v. 24), and αὐτόν (v. 25). Peter's preaching starts from the earthly Jesus.

Jesus has manifested God's power. It is through him that God works these mighty deeds, wonders, and signs. The verb ἀποδεδειγμένον has a wide range of meanings such as to display, demonstrate, endorse, and appoint. It is possible that Luke connotes the wide range of meanings here. I judge it to mean "to show," "to demonstrate." God has demonstrated that Jesus is God's unique agent by working mighty deeds, signs, and wonders through him. God is the source of Jesus' mighty deeds.[63]

Fellow Israelites should have known that God has worked wonders through Jesus among them. He is God's prophet.[64] Yet they killed him, but God raised him from death. Luke underlines the significant role of God in Jesus' earthly ministry, suffering, death, and resurrection. It is God who takes the initiative to demonstrate who Jesus is; it is God who works mighty deeds, signs, and wonders through Jesus; it is according to God's set plan and foreknowledge that you kill him; it is God who raises Jesus from the dead. Throughout the life of Jesus, God "remains the subject."[65]

This is the first time that Luke presents the contrast formula in regard to Jesus' death between the action of the Jerusalemites and the action of God. These Jews kill Jesus by fastening him to the cross, making use of lawless men (v. 23). But God raises him from the dead (v. 24).

---

63. Barrett, *Acts of the Apostles*, 141; Johnson, *Acts*, 50.

64. Johnson (*Acts*, 50) recognizes that the terms δυνάμεσι καὶ τέρασι καὶ σημείοις and ἐν μέσῳ ὑμῶν echo Moses' work as a prophet in Deut 34:10–12. Jesus is then a prophet through whom God works signs and wonders.

65. Gert J. Steyn, *Septuagint Quotations in the Context of Petrine and Pauline Speeches of the Acta Apostolorum* (Kampen, Netherlands: Kok Pharos, 1995) 101 n. 188.

This contrast formula appears more clearly in v. 36. Paradoxically the Jerusalemites have fulfilled God's set plan and foreknowledge.[66]

B. Scripture Proof Citation (vv. 25-28)

Verse 24 says that God raised Jesus, releasing him from death's throes, because it was impossible for him to be held by it. Jesus' resurrection was part of God's set plan. It was necessary because death could not hold Jesus. The causal γάρ in v. 25 explains the reason: because David prophesied that the Messiah would rise from dead. The prophecy of David in Ps 16:8-11 presents the reason why death could not hold Jesus. The introductory phrase Δαυὶδ γὰρ λέγει εἰς αὐτόν means "David referred to the Messiah when he wrote Psalm 16:8-11."[67] The pronoun αὐτόν means Jesus, the risen Lord, in the context of Acts.

Luke thinks that the author of this Psalm is David. It is a song of trust in God's help and providence in troubles. He quotes LXX Ps 8:8-11 exactly in vv. 25-28.[68] In Psalm 16, David gives thanks to God. He has set the Lord God "before me always." "The Lord is at my right hand, I shall not be shaken." It is for this reason that "my flesh too will live on in hope; for you will not abandon my soul to the netherworld, nor will you allow your holy one to see decay (vv. 26-27)." These two verses underline David's unwavering trust in Yahweh's steadfast faithfulness, even in death. God "has made known to me the paths of life; you will fill me with joy in your presence." Verses 26-27 can mean bodily resurrection. "At the time when the LXX came into being, the belief in the resurrection was thriving. It is thus not surprising to find traces of it here. The LXX then, appears at this point the better candidate for adoption by Luke in Acts."[69]

---

66. Matera, "Responsibility for the Death of Jesus in Acts," 78-79. Steyn (*Septuagint Quotations*, 102) writes, "There may be some implied antithetic parallelisms between v. 23 and v. 24." He presents them like this: (1) v. 23a, "God has handed Jesus over" versus v. 24a, "God has resurrected Jesus"; (2) v. 23b, "Jesus was crucified by the hand(s)of the lawless" versus v. 24b, "Jesus was released from the 'bands' of death"; (3) v. 23c "Jesus was killed by these lawless people" versus v. 24c, "Death does not have power over him."

67. Gregory V. Trull, "Peter's Interpretation of Psalm 16:8-11 in Acts 2:25-32," *BSac* 161 (2004) 432-48, here 439. He interprets λέγει εἰς as "with reference to." Jesus the risen Lord is the referent of David's prophecy in Ps 16:8-11.

68. Luke does not include the phrase τερπνότητες ἐν τῇ δεξιᾷ σου εἰς τέλος of LXX Ps 16:11c in his quotation, perhaps because he will quote a similar phrase κάθου ἐκ δεξιῶν μου in v. 34b from LXX Ps 109:1.

69. Steyn, *Septuagint Quotations*, 106.

It is important to present OT proof for Jesus' resurrection, since it is essential for Israel to recognize that Jesus' resurrection is rooted in Scripture. Luke presents Ps 16:8-11 to prove that David prophesied Jesus' resurrection. The author of the Psalm is David, but to whom does this Psalm refer? Whose soul will not be abandoned to the netherworld? Who is the holy one that will not see decay?

C. Interpretation of the Previous Scripture Citation (vv. 29-31)

Peter addresses his audience as "my brothers." He regards himself as a fellow Israelite who shares their religious heritage.

First, this Psalm cannot refer to David, because the presence of David's tomb proves that he could not have been speaking of himself. David died and was buried. Consequently David must have been speaking about another, who is the holy one of God.

Second, David is a prophet.[70] He knew the oath that God swore to him. God would set one of David's descendants upon his throne (v. 30). Luke alludes to Ps 132:11, which he implicitly quotes, ἐκ καρποῦ τῆς κοιλίας σου θήσομαι ἐπὶ τὸν θρόνον σου. This psalm celebrates the Davidic dynasty, in which David is called God's "Anointed One" (τοῦ χριστοῦ σου, Ps 132:10). Luke may also be alluding to Ps 89: 4-5. The allusion to 2 Sam 7:12-16 is clear in v. 30. In Luke 1:32-33, the allusion is to the promise made to David in 2 Sam 7:12-16 with regard to his everlasting dynasty.

Third, since Ps 16:8-11 cannot refer to David, he must have been speaking of someone else, since he was a prophet. With his prophetic foreknowledge, he must have been speaking of the resurrection of the Messiah. More specifically, Ps 16:10 refers to the Messiah, one of David's descendants. Therefore, David's prophecy in Ps 16:8-11 refers to the Messiah (the Anointed One from the House of David).

---

70. Fitzmyer (*Acts*, 258) writes, "David is never called a prophet in the OT, and there is little in the story of David that might serve as a springboard for such a title." He finds that the function of prophecy is attributed to David in the Qumran text and in Josephus's work. See Fitzmyer, "David, 'Being Therefore a Prophet...' (Acts 2:30)," *CBQ* 34 (1972) 332-39. Johnson (*Acts*, 51) writes, "That the author of the psalms was a prophet is axiomatic for Luke (see Luke 20:41-42; 24:44; Acts 1:16, 20; 4:25; 13:33-36)."

D. Christological Kerygma: Jesus' Resurrection, Exaltation, and the Coming of the Spirit at Pentecost (vv. 32–33)

Who is this Messiah whose soul is not abandoned to the netherworld and whose body does not experience corruption? This Jesus whom God raised from the dead is the Messiah. Jesus' resurrection confirms that his body is not abandoned to the netherworld, nor does his body suffer corruption. He has fulfilled the prophecy in his resurrection. He is the Messiah. Peter announces to his audience that we (the Twelve) are the witnesses of Jesus' resurrection. The risen Lord has appeared to them and shown himself to be alive (1:3). "Luke thus has Peter fulfill Jesus' prophecy in Luke 24:48 and Acts 1:8, and his own criterion of apostleship, that one should be a witness to the resurrection (Acts 1:22)."[71]

Jesus has been exalted to the right hand of God. The phrase "to the right hand" is alluded to in Ps 16:11b, which Luke does not quote in Acts 2:25–28. This phrase also anticipates the quotation in Acts 2:34b. The place at the "right hand" is the place where a king invites his favorites to sit (2 Kgs 2:19; 1 Chr 6:39; 1 Esdr 4:29; 9:43; Neh 8:4). In this sense, Jesus the risen Lord is a victorious one, who enjoys God's favor. God confirms his status by exalting him to sit at his right. The image of God's right hand signifies the source of "power, life, and salvation (Exod 15:6; LXX Pss 17:35; 25:10; 43:3; 47:10; 59:5; 97:1; 117:16; 137:7)."[72] Being exalted to or "by" the right hand of God, Jesus receives the promised Spirit from the Father. Through the Prophet Joel, God promised to pour his Spirit on all flesh (2:17–18). The risen Lord receives the promise, that is the Spirit, and he sends it out (ἐξέχεεν). Through the outpouring of the Spirit, the Galileans speak of the mighty deeds of God in tongues, and Peter proclaims the risen Lord. This is what the audience is hearing and seeing (v. 33).

E. Proof from Scripture (vv. 34–35)

Luke quotes LXX Ps 109:1 to prove that David was not exalted to the right hand of God. When David writes this Psalm, he does not refer to his own assumption into heaven. He must have been speaking of another, for it was not David who went up into heaven (v. 34). This is proved in the argument of vv. 29–31 that David's tomb is still among them. There is no "assumption" of David in the OT.[73] Rather, it is Jesus whom God has exalted to his right hand by raising him from the dead.

---

71. Johnson, *Acts*, 52.
72. Ibid.
73. Fitzmyer, *Acts*, 260.

The quotation in LXX Ps 109:1 reads, "The Lord said to my Lord: 'Sit at my right.'" The Lord is God. To whom does "my Lord" refer? Does it refer to David, since this Psalm is ascribed to David? David is not exalted to the right side of God. "My Lord," then, must not refer to David. It must refer to one who has been raised to the right of God. Jesus has been raised to the right of God. Therefore, he must be "my Lord" of LXX Ps 109:1.

LXX Psalm 109 is "a royal psalm commemorating the enthronement of a king of his dynasty, who is invited by Yahweh to ascend to the throne and assume a position of honor beside God."[74] "My Lord" in LXX Ps 109:1, then, refers to the risen Lord in his exaltation to the right of God, the Lord. God has given Jesus the Lord his victorious status. This prepares for the climatic proclamation in v. 36.

F. Christological Kerygma: God has Made Jesus both Lord and Messiah (v. 36)

Luke draws the conclusion for his arguments (οὖν) from Scripture: "Let the whole house of Israel know for sure that God has made Jesus both Lord and Messiah." This verse recalls v. 21, "Everyone who calls upon the name of the Lord will be saved." On the basis of LXX Ps 109:1, then, Peter proves that God has made Jesus the Lord. This christological title implies that Jesus, in his risen status, has been made equal to God. Jesus is the Lord who, like God in the OT, brings salvation to all who call upon his name.[75] Having been exalted to the right of God, he received the status of Lord. This prepares for Peter's call to repent and be baptized in the name of Jesus Christ (v. 38) for the forgiveness of sins since salvation comes by calling upon the name of the Lord Jesus Christ.[76]

---

74. Ibid.

75. Bock, *Acts*, 136. See also Witherington (*Acts*, 148) who writes that the word κύριος and its variants appear at least 104 times in Acts. It clearly refers to God 18 times and to Jesus 47 times. It is not clear whether other occurrences refer to God or Jesus. In the case of Acts 2:34, he writes, "Both God and Jesus are referred to as κύριος shows how flexible Luke was prepared to be in his use of the term κύριος." Matera (*New Testament Theology*, 67 n. 17) recognizes that in several instances it is not clear whether "Lord" refers to God or Jesus. He writes that this use "suggests that the relationship between God and Jesus is so close that Luke can use 'Lord' in this ambiguous way."

76. John J. Kilgallen ("'With many other words' (Acts 2, 40): Theological Assumption in Peter's Pentecost Speech," *Bib* 83 [2002] 70–87, here 87) concludes that "God gave His Spirit to Jesus of Nazareth, who has poured out the Spirit of God to cause prophecy. The significance, i.e., the purpose of this outpouring of the Spirit is that anyone who

Throughout the whole presentation, Luke compares David with Jesus. He refutes the thesis that David is the promised Messiah and Lord. David is a prophet. In Psalms 16 and 110, he does not refer to himself. Rather he prophesies the future coming of the Messiah and Lord, Jesus the risen one.

Verse 36 ends with a contrast formula between what God has done with what the Jerusalemites have done (ὑμεῖς ἐσταυρώσατε). This formula recalls the similar contrast in vv. 23–24. This contrast formula is part of many missionary discourses in Acts. On the one hand, the missionary discourses affirm that Jesus' passion, death, and resurrection have fulfilled God's set plan and foreknowledge; on the other hand, they call the audience to repentance for their role in putting Jesus to death. Luke ends his direct sermon with "You crucified this Jesus" (v. 36b). The purpose of this sermon is to make the audience recognize (vv. 14, 36) its ignorance of killing their Lord and Messiah and call for repentance.[77]

This sermon is part of "a recognition scene, whereby, in the manner of tragedy, persons who have acted blindly against their own best interests suddenly recognize their error. Accordingly, the speech is designed to produce the effect described following the disclosure in 2:36, 'Hearing, they were cut to the heart' (2:37), an indication that the hearers have, in fact, recognized their error and are ready for the call to repentance that follows."[78]

3. Call to Repentance and Promise of Salvation (vv. 37–40)

In v. 36, Peter ends his sermon with an accusation against his audience, "God has made him both Lord and Messiah, this Jesus whom you crucified." The purpose of this accusation is to highlight the sins of his audience and call for repentance. Peter's sermon is effective. His audience asks what they must do. He responds with an exhortation.

---

now calls on the name of the Lord Jesus will be saved."

77. Matera, "Responsibilty for the Death of Jesus in Acts," 78–79. See also Jacques Dupont, "Repentir et Conversion d'après les Actes des Apôtres" in *Etudes sur les Actes des Apôtres* (LD 45; Paris: Cerf, 1967) 421–57, esp. 436.

78. Tannehill, *Narrative Unity of Luke-Acts: Acts,* 35. See also Matera, "Responsibility for the Death of Jesus in Acts," 78.

A. The Audience is Touched and Asks for Advice (v. 37)

After having heard Peter's sermon that they have crucified the Lord and Messiah, the Jews in Jerusalem are cut to the heart. They have deep pain and remorse in their hearts for the sins they have committed against their Messiah. They ask Peter and the other apostles, "Brothers, what shall we do?" This verse recalls v. 14. Luke wants to show that the Jews recognize the apostles as their fellow Israelites. Now the apostles are the new leaders of the people of God. They are fulfilling what the risen Lord commissioned them to do. The audience wants to atone for what they have done in ignorance of their Messiah.

B. Peter's Response (vv. 38–39)

In response to his audience's request, Peter answers that they should (1) repent; (2) be baptized in the name of Jesus for the forgiveness of sins; and (3) receive the gift of the Spirit.

1) Repent and Be Baptized in the Name of Jesus the Messiah (v. 38a)

Peter responds to their question with a call to repentance. "Repent" (μετανοέω) and its noun form "repentance" (μετάνοια) are favorite Lucan terms. The verb means "to change one's mind." In the OT it has "a religious sense of culpability toward someone, God or another human being; it came to mean a 'reform of life,' especially a change from sinful conduct (Wis 11:23; 12:19)."[79] Luke often connects this verb with the "forgiveness of sins" as he does here in v. 38 (Luke 3:3; 24:47; Acts 2:38; 3:19; 5:31; 8:22; 26:18, 20). In addition to μετανοέω, Luke also uses ἐπιστρέφω (Acts 3:19; 9:35; 11:21; 14:15; 15:3, 19). The Hebrew word for ἐπιστρέφω is שׁוּב. It means to change the direction of one's life from moving away from God to a direction toward God. The starting point for repentance is confessing that they have crucified their Lord and Messiah.

Peter urges his audience to "be baptized in the name of Jesus the Messiah." The ritual of baptism is associated with repentance in John the Baptist's mission (Luke 3:7–16). In baptism, people are washed clean. In this context, the baptismal washing signifies that they have repented of their sins against their Messiah. Their sins are washed away, and they can draw near to God.[80] In baptism, they also publicly declare that they dedicate themselves to Jesus, the Messiah.

79. Fitzmyer, *Acts*, 265.
80. Bock, *Acts*, 142. Fitzmyer (*Acts*, 266) holds that the phrase "in(to) the name of Jesus" is a banking or commercial expression used by Luke to describe "baptism as a

The purpose of baptism in Jesus' name, then, is the forgiveness of sins.[81] By committing oneself to Jesus the Messiah in baptism, one is associated with the Messiah. The expression εἰς ἄφεσιν ἁμαρτιῶν means for the forgiveness of sins. In its religious sense, it means remission of debts. In baptism, one belongs to the Messiah, the savior, and one's debt is remitted.

2) Receive the Promise of the Lord: the Gift of the Holy Spirit
   (vv. 38b–39)

The goal of repenting and being baptized in the name of Jesus for the forgiveness of sins is to receive the gift of the Spirit; that is, the promise from God. By baptism in the name of Jesus the Messiah, one is committed to the risen Lord. Jesus has been raised at the right of the Father and received the promise of the Spirit from the Father (v. 33). Now he can pour out the Spirit on all who have been baptized in his name. The promise of the Spirit is a mark of the eschatological age (v. 17). The promise of the Spirit is for all, the Jews present at Pentecost in Jerusalem, their children, and those who are far off. It includes all the Jews even those who are in the diaspora.

c. Summary and Final Exhortation (v. 40)

Luke narrates that Peter testifies with many other words. This is a literary technique widely used in ancient literatures. It means that the words in the speech "do not exhaust what the speaker said."[82] The speaker delivers more than is presented in the speech. The verb διεμαρτύρατο is from διαμαρτύρομαι. It means to testify to something solemnly and emphatically. The verb παρακαλεῖν means to exhort, to appeal, to urge. These two

---

mode of ascription to Christ."

81. Fitzmyer (*Acts*, 266) writes, "For Luke the 'name of Jesus' connotes the real and effective representation of Jesus himself." The name of a person makes the person present. He has the authority to deliver God's salvation because he sits at the right hand of God. Jesus is thus the source of salvation for all who return to him and are baptized in his name.

82. Dibelius, *Book of Acts*, 77. Killgallen ("With many other words," 87) claims that probably because Luke wants this sermon to be brief, he assumes that Peter's audience and his readers know three things: (1) Jesus is the Son of David (Luke 1:32); (2) the Lord of Ps 110:1 is the Messiah (Luke 20:41–44); and (3) "When one speaks about the giving of the Spirit, one should talk of Father and Son, not simply of God and Jesus of Nazareth." (Luke 2:49 with 24:49). See also Barrett, *Acts of the Apostles*, 156.

verbs convey a sense of Christian preaching.[83] It includes bearing witness to the facts about Jesus and appealing for the audience to respond.

There are two possible translations of σώθητε, "be saved" or "save yourselves." I judge that it should be translated as "be saved." In the context of this sermon, the verb σώθητε (v. 40) recalls v. 21, "Everyone who calls on the name of the Lord will be saved." God's Spirit is for everyone whom the Lord calls. The audience needs to accept God's gift, the Spirit, and be saved. This meaning is confirmed in v. 47. Those who have responded to Peter's call and are baptized are called τοὺς σῳζομένους ("those who were being saved").

Peter's audience is called to be saved ἀπὸ τῆς γενεᾶς τῆς σκολιᾶς ταύτης. They must be saved from a larger population and be included as "part of a remnant people."[84] This phrase is drawn from Deut 32:5 or LXX Ps 77:8. Similar phrases appear in Luke 9:41 and 11:29. Peter exhorts his audience to believe in his message and be baptized. They should stand apart from those who refuse to believe in Jesus as the Messiah. Those Jews, who refuse to accept the salvation that Jesus brings, "are part of a corrupt generation that was complicit in the death of the Messiah (2:40).

Those who believe in Peter's testimony and are baptized in the name of Jesus the Messiah are saved from those who refuse to repent. Through the power of the Spirit at Pentecost, they form the reestablished Israel. The new community of the church is "a restored and repentant Israel," "God's covenant people."[85]

In summary, Peter's first missionary sermon explains the coming of the Spirit at Pentecost. The descent of the Spirit is the fulfillment of prophecy (LXX Joel 3:1–5a). It marks the beginning of the eschatological time. Everyone who calls on the name of the Lord will be saved. Through the prophecies of David, Peter proves that Jesus has been made Lord and Messiah through his resurrection. His audience is called to repent and be baptized in his name and receive the promise of the Father, the Spirit. Thus, believers in Jesus Christ form the reestablished Israel, the church.

---

83. Barrett, Ibid.
84. Johnson, *Acts*, 58.
85. Ibid.

II. THE LITERARY FUNCTION OF PETER'S INAUGURAL SERMON IN ACTS

Peter's inaugural missionary sermon is to the Jews at Pentecost. On the one hand, it explains the significance of the coming of the Spirit. On the other hand, it recalls what Jesus commissions his apostles to do after his resurrection. Furthermore, it goes beyond the context of the Pentecost event. Literarily, it presents a model for how the apostles will fulfill Jesus' commission to bear witness to his resurrection. In doing so, it specifies the character of the ministry of his apostles. They will prophesy, perform signs and wonders, and witness to the risen Lord. It lays the foundation for other missionary sermons in Acts. It also announces the main themes that Luke will explore in the rest of Acts.

A. *Peter's Inaugural Sermon Functions as a Model of How the Apostles Respond to Jesus' Instruction and Commission after Resurrection*

John the Baptist announces a baptism of Spirit and fire (Luke 3:16). Jesus assures his audience that the heavenly Father will give the Spirit to those who ask him (Luke 11:13). The risen Lord pledges to send the promise of his Father to his apostles (Luke 24:49; Acts 1:4, 8). These promises create a narrative need for fulfillment. The coming of the Spirit at Pentecost fulfills Jesus' promises.

Peter's speech is the result of Jesus' teaching after his resurrection (Luke 24:44–45; Acts 1:2–3) and the Spirit's empowerment (Acts 2:4). Jesus opens the minds of his apostles so that they understand the Scriptures and recognize that everything in them must be fulfilled. Peter's inaugural sermon is an example of how Peter, the representative of the apostles, has been transformed by the teaching of the risen Lord. This period of transition and preparation bears fruit. The Spirit enables Peter to bear witness to Jesus' resurrection with boldness. His sermon is a model of how Jesus' death and resurrection have fulfilled the Scriptures.

In his speech (Acts 2:14–40), Peter proclaims Jesus' resurrection (vv. 22–24) and uses LXX Ps 16:8–11 and 109:1 to prove it. He understands that it is by God's set plan and foreknowledge that Jesus was killed (v. 23). God raised him from the dead. Peter learns this from the risen Lord (Luke 24:46) and bears witness to it.

In the Gospel (24:47–48), Luke lays out the basic themes of the apostolic proclamation that Jesus' apostles will preach in Acts. In response to Jesus' commission, Peter preaches to the Jews at Pentecost: Repent and be baptized in the name of Jesus the Messiah for the forgiveness of sins and receive the gift of the Spirit (Acts 2:38). Jesus' apostles have been commissioned to preach repentance for the forgiveness of sins in Jesus' name. Now they preach repentance to those who refused to accept Jesus as their Messiah. The salvation that Jesus brings is the forgiveness of sins. At Pentecost, the Christian community is formed through baptism in Jesus' name, and they receive the gift of Spirit. Peter's sermon corresponds to Jesus' commission. It shows that Peter and the apostles begin to fulfill what Jesus has commissioned them to proclaim. This conformity guarantees the authority of Peter's preaching.

B. Peter's Sermon Functions as a Foundation for the Missionary Sermons in Acts

Luke sets Peter's sermon at Pentecost at the beginning of the apostles' mission to witness to Jesus' resurrection. Scholars recognize that "Acts 2 comes to us as the most finished and polished specimen of the apostolic preaching, placed as it were in the shop window of the Jerusalem Church and of Luke's narrative."[86] Acts 2:14–40 is the "keynote address" of Acts.[87] "The Pentecost speech of Peter is a very good presentation of the truth about Jesus, a representative presentation which at the same time shows the strength of a solid witness to Jesus and offers itself as a typical, though not exhaustive example of the bases of early post-pentecostal successful and convincing preaching."[88] It has a significant literary function in Acts.

Peter's Pentecost sermon functions as a foundation of the missionary sermons in Acts in three ways. First, this sermon is an example of how to prove Jesus' resurrection from Scripture. Peter proclaims God's mighty deeds in Jesus the Nazorean by raising him from dead. He focuses on God's mighty deeds in Jesus (2:11). Jesus is commended by

---

86. John A. T. Robinson, "Most Primitive Christology of All," *JTS* 7 (1956) 177–89, here 185.

87. Richard F. Zehnle, *Peter's Pentecost Discourse: Tradition and Lukan Reinterpretation in Peter's Speeches of Acts 2 and 3* (SBLMS 15; ed. Robert A. Kraft; Nashville: Abingdon, 1971) 17. See also David L. Tiede, "Acts 2:1–47," *Int* 33 (1979) 62–67, here 63. Talbert (*Reading Acts,* 47) writes, "In Acts as a whole, Peter's speech functions as a frontpiece, just as Jesus' speech in Luke 4:16–27 does in the third Gospel."

88. Kilgallen, "With many other words," 71–72.

God (v. 22). He uses LXX Psalms 16 and 109 to proclaim that David prophesied Jesus' resurrection. This is the foundation of other preaching about Jesus' resurrection. In the following narrative, Luke mentions that the apostles bear witness to Jesus' resurrection (4:33). He does not need to repeat this proof from Scripture.

Second, Peter proclaims Jesus as Lord and Messiah. At the beginning of the apostles' public announcement, it is essential to rectify their misconceptions and accusations. By identifying Jesus as the Lord, Peter proclaims that he enjoys God's own status. God gives salvation through the risen Lord. This lays the foundation for the call to believe in the Lord (5:14; 9:42; 18:8; 20:21), proclaim the Lord (11:20–21), and be saved through the grace of the Lord (15:11) in the following narratives.[89]

This is the first time that Jesus is called Messiah in Acts (vv. 31, 36). Peter proves through Scripture that Jesus is the promised Messiah of Israel. He is God's agent to bring salvation to Israel. The presentation of Jesus, as the promised Messiah, is integral for the missionary sermons to Jews. Luke summarizes the apostles' teaching as they proclaim Jesus as the Messiah (5:42). The word they preach to the Samaritans is to proclaim the Messiah (8:5). Luke does not need to present the argument that Jesus is the Messiah since Peter's sermon has already proved it.

Third, Peter's inaugural sermon lays the foundation for other missionary speeches in Acts. There are similar patterns in them.[90] Most speeches are related to the narrative settings. Luke uses them to interpret the theological significances of these events. There are some variations in presenting these speeches. Different speeches, then, function differently in Acts.[91] Yet Peter's keynote sermon presents a paradigm for the missionary sermons in Acts. The paradigm is an address connected with a corresponding event (2:15–16), quotations from the OT (Joel 3:1–5a at

---

89. Darrell L. Bock, "Jesus as Lord in Acts and in the Gospel Message," *BSac* 143 (1986) 146–54, here 151.

90. Schweizer, "Concerning the Speeches in Acts," 210–12; Dibelius, *Book of Acts*, 67; Soards, *Speeches in Acts*, 11; Fitzmyer, *Acts*, 107.

91. Robert C. Tannehill, ("The Functions of Peter's Mission Speeches in the Narrative of Acts," in *The Shape of Luke's Story: Essays on Luke-Acts*, 169–84, here 171) lists five general functions of the speeches. First, they provide reviews of key events in Jesus' story and previews of new events, interpreting them theologically; second, they interpret the significance of events taking place at the time of the speech; third, they have a reinforcing function in repeating certain themes; fourth, they complement one another in providing new details or expanding new themes; fifth, they present new understandings of Scripture.

vv. 17–21), christological or theological kerygma (2:22–24), sometimes a further OT passage which is quoted as a proof of the kerymatic preaching (Ps 16:8–11 at vv. 25–28), and a call for conversion (v. 38–39). Although there are some variations or changes of order in these elements of the speeches, Luke uses Scripture to proclaim that Jesus has been raised from the dead. He is the Messiah, and the audience is called to repent. This is the fundamental paradigm of the missionary speeches.

Luke uses this sermon as one of the models of how the apostles preach. Since Luke has presented this sermon, later he uses some terms and phrases to recall the sermons that Peter has preached. These terms and phrases are "to teach" or " to teach in the name of the Lord" (4:18; 5:21, 25, 28), to speak what the apostles "have seen and heard" (4:20), "to speak your word with all boldness" (4:29), "to speak the word of God" or "the word of God" (4:31; 6:7; 8:4, 14, 25), "to bear witness to the resurrection of the Lord Jesus" (4:33), "to proclaim the Messiah" (8:5) or "to proclaim Jesus" (8:35) or preach the good news (8:25, 40) and the name of Jesus Christ (8:12). Luke also uses a short speech in 5:30–32 to recall Peter's inaugural sermon to the Jews in Acts.

C. Peter's Sermon Announces the Main Themes of Acts

Peter's sermon functions as an explanation of the Pentecost event. It also functions as a foundation for the recurrent theme of Pentecost in the rest of Acts. The Pentecost event marks the beginning of a new age—the eschatological age. Luke uses the prophecy of Joel 3:1–5a to describe the eschatological activity of God's Spirit among the Christians in this new age. It announces the nature of their mission, to prophesy God's mighty deeds in Jesus of Nazareth. It presents the themes that Luke will explore in the rest of Acts.

1. The Theme of the Spirit

Peter's sermon explains the coming of God's Spirit upon the assembly. This is the fulfillment of the prophecy of Joel 3:1–5a. Now it is Jesus who pours forth (ἐξέχεεν) what God will do in the last days. The Spirit is related to the risen Lord. He is the one who sends God's Spirit in this new age. This grounds the relationship of the coming of the Spirit with the risen Lord.

The descent of the Spirit at Pentecost initiates the coming of the Spirit upon all flesh. The subsequent narrative demonstrates how the

Spirit comes upon different groups of people. It shows that the Spirit is the guiding force of the new community.

> The Spirit comes upon the community in Jerusalem to strengthen it in persecutions (4:31); inspires Stephen with the courage to face martyrdom (7:55); singles out Barnabas and Saul for their first mission (13:2); inspires the edict of the council at Jerusalem (15:28); directs the second journey of Paul (16:6f.); inspires Paul to start on his way to Jerusalem (19:21); and makes known to him what awaits him there (20:22f.; 21:4, 11).[92]

The Spirit confirms the mission to Samaria (8:16–17). This is the first mission outside of Jerusalem. In the story of Cornelius, when Peter delivers a speech, the Spirit falls upon all who are listening to the word. They start to speak in tongues to glorify God (10:44–46). It is the Spirit that confirms Peter's understanding of the vision that he sees. At the coming of the Spirit to the Gentiles, Peter grasps that this event is similar to what happened to the Jews at Pentecost. God gives the Gentiles the same gift of the Spirit that he gave to the Jewish Christians (11:15).

After Paul receives the Spirit (9:17), he is sent by the Spirit on his mission (13:2). When Paul lays his hands on the Ephesians who have been baptized with the baptism of John, the Spirit comes upon them and they speak in tongues and prophesy. The Spirit confirms Paul's mission. It is the Spirit who guides the mission of the Church and confirms the mission of Jesus' followers. The Pentecost sermon sets the tone for the significant role of the Spirit. In the last days, God's Spirit will come upon all flesh. Through the risen Lord, God sends his Spirit to all and guides the mission of the Church through his Spirit.[93]

---

92. Zehnle, *Peter's Pentecost Discourse*, 126. See also F. Scott Spencer, *The Gospel of Luke and Acts of the Apostles* (Nashville: Abingdon, 2008) 218–32; Earl Richard, "Pentecost as a Recurrent Theme in Luke-Acts," in *New Views on Luke-Acts* (ed. Earl Richard; Collegeville: Liturgical Press, 1990) 133–49.

93. Luke T. Johnson (*The Literary Function of Possessions in Luke-Acts* [SBLDS 39; Missoula, MT: Scholars Press, 1977] 40–41) writes, "Acts can rightly be called the Book of the Holy Spirit. Not only does the Spirit actively intervene at every critical stage of the mission (cf. e.g. 8:29, 39; 10:19; 11:12; 13:2, 4; 16:6, 7; 19:1; 20:22), but it is the gift of the Holy Spirit which initiates the mission and gives it its shape. Luke includes in his narrative five separate accounts of the bestowal of the Spirit (2:1–12; 4:28–311; 8:15; 10:44; 19:6)."

2. The Theme of the Character of the Apostles' Mission: Prophesy, Perform Signs and Wonders in the Name of the Lord

At the end of Acts 2:18, Luke adds "they shall prophesy" to the LXX Joel 3:2. This addition emphasizes the element of prophecy already present in v. 17. Luke underlines that the purpose of the pouring out of the Spirit is to empower Jesus' witnesses to prophesy. The nature of the Spirit is "the Spirit of prophecy."[94] Luke stresses that the Spirit, the source of prophecy in the OT, "will produce similar effects on a more grandiose scale in the future."[95] The apostles, filled with the Spirit, will proclaim God's mighty deeds in Jesus (2:11, 22–24), bear witness to his resurrection, and call their listeners to conversion. The disciples are commissioned to a prophetic proclamation of the risen Lord.

Luke confirms the relationship between the Spirit and the prophetic preaching. Peter is filled with the Spirit and proclaims μετὰ παρρησίας (2:29) that Jesus is Lord and Messiah (2:36). Thus, he is fulfilling his role as witness to Jesus' resurrection (1:8; 2:32). "Filled with the Spirit," Peter delivers a speech to the people in Jerusalem (4:8). Wisdom and the Spirit make Stephen's word powerful (6:10). After being filled with Spirit, Paul begins to proclaim Jesus in the synagogues (9:17–20). The same Spirit enables Barnabas to preach (11:23–24). When their preaching arouses hostility, the Christian community prays to God that they might proclaim the Word with all boldness. They are all filled with the Spirit and continue to speak the Word of God with boldness (4: 29–31). The Spirit's work is a work of the Word. The Spirit empowers Jesus' witnesses to preach with boldness.[96] The nature of the mission of Jesus' followers is to proclaim the risen Lord.

With the addition of "signs" at 2:19 the expression "signs and wonders" emerges in Acts. "[T]his Spirit of Prophecy is manifested in the working of signs and wonders."[97] Jesus' apostles demonstrate the power of their prophetic preaching by working signs and wonders. In Acts 7:36,

---

94. Johnson, *Literary Function of Possessions in Luke-Acts*, 44.

95. Alexander Kerrigan, "The 'Sensus Plenior' of Joel, III, 1-5 in Act., II, 14–36," in *Sacra Pagina: Miscellanea Biblica Congressus Internationalis Catholici de Re Biblica* (ed. J. Coppens, A. Descamps, and E. Massaux; BETL 12–13; Gembloux: J. Duculot, 1959) 295–313, here 301.

96. Daniel Marguerat, *The First Christian Historian: Writing the "Acts of the Apostles"* (trans. Ken McKinney, Gregory J. Laughery and Richard Bauckham; SNTSMS 121; Cambridge: Cambridge University Press, 2002) 118–19.

97. Johnson, *Literary Function of Possessions in Luke-Acts*, 45.

Stephen mentions that Moses does signs and wonders in Egypt. God works signs and wonders through Moses in leading the Israelites out of Egypt (Exod 4:8, 9, 17, 28, 30; 7:3, 9; 10:1, 2; 11:9–10). Peter proclaims that God works mighty deeds, signs, and wonders through Jesus (2:22). Similarly, Jesus' disciples perform signs and wonders (2:43; 4:30; 5:12; 6:8; 14:3; 15:12). Through these signs and wonders, they demonstrate that they are filled with the Spirit.

After being anointed with the Spirit, Jesus is filled with God's power and goes out to do good and to heal those oppressed by evil (Acts 10:38; Luke 4:31–41). With the power of the Spirit that comes from Jesus, Peter heals a lame man (Acts 3:1–10; Luke 5:17–26). This healing and the apostles' preaching of the risen Lord result in rejection in Jerusalem (4:1–3). Like Jesus, his apostles are filled with the Spirit. They proclaim God's word in bearing witness to Jesus' resurrection. They also perform signs and wonders. Their healing and proclamation of the risen Lord, however, causes a mixed response of acceptance and rejection. They are depicted as prophets who prophesy about God's mighty deeds in Jesus Christ.[98] "The apostles are men filled with the Holy Spirit, who speak God's Word by witnessing boldly to the resurrection of Jesus, and who demonstrate the power of their message by working signs and wonders."[99] Johnson writes that Luke

> makes the Joel prophecy a programmatic statement for the rest of the narrative: the reader will recognize those who are 'filled with the Holy Spirit' and who 'work signs and wonders among the people' as prophets in the line of Moses, just as the description of Jesus immediately after the citation as one who worked 'powerful deeds, wonders and signs' during his ministry mark *him* as a prophet.[100]

3. The Theme of Salvation in the Name of the Lord

Peter proclaims that everyone who calls on the name of the Lord will be saved (v. 21). He proves that through the resurrection God has made Jesus both Lord and Messiah (v. 36). Therefore, everyone is called to be baptized in the name of Jesus Christ for the forgiveness of sins and receive the gift of the Spirit (v. 38). Everyone is exhorted to be saved

---

98. Ibid., 77.
99. Ibid., 48.
100. Johnson, *Acts*, 54.

from this corrupt generation (v. 40). Peter's Pentecost sermon is a sermon about salvation in Jesus' name; that is; "in raising Jesus from the dead, God has made him the source of salvation for all who believe in his name."[101]

Salvation involves forgiveness of sins. Peter exhorts his audience to repent from their sin of rejecting the Messiah. Salvation is also connected with healing. The healing of the lame man is "in the name of Jesus Christ the Nazorean" (4:10). The name of Jesus is the power behind the healing (3:6, 16; 4:7). He concludes, "There is no salvation in anyone else, for there is no other name under heaven given to human beings by which we are to be saved" (4:12). The healing of the lame man fulfills the promise made in 2:21 and functions as an example of salvation through Jesus' name. It is for Jesus' name that the apostles are threatened by the rulers (4:17, 18; 5:28, 40, 41). It is through the name of Jesus that the apostles heal and work signs and wonders (4:30). "The passages cited in Acts 2–5 are part of an interconnected narrative sequence that is shaped with the prophecy of 2:21 in mind."[102] Christians are those who "call upon the name" (9:14, 21; 22:16).

After Chapter Five, the name of Jesus is mentioned with the mission of Philip in Samaria (8:12, 16) and then with Paul's call and early preaching (9:14, 15, 16, 21, 27, 28). This is "perhaps to emphasize the continuity of the preaching of Philip and Paul with the preaching of the apostles."[103] The name of Jesus continues to appear in 10:43, 48; 15:26; 16:18; 19:5, 13, 17; 21:13; 22:16; 26:9 in Acts. The apostles are to preach Jesus and salvation in his name.

4. The Theme of God's Set Plan and Foreknowledge in Jesus

According to Acts, the Jews in Jerusalem crucified Jesus (vv. 23, 36). But God has raised him from death (vv. 24, 32). This is the first time that the contrast form is presented in Acts. Peter uses Scripture to expound God's set plan and foreknowledge (v. 23).[104] Jesus' suffering, death, and

---

101. Matera, *New Testament Theology*, 72.

102. Tannehill, *Narrative Unity of Luke-Acts: Acts*, 31.

103. Ibid., 49.

104. David P. Moessner, "Two Lords 'at the Right Hand'? The Psalms and an Intertextual Reading of Peter's Pentecost Speech (Acts 2:14–36)," in *Literary Studies in Luke-Acts: Essays in Honor of Joseph B. Tyson* (ed. Richard P. Thompson and Thomas E. Philips; Macon, GA: Mercer University Press, 1998) 215–32, here 232. He writes, "Curiously, many contemporary commentators place much emphasis, and rightly so,

resurrection fulfill everything written about him in the Scriptures (Luke 24:44). This happens according to God's plan (4:28; 13:36; 20:27). This is the foundation of the contrasts in 3:15, 17–18; 4:10–11; 5:30; 10:39–40; 13:28–30.

On the one hand, the contrast form reveals the ignorance of the Jews in crucifying Jesus the Messiah. On the other hand, it demonstrates God's plan in Jesus Christ. God's plan moves to its fulfillment in Jesus Christ. Yet "the plan of God has breadth beyond the will and work of God in history in relationship to Jesus alone."[105] Jesus fulfills God's plan in his death, resurrection, and exaltation. He also "inaugurates the ongoing testimony to God's saving work" in his followers.[106] God's plan continues to operate in the ministry of Jesus' apostles. They link God's work in Jesus in the past with the present reality of God's work.[107]

Luke uses δεῖ to indicate divine necessity—God's plan. Peter recognizes God's plan in the death of Judas (1:16) and the selection of his successor (1:21). He interprets his mission as necessarily obeying God's plan (5:29). Paul's ministry is "to declare the entire plan of God" (20:27). He must visit Rome and bear witness there (19:21; 23:11). God's plan is the guiding thread in the narrative of Acts. Jesus does everything according to God's plan, so do his followers.

5. The Theme of Repentance for the Forgiveness of Sins

The risen Lord commands his disciples to preach repentance in his name for the forgiveness of sins (Luke 24:47). Peter's Pentecost sermon aims to convince the Jews in Jerusalem that they unknowingly killed their

---

on the programmatic function of the Joel text, and yet tend to ignore his second longest citation altogether. But would it not make more 'sense' in the rhetoric of the speech to interpret Peter as expatiating upon 'the determined plan and foreknowledge of God,' remembering Jesus' words (Luke 24:46), how it is that 'the Psalms are written about me,' namely that 'the Christ must suffer and on the third day rise from the dead' (v. 46)?" (pp. 222–23)

105. Soards, *Speeches in Acts*, 187.
106. Ibid., 188.
107. Marion L. Soards (*The Passion according to Luke: The Special Material of Luke 22* [JSNTSup 14; Sheffield: JSOT Press, 1987] 159) writes, "Luke can say at Acts 9:34 that Jesus Christ heals and at 26:22–23 that Christ proclaims light to his own people and to the Gentiles. Thus the patterns of human response to Jesus that were seen throughout his earthly ministry, and which culminated in the events of the Passion, continue after Jesus' death and resurrection; for, while Jesus is exalted into heaven, humanity continues to accept or reject him as he ministers among and through the disciples."

promised Messiah. He calls for repentance so that they can be saved. Salvation is a central theme in Acts. It means "the fulfillment of God's covenant promise and the restoration of God's people" for the Israelites. For the Gentiles, it means "to become part of the renewed and reestablished people of God."[108] The salvation promised by the prophets in the OT and the forgiveness of sins proclaimed by John the Baptist are given to Israel at Pentecost. The gift is given to those in Jerusalem and in the diaspora. This is "a word of restoration of Israel, reestablishing the people of God through whom salvation and repentance will in time also be proclaimed to the Gentiles (cf. Acts 11:18: 'Then to the Gentiles also God has given repentance')."[109]

At Pentecost, the presence of the Spirit offers the opportunity for repentance and the forgiveness of sins to all the Israelites. They need to recognize their blindness and ignorance in denying their promised Messiah. Their proper response is to repent and be baptized in the name of Jesus Christ. The audience at Pentecost realizes their wrongdoings; they are cut to the heart. About three thousand of them accept the message of repentance and are baptized. This is the reestablishment of a repentant Israel.[110] The mission of Jesus' followers is to proclaim his resurrection and call people to repentance for the forgiveness of sins. Peter proclaims repentance to the Jews in Jerusalem (2:38; 3:19; 5:31) and to the Gentiles (11:18). Peter functions as "a preacher of repentance."[111]

Paul urges his audience at Antioch to believe in the risen Lord for the forgiveness of sins, lest they become scoffers (13:40–41). God has overlooked the times of ignorance, but now he demands that all people everywhere repent (17:30). He summarizes his mission as "I earnestly bore witness for both Jews and Greeks to repentance before God and to faith in our Lord Jesus" (20:21). Yet there are some stiff-necked people who refuse to believe in Jesus (7:51). They have become stubborn (28:25–27). Jesus' followers call the Israelites to be saved from this corrupt generation (2:40) and become part of the reestablished Israel.

---

108. Matera, *New Testament Theology*, 71.

109. Tiede, "Acts 2:1–47," 66.

110. Tiede ("Acts 2:1–47," 65) writes that faith is "found first in Jerusalem and that the subsequent mission to Samaria, to the diaspora, and even to the Gentile world was built upon the continuity of this faith of believing Israel."

111. Tannehill, *Narrative Unity of Luke-Acts: Acts*, 41.

6. The Theme of Universal Salvation in Jesus Christ the Lord

The universal nature of the Pentecost event is clear. Both Jews and converts to Judaism from every nation under heaven are represented at Pentecost (2:5, 11). God will pour out his Spirit on all flesh (2:17), sons and daughters, young and old, male and female servants. Everyone who calls on the name of the Lord will be saved (2:17–21). The whole house of Israel should know that Jesus is Lord and Messiah (2:36). Therefore, everyone is called to repent and be baptized in the name of Jesus Christ for the forgiveness of sins in order to receive the gift of the Spirit. This promise of the Spirit is made to them, their children, and to all those who are far off, whomever the Lord will call (2:39). "Those who are far off," probably echoes Isa 57:19. They are diaspora Jews or God-fearers who are not present for the assembly. "In the development of Luke, however, the expression looks to anyone who responds, which eventually would include Gentiles."[112]

The mission is extended to Samaria (8:5). In the episode of Cornelius, Peter realizes that God shows no partiality. Rather, in every nation whoever fears him and acts uprightly is acceptable to him. The Spirit comes upon Gentiles and thus confirms that the promise of the Spirit is also for them. The Gentiles receive the Spirit as did the Jews at Pentecost (10:35, 454–48).

Paul also proclaims that every believer is justified in Jesus Christ (13:39). After his rejection at Antioch, he says that he will go to the Gentiles. The Lord commanded Paul and Barnabas to be a light to the Gentiles, an instrument of salvation to the ends of the earth (13:47). At the end of the first mission, Paul and Barnabas report how God opened the door of faith to the Gentiles (14:27). Paul brings Jesus' name to Gentiles, kings, and Israelites (9:15). He brings salvation to Rome, where he receives all who come to him, and he proclaims the kingdom of God and teaches about the Lord Jesus Christ (28:31). The salvation that Jesus brings is universal. Luke narrates that salvation in Jesus' name begins in Jerusalem, moves forward to Samaria, and finally reaches Rome. Both Jews and Gentiles have access to salvation in Jesus' name.

To summarize, the Pentecost sermon is the inaugural sermon that Peter preaches to Jews from all over the world. This sermon explains the outpouring of the Spirit at Pentecost. It shows that the apostles learn

---

112. Bock, *Acts*, 145. See also Fitzmyer, *Acts*, 267.

from the instruction of the risen Lord and begin to fulfill their commission. This sermon functions as a model of how the disciples respond to the instruction and commission of the risen Lord. It is the inaugural missionary sermon to the Jews in Acts. It lays the foundation for other missionary sermons and abbreviated sermons related to Jesus' resurrection. The passage of Joel 3:1–5a functions as a programmatic statement concerning the nature of the outpouring of the Spirit. Jesus' disciples are filled with the Spirit. Their mission is to prophesy, to do signs and wonders in the name of Jesus Christ, and to bear witness to his resurrection. This sermon also functions as a keynote sermon to announce the main themes that will be explored in the rest of Acts.

III. CONCLUSION

A. The Parallel between the Literary Context of Jesus' Inaugural Sermon in Luke 4:16–30 and Peter's in Acts 2:14–40

There is a parallel between the literary context of Jesus' sermon in Luke 4:16–30 and Peter's Sermon in Acts 2:14–40. Preparation is involved in the lead-up to both inaugural sermons. Luke uses four elements to prepare for Jesus' sermon. They are Jesus' prayer (3:21), the descent of the Spirit (3:22), Jesus' genealogy (3:23–37), and his temptation (4:1–13). Luke also prepares Peter's sermon with four elements: forty days' instruction by the risen Lord, ending with the ascension (Acts 1:1–12); prayer of the Christian community (1:13–14); choice of Judas's successor (1:15–26); and the coming of the Spirit (2:1–4) upon the assembly of people from all the nations (2:5–13).

Except for the forty days' instruction given by the risen Lord to his apostles, there is a parallel context between the two inaugural sermons. First, in each the coming of the Spirit is prepared for in prayer. Jesus is praying when the Spirit comes, and so too are Jesus' apostles and the first community in Jerusalem.

Second, after prayer, the Spirit comes upon Jesus at his baptism and on Jesus' apostles at Pentecost. The Spirit comes upon Jesus in bodily form as a dove and as tongues of fire upon his disciples. The Spirit comes with a voice. At Jesus' baptism, it is the voice of the Father to Jesus, "You are my beloved Son; with you I am well pleased." At the baptism of the Spirit of Jesus' disciples, the Spirit comes with a noise like that of strong wind. As a result, those who are filled with the Spirit begin to speak in different tongues.

Third, Jesus' genealogy traces Jesus' origin to Abraham, Adam, and God. Jesus is the final fulfillment of all those who have gone before him. He is the Son of God, "the prophet who sums up all the promises and hopes of the people before him."[113] In Acts, Luke presents all the nations of the world as being gathered in Jerusalem. Jesus' successors will carry salvation in Jesus to these nations.[114] Thus, the list of the nations signifies the scope of the disciples' mission in Acts.

In each case, there is some preparation of the inaugural sermons. There is a parallel literary pattern: Jesus' prayer (Luke 3:21) and prayer of the Christian community (Acts 1:13-14), the coming of the Spirit upon Jesus (Luke 3:22) and the apostles (Acts 2:1-4), Jesus' genealogy (Luke 3:23-37) and the list of the nations of Jews at Pentecost (Acts 2:9-11), and the deliverance of the inaugural sermons by Jesus (Luke 4:16-30) and Peter (Acts 2:14-40).[115]

Jesus' inaugural sermon is followed by a rejection by his compatriots. Peter's sermon is first received with success. It lays the foundation of faith in Jerusalem. Gradually the apostles come into conflict with the leaders in Jerusalem. In Acts 7, after the martyrdom of Stephen, a great persecution arises against the Christians in Jerusalem.

---

113. Johnson, *Acts*, 47.

114. Johnson (*Acts*, 47) writes, "Immediately after the gift of the Spirit in Jesus' baptism (Luke 3:21-22), the generations of Jews are traced all the way back to Abraham, and even further, to Adam. Now, after this 'baptism in the Spirit' of the apostles and their company, Luke lists all the lands from which Jews have gathered. The parallelism fits the pattern of Luke's story: Jesus is the prophet who sums up all the promises and hopes of the people before him, in his apostolic successors, that promise and hope (now sealed by the Spirit) will be carried to all the nations of the earth."

115. There is no parallel between Jesus' temptation (Luke 4:1-13) and the choice of a successor of Judas (Acts 1:15-26). Yet two points can be compared in these two passages. They are Jesus and his disciples' understanding of Scripture and their identities. Jesus understands Scripture. He rebuffs the devil by using Scripture (Deut 8:3; 6:13, 16). He affirms his identity as God's beloved Son and he does God's will. In the choice of a successor of Judas, Peter understands Scripture after Jesus' instruction. He sees Judas' failing in his ministry as the fulfillment of Scripture. He presents the true identity of Jesus' disciples as witnesses of Jesus' resurrection.

B. The Literary Functions of Jesus' and Peter's Inaugural Sermons

Both sermons are delivered by the speakers who have been empowered by the Spirit (Luke 4:14; Acts 2:4). After the lead-up, Luke sets the two sermons at the start of Jesus' and his followers' public missions. Jesus delivers his first public sermon to his compatriots and Peter speaks to his Jewish audience in Jerusalem. The setting of the two sermons is literarily significant to Luke-Acts.

First, both sermons function as model sermons. For Jesus, Luke narrates that Jesus has already taught in the synagogues in the region of Galilee (Luke 4:14–15). Yet he does not present the content of Jesus' teaching. The sermon in 4:16–30 serves as a model of how Jesus teaches in the synagogues of Galilee. In Acts, Jesus has instructed his followers for forty days, explaining to them that his death has fulfilled the Scriptures. He further commissions them to be his witnesses and to preach repentance for the forgiveness of sins. Yet Luke does not present the content of the preaching until Peter delivers his inaugural sermon to the Jews in Jerusalem at Pentecost. This sermon functions as the model of how the disciples showed response to Jesus' instruction and commission after the resurrection.

Second, both sermons use Scripture passages to describe the character of the ministry that Jesus and his disciples will carry out. Jesus' ministry is to proclaim the good news of the kingdom of God to the poor. He comes to proclaim God's salvation—forgiveness of sins. Jesus' disciples are filled with the Spirit to prophesy, to bear witness to his resurrection, and to work signs and wonders in his name.

Third, both sermons announce the main themes that will be explored in the rest of Luke-Acts. Jesus' sermon presents the themes that he will develop in Luke. Several of these themes continue to be dealt with in Acts. Peter's sermon summarizes the main themes that he will develop in Acts. There are some connections with the themes in the Gospel but there are some new themes as well.

Both sermons announce the theme of the Spirit. In Luke, Jesus is filled with the Spirit and begins his ministry. In Acts, God's Spirit is poured out on Jesus' disciples through the risen Lord. The Spirit guides the mission of the community.

Both Luke and Acts announce the identity of Jesus and his disciples. Jesus is a prophet like Moses. His apostles are witnesses to his resurrection. They are in the line of the prophets. Like Jesus, his apostles meet rejection and conflict with the Jewish leaders in Jerusalem.

Both emphasize forgiveness of sins. Jesus brings forgiveness of sins. He commissions his apostles to preach it. In Acts salvation, that is, the forgiveness of sins, comes from believing in Jesus' name.

Both announce the theme of fulfillment. In the Gospel, Jesus fulfills the prophecy of Isaiah. In Acts, Jesus' disciples preach that the suffering, death, and resurrection of Jesus happened according to God's set plan and foreknowledge. Their ministry is to fulfill God's plan.

Both announce the theme of mission to the Gentiles. In Luke, Jesus sets the direction by bringing salvation to towns other than his hometown. In Acts, salvation is for all who call upon the name of the Lord. Everyone is called to repent and be baptized in the name of Jesus Christ. Salvation has a universal character. The themes presented in Peter's sermons continue the themes in Jesus' sermon and develop them to a fuller degree. The preacher in Luke becomes the one proclaimed in Acts. Jesus is the center of the church's preaching.

Fourth, Peter's sermon also functions as a foundation for the missionary sermons that follow in Acts. It is the most finished and polished example of apostolic preaching. It is the best example of proving Jesus' resurrection through Scripture. It proves that Jesus is Lord and Messiah.

Finally, the coming of the Spirit is prepared for in prayer (Luke 3:21–22; Acts 1:14; 2:2–4). Both sermons are delivered as the result of being filled with the Spirit. Both sermons contain a scriptural quotation of some length, describing the character of the mission. The subsequent narrative is to fulfill the mission that is described in the inaugural sermons. They all present the main themes that will be explored in the rest of the narrative.

Having studied the literary functions of the two inaugural sermons by Jesus (Luke 4:16–30) and Peter (Acts 2:14–40), I have drawn the conclusion that Luke is a skillful writer who carefully composes inaugural sermons for the major characters in Luke-Acts. Jesus' inaugural sermon has a significant literary function in the Gospel of Luke, especially with regard to the nature of Jesus' mission in Luke. Peter's inaugural sermon has a significant literary function in Acts, especially in related to Peter's mission in Acts.

Just as Jesus is the major figure in Luke, Peter plays the major role in the first half of Acts, and Paul is the dominant figure, the hero, in the second half of Acts (13:1–28:28). Like Jesus and Peter, Paul delivers an inaugural sermon to the Jews in Antioch of Pisidia (Acts 13:16–41). I will study the literary function of Paul's inaugural sermon to determine whether it also has a significant literary function in Paul's mission among the Jews in Acts. In order to do so, I will first do an exegetical study of this sermon (Chapter Four) and then study its literary function (Chapter Five).

4

Paul's Inaugural Sermon to the Jews in Antioch of Pisidia in Acts 13:16–41

INTRODUCTION

AFTER STUDYING JESUS' INAUGURAL sermon in Luke 4:16–30 and Peter's in Acts 2:14–40, I have concluded that these two sermons have significant literary functions in Luke-Acts. In this chapter, I will study Paul's inaugural sermon to the Jews in Antioch of Pisidia as related in Acts 13:16–41. In order to do so, I will first study its remote and immediate literary contexts. In the second part, I will present a structure for this sermon. In the third part, I will provide a detailed exegesis of it. At the end, I will draw a brief conclusion.

I. THE LITERARY CONTEXT OF ACTS 13:16–41

A. *The Remote Context: From Saul the Persecutor to Paul the Proclaimer of Jesus*

1. Saul at the Martyrdom of Stephen

Saul is mentioned for the first time in Acts at the martyrdom of Stephen (7:58). Those who hear Stephen's speech are infuriated and drag him out of the city and stone him to death. Witnesses pile their cloaks at the feet of a young man named Saul. At Stephen's martyrdom, then, Luke directs our attention away from Stephen to Saul. This is a narrative technique intended "to introduce a significant new character first as a minor character, a literary method to unify the narrative."[1]

---

1. Tannehill, *Narrative Unity of Luke-Acts: Acts,* 99. This narrative technique is used

There are different interpretations of the act of piling the cloaks at the feet of someone. Lüdemann writes, "The great missionary is introduced in the lowly role of a bystander."[2] Johnson states that the phrase "at the feet" is "suggestive in light of Luke's use of it in 4:35, 37, and 5:1. If he uses the gesture consistently, it signifies recognition of Paul as a leader of those opposed to Stephen, a position that he will immediately assume in 8:3."[3] Fitzmyer thinks that the meaning of this symbolic act "escapes us today."[4] Paul refers to this detail in 22:20. The act of piling the cloaks at the feet of Paul shows his approval and participation in the death of Stephen. Moreover, Johnson writes, "It suggests that Paul may well have been the instigator of the trouble in the first place."[5]

Luke describes Saul's role in the Jerusalem Christian community as "the arch-persecutor."[6] He continues to ravage the church, entering house after house and dragging out both men and women and handing them over for imprisonment. The verbs λυμαίνω and σύρω suggest "arbitrary and violent anger" and "physical harm and insult" that Saul inflicted on the Christians in Jerusalem.[7] Saul is introduced negatively, for he is associated with Stephen's death. He is the arch-persecutor of the newly founded church community in Jerusalem.

In emphasizing Saul's violent persecution of the church, Luke prepares for the narrative of Saul's conversion in Acts 9.[8] But more importantly, he prepares for what happens in the following verse: "those who had been scattered went about preaching the word."[9] The act of persecuting Christians has an unexpected good effect, however, enabling Christians to carry their witness beyond Jerusalem.[10] "God's possibili-

---

in the appearance of Barnabas in 4:36–37, who reappears as a major figure in introducing Saul to the apostles (9:27).

2. Lüdemann, *Acts,* 104.

3. Johnson, *Acts,* 140.

4. Fitzmyer, *Acts,* 394.

5. Johnson (*Acts,* 141) lists three reasons for this: Saul was from Cilicia, as were some of those who attacked Stephen (6:9); the symbolic act of putting their cloaks at the feet of Saul is a recognition of his authority; Saul is described as the leader of the persecution that follows (8:3).

6. Haenchen, *Acts,* 294.

7. Johnson, *Acts,* 142.

8. Lüdemann, *Acts,* 105; Johnson, *Acts,* 144.

9. Fitzmyer, *Acts,* 397.

10. Ibid.

ties are not exhausted when humans reject the offered salvation with violence."[11]

2. The Call of Saul (9:1-19a)

In 9:1, Luke picks up the thread of the narrative about Saul's persecution of the church in Jerusalem in 8:3 with the adverb ἔτι ("still"). Saul was first introduced as one who associated with the murderers of Stephen (7:58). Now he becomes the main representative of those who condemned Stephen, whom Luke described as stiff-necked in 7:51-52, for he is the one who is breathing murderous threats against the Lord's disciples (φονεῖς 7:52, φόνου 9:1; ἐδίωξαν 7:52, διώκεις 9:4).[12] He even wants to extend the persecution beyond Jerusalem to Damascus. Surprisingly, Saul the persecutor is transformed and commissioned to proclaim the name he had persecuted. He will bear witness to "the name" before Gentiles, kings, and Israelites, and he will suffer for the name to which he is going to bear witness.

The story of Paul's encounter with the risen Lord is important for Luke. Accordingly, he recounts it three times (Acts 9, 22, and 26). Haenchen and other commentators explain the different accounts as the result of different sources.[13] Chapter 9 is narrated in the third person. It is Luke's dramatization of Saul's experience on the road to Damascus.[14] In this account, the role of "ecclesial mediation" is specified.[15] This account of Saul's call shows how the Lord has transformed the great persecutor into a great missionary.

The event at Damascus starts with the initiative of Saul, who approaches the high priest for letters that will authorize him to persecute the Christians in the diaspora synagogues in Damascus. Throughout the diaspora, the synagogue as a house of prayer was the gathering place for Jews. The story that Saul goes to the synagogue to persecute Christian Jews shows that Christian Jews still went to synagogues for worship. It also indicates that the leaders of the synagogues in the diaspora are

---

11. Tannehill, *Narrative Unity of Luke-Acts: Acts*, 101.

12. Ibid., 114.

13. Haenchen, *Acts*, 325-27. The three speeches have different purposes. The other two accounts in chap. 22 and 26 are defense speeches. Luke uses these two speeches to defend Paul from the charge that he speaks against Moses, the law, and the temple.

14. Fitzmyer, *Acts*, 421.

15. Marguerat, *First Christian Historian*, 191.

Paul's Inaugural Sermon to the Jews in Antioch   113

thought to have authority over Christian Jews.[16] There is not yet a clear distinction between Christian Jews and non-Christian Jews.

Luke does not specify why Saul persecuted the Christians. It is not unreasonable to assume, however, that Saul regards them as "heretics or apostates from orthodox Judaism."[17] As a Jew, he waits for the coming of the Messiah. Yet Christians proclaim that the crucified Jesus is the Messiah. For Saul, Christianity is a heterodox movement that presents a threat to Jewish faith. He cannot reconcile his faith with the new Way of the Christians.

On the road to Damascus, a light from heaven flashes around Saul. In the OT, the flashing of lightning is a feature of theophanies (Exod 19:16; 2 Sam 22:15; Ps 17:14; 76:18; 96:4; 143:6; Ezek 1:4, 7, 13; Dan 10:6).[18] Here it is a "revelatory Christophany," a "manifestation of God's Son" to Saul.[19] Besides the light from heaven, there is a voice saying, "Saul, Saul, why are you persecuting me?" Saul replies, "Who are you, sir?" The voice replies, "I am Jesus, whom you are persecuting." In this response, the crucified Jesus whom Saul persecutes identifies himself with his disciples, the men and women who belong to the Way. Furthermore, Luke wants to "identify Saul with those previously accused of Jesus' rejection and death in the speeches of Peter and Stephen." In other words, Saul is identified as the one who aligned himself with the persecutors of Jesus and Stephen.[20] He is an enemy of Jesus' followers.

After the appearance, the risen Lord commands Saul to go to the city where he will be told what he must do. The powerful persecutor has become powerless. Blind, he is led by his companions, and he neither eats nor drinks. This state is a "holy period of transition," a time of repentance and preparation for a further revelation in the future.[21] Neither to eat nor drink for three days also has a symbolic meaning that suggests death.[22] Saul's identity as a persecutor will be destroyed, and a new

---

16. Fitzmyer, *Acts*, 423.
17. Ibid., 424.
18. Johnson, *Acts*, 163.
19. Fitzmyer, *Acts*, 420.
20. Tannehill, *Narrative Unity of Luke-Acts: Acts*, 114.
21. Johnson, *Acts*, 164; Fitzmyer, *Acts*, 426.
22. Flichy (*La Figure de Paul dans les Actes des Apôtres*, 80) writes, "La dimension symbolique est également présente pour ce qui concerne le jeûne ne pas boire ni manger pendant trois jours est synonyme de mort. La rencontre avec le Christ qui introduit

identity as a chosen vessel will be given to him in v. 15. The Damascus road event is the end of his plan to destroy the Christian community and the reconstitution of his identity.[23] Saul will be a prophet for the restored Israel.[24]

It is Christ who sends Ananias to heal Saul, to baptize him, and to accept him into the Christian community. The risen Lord's command to Ananias to go to Saul meets resistance because Ananias knows of Saul's identity as a persecutor. Tannehill notes that Luke takes time to present Ananias's reaction of resistance and the Lord's corrective response. It shows that Ananias's fear of the persecutor must be overcome. The Lord's work is revealed through events that overthrow normal human expectations. Not only Ananias but even the Christian community in Jerusalem has difficulty in accepting Saul's conversion (9:26). "Human disbelief highlights the amazing transformation of Saul worked by the Lord."[25] Tannehill writes:

> The narrative seeks to heighten the sense of surprise by rhetorical reversal in the dialogue between Ananias and the Lord. Ananias protests that Saul has come to inflict suffering on "those calling upon your name," but the Lord replies that Saul is a chosen instrument "to bear my name" and he himself "must suffer for my name." The persecutor is about to become not only a Christian but also an outstanding example of one who endures persecution in order to fulfill his mission, much to Ananias' surprise.[26]

Saul's new identity is as a chosen vessel of the Lord. Literally, σκεῦος ἐκλογῆς ἐστίν μοι οὗτος means "this one is for me a vessel of

---

Saul à une nouvelle vie suppose la mort de son existence précédente."

23. Marguerat, *First Christian Historian*, 192.

24. Rebecca I. Denova (*The Things Accomplished among Us: Prophetic Tradition in the Structural Pattern of Luke-Acts* [JSNTSup 141; Sheffield: Sheffield Academic Press, 1997] 179-84) recognizes that Saul's status as a prophet of Israel is demonstrated in the stories of his call on the way to Damascus. In the prophetic tradition, prophets are often struck "mute" when they encounter God. Saul is struck blind as the result of being an enemy of God, just as the Syrians are struck blind (2 Kgs 6:18). "Once the Syrians have served their purpose as an instrument to display the power of the God of Israel, their sight is restored, just as Paul's sight is restored when he learns that he will be an instrument chosen by the Lord (Acts 9. 15-18)" (p. 180). See also Krister Stendahl, *Paul among Jews and Gentiles* (Philadelphia: Fortress, 1976) 7-23; Charles Hedrick, "Paul's Conversion/Call: A Comparative Analysis of the Three Reports in Acts," *JBL* 100 (1981) 415-32.

25. Tannehill, *Narrative Unity of Luke-Acts*: Acts, 116.

26. Ibid., 117.

election." This explains the purpose of the "unique post-pentecostal appearance of the risen Lord" to Saul.[27] The risen Lord chooses Saul, the persecutor of those who call upon the name, as an instrument for spreading his name. This call is similar to the call of the prophets in the OT (Isa 6:9; Jer 1:9–10; Ezek 2:3–4). The verb ἐκλέγω "call," "choose," is used for selecting the twelve (Luke 6:13; Acts 1:2, 24), the seven (Acts 6:5), and Peter as God's instruments (15:7, 22, 25). This verb usually refers to a person chosen for a special role or mission. Saul, then, has been chosen for a special reason.[28] He is the chosen instrument destined to carry the Lord's name before Gentiles, kings, and the children of Israel. This is all the more dramatic and stunning, for the risen Lord has chosen the former persecutor and totally transformed him.

As in Acts 1:8, the Lord's words to Saul in 9:15–16 present a programmatic prophecy for Saul's missionary career. He will preach the name of Lord to Jews (13:5, 15–41; 14:1–7; 17:1–3, 10–11, 16–17; 18:4–5, 18–19; 19:8; 28: 17–29), to king Agrippa (25:23–26:29), and to Gentiles (14:8–20; 15:3;17:22–31). Saul's future role will be universal in scope. He will not only be an apostle to the Gentiles, he will also bear witness to "kings" and "the children of Israel."[29]

In the narrative of Paul's mission, beginning with Acts 13, he preaches to Jews first and then to Gentiles. Tannehill recognizes that the order in 9:15 is the reverse of this. He thinks that putting "Gentiles" at the beginning of the list is intended to emphasize the importance of preaching to the Gentiles, for it indicates a new development at this point in the narrative.[30] Yet Johnson correctly writes, "What is most striking in the statement, however, is the climactic position of 'children of Israel.' They are not left behind in Paul's mission; he continues to preach to his fellow Jews until the very end of the story (28:23–28)."[31]

The reference to "Gentiles" and "children of Israel" in 9:15 is the "first indication of the comprehensive scope of Paul's mission."[32] In the later narrations of Paul's call, Paul is destined to be a witness "to all persons" (22:15), and he is sent to both the Jewish "people" and to the

27. Fitzmyer, *Acts*, 428.
28. Tannehill, *Narrative Unity of Luke-Act: Acts*, 117.
29. Fitzmyer, *Acts*, 428.
30. Tannehill, *Narrative Unity of Luke-Act: Acts*, 119.
31. Johnson, *Acts*, 165.
32. Tannehill, *Narrative Unity of Luke-Acts: Acts*, 119.

"Gentiles" (26:17). As a prisoner Paul continues to preach to all who come to him (28:30-31). The inclusion of both Gentiles and the children of God is a major theme in the Lukan description of Paul's mission.[33]

"For I myself will show him how much he has to suffer for my name." The conjunction γάρ ("for") connects this verse (9:16) to the preceding one and associates the bearing of Jesus' name with suffering for the name. The suffering results from his mission to carry the Lord's name to Gentiles, kings, and the children of Israel.[34] The risen Lord stresses the fellowship of suffering that Christ and his followers must endure. The divine "must" directly and deliberately places Saul in the line of suffering prophets like Moses, Jesus, Jesus' disciples, and Stephen. The portrait of a suffering Saul is important in Acts. Like an arc, it stretches from Saul's call to his imprisonments at the end of Acts.[35] This statement of Saul's suffering (9:15-16) has a proleptic function in the narrative similar to the text of 1:8.

Ananias goes to Saul, lays his hands on him, and cures him. Saul gets up and is baptized, and he starts to take food again. After taking it, he regains his strength. This signifies a new birth for Saul, who has been totally transformed by the risen Lord. Saul is legitimized to become a witness to the risen Lord.

3. Saul the Preacher of the Risen Lord in Damascus (9:19b-25)

After staying with the disciples in Damascus for some days, Saul immediately begins to proclaim in the synagogue that Jesus is the Son of God (9:20). By the use of the adverb εὐθέως ("immediately") and the imperfect tense ἐκήρυσσεν ("he started to preach"), Luke emphasizes that Saul immediately fulfills his role as a preacher of the risen Lord without any consultation or approval of the twelve. Saul directly receives his call from the risen Lord to preach to the Jews and carry his name to "the children of Israel." Nothing is said about Saul trying to preach to Gentiles.[36]

---

33. Ibid.

34. Ibid., 117-18.

35. Volker Stolle, *Der Zeuge als Angeklagter: Untersuchungen zum Paulus-Bild des Lukas* (BWANT 102; Stuttgart: Kohlhammer, 1973) 164.

36. Fitzmyer (*Acts*, 433) writes, "The reason is that Luke has not yet told about the inauguration of the Gentile mission; that comes with the mission of Peter in chap. 10."

The synagogue in Damascus was originally the place where Saul intended to arrest those who followed the Way. Now, in the synagogue, he proclaims the very Jesus whom he wanted to destroy. Jervell writes, "Seine Verkündigung fand in den Synagogen statt, wohin er ursprünglich mit dem Auftrag gekommen war, die Christen zu bekämpfen und zu verhaften. Nun ist und bleibt die Synagoge die Gemeinde die Ort der Verkündigung. Und Paulus ist von Anfang an Judenmissionar."[37] Saul's abrupt conversion surprises everybody. But here Luke "establishes the pattern for Paul's preaching throughout the rest of the narrative: Paul always begins in the synagogues and only when rejected there does he move to other venues (13:5, 13–16; 14:1; 16:13, 16; 17:1; 18:4; 19:8).[38]

The subject of Saul's preaching is Jesus. He proclaims that Jesus is the Son of God. In Acts, this is the only explicit use of the title for Jesus, except the textually suspect 8:37. This is a familiar title of Jesus in the Gospel of Luke (1:32, 35; 3:22; 4:3, 9, 41; 22:70). It is most probably an early kerygmatic title of Jesus since it appears in pre-Pauline fragments of the kerygma in 1 Thess 1:10 and Rom 1:3-4. In the OT, the title "Son of God" is used in different ways. For example, it can be used as a title of adoption for a Davidic king (2 Sam 7:14; Ps 2:7). When Luke adopts this title in Acts, "he relates it to the resurrection, applying Ps 2:7 to Jesus, whom God raised 'from the dead' (13:33-34)." But "in the Lukan writings, 'Son of God' attributes to Jesus a unique relationship with Yahweh, the God of Israel."[39]

Saul's preaching in the synagogue of Damascus astounds everyone who hears his teaching. They are amazed by such a dramatic transformation of the persecutor. Yet Saul becomes even more powerful in his preaching. He confounds the Jews in Damascus with proofs that Jesus is the Messiah. The verb συμβιβάζειν means to "demonstrate," to "prove," or to "teach," "instruct." Here Saul affirms that Jesus is the Messiah, and

---

37. Jacob Jervell, *Die Apostelgeschichte* (Göttingen: Vandenhoeck & Ruprecht, 1998) 285.

38. Johnson, *Acts*, 170.

39. Fitzmyer, *Luke I-IX*, 206-7. He writes, "Luke does not intend that Jesus should be recognized as God's son merely in the adoptive sense in which a king on David's throne could be called his son (2 Sam 7:14; 1 Chr 17:13); his explicit relation of the title to the conception of Jesus connotes much more." Fitzmyer notes that the term "son(s) of God" is used with diverse nuances. It means "angels of God" (Gen 6:2; Job 1:6; 2:1; Ps 19:1; Dan 3:25), and is used as a title of Israel in a collective sense (Exod 4:22) or for an individual Jew (Sir 4:10) (p. 206).

he brings forth evidence from Scripture to prove this. The arguments are based on the texts of LXX Ps 109:1 and Ps 2:7.[40] Luke probably regards the title "Messiah" as equivalent to the title "Son of God" in v. 20.[41] However, Fitzmyer notes, "Both in OT origin and in Palestinian usage and connotation the two titles were different. For their proper understanding in the NT, they should be kept distinct and not equated or conflated."[42]

On the one hand, Saul's preaching of Jesus as the Messiah shows the continuity of his preaching and the preaching of others. The title "Son of God" is also a familiar title in the Lukan gospel. On the other hand, Saul's preaching here about Jesus as the "Son of God" and "Messiah" is very brief. It will need further detailed demonstration from Scripture that by his resurrection Jesus has become the Son of God and the Messiah promised to Israel. This summary of Saul's preaching to the Jews in the synagogue of Damascus has a proleptic function inasmuch as it foreshadows what Paul will say in the speech at Antioch. It also relates Saul's preaching to the witnesses of the gospel, and it anticipates a fuller demonstration that Jesus is the Messiah.

After a considerable time, the Jews conspire to kill Saul. His bearing witness to the name of Jesus has brought him suffering (9:15-16). The brief narrative of the Jews plotting to kill Saul confirms the Lord's words about Saul's suffering for bearing witness to the name of the Lord. When the Jews plot to kill Saul, he escapes from Damascus and goes to Jerusalem.

4. Saul's Visit to Jerusalem (9:25-31)

There is a similarity between the events in Jerusalem and those in Damascus. The disbelief of the disciples in Jerusalem toward Saul (9:26) parallels Ananias's hesitation to believe (9:13-14); Barnabas's reassurance (9:27) recalls the reassurance of the Lord (9:15-16); Saul's attempt

---

40. Barrett, *Acts of the Apostles*, 465.

41. Ibid. Jervell (*Apostelgeschichte*, 284) also interprets these two titles as identical in meaning; see also Haenchen, *Acts*, 331.

42. Fitzmyer, *Acts*, 435; Fitzmyer (*Luke I–IX, 197–99*) explains that the title Messiah is derived from Palestinian Judaism. First it was predicated of certain historical persons regarded as anointed agents of Yahweh who can bring service or protection for their people. Later it referred to the expectation of a future David or an anointed figure sent by God. When Luke wrote his gospel, Christ had also become a name of Jesus of Nazareth. In Acts, this title is expressly linked to Jesus' resurrection. Jesus in his resurrection has become the anointed agent from God announcing a new salvation of God.

to associate with the disciples in Jerusalem (9:28b) resembles his association with the disciples in Damascus (9:19b); Saul's bold preaching in Jerusalem (9:28b-29a) follows his preaching in the Damascus synagogue (9:20-22). In each instance Saul's preaching results in a plot to kill him, but this plot becomes known and Saul is able to escape with the help of the Christians (9:20-25, 28-30).[43]

Tannehill notes that the similarity of events in Damascus and Jerusalem is underscored by the wording in 9:27-29. Barnabas told the disciples in Jerusalem how he preached boldly in the name of Jesus. Luke uses the same wording to describe Saul's preaching in Jerusalem. Furthermore, the same word "to do away," "to kill," is echoed through repetition in Damascus and Jerusalem.[44]

Saul preaches boldly. The verb παρρησιάζομαι appears here in 9:27-28 and another five times (13:46;14:3; 18:26; 19:8; 26:26) in Acts. The noun παρρησία occurs five times in Acts (2:29; 4:13, 29, 31; 28:31). Barrett interprets this word in this way. "It always denotes bold, open Christian proclamation." He continues, "[I]t points rather to a blunt statement of the truth regardless of the consequences."[45] This is a favorite Lukan word. Luke uses παρρησία when referring to Paul's preaching ministry (9:27-28; 13:46; 14:3; 19:8; 26:26; 28:31). It is also used to refer to the preaching of the apostles, especially Peter's (2:29; 4:13, 29, 31). Saul continues to preach boldly to Jews as Peter did in Jerusalem. He starts his mission by preaching boldly to the Jews in Damascus and Jerusalem. He will continue to preach boldly in Antioch of Pisidia (13:46), in the diaspora, until the end of Acts (28:31).

In 9:28, there is a short summary of Saul's new relationship with the apostles and other disciples. Saul is accepted by the Jerusalem Christians and continues his bold proclamation and testimony among the Jews in Jerusalem. He starts to debate with the Greek-speaking Jews. This is a narrative reversal. Luke has Saul debate with the same group to which he belonged and which executed Stephen (6:9-14).[46] As happened to him in Damascus, Saul now meets the same reaction of resistance and threat of death because of his preaching.

---

43. David Gill, "The Structure of Acts 9," *Bib* 55 (1974) 546-48.
44. Tannehill, *Narrative Unity of Luke-Acts: Acts*, 122.
45. Barrett, *Acts of the Apostles*, 469.
46. Johnson, *Acts*, 172.

When Saul is in Jerusalem, he assumes the role of the martyr Stephen, debating with Hellenistic Jews who plot to kill him (6:9–11; 9:29). Later, he will face accusations similar to the accusations against Stephen (6:13; 21:28).[47] The persecutor who witnessed the martyrdom of Stephen becomes the one who assumes the vacant role of Stephen and so continues his mission.

Luke wants Saul to come to Jerusalem. In doing so, he does not intend to legitimate Saul's mission nor does he want to relativize Saul's significance. Rather, he brings him to Jerusalem, "because *all* of the missionaries in Acts are brought into connection with the Jerusalem leadership as quickly as possible. Luke's interest is in showing how the gospel moved out into the Gentile world in continuity with the restored people of God in Jerusalem."[48]

Saul is sent off to Tarsus (9:30), from where Barnabas will fetch him (11:25). In this way geographical locations are used to link the otherwise broken narratives. In 9:31, the section closes with a summary statement of the situation of the church. Although the newly found church is persecuted, the gospel makes great progress into Judea, Galilee, and Samaria. Saul has been transformed into a preacher of the Lord. Yet it is God who continues to increase the growth of the church. From now on, Saul will fulfill his commission of carrying the name of the Lord before Gentiles, kings, and the children of Israel.

In Acts 11:19, Luke continues the narrative line left off in 8:4 with the frequently used verb διασπείρω. In between, he narrates the legitimacy of the Gentile mission initiated by Peter. Thus, Luke prepares Paul's mission in Antioch. Just as the church of Jerusalem sent Peter and John to oversee the evangelization in Samaria (8:14–24), so it now sends Barnabas to Antioch to oversee the church there (11:22–26).

Barnabas fetches Saul from Tarsus (9:30). For a whole year Barnabas and Saul teach a large number of people in Antioch (11:25–26). By having Barnabas recruit Saul to teach in Antioch, Luke indicates that Saul is accepted by the church leadership of Jerusalem. Then, by having him and Barnabas deliver the collection to the needy in the church of Jerusalem, Luke demonstrates Saul's unity and solidarity with the church in Jerusalem (12:25). Although Luke has Saul and Barnabas teach a large number of people in Antioch for a whole year, he does not recount the

---

47. Tannehill, *Narrative Unity of Luke-Acts: Acts,* 114.
48. Johnson, *Acts,* 174.

content of their preaching. This creates an expectation within the reader who wants to know the full content of Saul's preaching.

B. The Immediate Context: Paul the Missionary to the Jews during His First Missionary Journey (13:1–14:28)

The immediate context of Paul's inaugural sermon is his first missionary journey. When Barnabas and Saul are in Antioch, as they are worshiping the Lord and fasting, the Spirit speaks to the community, "Set apart for me Barnabas and Saul, for the work to which I have called them" (13:2). Thus, the Spirit-guided missionary journey of Barnabas and Saul is inaugurated. This, then, is the formal commission of Saul by the Spirit to begin his missionary work. The commission by the Spirit happens at a prayer service, thereby allowing Luke to emphasize that it is through prayer that Saul and Barnabas are commissioned by the Spirit to begin their mission.[49] This sermon to the Jews in Antioch of Pisidia (13:16–41) is Paul's major speech during his first missionary journey.

The Spirit appoints Saul and Barnabas and empowers them to do the work for which they have been called. Saul will now fulfill the call of the Lord to bring his name to all peoples (9:15). In Antioch they are commended to the grace of God for this work, and it is to Antioch they will return when they finish their first missionary journey (14:26).

In 13:9, the name "Paul" is used for the first time.[50] This is Paul's Roman name. The use of the Semitic name "Saul" suggests that Luke wants to show "that the well-known Christian Paul had deep roots in Judaism. This, he may have considered, was now sufficiently demonstrated."[51] In this context he meets a Roman proconsul, and he starts to evangelize the Jews and Gentiles beyond Jerusalem in the diaspora. Therefore, it is appropriate for Luke to introduce Paul's Roman name.

There is a change of order of the names of Barnabas and Saul as well. The order of their names is changed: from "Barnabas and Saul" (13:2, 7) to "Paul and his companions" (13:13) and "Paul and Barnabas"

---

49. Philippe Bossuyt (*L'Esprit en Actes: Lire les Actes des Apôtres* [Le Livre et le Rouleau 3; Bruxelles: Éditions Lessius, 1998] 69) writes, "Barnabas et Shaoul ne sont pas envoyés par l'assemblée d'Antioche mais par L'Esprit Saint."

50. Fitzmyer (*Paul and His Theology*, 2) writes, "More likely, the Apostle was called *Paulos* from birth, and *Saul* was the *signum* or *supernomen*, 'added name,' used in Jewish circles. . . . There is no evidence that 'Saul' was changed to 'Paul' at the time of his conversion; indeed, *Saulos* is used in Acts even after this event. The change in 13:9 is probably due to different sources of Luke's information."

51. Barrett, *Acts of the Apostle*, 616.

(13:43). The change of order shows the changed role of Paul in proclaiming the good news in the diaspora. Barnabas is not even mentioned in the introductory material (13:16). It is Paul who delivers the sermon in the synagogue of Antioch of Pisidia. He now becomes the main actor in Acts. He is the dominant figure of the second half of Acts.

Paul has been preaching and teaching for some time and in many places. After being baptized by Ananias, he begins to preach in the synagogue of Damascus (9:20); then he preaches in Jerusalem (9:28); later, he and Barnabas teach a large number of people in Antioch for a whole year (11:26). After being sent by the Spirit from Antioch, Saul and Barnabas arrive in Salamis and proclaim the word of God in the synagogue of the Jews (13:5). However, until this point in the narrative, no specific content has been recorded with regard to Saul's proclamation to the Jews in synagogues.[52] Readers are anxious to know the detailed content of what he preaches in his mission. They are looking for an example of the message he preaches. The "dramatic portrayal of this preaching is reserved for the major scene that follows in 13:14–43."[53] Accordingly, Luke presents Paul's inaugural sermon to the Jews at the beginning of his first missionary journey in Antioch of Pisidia.

To summarize, in order to prepare the persecutor Saul to become a chosen vessel to bear the Lord's name to all peoples, the Lord transforms him. The preparation of Paul includes the appearance of the Lord to Paul, Paul's praying in blindness, his being filled with the Spirit and being baptized, and his commission by the Spirit. Saul begins to fulfill his call to preach in Damascus, in Jerusalem, and in Antioch. In a prayer setting, the community in Antioch sent off Saul and Barnabas. Paul is now ready to bring the name of the Lord to all the peoples.

II. THE STRUCTURE OF ACTS 13:16–41

The setting of the sermon is in a synagogue in the diaspora on a Sabbath at which Paul and Barnabas are present. The structure of this sermon is marked by the threefold direct address to the audience in vv. 16, 26, and 38. These linguistic markers structure this sermon in three parts. This sermon ends in v. 41.

---

52. Only summaries of the content of Saul's proclamations about Jesus are presented. Paul proclaimed that Jesus is "the Son of God," and "Messiah" in Damascus (9:20, 22).

53. Tannehill, *Narrative Unity of Luke-Acts: Acts,* 161.

Like Peter, Paul has become a keen interpreter of Scripture. Now he delivers his inaugural sermon to both Jews and God-fearers. In the first part, he presents a history of Israel (vv. 16b–25). In the second part, Paul's kerygmatic teaching focuses on the fulfillment of the promise in Jesus' resurrection with proof from Scripture (vv. 26–37). In the third part, Paul calls for faith in Jesus Christ, which results in the forgiveness of sins and concludes with a warning of the consequences of disbelief (vv. 38–41).[54]

The structure of the sermon is as follows:

A. God's graciousness and promise to Israel in Israel's history (vv. 16b–25)

    1. Address and appeal for a hearing (v. 16b)

    2. God's graciousness and promise to Israel (vv. 17–23):

        a. God's election of and graciousness toward Israel (vv. 17–20)

        b. Israel's call for a king and God's promise of a savior (vv. 21–23)

    3. The witness of John the Baptist (vv. 24–25)

B. The message of salvation

    1. Address and declaration (v. 26)

    2. Christological kerygma (vv. 27–31)

    3. Jesus is the fulfillment of the promise: proof from Scripture (vv. 32–35)

    4. A contrast: Jesus fulfills what David did not fulfill (vv. 36–37)

C. The meaning of salvation and a concluding warning

    1. Appeal and address (v. 38a)

---

54. Fitzmyer, *Acts*, 507. Flichy, *La Figure de Paul dans les Actes des Apôtres*, 186. Dumais, *Langage de L'Évangélisation*, 64–65. Elleul ("Antioche de Pisidie," 5) writes, "A trois reprises (v. 16, 26 et 38) Paul apostrophe ses auditeurs. Il est clair que dans l'art oratoire, ce genre d'appel est un moyen technique fort courant pour attirer l'attention, pour souligner une idée importante, pour marquer un nouveau développement. Nous les considérerons donc comme les indices de sections différentes et proposons de diviser le texte en trois parties:16–25, 26–37 et 38–41."

2. The meaning of salvation: forgiveness of sins, justification by faith (vv. 38-39)
3. A stern warning from the OT (vv. 40-41)

III. A DETAILED EXEGESIS OF ACTS 13:16-41

Luke arranges Paul's first missionary sermon to diaspora Jews and God-fearers in a setting of a synagogue Sabbath service. The synagogue is a significant Jewish institution. It is a place for reading, studying Scripture, and praying. It is also a meeting place for Jews for some social activities.[55] It is the place where Paul can find a congregation of Jews and preach to them. Luke gives a brief report that Paul and Barnabas preached in the Jewish synagogue of Cyprus (13:5). He describes a setting of Sabbath service in Antioch (v. 15).[56] He then presents Paul's first sermon to diaspora Jews. The setting for Paul's inaugural sermon "deliberately mirrors that of Jesus' first speech in Luke 4:16-30."[57] Jesus enters the synagogue according to his custom (Luke 4:16), and so does Paul (Acts 13:14; 17:2). Luke emphasizes that Paul evangelizes diaspora Jews first (13:5). This narrative motif will dominate this episode and the ending of Paul's sermon (13:46).[58]

The central part of the synagogue service includes reading the law and the prophets followed by a sermon.[59] In contrast to Luke 4:18-19, Luke does not present the specific texts read at this service. Rather, the synagogue leaders invite Paul and Barnabas to speak a word of exhorta-

---

55. Barrett, *Acts of the Apostles*, 323; see also *The New Testament Background: Selected Documents* (ed. C. K. Barrett; London: SPCK, 1987) 53-55, 204-6, 211; Fitzmyer, *Acts*, 357; Howard C. Kee, "The Transformation of the Synagogue after 70 C.E.: Its Import for Early Christianity," *NTS* 36 (1990) 1-24; Lee I. Levine, "The Nature and Origin of the Palestinian Synagogue Reconsidered," *JBL* 115 (1996) 425-48; Rainer Riesner, "Synagogue in Jerusalem," in *The Book of Acts in Its Palestinian Setting* (BAFCS 4; ed. Richard Bauckham; Grand Rapids, MI: Eerdmans, 1995) 179-210.

56. Franklin S. Spencer, *Journeying through Acts: A Literary-Cultural Reading* (Peabody, MA: Hendrickson, 2004) 154.

57. Johnson, *Acts*, 230.

58. Fitzmyer, *Acts*, 500, 509. See also Mikeal C. Parsons, *Acts* (Paideia Commentaries on the New Testament; Grand Rapids, MI: Baker Academic Press, 2008) 191.

59. Fredrick F. Bruce, *The Acts of the Apostles: The Greek Text with Introduction and Commentary* (3rd ed.; Grand Rapids, MI: Eerdmans, 1990) 302; see also Fitzmyer, *Acts*, 509; Johnson, *Acts*, 230; Barrett, *Acts of the Apostles*, 628; Malina & Pilch, *Book of Acts*, 92-93.

tion (λόγος παρακλήσεως).⁶⁰ The same expression is used in Heb 13:22 to describe the hortatory message of the Epistle to the Hebrews.⁶¹ This term has a technical meaning for an exhortation or sermon based on the readings in a Sabbath service.⁶² It interprets the contemporary relevance and meaning of the Scripture texts after they have been read.⁶³ "A word of exhortation," then, describes Paul's sermon in vv. 16b–41.⁶⁴ Luke uses the noun form παρακλήσεως (13:15) and the verb παρεκάλουν (13:42) to frame Paul's sermon. Paul is depicted as a Greek orator as he stands up and makes a gesture for silence and attention.

A. God's Graciousness and Promise to Israel in Israel's History (vv. 16b–25)

Luke carefully crafts this sermon so that it will be persuasive to Paul's Jewish audience in the diaspora. In doing so, he selects materials and

---

60. Bruce (*Acts: The Greek Text*, 302) thinks that leaders of the synagogue were chosen from the elders of the congregation to take charge of public worship. They find suitable persons to lead prayers, to read lections, and to preach or to invite suitable person to address the congregation. Usually there is one leader in a synagogue (Luke 13:14; Acts 18:8, 17). Sometimes there are more than one (Mark 5:22). See also David G. Peterson, *The Acts of the Apostles* (Grand Rapids, MI: Eerdmans, 2009) 386 n. 55; Barrett, *Acts of the Apostles*, 629; Johnson, *Acts*, 230; Anton Deutschmann, *Synagoge und Gemeindebildung: Christliche Gemeinde und Israel am Beispiel von Apg 13, 42–52* (Biblische Untersuchungen 30; Regensburg: Verlag Friedrich Pustet, 2001) 36–39.

61. Jervell (*Apostelgeschichte*, 353) writes, "Sie wird hier als λόγος παρακλήσεως bezeichnet, was nicht Trostworte, sondern Ermahnungsworte bedeutet, Hebr 13, 22."

62. Witherington, *Acts*, 406–7 n. 190. Dumais (*Langage de L'Évangélisation*, 69) thinks that the term λόγος παρακλήσεως used in Heb 13:22 and Acts 13:15 should not be understood as a simple moral exhortation. He quotes Otto Michel (*Der Brief an die Hebräer* [KEK 13; Göttingen: Vandenhoeck & Ruprecht, 1966] 542–43) and writes that this term means "une espèce particulière d'instruction exégétique et parénétique." See also Beverly Roberts Gaventa, *The Acts of the Apostles* (ANTC; Nashville: Abingdon, 2003) 197; Johnson, *Acts*, 230; Barrett, *Acts of the Apostles*, 629; Fitzmyer, *Acts*, 510. Otto Glombitza ("Akta XIII. 15–41: Analyse einer lukanischen Predigt vor Juden," *NTS* 5 [1959] 306–17, here 309) claims that this is a technical term that means a messianic interpretation of the OT as in Luke 4:16–30. I do not agree with this interpretation.

63. Robert W. Wall, "The Acts of the Apostles: Introduction, Commentary, and Reflections," in *The New Interpreter's Bible*: Vol., X (ed. Leander E. Keck; Nashville: Abingdon, 2002) 191.

64. Most commentators (Fitzmyer, Barrett, Johnson, Witherington) regard the entire sermon as a "word of exhortation." Pillai (*Early Missionary Preaching*, 55) limits it to vv. 17–22, a narration of God's saving acts. Wall ("Acts," 191) interprets this term as "an edifying homily concerning God's saving acts in the history of Israel." Therefore, he also limits it in the first part of the sermon (vv. 17–25).

adapts them to his purpose. He presents Paul as reciting Israel's history beginning with God's choosing their ancestors.⁶⁵ He then narrates God's graciousness in leading the Israelites out of Egypt, their wandering in the wilderness, the possession of the land, the period of the judges, the prophet Samuel, and kings Saul and David.⁶⁶ The history reaches its climax with the promise of the savior, Jesus (v. 23).

1. Address and Appeal for a Hearing (v. 16b)

In response to the invitation to speak a word of exhortation to the people, Paul stands up and addresses not only Israelites but "those who fear God" as well. "The congregation of the diaspora synagogue is different from those addressed during the church's Palestinian mission."⁶⁷ The salutation ἄνδρες 'Ισραηλῖται means "fellow Israelites" (2:22; 3:12; 5:35; 13:16; 21:28). It is a salutation of a Jew to fellow Jews. Since Paul will give a retrospective review of God's graciousness in Israel's history, it is significant that he addresses his audience as fellow Israelites. But who are "those who fear God?" Are they Jews or Gentiles?

There is debate whether these God-fearers are Gentile sympathizers or Jewish proselytes.⁶⁸ Fitzmyer interprets φοβούμενος τὸν θεόν (10:22, 35; 13:16, 26) and σεβόμενος τὸν θεόν (13:50; 16:14; 17:4, 17; 18:7; cf. 18:13; 19:27) as quasi-technical phrases to denote " 'God-fearers,' non-Jews sympathetic to Judaism, those who did not submit to circumcision or observe the Torah in its entirety, but who did agree with the ethical monotheism of the Jews and attended their synagogue services."⁶⁹ Barrett

---

65. Dumais, *Langage de L'Evangélisation*, 279; see also Tannehill, *Narrative Unity of Luke-Acts: Acts*, 165–66.

66. Gaventa, *Acts*, 198.

67. Wall, "Acts," 191.

68. Max Wilcox, "The 'God-fearers' in Acts: A Reconsideration," *JSNT* 13 (1981) 102–22; Thomas Finn, "The God-Fearers Reconsidered," *CBQ* 47 (1985) 75–84; Thomas Kraabel, "The God-Fearers–A Literary and Theological Invention," *BAR* 12 (1986) 46–53; Irina Levinskaya, *The Book of Acts in Its Diaspora Setting* (BAFCS 5; Grand Rapids, MI: Eerdmans, 1996) 120–26; Jerome Murphy-O'Connor, "Lots of God-Fearers? *Theosebeis* in the Aphrodisias Inscription," *RB* 99 (1992) 418–24; Bernd Wander, *Gottesfürchtige und Sympathisanten* (WUNT 104; Tübingen: Mohr Siebeck, 1998); J. Brian Tucker, "God-Fearers: Literary Foil or Historical Reality in the Book of Acts," *JBS* 5 (2005) 21–39. For further bibliography, see Fitzmyer, *Acts*, 450; Pervo, *Acts*, 332.

69. Fitzmyer, *Acts*, 449–50. See also Jervell (*Apostelgeschichte*, 353); Buss (*Missionspredigt*, 34–35); Tucker, "God-Fearers," 23–28.

interprets it in v. 16 as Jewish "proselytes," or an additional reference to Jews, "My fellow Jews, yes, you who fear God as no other nation does."[70] Based on the context and the content of this sermon, David L. Woodall interprets this phrase as an additional reference to Israel.[71]

The concept "God-fearers" connoted diverse meanings in antiquity. It included devout Jews as well as "an umbrella term for Gentiles with varied interests in Judaism."[72] Luke may be aware of such Gentiles and sees them as a great opportunity for Christian evangelists.[73] In most cases, the gospel is preached to this group of Gentile sympathizers with Judaism in Acts.[74] It is true that Luke may regard the God-fearers as part of the Israelites, although they are not "in the fullest sense of the term 'Israelites.'"[75] It is also possible that some of the God-fearers are proselytes (13:43).[76] In the context of 13:16–41, I judge them to be Gentile sympathizers.

These Gentile sympathizers exemplify Paul's teaching that "every believer is justified in him (the risen Lord)" (v. 39).[77] Besides teaching in a Jewish synagogue in Salamis, Paul also preached to Sergius Paulus (13:7). He came to believe because of Paul's teaching about the Lord (v. 12). It is possible that when Paul addresses his audience in Antioch of Pisidia he bears these two groups in mind. Thereby, he emphasizes that the salvation won by Jesus is open to all.

70. Barrett, *Acts of the Apostles*, 631.

71. David L. Woodall, "Israel in the Book of Acts: The Foundation of Lukan Ecclesiology" (Ph.D. diss., Trinity Evangelical Divinity School, 1998) 202–4. The reasons why he concludes this are: (a) the leaders of the synagogue invite a speaker to speak to τὸν λαόν, the people of Israel (vv. 13, 15, 17, 31); (b) the content of the sermon concerns Israel (vv. 17, 23, 24); (c) the first person plural pronouns identify Paul and Barnabas with the Jewish people (vv. 17, 26, 32–33); (d) the second person plural pronouns of vv. 32, 34, 38, 41 connect "you" the Jewish audience with "us" Paul and Barnabas; (e) a reference to Gentiles comes in v. 38 in the text, and it is not clear whether they are part of the synagogue.

72. Tucker, "God-Fearers," 38.

73. Barrett, *Acts of the Apostles*, 501.

74. Matera, *New Testament Theology*, 80 n. 37.

75. Johnson, *Acts*, 230.

76. Peterson, *Acts*, 386 n. 58. Malina & Pilch (*Books of Acts*, 93–95) writes, "Paul is addressing Israelites exclusively, the only ones who would be allowed into the club or community center ('synagogue'). The phrases would refer to sophisticated, practicing Israelites who would be fully cognizant of the traditions Paul cites, and other Israelites less sophisticated and familiar with the traditions. Certainly no non-Israelites could appreciate Paul's masterful use of Israelite traditions, that is, Scripture."

77. Buss, *Missionspredigt*, 35; see also Soards, *Speeches in Acts*, 81–82.

2. God's Graciousness and Promise to Israel (vv. 17-23)

Paul presents a recital of Israel's history to the diaspora Jews. In doing so, he presents a positive view of their history. In this diaspora setting, he is not polemical or accusatory against Jews.[78] He "draws out Jesus' connection to the Davidic dynasty as royal Messiah rather than Stephen's primary emphasis on Jesus as the messianic prophet-like-Moses."[79]

Paul's summary of Israel's history, however, is selective. It begins with God's election of Israel's ancestors and God's graciousness toward them. When it comes to King David, the recitation of Israel's history slows down. Finally, Israel's history reaches a climax when, according to God's promise to David, one of his descendants (Jesus) is brought to Israel (v. 23). Paul emphasizes "the faithfulness of 'the God of this people' in the past and supremely in the present, through the fulfillment in Jesus of the ancient promises."[80] Except for the verb ᾐτήσαντο in v. 21, God is the subject of all the verbs in vv. 17-23.

A. God's Election of Israel and Graciousness toward Israel (vv. 17-20)

In his sketch of Israel's history, Luke does not quote directly from the OT. Rather, he alludes to a number of conflated texts. This conflation serves to give a biblical tone to this sermon.[81] The titile ὁ θεός appears six times (vv. 17, 21, 23, 30, 33, 37), Ισραήλ three times (vv. 17, 23, 24), and λαός four times (vv. 17 [2x], 24, 31) in Paul's sermon. This recital of Israel's history recounts how the God of Israel has shown his kindness to his people throughout their history. It is God who initiates this special relationship with Israel. Through this election, God shows that he is the God of Israel.[82]

---

78. Bruce, *Acts: The Greek Text*, 303. This speech is often compared with Stephen's speech which also recounts their history (7:2-50). Stephen's speech, however, is a defense speech. He recites Israel's history to show the people, the elders, the scribes, and the high priest in Jerusalem that they have always rebelled against God. Like their ancestors, they are disobedient and so they reject Stephen's witness (7:51-53).

79. Walls, "Acts," 191.

80. Bruce, *Acts: The Greek Text*, 303.

81. Haenchen, *Acts*, 104. Dumais, *Langage de L'Evangélisation*, 90-95. Soards (*Speeches in Acts*, 82) points to some texts from the OT. They are Exodus 6, Deuteronomy 1 and 7, Joshua 14-17, 1 Samuel 7-10, 15-16, 2 Samuel 7 and 22, and LXX Psalm 77.

82. Bock, *Acts*, 451; Fitzmyer, *Acts*, 510; Barrett, *Acts of the Apostles*, 631. Johnson (*Acts*, 230) recognizes, "The theme of Israel as 'the people of God' is central to Luke's

Paul stresses that God chose "our fathers" (Exod 6:6, 8; 12:51; Deut 4:37; 7:7; 10:15; LXX Ps 32:12; 136:11–12). He uses the pronouns ἡμῶν (v. 17) and ἡμῖν (v. 26, 33) to identify himself with his addressees. The word πατέρας is repeated in vv. 32, 36. In this way Paul adapts his sermon to build connections with his audience. He and his audience share the same ancestry. This common heritage helps to develop Paul's argument in v. 23 that they share the same promise and the fulfillment of this promise in Jesus the savior.

Paul does not mention the names of the patriarchs, and he summarizes the history before the Exodus in a short note of God's election.[83] He quickly moves to God's saving action when the Israelites sojourned in Egypt. God raised them up (ὕψωσεν) when they were in Egypt, a foreign land. The verb ὕψωσεν was used for Jesus' exaltation in Acts 2:33 and 5:31. This verb now prepares the audience to reread Israel's history from the point of view of Jesus' exaltation.[84] The people of Israel were slaves and persecuted, but God made them great in number (Exod 1:20) and victorious against the Egyptians. With an uplifted arm, God led them out of the land of Egypt (Exod 6:1, 6, 8; 12:51; Deut 4:34; 5:15; 9:26). This is fitting for Paul's diaspora audience. Like the Israelites in Egypt, they live in the diaspora outside of the territory of Israel.

There is a textual variant in v. 18. Some MSS P⁷⁴, A, C*, E, Ψ, 33. 181 read ἐτροφοφόρησεν ("he nourished," "fed with food," or "cared for"). But other MSS ℵ, B, C2, D, 36, 81, 307, 453, and 1739) read ἐτροποφόρησεν ("put up with," "bore with"). The external evidence is almost evenly balanced between the two variants. Here, Luke alludes to Deut 1:31. The LXX presents the same two variants in rendering the MT נָשָׂא, which it translated as ὡς ἐτροφοφόρησέν (ἐτροποφόρησέ) σε κύριος ὁ θεός σου.[85]

---

literary and religious purposes."

83. He mentions only the name of Abraham in v. 26.

84. Flichy (*La Figure de Paul dans les Actes des Apôtres*, 192) writes, "La stratégie rhétorique de Paul se dévoile par làau lecteur: jouant sur la polysémie du verbe ὑψόω pour relire l'histoire d'Israël àpartir de la résurrection du Christ, il prépare son auditoire àentendre l'histoire d' « élévation » qui lui est familière comme une histoire de résurrection."

85. Metzger (*Textual Commentary*, 357) writes, "[O]ne has the feeling that in the context it is more likely that reference should be made to God's interposition and efforts in behalf of the Israelites rather than his forbearance in the face of their ingratitude; the problem is whether the greater appropriateness was sensed by the author or by copyists. On balance it seemed best to adopt the reading that differs from the prevailing Septuagint text, on the ground that scribes would have been more likely to accommo-

130   PAUL AMONG JEWS

The verb ἐτροφοφόρησεν occurs in B and twenty-eight other MSS. It is more likely that Luke adopts this prevailing LXX reading of Deut 1:31 suggesting that ἐτροφοφόρησεν is original.

In the present context, the emphasis is on how God showed his graciousness to Israel. The sermon does not speak of the sins of Israel in the desert. Rather, it speaks of God as the one who provides benefits for his people.[86] I judge ἐτροφοφόρησεν to be original. If ἐτροποφόρησεν were original, it would be in tension with the positive recollection of Israel's history narrated in v. 19. In this speech Paul does not focus on the behavior of the Israelites. He focuses on how God cared for them for forty years in the desert.

The verb ἐτροποφόρησεν may have been introduced here under the influence of Stephen's negative presentation of Israel's rebellion in the desert (7:39–43). In this part of Paul's sermon (13:18–20a), he follows the plot of Stephen's presentation (7:39–45). After the sojourn in the desert (7:39–43; 13:18), then Stephen and Paul narrate the overthrow of the seven nations in the land of Canaan and the inheritance of the promised land by the Israelites (7:45; 13:19–20a). It may also be that the prevailing experience of Israel's lack of faith in the desert came into play (Num 14:33–34). In the context of this sermon (13:16–41), the rejection of Jews against Paul's message the next Sabbath could explain the appearance of ἐτροποφόρησεν. Probably, in the course of separation between Jews and Christians, certain later copyists hold anti-Jewish view and consequently they change from ἐτροφοφόρησεν to ἐτροποφόρησεν to express a more negative view toward Jews. Phonetically, the two words were pronounced the same. This might cause confusions as well.

God continues to be the sole actor in Israel's history. The history continues with a positive theme. God destroyed seven nations in the land of Canaan and gave them their land as an inheritance (Deut 7:1) for about four hundred and fifty years. God led the Israelites out of the land of Egypt, nourished them in the desert, and made them inherit the

---

date the two than to make them diverge."

86. Pervo, *Acts*, 335–36 n. 44; Johnson, *Acts*, 231; Barrett, *Acts of the Apostles*, 632; Flichy, *La Figure de Paul dans les Actes des Apôtres*, 192; Pichler, *Paulusrezeption*, 145–46; Pillai, *Early Missionary Preaching*, 85; Witherington (*Acts*, 410) writes, "The positive context favors the reading 'cared for,' and this is in fact the better-attested reading for Deut. 1:31."

land of Canaan as their land. God led the Israelites to the promised land in Canaan.

The phrase ὡς ἔτεσιν τετρακοσίοις καὶ πεντήκοντα employs a dative of duration of time, "for about 450 years."[87] Fitzmyer thinks that it refers to four hundred years in Egypt (Gen 15:13, see also Acts 7:6), forty years in the desert (Num 14:33–34; Acts 13:18), and ten years in the conquest of Canaan (Joshua 14) before the appearance of judges. This interpretation is preferred by most scholars.[88] In the narrations of Israel's history, "apparently some meticulous attention is paid to periods of time (13:18, 20, 21; see 7:6, 23, 30, 36, 42), probably in order to lend the speeches historical verisimilitude."[89] In this sermon, the periods of times show that God, as the subject of all the actions in Israel's history, is in control. Everything happens according to God's timetable.

After these things, God gave them judges until the prophet Samuel. God gave the people judges and a prophet as their leaders to guide his chosen people. Judges were appointed before the monarchy (Judg 2:16, 18, 19; Ruth 1:1; 1 Chr 17:10). Samuel was regarded as "the last judge" (1 Sam 7:15) and as "the first in the prophetic succession after Moses (1 Sam 3:20)."[90] It seems that Paul wants to move on quickly to the narration of the coming King David in Israel's history.

B. Israel's Call for a King and God's Promise of a Savior to Them (vv. 21–23)

Samuel is mentioned at the end of v. 20 because he was the one that the people asked for a king (1 Sam 8:6). Although kingship was presented quite negatively in parts of the OT (1 Sam 12:1–25), Paul does not mention that Samuel was unwilling to meet their request in the beginning (1 Sam 8:7–8). The people asked for a king, and God gave them a king, Saul (1 Sam 9:1–2). God manifests no negative judgment toward this

---

87. Bruce (*Acts: The Greek Text*, 304) interprets this phrase as dative of point of time, not duration. It means in the 450th year, God gave them their land as a possession. This interpretation is not correct. It appears five times in the NT and denotes dative of duration.

88. Fitzmyer, *Acts*, 511; see also Wilfried Eckey, *Die Apostelgeschichte: Der Weg des Evangeliums von Jerusalem nach Rom* (Neukirchen-Vluyn: Neukirchener, 2000) 1. 297.

89. Johnson, *Acts*, 231.

90. Bruce, *Acts: The Greek Text*, 305. Johnson (*Acts*, 231) writes, "Luke's periodization here recalls Acts 3:24: 'indeed all the prophets who spoke from Samuel onwards also announced these days.'"

request. Rather, he shows his continuous graciousness and providence in granting them a king.[91]

Paul introduces Saul as a son of Kish, a man of the tribe of Benjamin (1 Sam 10:1, 20–21, 24; 11:15; 13:1). Paul is also called Saul (Acts 9:19; 13:9), and he is also from the tribe of Benjamin, according to Phil 3:5 and Rom 11:1. Saul was removed from his office (v. 22). It is hard to reconstruct how long he reigned as a king of Israel. The "forty-year" kingship of Saul is not mentioned in the OT. Josephus mentions that Saul reigned for eighteen years during the time of Samuel and twenty-two years thereafter (A. J. 6.14.9 §378; but cf. A. J. 10.8.4 §143, where Saul's reign is twenty years).[92]

Saul serves as "a transitional figure" in Israel's history to prepare for the coming of King David.[93] He will be compared with David in v. 22. God removed Saul and raised up David as the king of Israel. Paul does not say that Saul acted foolishly and disobeyed God. The narration shows God's authority in removing one king and raising David to the kingship. Saul has finished his course as a precursor of David, and he is set aside. Paul's audience in the synagogue knows the disloyalty of King Saul. The verb "remove" him from kingship may have the connotation that anyone who is not faithful to God will be set aside by God.

God raised up (ἤγειρεν) David as king. This does not mean God raised David from death but that God brought him forward to be a king (1 Sam 16:11–13). The choice of ἐγείρω is significant. Paul uses this verb to depict Jesus' resurrection in vv. 30, 37 (see also Luke 9:22; 24:6; Acts 3:15; 4:10; 5:30; 10:40). The application of the verb ἤγειρεν shows "a typological connection is already being forged."[94]

God said and bore witness to David. The participle μαρτυρήσας echoes the prevailing theme of witness in Acts (1:8). God testified about David, "I have found David, son of Jesse, a man after my heart, who will do all my will." This is not a quotation from a single text but a conflation of three scriptural phrases from LXX Ps 88:21 (εὗρον Δαυίδ), 1 Sam

---

91. Johnson, *Acts*, 231–32; Fitzmyer, *Acts*, 512; Peterson, *Acts*, 388. However, Soards (*Speeches in Acts*, 82) thinks that there is a negative tone here. He writes, "Then the speech notes a negative moment in Israel's history, when the people called for a king. That Israel's request is not a positive development becomes clear from the following remarks. Thus, this portion of the speech has a polemical undertone."

92. Fitzmyer, *Acts*, 512; Barrett, *Acts of the Apostles*, 635.

93. Bock, *Acts*, 452.

94. Johnson, *Acts*, 232.

13:14 (ἄνθρωπον κατὰ τὴν καρδίαν αὐτοῦ), and Isa 44:28 (καὶ πάντα τὰ θελήματά μου ποιήσει).[95] Thus "Israel's history is narrated in such a fashion that it is oriented towards David as its culmination (v. 22)."[96] Instead of presenting a negative and polemical image of kingship, this verse heralds the climax of Israel's messianic hopes.

From David, Paul moves on to Jesus. The connection between the two is emphasized. The phrase τούτου ὁ θεὸς ἀπὸ τοῦ σπέρματος lays emphasis on David. It is from this man's (David's) offspring that God brought forth for Israel a savior, Jesus. The concept of promise is presented. The promise to David is not directly mentioned. The promise in 2 Sam 7:12 comes to mind.[97] God promised David that he would raise up one of his descendants to succeed David and establish his kingdom forever (2 Sam 22:51). In Israel's history, this promise was understood to refer to the coming of a *future* "David" (Jer 30:9; Hos 3:5; Ezek 37:24-25) and even to the coming of "Messiah" (Dan 9:25; Ps 17:21-34).[98] Buss warns against interpreting this promise against the background of the Davidic promise in 2 Sam 7:12. He argues that the promise refers to a "savior" for Israel and concludes that Luke regards the whole OT as the promise to Israel.[99]

Through the promise Paul connects David and his descendant Jesus, and this promise is related to David. The word ἐπαγγελία appears

---

95. Steyn, *Septuagint Quotations*, 164. Barrett (*Acts of the Apostles*, 636) thinks this conflated passage is probably quoted from memory. Fitzmyer (*Acts*, 512) holds that the phrase "he will do all my wills" is originally applied to the Persian king Cyrus. He is a shepherd and called the Lord's "anointed one" (Isa 45:1). Here David is also called מָשִׁיחַ., a man after God's heart.

96. Jervell, *Theology of the Acts of the Apostles*, 67.

97. Dumais, *Langage de L'Evangélisation*, 220-22; Mark L. Strauss, *The Davidic Messiah in Luke-Acts : The Promise and Its Fulfillment in Lukan Christology* (JSNTSup 110, Sheffield: Sheffield Academic Press, 1995) 155; Fitzmyer, *Acts*, 512; Barrett, *Acts of the Apostles*, 636; Johnson, *Acts*, 232.

98. Fitzmyer, *Acts*, 512-13.

99. Buss (*Missionspredigt*, 48) writes, "Die Annahme, daß Lukas Apg 13, 17-23 in Anlehnung an 2 Sam 7, 6-16 redigiert habe, ist nicht mehr als eine kaum zu beweisende Hypothese." He concludes, "Wir betonen dies, um davor zu warnen, die ganze Rede nur auf dem Hintergrund des David-Bundes zu interpretieren, wo doch vielmehr Lukas das ganze AT al seine einzige ἐπαγγελία vor Augen hat" (p. 49). Flichy (*La Figure de Paul dans les Actes des Apôtres*, 195) has a similar but different interpretation of the promise. She writes, "Ainsi ; au-delà de la promesse d'une descendance et d'une royauté « pour toujours » faite à David, c'est également la promesse faite à Abraham et àses descendants d'une bénédiction et d'une alliance éternelle qui s'accomplit en Jésus."

in v. 32 and implicitly in v. 33 (ταύτην). God has fulfilled the promise made to the ancestors by raising Jesus.[100] In v. 22, David was presented as the culmination of Israel's history. Now Jesus is seen as the culmination of God's promise to Israel. The salvation begun with God's election of the ancestors and continued until David comes to completion in Jesus. "God has fulfilled his promise to Israel, especially as represented by the house of David, bringing to his people a Savior."[101]

Some MSS (C D 33. 36, etc) read ἤγειρε instead of ἤγαγεν. From the external evidence (P[74] ℵ A B E Ψ), it seems that ἤγαγεν is the original reading. The variant ἤγειρε, however, shows that the copyist saw the connection between this verse with the raising of David in v. 22 and God's raising Jesus in v. 30, and possibly 2 Sam 7:12 (ἀναστήσω τὸ σπέρμα σου).

The words ἤγαγεν and Ἰσραήλ in v. 23 form an inclusion with v. 17. God, as savior, begins Israel's history by leading the Israelites out of Egypt. He continues to guide Israel's history, and he brings a savior Jesus to Israel. "Paul souligne ainsi, à l'attention de son public, que son inscription dans l'histoire n'a pas fait varier le nom de son destinataire."[102]

Paul introduces Jesus into his sermon. He not only mentions God's promise, he proclaims that the promise has been fulfilled in Jesus as well. This is new to the Israelites. Jesus is the one whom God promised to David. This is also potentially controversial to his audience. Paul does not use the explicitly Jewish concepts as "Messiah" or the term "king."[103] Rather, he applies the title "savior" to Jesus. Yet he does not define the meaning of this term. In the OT, this term is used of God as a deliverer (Judg 3:9, 15; 1 Sam 10:19; Isa 45:15, 21). In Luke 2:11, Acts 5:31, and 13:23, Jesus is called savior. The identity of Jesus as "savior" anticipates "the forgiveness of sins" that comes through him that will be mentioned in v. 38.

3. The Witness of John the Baptist (vv. 24–25)

In order to connect Jesus with David, Paul's narration moves from David to Jesus. Just as Saul was presented as a precursor of King David, so John

---

100. Kilgallen ("Acts 13, 38–39: Culmination of Paul's Speech in Pisidia," 489–90) makes the same point.
101. Barrett, *Acts of the Apostles*, 636–37.
102. Flichy, *La Figure de Paul dans les Actes des Apôtres*, 195.
103. Pervo, *Acts*, 337.

the Baptist is presented as the herald of Jesus' coming. And just as Saul was removed from kingship, so John, after he fulfilled his course, faded away. And just as Paul compared Saul with David, so he compares John with Jesus (v. 25). Just as David was a man after God's own heart who carried out God's will, so Jesus carried out God's will.

John is the last figure who belongs to the time of promise before the coming of the final fulfillment of God's promise in Jesus' resurrection. He came before Jesus to prepare for the coming of the Lord. He preached a baptism of repentance to all the people of Israel (Luke 3:1-20). Thus, he was preparing Israel to meet its Messiah. He made it clear that Israel was estranged from God, and he challenged Israel to repent and be reconciled with God in order to receive the forgiveness of sins that is offered by Jesus (Acts 13:38-39).[104]

John bore witness to the one who would come after him. John made it clear that he was not the one who came to fulfill the promise. He did not consider himself worthy to do a slave's task and untie the sandals of the one who is to come. John was a prophet who recognized the greatness of Jesus. This echoes Luke 3:15-16, a text in which people wondered whether John might be the coming Messiah. John's witness is meant to dispel any questions about the messianic character of Jesus' contemporary.[105] Verses 24-25, then, serve as "an historical testimony to the identity of Jesus."[106]

To summarize, contrary to Dibelius who thinks that this section (vv. 16-25) has no connection with the sermon, this retelling of Israel's history is significant for Paul's sermon.[107] The rehearsal of the history serves as a *captatio benevolentiae*.[108] In this section, Paul presents some major concepts that he will develop in his sermon. The rehearsal of Israel's history leads to the coming of Jesus, the savior of Israel. He presents the significant term "promise" and Jesus as the savior who comes to

104. Peterson, *Acts*, 389. Witherington, *Acts*, 410.

105. Jervell, *Apostelgeschichte*, 357; Witherington, *Acts*, 411; Dumais, *Langage de L'Evangélisation*, 279.

106. Strauss, *Davidic Messiah in Luke-Acts*, 160.

107. Dibelius, *Book of Acts*, 68. This understanding is criticized by Pillai (*Early Missionary Preaching*, 84) and DeSilva ("Paul's Sermon in Antioch of Pisidia," 37).

108. Buss, *Missionspredigt*, 48. It is true that it fits the audience of diaspora Jews. Paul relates to his audience by beginning the story of God's election of their ancestors, God's leading them out of Egypt and their entrance into the promised land. God is the one who has guided the history of Israel. God has fulfilled all his promises.

fulfill this promise. Throughout the sermon, the unifying thread is the promise to David and its fulfillment in Jesus' resurrection.

B. The Message of Salvation: Fulfillment of the Promise in Jesus' Resurrection (vv. 26-37)

In this part, Paul focuses on the message of salvation to his audience. He proclaims Jesus' death, burial, resurrection, and appearances. In Jesus' resurrection, God has fulfilled the promise to their ancestors. Paul, then, proves Jesus' resurrection on the basis of certain scriptural passages.

1. Address and Declaration (v. 26)

The second section begins with a direct address to the mixed audience: "Brothers, children of the family of Abraham, and you who are God-fearers." The new element of the greeting is "children of the family of Abraham" (Acts 7:2; Luke 3:8). This address corresponds to v. 16. Paul and his audience share common ancestors whom God has elected. Paul emphasizes that they are all descendants of father Abraham. The theme of election in v. 17, then, is renewed in v. 23. "Not only the promise of David but also the election of Israel remains an important premise of the speech as a whole."[109]

This opening address also develops the concept of salvation alluded to in v. 23 where Paul identifies Jesus as "savior." Now Paul speaks of the message of salvation that Jesus has brought. In v. 47 Paul and Barnabas will summarize the subject and goal of their preaching as "salvation." The notion of salvation is significant in Peter's inaugural sermon as well (2:22-24). Paul identifies his preaching as a "message of salvation." The word λόγος, which refers to the message of disciples' proclamation, may be an allusion to Ps 107:20, ἀπέστειλεν τὸν λόγον αὐτοῦ καὶ ἰάσατο αὐτούς. It is a Lucan literary variant for other expressions in 5:20; 6:2, 7; 16:32; 19:10, all descriptions of the Christian gospel and the benefits that it brings.[110]

---

109. Tannehill, *Narrative Unity of Luke-Acts: Acts*, 168. Buss (*Missionspredigt*, 63) interprets the address "children of Abraham" as a warning as well. God can raise children to Abraham from these stones (Luke 3:8). God can also call Gentiles for salvation (Acts 13:47). He thinks that "those who are God-fearers" are "brothers" as well in this direct address (v. 26).

110. Fitzmyer, *Acts*, 514.

This salvation is for us. The pronoun ἡμῖν is put in the emphatic position. Paul uses the pronoun ἡμῖν to identify himself with his audience as a diaspora Jew. Paul emphasizes that salvation has come to his contemporaries, his audience. There is a contrast between diaspora Jews (ἡμῖν) and the Jerusalemite Jews. The particle γάρ connects the two. This means that the message of salvation has been sent out to us (diaspora Jews) because the Jerusalemite Jews have rejected Jesus. A similar construction is used in 28:28, "This salvation from God has been sent to the Gentiles."[111]

2. Christological Kerygma (vv. 27-31)

Christological kerygma is a central part in the sermons of the first half of Acts (2:22-24; 3:13-15; 5:30-31; 10:37-41). There are some difficulties in understanding v. 27. First, the pronoun τοῦτον is ambiguous. Grammatically, it refers to the closest proper noun, which is ὁ λόγος in v. 26. In this context, however, Paul has Jesus (Ἰησοῦς) of v. 23 in mind. The Jerusalem Jews and their leaders failed to recognize Jesus as the savior of Israel. The D-text read μὴ συνιέντες τὰς γραφάς ("not understanding the Scriptures") in an attempt to clarify the pronoun τοῦτον. Second, grammatically the participle ἀγνοήσαντες can have two objects, the pronoun τοῦτον and τὰς φωνὰς τῶν προφητῶν. The latter can also be the object of ἐπλήρωσαν. Verses 27-28 can be rendered in this way, "For those who live in Jerusalem and their leaders failed to recognize him (Jesus). They did not understand the oracles of the prophets that were read Sabbath after Sabbath. Thus, they fulfilled them (oracles) by condemning him (Jesus), though they had not found any cause worthy of death. They demanded of Pilate to have him killed."[112]

---

111. Johnson, *Acts*, 233. He thinks the reading of ὑμῖν might make more sense, since there is a deliberate contrast between the Jews in Antioch of Pisidia and those in Jerusalem. From the external evidences, ἡμῖν is read in MSS P⁷⁴ ℵ, A, B, D, 33, 81, and 614. The first person plural is probably original. The two pronouns were pronounced the same.

112. See similar translations by Pervo, *Acts*, 338; Haenchen, *Acts*, 410; DeSilva, "Paul's Sermon in Antioch of Pisidia," 39. See Eldon J. Epp, "The 'Ignorance Motif' in Acts and Anti-Judaic Tendencies in Codex Bezae," in *HTR* 55 (1962) 51-62. Barrett (*Acts of the Apostles*, 620) translates the two verses in this way. "For the inhabitants of Jerusalem and their rulers, though they did not recognize him or the words of the prophets, which are read every Sabbath, sat in judgment upon him and so fulfilled the prophetic message. Though they found no charge against him they asked Pilate that he should be killed."

The recognition of Jesus as the Messiah is related to a correct understanding of the oracles of the prophets (Luke 24:44; Acts 8:34; 17:10–11). The center of these oracles is the promise that God raised Jesus as the savior of Israel (v. 23). According to Paul, the Jews read the prophets every Sabbath but they did not recognize Jesus in these prophecies. This remark leads Paul to show in vv. 32–35, through a correct understanding of the Scriptures, that Jesus is the Messiah.

Paul distinguishes the Jews in the diaspora from those in Jerusalem. The message of salvation has been sent out to the Jewish populace in the diaspora because those in Jerusalem failed to recognize Jesus. Indeed they fulfilled the prophecies by condemning Jesus. Paul does not blame the diaspora Jews for this since he does not want to enflame them. Accordingly, he softens his remarks and focuses his attention on the ignorance of the Jews in Jerusalem.

The motif of ignorance is a significant aspect for the rejection of Jesus by the Jews in Jerusalem (3:17). Because of their ignorance and failure to understand the Scriptures, they unwittingly fulfilled the prophecies concerning Jesus the Messiah. The purpose of narrating what the Jews in Jerusalem did is to warn those in the diaspora lest they fail to recognize Jesus as the Messiah. Paul's preaching to the Jews in the diaspora provides a second chance for them to accept Jesus as the Messiah. This warning becomes clearer at the end of the sermon (v. 41).

"They" found no cause worthy of death against Jesus. Here "they" must refer to the Jews in Jerusalem and their leaders (v. 27). This emphasizes Jesus' innocence. The term αἰτία θανάτου means *causa capitalis*, a capital charge.[113] The language of εὑρόντες and αἰτίαν θανάτου echoes Pilate's triple announcement in the Passion Narrative of Jesus' innocence (Luke 23:4, 14, 22). The use of ᾐτήσαντο recalls the verb αἰτέομαι in Luke 23:23–25 and Acts 3:14. In the Lukan Passion Narrative, Pilate did not find cause to put Jesus to death. Here, Paul underlines that Jerusalemite Jews and their leaders could not find any evidence against Jesus either.

The emphasis on Jesus' innocence has an apologetic function. Jesus was not put to death because he was guilty of a capital offense. He died to fulfill what is written about him in the Scriptures. Jesus' followers, especially Paul, will experience what he has experienced as the authorities explicitly or implicitly acknowledge the innocence of Christian preachers (16:35–39; 18:14–16; 19:31, 37; 23:29; 25:14–19; 26:3).

---

113. Barrett, *Acts of the Apostles*, 640.

Despite the injustice against the innocent one, Jesus' death on the cross is the fulfillment of the Scriptures. In v. 27, Paul presents a summary of Jesus' death as a fulfillment of the oracles of the prophets. In v. 29, everything the Jews and their leaders did unwittingly fulfilled all the things written about him in the Scriptures. According to Luke, it was necessary for the Messiah to suffer these things (Luke 22:37; 24:26-27) since everything written about him in the Scriptures had to be fulfilled (24:44).

"They took him from the tree and placed him in a tomb."[114] In this section (vv. 27-29), there is no change of subject. The Jerusalemite Jews and their leaders are the only subjects so far. In omitting some details of Jesus' passion account (Luke 23:53), Luke has actually shortened the account.[115] Most probably, this is to build a strong contrast between what human beings, here the Jerusalemite Jews and their leaders, have done to Jesus (vv. 27-29) and what God has done (v. 30).[116] Human beings had Jesus killed and buried in a tomb. They destroyed Jesus and put him to death. But God raised him from the dead.

The mention of Jesus' resurrection in v. 30 is brief, since it will be developed further in vv. 32-37. The narration focuses on the risen Lord's appearances and the witness of his disciples in Jerusalem. In this speech, Paul echoes what Peter preached earlier, thereby showing the continuity and consistency of Paul's preaching. In Acts 1:3, the risen Lord appeared to his apostles for forty days. Paul does not need to repeat the number of days in this short presentation.

---

114. Fitzmyer (*Acts*, 515) interprets the participle καθελόντες and third plural aorist form ἔθηκαν as "indefinite or generic." They are used as a substitute for the passive "he was taken down." Bruce (*Acts: The Greek Text*) thinks the plural form is a generalizing plural. In Luke 23:53 it is Joseph of Arimathaea who took Jesus' body down and buried it in the tomb; in John 19:38-42 Nicodemus joined him in doing so. "As both of them were members of the Sanhedrin, their action could have been seen as undertaken on behalf of the court as a whole" (p. 308).

115. Haenchen, *Acts*, 410. See also Barrett (*Acts of the Apostles*, 641-42). Peterson (*Acts*, 391) writes, "[T]he story is simplified here by attributing the burial to those who carried out all that was written about him (cf. Is. 53:9)." Probably it is too short to be fully understood. The Western text tries to add more information for clarification.

116. Fitzmyer (*Acts*, 515) has a similar understanding of the function of contrast between what human beings have done to Jesus and God has done to him. Gaventa (*Acts*, 199) understands the narration that the Jerusalemites themselves took Jesus down from the tree placed him in a tomb to serve "the speech's rhetorical purpose of highlighting the offense of Jerusalem in Jesus' death."

Beginning with the baptism of John (1:22), Jesus' disciples accompanied him from Galilee to Jerusalem. Accordingly, they were eyewitnesses of Jesus' whole ministry, as well as of his passion and resurrection in Jerusalem. They are now his witnesses to the people of Israel (Luke 24:48; Acts 1:8; 2:32; 3:15; 5:32; 10:39, 41).[117] "The 'people' are not only the inhabitants of Jerusalem (13:27), but also those of Judea, Samaria, and areas of the eastern Mediterranean to which the Word has already spread."[118]

3. Jesus Is the Fulfillment of the Promise: Proof from Scripture (vv. 32–35)

"We too are proclaiming to you the good news: the promise to our ancestors has been fulfilled." The conjunction καί (v. 32) links the emphatic pronoun ἡμεῖς with μάρτυρες αὐτοῦ (v. 31). This relates the present role of Paul and Barnabas to the role of the witnesses from Galilee in v. 31. Jesus' apostles proclaimed the good news to the people of Israel in Jerusalem (2:1–8:4), Judea, and Samaria (8:5–40), and even to Gentiles (9:1–12:25). Like Jesus' apostles, Paul and Barnabas continue to bear witness to diaspora Jews and God-fearers (v. 26). Paul wants to highlight that he is not bringing a new message to the Jews in Antioch. Rather, he continues to preach the same message to the people of Israel, even though he is preaching to Jews in diaspora. His mission is in continuity with that of Jesus' apostles.

The good news that Paul preaches is the realization of the promise to their ancestors. The promise is mentioned in v. 23: From David's descendants, God would bring a savior for Israel. Paul proclaims that God has fulfilled this promise by raising Jesus from the dead. Paul summarizes the good news that he proclaims in three ways. First, in vv. 32b–33a he notes that God has fulfilled the promise he made to their ancestors, to them,

---

117. Metzger (*Textual Commentary*, 361) discusses the evidence for and against the inclusion of νῦν in v. 31. On the one hand, its different position, its expanded form ἄχρι νῦν in D, and its omission by B suggest that it was added later. On the other hand, the fact that in similar passages (2:32; 3:15; 5:32; 10:39) νῦν is not present suggests that it was not added later by scribes; rather, it was original. "Its absence in some witnesses may be accounted for either because it was regarded as unnecessary, or because the apostles not only now first, but for a long time past, were witnesses." I judge that the inclusion of νῦν in v. 31 is original. Luke shows the continuity of Paul's witness with that of Jesus' disciples. They are now witnesses. Paul joins them to bear witness to the Jews in diaspora. The presence of νῦν may also prepare for the Jerusalem Council in Acts 15. See also Barrett, *Acts of the Apostles*, 644.

118. Fitzmyer, *Acts*, 516.

and to their children. Second, God has fulfilled this by raising Jesus; this is supported by a scriptural proof from Ps 2:7 in v. 33b. Third, Jesus, has been raised from the dead; his body did not see decay. This is supported by quotations from Isa 55:3 and LXX Ps 15:10 in vv. 34–35.[119]

There is a debate as to whether τοῖς τέκνοις αὐτῶν ἡμῖν or τοῖς τέκνοις ἡμῶν is original in v. 33. The pronoun ἡμῶν is attested in P[74] ℵ A B C* D (Ψ *pc* p) lat. According to the external evidences, ἡμῶν could be the original reading. Yet this reading does not make any sense in this context. Consequently, most commentators regard ἡμῶν as an early corruption of the text,[120] and they argue that τοῖς τέκνοις αὐτῶν ἡμῖν is original, although the external evidences (C3 E 33. 1739 sy) is not as strong.[121] I judge τοῖς τέκνοις ἡμῖν to be original. Probably, there was a primitive scribal error in copying ἡμῖν to ἡμῶν. It is also possible that this error is influenced by ἡμῶν in v. 17 πατέρας ἡμῶν. The phrase τοῖς τέκνοις ἡμῖν can mean "to their (ancestors') children, us."[122] Some scribes may have thought it was not clear, so they add αὐτῶν after τοῖς τέκνοις for clarification.[123]

The verb εὐαγγελιζόμεθα takes three objects. They are ὑμᾶς, τὴν ἐπαγγελίαν in v. 32, and the ὅτι clause in v. 33. Paul proclaims the good news that God has fulfilled the promise for us, their (ancestors') children, by raising Jesus. The motif of fulfillment is repeated for the third time (vv. 27, 29, 33). The fulfillment of the promise is the result of God's raising Jesus.

---

119. Steyn, *Septuagint Quotations*, 168–69.

120. Haenchen, *Acts*, 411; see also Pichler, *Paulusrezeption*, 173; Metzger, *Textual Commentary*, 362 n. 23; Bruce, *Acts: The Greek Text*, 309. However, most recently Peterson (*Acts*, 391 n. 78) judges that ἡμῶν has a strong claim to be the original, since it is attested in the best manuscripts and it is a harder reading as well.

121. Commentators like Fitzmyer (*Acts*, 516), Johnson (*Acts*, 234), and Peterson (*Acts*, 391) take this view. For further manuscript witnesses, see *New Testament Greek Manuscripts: The Acts of the Apostles* (ed. Reuben Swanson; Pasadena, CA: William Carey International University Press, 1998) 228.

122. Wallace, *Greek Grammar beyond the Basics*, 215–16. He explains that the article has the function of a possessive pronoun. He writes, "The article sometimes used in contexts in which possession is implied. The article itself does not involve possession, but this notion can be inferred from the presence of the article alone in certain contexts" (p. 215).

123. See the similar views of Barrett (*Acts of the Apostles*, 645), Buss (*Missionspredigt*, 89), and Haenchen (*Acts*, 411).

The meaning of ἀναστήσας is debated. Does it mean "bringing up Jesus on the stage of Israel history?" (view 1) or "raising Jesus from the dead" (view 2). Bruce argues that it means the former.[124] Most commentators interpret it as the latter. Strauss combines the two and suggests, "While taking Ps. 2.7 as a prophecy fulfilled at the resurrection (as in view 2), Luke introduces the verse primarily to prove that Jesus is the Son of God, and hence the messiah, who fulfills the promises to David in his whole life, death and resurrection (as in view 1)."[125] It is true that the promise that God brought Jesus to Israel is presented in v. 23. Yet from v. 26 onward, Paul speaks of Jesus' death and resurrection (vv. 26–37). In the next verse (v. 34), Paul uses the same verb ἀνίστημι to indicate that God raised Jesus from the dead. If this verb means that God brought Jesus onto the stage of Israel, the thought of God's raising Jesus from the dead would be interrupted.[126] Strauss further explains,

> Luke probably uses ἀναστήσας to refer to the whole Jesus event. Jesus' whole life, death and resurrection were κατ' ἐπαγγελίαν (v. 23), that is, they were part of the fulfillment of God's promise to David. While this fulfillment begins with Jesus' coming onto the scene of history, it also encompasses the resurrection—the climax of his 'raising up'.[127]

Steyn understands the verb ἀνίστημι as the exalted status of the risen Lord.[128] God has fulfilled his promise to David by raising Jesus from the dead and exalting him to his right hand. His exalted status

---

124. In analyzing Acts 3:22 and 7:37, Bruce (*Acts: The Greek Text*, 309) writes, "The promise of v. 23, whose fulfillment is here announced, points forward to the 'bringing to Israel of a Savior, Jesus.'"

125. Strauss, *Davidic Messiah in Luke-Acts*, 164.

126. Eduard Schweizer, "The Concept of the Davidic 'Son of God' in Acts and Its Old Testament Background," in *Studies in Luke-Acts* (ed. Leander Keck and J. Louis Martyn; Philadelphia: Fortress, 1980) 186. See also O'Toole, "Christ's Resurrection in Acts 13, 13–52," 366; Steyn, *Septuagint Quotations*, 173 n. 82; Evald Lövestam, *Son and Savior: A Study of Acts 13, 32–37 with an Appendix: 'Son of God' in the Synoptic Gospels* (ConNT 18; trans. Michael J. Petry; Lund: C. W. K. Gleerup and Copenhagen: Ejnar Munksgaard, 1961) 9.

127. Strauss, *Davidic Messiah in Luke-Acts*, 164.

128. Steyn (*Septuagint Quotations*, 173–76) thinks that uses of Ps 2:7 in Heb 1:5 and 5:5 help to clarify the meaning of ἀναστήσας. In the two verses, Ps 2:7 is used to describe the exalted status of the Son at the right hand of the Father. For Luke, there is no clear distinction between resurrection and exaltation. He understands them as part of one process. Accordingly, Luke uses ἀναστήσας to refer to Jesus' resurrection and exaltation.

confirms that he is the savior for Israel. It is important to bear all these elements in mind.

In vv. 33-35, Paul quotes three OT texts to prove that God raised Jesus. The first is Ps 2:7 in v. 34.[129] This is an exact quotation from LXX Ps 2:7. This psalm is a royal psalm composed for the enthronement of a Davidic king. It is possible that when Luke quotes this psalm, he has the whole psalm in mind. Ps 2:1-2 is quoted in Acts 4:25-28. In the context of Acts 13:26-37, the Jerusalemite Jews and their leaders killed Jesus, but God vindicated Jesus their king by raising him from the dead.

"You are my son, today I have begotten you." In raising Jesus, God has exalted him as his Son. The proclamation of Jesus' sonship confirms his messianic identity. The promise in 2 Sam 7:14-16 proclaims that one of David's descendants will be "raised up," (ἀναστήσω in v. 12) and he shall be God's "son," (v. 14) and his "throne," "house," and "kingdom" will last "for all eternity" (v. 16). People await the fulfillment of the Davidic prophecies: "a Messianic figure, God's son of Davidic descent, who will rule over Israel in the latter days."[130] In the annunciation, the angel said to Mary about Jesus, "The Lord God will give him the throne of his father David" (Luke 1:32). The promise is referred to again in Acts 2:30 and 13:22-23. In vv. 32-33, Paul announces its fulfillment in Jesus' being raised.

Paul confirms Jesus' identity as the Davidic Messiah (Luke 3:22; 9:35) by quoting Ps 2:7. Through Jesus' resurrection God has enthroned Jesus. The enthronement ritual that was practiced in Israel has been moved to the heavenly sphere. The psalm helps the Lukan readers to comprehend the significance of Jesus' resurrection.

"Today" refers to the day of Jesus' resurrection in this context. On the day of Jesus' resurrection, Jesus' being exalted is "just as it was said of old that God had begotten the historical unnamed king of the Davidic dynasty at his enthronement."[131] The citation of Ps 2:7 in v. 33 serves two

---

129. There are some textual issues here. The text ἐν τῷ ψαλμῷ γέγραπται τῷ δευτέρῳ is in the most reliable manuscripts (P⁷⁴ ℵ A B C Ψ 33. 81. 945. 1739 *al*). Some texts read "in the first psalm," others, "in the psalms." The confusion comes from the fact that in the patristic period Psalms 1 and 2 were joined together. There is no clear date when psalms were numbered. I follow the external evidence and take "the second psalm" to be original.

130. Schweizer, "The Concept of the Davidic 'Son of God' in Acts and Its Old Testament Background," 191. See further the connection between the promise in Acts 13:33 and 2 Sam 7:14 by Dumais (*Langage de L'Evangélisation*, 187-96).

131. Fitzmyer, *Acts*, 517.

purposes: first, it confirms Jesus' messianic identity. He is the Messiah who fulfills the promise made to the ancestors. Second, it prepares for the discussion of Jesus' resurrection.[132]

Most commentators interpret vv. 34–37 as the scriptural proof of Jesus' resurrection. The particle ὅτι at the beginning of v. 34 parallels the ὅτι in v. 33. The particle δέ has an explicative function.[133] In v. 34, Paul further interprets the meaning of "raising up Jesus" in v. 33 as God raised him from the dead. In this case, the particle ὅτι can mean "because." Thus, Psalm 2 is used to interpret Jesus' exaltation by the Father at the resurrection. Jesus' resurrection means that his body will never decay. Here, decay refers to death. Paul presents two scriptural passages to prove that the Messiah will not see decay. Verses 34–35 can be translated, "Because he (God) raised him (Jesus) from the dead, never to return to decay, he said in this way, 'I will give you the faithful covenant promises to David'; that is why he declared in another place, 'You will not give your holy one to see decay.'"

The scriptural proof, "I will give you the faithful covenant promises to David," is a reference to LXX Isa 55:3b.[134] This is part of a quotation of LXX Isa 55:3, "I will make with you an everlasting covenant, the assured holy things for David." Only the last five words are quoted in Acts 13:34 (τὰ ὅσια Δαυιδ τὰ πιστά). The corresponding MT text has דָוִד הַנֶּאֱמָנִים חַסְדֵי. The word חֶסֶד is usually translated as ἔλεος in the LXX, which means covenantal faithfulness. The plural form חֲסָדִים is translated as τὰ ἐλέη. Perhaps the noun חֶסֶד, was confused with its plural construct state חֲסִידֵי, which means holy things and consequently it is translated

---

132. Strauss, *Davidic Messiah in Luke-Acts*, 164.

133. Buss (*Missionspredigt*, 98-99). He thinks he combination of ὅτι δέ can be translated as "im Hinblick auf, in bezug auf . . ." It is something like περί plus genitive (p. 99). See also Bock, *Proclamation from Prophecy and Pattern: Lucan Old Testament Christology* (JSNTSup 12; Sheffield: Sheffield Academic Press, 1987) 248.

134. Hans Conzelmann (*Acts of the Apostles: A Commentary on the Acts of the Apostles* [Hermenia; trans. James Limburg, A. Thomas Kraabel and Donald H. Juel; Philadelphia: Fortress, 1987] 105) thinks that Isa 55:3b is cited in such a fragmentary way that the quotation is unintelligible by itself. According to H. G. M. Williamson ("'The Sure Mercies of David': Subjective or Objective Genitive?" *JSS* 23 [1978] 31-49, here 49), the majority of critics accept the reference of LXX Isa 55:3b and some even claim that it is a fairly accurate translation of MT.

as τὰ ὅσια.¹³⁵ But this change may have been intentional by Luke.¹³⁶ It is possible that Luke uses τὰ ὅσια in order to connect it with τὸν ὅσιον in v. 35 by employing the exegetical rule *gezerah shewa*. He connects the holy things with the holy one.

There are different interpretations of τὰ ὅσια Δαυιδ τὰ πιστά. Some interpret τὰ ὅσια Δαυιδ as acts of covenant kindness and love (holiness) performed by David. Therefore, David is the subject.¹³⁷ Most commentators think David is an objective genitive.

It means God's τὰ ὅσια to or for David.¹³⁸ The phrase τὰ ὅσια Δαυιδ τὰ πιστά can mean "unfailing divine assurances or decrees relating to David." They are God's promises to David.¹³⁹ The word ὅσια appears only in LXX Deut 29:18, in which יְהִי־לִי שָׁלוֹם is rendered as ὅσιά μοι γένοιτο. The word שָׁלוֹם is translated as ὅσια. Dupont and Lövestam have studied this word in Greek inscriptions from Cnidus. There it is "used as a general expression for blessings and good gifts, which may be expected from the deity."¹⁴⁰ Luke borrows this meaning from his Hellenistic religious context and uses it to denote divine benefits bestowed by God.

Lövestam argues persuasively that both the Hebrew dysx and its rendering in Greek ὅσια have a covenant background. By studying Pss 89:4–5, 132:11, and Isa 9:1–7, he concludes that τὰ ὅσια refers to the covenantal promise that God made with the house of David. They are "messianic

---

135. Jacques Dupont, "ΤΑ ʿΟΣΙΑ ΔΑΥΙΔ ΤΑ ΠΙΣΤΑ" in *Etudes sur les Actes des Apôtres* (ed. Jacques Dupont ; Paris: Cerf, 1967) 337–65, here 343. But Fitzmyer (*Acts*, 517) writes, "The Greek form of the LXX is a fairly accurate translation of the Hebrew MT and of 1QIsaa 45:22–23." His judgment is probably based on his book review of Lövestam's book entitled *Son and Savior: A Study of Acts 13, 32–37*. See the book review by Fitzmyer in *TS* 81 (1962) 467–69.

136. Strauss, *Davidic Messiah in Luke-Acts*, 168.

137. A. Caquot, "Les «Graces de David»: A Propos d'Isaie 55/3b," *Sem* 35 (1965) 45–59; W. A. M. Beuken, "Isa. 55, 3–5: The Reinterpretation of David," *Bijdr* 35 (1975) 49–64; Peter J. Gentry, "Rethinking the 'Sure Mercies of David' in Isaiah 55:3," *WTJ* 69 (2007) 279–304.

138. Williamson "'The Sure Mercies of David,'" 31–49; Lövestam, *Son and Savior*, 69; Walter C. Kaiser, Jr., "The Unfailing Kindness Promised to David: Isaiah 55.3," *JSOT* 45 (1989) 91–98; Lövestam, *Son and Savior*, 55; Fitzmyer, *Acts*, 517; Johnson, *Acts*, 235. More different interpretations are presented by Bock (*Proclamation from Prophecy and Pattern*, 249–54) and Strauss (*Davidic Messiah in Luke-Acts*, 166–72).

139. BDAG, s. v. ὅσις.

140. Lövestam, *Son and Savior*, 75. Dupont ("ΤΑ ʿΟΣΙΑ ΔΑΥΙΔ ΤΑ ΠΙΣΤΑ," 344) interprets this word as, "les bienfaits qu'on peut attendre de Dieu."

salvation blessings" (Heilsgüter).¹⁴¹ Thus, τὰ ὅσια means God's divine blessings and promise narrated in 2 Sam 7:5-16. The plural form is appropriate "since these blessings are multi-faceted, comprising the covenant promises of an heir, perpetual favour from God (for that heir), an eternal house, throne and kingdom, and rest and protection from enemies."¹⁴² Most probably, the covenantal promises are the resurrection of Jesus and his incorruptibility that guarantee the eternal promise of God's faithful love for Israel. Several commentators interpret the covenantal promises with forgiveness of sins and justification in Jesus in vv. 38-39.¹⁴³

In the context of Isa 55:3, God renews his covenant with his people Israel. This covenant is not a covenant of a binding agreement between two equal partners. Rather, it is "a covenant promise which God as giver confers upon his people Israel, the receiver."¹⁴⁴ In Acts 13:34, the LXX καὶ διαθήσομαι ὑμῖν διαθήκην αἰώνιον is rendered as δώσω ὑμῖν. In this way Luke emphasizes that God is the giver of the promise to David. In vv. 23 and 33, he underlines that God fulfills his promise.

This covenantal promise is everlasting (Isa 55:3). In 2 Sam 13-16, the term עַד־עוֹלָם; appears three times. This aspect is emphasized in other passages (Ps 89:30; 1 Macc 2:57; Ps 17:4). This covenant is trustworthy, faithful, reliable, and assured (הַנֶּאֱמָנִים;, τὰ πιστά). God will keep his promise (2 Sam 7:15-16; Ps 89:34-36) since he is trustworthy. God sent this everlasting assured promise of David to "you," the people of Israel (Isa 55:3). Now this promise is fulfilled for "you" (pl.) Paul's audience here and for all the Jews.

Jesus' resurrection confirms his identity as God's Son, the Messiah. His incorruptibility guarantees the fulfillment of God's everlasting and trustworthy promise to David and his descendants. Since Jesus is raised

---

141. Ibid., 73-81. He further argues that even the Hebrew ~Alv', which is translated as ὅσια in Deut 29:18, has a covenant connotation.

142. Strauss, *Davidic Messiah in Luke-Acts*, 170-71.

143. Dupont, "ΤΑ 'ΟΣΙΑ ΔΑΥΙΔ ΤΑ ΠΙΣΤΑ," 355. Kilgallen, "Acts 13, 38-39: Culmination of Paul's Speech in Pisidia," 495.

144. Lövestam, *Son and Savior*, 54-55, 80. Gentry ("Rethinking the 'Sure Mercies of David' in Isaiah 55:3," 283) claims that in Isa 55:14-15, the author shows that the covenant made with David will only be fulfilled by both a faithful father (Yahweh keeps his promises) and a faithful son (the obedience of the king to Yahweh's Torah). He concludes that this covenant is conditional and "faithfulness and obedience in the father-son relationship are crucial."

from the dead, he will never see decay, for the trustworthy God will not allow his holy one to see it (v. 35).

Paul connects the quotation from Isa 55:3 with LXX Ps 15:10 by διότι ("that is why," or "therefore"). "You will not allow your holy one to see decay." This psalm is used only here and Acts 2. The prominence of διαφθοράν in vv. 34–36 is noticeable. It appears six times in the NT, only in Acts. Paul uses this word four times in these three verses. The idea of incorruptibility is pointed out clearly. The incorruptibility of Jesus' body is connected with the resurrection of his body from the dead.

4. A Contrast: Jesus Fulfills What David Did Not Fulfill (vv. 36–37)

In LXX Ps 15:10, David prophesies that God will not allow his 'holy one' to see decay. In its historical context, this text refers to David since Paul mentions the faithful promises to David in v. 34. But after David served God's purpose in his own generation, he fell asleep with his ancestors and did see decay. But the one whom God raised did not see decay. There is a contrast between David and the one whom God raised from the dead. This prophecy cannot apply to David then. It must apply to the one whom God raised from the dead. The risen Lord is the holy one who did not see decay. He is the one who fulfilled God's covenantal promises to David. By raising Jesus from the dead, God has shown his faithfulness to his promise to David. God has fulfilled the promise made to David. He has raised Jesus as the Messiah, the savior, the Holy One for all.

C. The Meaning of Salvation and a Concluding Warning (vv. 38–41)

Paul's narration of Israel's history has focused on God's kindness toward the Israelites. This history came to its climax when God brought Jesus as a savior for the whole of Israel according to his promise (v. 23). This promise was fulfilled in raising Jesus from the dead. As a result, it is clear that Jesus is the Son of God, the Messiah, for he did not see decay. He is God's holy one, through whom God delivers his covenantal promises to David. Paul expounds how this sermon is applicable for his audience in Antioch. The particle οὖν indicates that Paul is drawing a conclusion from his speech in response to speak a word of encouragement to the people. According to Kilgallen, vv. 38–39 is the climax of the speech.[145]

---

145. Kilgallen, "Acts 13, 38–39: Culmination of Paul's Speech in Pisidia," 483–84.

1. Appeal and Address (v. 38a)

Paul addresses his audience as ἄνδρες ἀδελφοί. This address may include fellow Israelites and God-fearers. It is possible that he focuses on the Jews in the synagogue, since he will discuss justification and the role of the law in what follows. But Paul probably wants to include everyone in this address, since he mentions the universality of salvation that Jesus brings in v. 39.

2. The Meaning of Salvation: Forgiveness of Sins, Justification by Faith (vv. 38-39)

David served his purpose in the past. He died and saw decay, but God raised Jesus, one of David's descendants who lives "forever and thus functions as the savior for all Israel, for all time and every place."[146] He is the mediator of salvation through whom forgiveness of sins is proclaimed to all. Just as David served as a king for the Israelites in the past, so now Jesus, the risen Lord, has become a savior for all the generations. David is no longer the mediator of God's salvation.

Paul begins that "through him (Christ) forgiveness of sins is being proclaimed to you, and from everything of which you cannot be justified by the Law of Moses, through him everyone who believes is justified." Witherington argues that the prepositional phrase ἀπὸ πάντων ὧν οὐκ ἠδυνήθητε ἐν νόμῳ Μωϋσέως δικαιωθῆναι suggests that the Mosaic Law brought forgiveness for some sins, but not all. Accordingly, faith in Jesus brings forgiveness for those things from which the law cannot bring forgiveness.[147] Fitzmyer, however, thinks that this is a "misreading of Luke."[148] Haenchen writes, "Anyone who . . . makes the author here develop a doctrine that an incomplete justification through the law is completed by a justification through faith imputes to him a venture into problems which were foreign to him."[149]

In light of the above discussion, it seems best to hold that Paul is affirming that Mosaic Law has lost its function to be a means of justifica-

---

146. Ibid., 491.

147. Witherington, *Acts*, 413. Johnson (*Acts*, 236) writes, "It is not certain whether the phrase 'from all the things which by the Law of Moses' is intended to mean that a) the Law offered forgiveness and righteousness in some cases but not all; or, b) the Law was insufficient as a whole with regard to forgiveness and righteousness."

148. Fitzmyer, *Acts*, 519.

149. Haenchen, *Acts*, 412 n. 4.

tion for all the people. The risen Lord has replaced the role of the Law. Everyone who believes in the risen Lord is justified. There is a contrast between the role of the risen Lord and the role of the Mosaic Law. Paul emphasizes the unique role of the risen Lord in bringing God's salvation, for by his resurrection Jesus has become the sole savior for all people in all time.[150]

The effect of Jesus' death and resurrection is the forgiveness of sins. This is the message that risen Lord commanded his apostles to preach (Luke 24:47). This is faithfully carried out by Jesus' witnesses (Acts 2:38; 5:31;10:43 and 26:18). Paul shows his consistency by preaching the same message. Luke may have borrowed the term "to be justified" from some Pauline letters.[151] The verb δικαιόω is a judicial term. It refers to the declaration of acquittal that a judge renders. Here, it means that God has acquitted or declared innocent of humans so that humanity is now in a right relationship with God. In effect, Luke develops "the theme of forgiveness of sins by incorporating the Pauline terminology of justification."[152] He makes justification almost a form of "forgiveness of sins."[153] Whether he knew of the contrast Paul draws between faith and deeds of the law is not clear. But "he makes Paul declare the inadequacy of the pursuit of uprightness or righteousness in God's sight by performing deeds prescribed by the Mosaic Law."[154]

Paul stresses that the Law of Moses cannot free people from sin. This is similar to Peter's statement in 15:7–11. The prepositional phrases διὰ τούτου, ἐν νόμῳ and ἐν τούτῳ function instrumentally. The demonstratives τούτου and τούτῳ refer to "him" "Jesus." Jesus replaces the Law of Moses, for he is the savior for all who believe in him. He is an eternal savior for both Jews and Gentiles. This is the message of Paul's exhortation: Salvation comes to those who believe in the risen Lord. This salvation is open to all who have faith in him.

---

150. Matera, *New Testament Theology*, 88. He notes that there are two references to Paul's teaching on justification in Acts 13:38–39 and 15:11. They hardly have the theological force and depth of Paul's teaching in Pauline letters. "But they do attest to Luke's understanding that there is no salvation apart from Christ" (p. 88).

151. Pervo (*Acts*, 340 n. 87) writes, "There is almost universal consensus that vv. 38–39 indicate Luke's familiarity with Pauline thought."

152. Barrett, *Acts of the Apostles*, 650.

153. Fitzmyer, *Acts*, 518.

154. Ibid.

3. A Stern Warning from the OT (vv. 40-41)

Following the call to believe in Jesus the Lord so that they may obtain the forgiveness of sins and justification, Paul concludes his sermon with a warning by quoting Hab 1:5. Like the OT prophets, he warns his audience not to reject his proclamation. They must not scoff at God's message.

In the text of Habakkuk, the Lord God rebukes the Israelites because they are behaving as scoffers, refusing to believe in God and his mighty deeds. Consequently, they will perish in the attack of the Chaldeans. They have remained obdurate although they have seen God's mighty deeds in history. Such unbelief is a danger for the Jews in Antioch of Pisidia.[155]

The MT of Hab 1:5 reads בַגּוֹיִם ("among the nations"). The LXX reads καταφρονηταί ("scoffers"). Paul cites the LXX form to warn his audience not to scoff at God's message. The response of being amazed (θαυμάσατε) has been used to characterize an ambivalent response to salvation (2:7; 3:12; 4:13; 7:31).[156] "The careful reader of Acts may well anticipate the uncertain response to Paul's speech and recognize that those who respond to his gospel in 'wonder' (or certainly with 'jealousy') rather than in faith are marked as outsiders to the salvation of God."[157]

The word ἔργον is added for the second time before ὃ οὐ μὴ πιστεύσητε ἐάν τις ἐκδιηγῆται in Acts 13:41. It has been interpreted as "Jesus' resurrection" or what God has fulfilled in Christ by raising him from the dead. The word ἔργον is used in 13:2 to denote the work that the risen Lord has called Paul and Barnabas to accomplish. They are called to preach the fulfillment of the promise that God made with their ancestors by raising Jesus from the dead and making him the savior for all who believe in him. "In effect, Paul is saying to the synagogue audience that they should not spurn the 'word of salvation' now being addressed to them, but should respond to it with faith in Christ."[158] In other words, they must choose "which side of the prophetic cause they will embrace, that of the scornful opponents of Jesus, like those of Jerusalem, or that of the believing disciples, like Paul and associates."[159] If they refuse to believe, they will be destroyed in the coming judgment of God (3:22-23; 4:11-12; 10:42; 17:30-31).

---

155. Peterson, *Acts*, 395.

156. Robert W. Wall, "The Function of LXX Habakkuk 1:5 in the Book of Acts," *BBR* 10 (2000) 252.

157. Ibid.

158. Fitzmyer, *Acts*, 519.

159. Spencer, *Acts* (Sheffield: Sheffield Academic Press, 1997) 146.

IV. CONCLUSION

After being called by the Lord to be his chosen vessel to carry the name of the Lord before Gentiles, kings, and Israelites, Paul begins his mission among his people Israel. He preaches in the synagogue of Damascus (9:20), and later in Jerusalem (9:22). He teaches a large number of people in Antioch of Pisidia for a year (11:26). But no specific content of his preaching is mentioned. Luke only provides his readers summaries such as: Paul proclaims that Jesus is the Son of God (9:20); he proves that Jesus is the Messiah (9:22); or simply he preaches the name of the Lord (9:28). Accordingly, Luke creates an expectation within his readers who are waiting for a more detailed account of Paul's preaching.

During Paul's first missionary journey, Luke mentions that Paul and Barnabas proclaimed the word of God in the synagogue of Salamis (13:5). But he still does not present a detailed account of Paul's preaching. This allows this expectation about the detailed content of Paul's preaching to grow until the dramatic presentation of Paul's sermon in Antioch of Pisidia.

The sermon that Paul delivers at Antioch of Pisidia (13:16–41) is his first full account of his preaching among Jews in Acts. Although there are some previews of Paul's preaching, there is no full scale presentation of it. The sermon in Antioch serves as a keynote speech to inaugurate Paul's preaching. Through this sermon, Luke wants to present what Paul preached earlier in Damascus, Jerusalem, Salamis, and Antioch of Pisidia. This sermon serves as a model of what Paul preached on a regular basis to the diaspora Jews.

Luke not only presents the specific content of what Paul preached earlier, he also presents the main theological themes Paul develops, namely, Jesus is the fulfillment of the promise that God made to David. This speech plays a significant role in Paul's ministry to Israel in Acts. In the next chapter, I will study the significance of this sermon for understanding Paul's ministry to Israel in the rest of Acts.

5

The Significance of Paul's Inaugural Sermon for Understanding His Ministry to Israel

INTRODUCTION

AFTER STUDYING JESUS' AND Peter's inaugural sermons, I concluded that both sermons have significant literary functions in Luke-Acts. Luke presents these sermons as model speeches for Jesus and Peter.

Although Jesus taught in the synagogue before his first public sermon (Luke 4:14–15), Luke does not present the content of his teaching. Jesus' inaugural sermon, however, serves as a model for what Jesus taught in Galilee. After this sermon, Jesus preaches in Capernaum in synagogues on the Sabbath (4:31). People are amazed at his teaching (4:22, 32). Jesus continues to preach in synagogues (6:6; 13:10). Yet Luke does not specify Jesus' teaching. Jesus' inaugural sermon is the model of how he preaches regularly in synagogues. His message is the fulfillment of Israel's scriptures.

In the same way, Peter's inaugural sermon at Pentecost serves as a model of how he preaches to the Jews. Later he continues to bear witness to the Lord. This sermon lays the foundation of his missionary sermons in Acts.

Besides serving as model sermons, the inaugural sermons of Acts serve as an introduction to the main characters of Luke-Acts. Luke brings his main characters onto the stage and has them deliver their first public sermon at the outset of their ministry. Through these sermons, the main characters are put in the spotlight and their ministry is inaugurated.

Jesus' inaugural sermon serves as an illustration of the nature of his ministry: to preach the good news of the kingdom of God to the poor. Luke demonstrates that Jesus fulfills his ministry as presented in his inaugural sermon in the rest of the Gospel. In the same way, Peter's inaugural sermon prepares for his ministry in the rest of Acts: to bear witness to the Lord and to perform signs and wonders in the name of the

Lord. These sermons of Jesus and Peter are programmatic for what each will do in his ministry.

In Chapter Four, I studied Paul's inaugural sermon to the Jews in Antioch of Pisidia (Acts 13:16-41). In light of the literary function of Jesus' and Peter's inaugural sermons, I will now argue that Paul's inaugural sermon functions in a similar way. This inaugural sermon serves as a model of how Paul regularly preached to diaspora Jews. Consequently, it is significant for understanding Paul's ministry to Israel in Acts.

When Paul is understood merely as an apostle to the Gentiles in Acts, there is a danger of viewing him as a rival of Peter who is viewed as the apostle to the Jews. This misconception is clear in the tendency criticism supported by the Tübingen School. Another example of this occurs when Wilckens argues that Paul's inaugural sermon is the turning point of Acts, his last call to the Jews. From this point on, according to Wilckens, Paul abandons his fellow Jews and starts his mission to the Gentiles. This theory, however, can be challenged since Paul continues to preach to Jews in their synagogues after his sermon in Antioch.

In this chapter I will study the significance of Paul's inaugural sermon for understanding his ministry to Israel in Acts. In order to do so, I will review the current research on Paul and his ministry to Israel. Next, I will study the significance of Paul's inaugural sermon for his ministry to Israel from a narrative-critical point of view. In doing so, I will focus on three aspects of Paul's ministry in Acts: Paul's ministry to Israel during his first missionary journey (13:42-14:28); Paul's ministry to Israel during his second and third missionary journeys (15:40-20:38); and Paul the prisoner as a witness to the Lord in Jerusalem, Caesarea, and Rome (21:1-28:31). Finally, I will draw some conclusions regarding Paul's ministry to Israel in Acts.

I. AN OVERVIEW OF CURRENT RESEARCH

According to Joseph B. Tyson, "The contemporary discussion of the understanding of Jews and Judaism in Luke-Acts seems to have been initiated by Jacob Jervell."[1] Jervell challenged the so-called consensus in-

---

1. Joseph B. Tyson, "Jews and Judaism in Luke-Acts: Reading as a God-fearer," *NTS* 41 (1995) 19-38, here 19. Some further studies on the topic of Luke's portrayal of Jews and Judaism are: idem, *Images of Judaism in Luke-Acts* (Columbia, SC: University of South Carolina Press, 1992); Thomas E. Phillips, "Subtlety as Literary Technique in Luke's Characterization of Jews and Judaism," in *Literary Studies in Luke-Acts* (ed.

terpretation with regard to the mission to the Jews that "Luke describes the rejection of the Christian proclamation on the part of the Jewish people. Only after and because Israel has rejected the gospel, and for that reason has itself been rejected, do the missionaries turn to Gentiles."[2] This consensus view has an anti-Jewish tendency inasmuch as it accuses the Israelites of rejecting the gospel and so being rejected by God.

Jack T. Sanders is "the most outspoken proponent of the view that Luke-Acts is an anti-Jewish writing."[3] Sanders writes, "Throughout Luke-Acts, therefore, the hostility of non-Christian Jews towards Christianity and of Jewish Christians towards Gentile Christianity is provoked by the inclusion of Gentiles."[4] In Sanders's view, by emphasizing the connection with Jerusalem, Luke tries to show that a "direct line of continuity runs from Moses and the prophets to the Church."[5] The hostility of the Jews against Christianity because of the inclusion of the Gentiles shows that "it is not Christianity that has rejected Judaism, but Judaism that has rejected Christianity."[6]

Jervell does not agree with this anti-Jewish understanding of Acts. He thinks that "the interplay of mass conversions and opposition from the Jews demonstrates that Israel has not rejected the gospel, but has

---

Richard P. Thompson and Thomas E. Phillips; Macon, GA: Mercer University Press, 1998) 313–26; M. Bachmann, "Die Stephanusepisode (Apg 6,1–8,3): Ihre Bedeutung für die Lukanische Sicht des Jerusalemischen Tempels und des Judentums," in *The Unity of Luke-Acts* (ed. J. Verheyden; BETL 142; Leuven: Leuven University Press, 1999) 545–62; Robert L. Brawley, "Ethical Borderlines between Rejection and Hope: Interpreting the Jews in Luke-Acts," *CTM* 6 (2000) 415–23; G. P. Carras, "Observant Jews in the Story of Luke and Acts: Paul, Jesus, and Other Jews," in *The Unity of Luke-Acts*, 693–708; Jay Eldon Epp, "Anti-Judaic Tendency in the D-Text of Acts: Forty Years of Conversion," in *The Book of Acts as Church History* (ed. Tobias Nicklas and Michael Tilly; BZNW 120; Berlin: Walter de Gruyter, 2003) 111–46; Joachim Jeska, *Die Geschichte Israels in der Sicht des Lukas* (FRLANT 195; Göttingen: Vandenhoeck & Reprecht, 2001).

2. Jacob Jervell, "The Divided People of God: The Restoration of Israel and Salvation for the Gentiles," in *Luke and the People of God: A New Look at Luke-Acts* (Minneapolis: Augsburg, 1979) 41–74, here 41.

3. Tyson, "Jews and Judaism in Luke-Acts," 21.

4. Jack T. Sanders, *The Jews in Luke-Acts* (Philadelphia: Fortress, 1987) 316. See idem, "The Parable of the Pounds and Lucan Anti-Semitism," *TS* 42 (1981) 660–68, here 667; idem, "The Jewish People in Luke-Acts," in *Luke-Acts and the Jewish People: Eight Critical Perspectives* (ed. Joseph B. Tyson; Minneapolis: Augsburg, 1988) 51–75.

5. Ibid., 33.

6. Ibid.

become divided over the issue."⁷ Both Christian Jews and non-Christian Jews claim the heritage of Israel. Both parties claim to be the only true people of God. Christian Jews experienced difficulties because they were accused by non-Christian Jews of abandoning their Jewish heritage. Consequently, some of the Jewish Christians experienced confusions with their Jewish identity and their claim to be loyal Jews. According to Jervell, "In the last decades of the first century many Christian Jews left the church and returned to the synagogue. There was obviously a relapse into Judaism. Luke is writing Acts in order to prevent such a relapse."⁸

Luke tries to prove that Christianity is the true Israel, for the Christians are "law-observant people."⁹ The law is the sign of the people of Israel. There is neither a rejection of Jews as a whole nor a negative view toward Judaism in Acts. Rather, Jervell points to positive attitudes toward Jews and the Jewish religion. Throughout Acts there are reports of mass conversions of Jews.

In repudiating the view that Luke narrates a story of rejection of the Jews and a successful mission to the Gentiles in Acts, Jervell points out that no mission takes place among heathens, for the history of the Gentiles is a history of idolatry in Acts (14:14–18; 17:16). "The Gentiles admitted to the church are the God-fearers, only these are acceptable to God; of these Cornelius is the paradigm (10:34f., further 10:1ff., 22)."¹⁰ Since the 1960s this thesis has been amplified by David Tiede, Donald Juel, Robert Tannehill, Robert Brawley, and David Moessner.

Because there are different understandings of how Luke-Acts views the Jews, there are different understandings of Paul's mission among the Jews. For Jervell, Paul is not depicted in Acts as "the apostle to the Gentiles, but as the apostle to the Jews and to the world, which is to

---

7. Jacob Jervell, *The Theology of the Acts of the Apostles* (New Testament Theology; ed. James D. G. Dunn; Cambridge: Cambridge University Press, 1996) 15. Jervell ("The Divided People of God," 41–74) claims that the Gentile mission originated because of Jewish acceptance of the gospel. See also Gerhard Lohfink, *Die Sammlung Israels. Eine Untersuchung zur lukanischen Ekklesiologie* (StANT 34; München: Kösel-Verlag, 1975) 55; Augustin George, "Israël dans l'oeuvre de Luc," *RB* 75 (1968) 481–525.

8. Ibid., 16. Jervell ("The Church of Jews and Godfearers," in *Luke-Acts and the Jewish People,* 11–20) holds that the Jews and God-fearers (Gentiles sympathizers) constituted the Church community of Luke-Acts. The God-fearers have strong ties to Israel and the Law and are members of the synagogue but are not circumcised. There were no "pure" Gentiles—pagans in the church community in Acts.

9. Ibid.

10. Ibid., 20.

say the Dispersion."[11] Jervell demonstrates that Paul proclaims, from synagogue to synagogue, that Jesus is the promised Messiah, giving evidence of this from the Scriptures. Through Paul's speeches, in which he defends his Jewishness, Luke rejects the accusations that Paul opposed Israel, the law, and the temple (21:28; 24:13–16; 26:22; 28:17).[12] Paul is the teacher of Israel.[13] Accordingly, Luke presents Paul as a missionary to Israel in Acts.

Robert L. Brawley follows a similar line of Jervell when he writes, "Acts presents Paul as completely Jewish and his gospel as complete in Jewish terms over against Jews and Christians who oppose Pauline universalism."[14] He thinks that Luke tries to repudiate Jewish opponents "who seek to influence both Jews and Gentiles by maligning Paul and his message."[15] Tannehill emphasizes that the Jewish people remain a central concern throughout Luke-Acts. Luke depicts Paul as an apostle to both Jews and Gentiles in Acts.[16]

According to Brawley, scholars who do not recognize the Jewish characterization of Paul in Acts fail to read the second half of Acts as "Paul's mission in the diaspora that includes gentiles." Rather, they regard this mission as "Pauline gentile mission *per se*." Accordingly, "Acts has been read as a reflection of Luke's repudiation of the Jews." Furthermore, they fail to recognize that the Lukan portrait of Paul in Acts is "both apologetic and irenic." These points of view are not mutually exclusive. Luke's apparent rejection of the Jews is really "part of his explanation of the Pauline mission among gentiles." Therefore, Paul's attitude is actually "innocuous to genuine Judaism as he understands it."[17]

Robert Maddox approaches the Lukan Paul by focusing on the material in which Luke presents Paul. He divides the Lukan sketch of Paul's

---

11. Ibid., 14.

12. Ibid., 12.

13. Jacob Jervell, "Paul: The Teacher of Israel, the Apologetic Speeches of Paul in Acts," in *Luke and the People of God*, 153–83.

14. Robert L. Brawley, *Luke-Acts and the Jews: Conflict, Apology, and Conciliation* (SBLMS 33; Atlanta, GA: Scholars Press, 1987) 83.

15. Ibid.

16. Robert Tannehill, "The Story of Israel within the Lukan Narrative," in *Jesus and the Heritage of Israel: Luke's Narrative Claim upon Israel's Legacy* (*Luke the Interpreter of Israel*, vol. 1; ed. David P. Moessner; Harrisburg, PA: Trinity Press International, 1999) 325–39, here 329.

17. Brawley, *Luke-Acts and the Jews*, 83.

career after his conversion into three periods. The first period is his missionary work in Cilicia and Syria; the second is his missionary journeys; and the third is his imprisonment in Acts 21–28. Maddox notes, "Luke describes this period of imprisonment at greater length than that of the mission." He continues, "Paul's imprisonment serves as the climax not only of Acts but of Luke's whole work."[18] He concludes that the Lukan community was under serious persecution. In Acts Paul is depicted as the one who is persecuted and suffers. He "stands as a representative and symbol of Christianity."[19] Luke presents Paul as he does to remind his community that all Christians are expected to be persecuted and suffer for the name of the Lord. In Maddox's view, Paul is a witness to suffering.

John Lentz, Jr. argues that the portrayal of Paul as "a loyal Jew" is neither conclusive nor satisfying. He writes, "While the Paul of Acts does indeed point with pride in his strict Jewish upbringing, he also is very proud of his Roman citizenship and his citizenship of the city of Tarsus."[20] Accordingly he approaches the portrayal of Paul in Acts through a socio cultural method. He concludes that "Luke portrayed Paul as a man of high social status and moral virtue."[21] The Lukan Paul has "high credentials" and personifies the man of "classical virtues."[22]

Bruce Malina and Jerome Neyrey, in their book *Portraits of Paul*, use a similar method and conclude that Paul is portrayed as the personification of the social ideal in the first-century Mediterranean cultural matrix.[23] In their *Social-Science Commentary on the Book of Acts*, Malina and Pilch claim that Acts was composed for first-century Jews. "The protagonists of the story are witnesses to what the God of Israel has done in and to Jesus of Nazareth, Israel's Messiah to come. *Messiah* is an exclusively Israelite social role."[24]

---

18. Robert Maddox, *The Purpose of Luke-Acts* (FRLANT 126; Göttingen: Vandenhoeck & Ruprecht, 1982) 76.

19. Ibid., 80.

20. John C. Lentz, Jr., *Luke's Portrait of Paul* (SNTSMS 77; Cambridge: Cambridge University Press, 1993) 1.

21. Ibid., 3.

22. Ibid.

23. Bruce J. Malina and Jerome H. Neyrey, *Portraits of Paul* (Louisville, KY: Westminster John Knox, 1996).

24. Malina and Pilch, *Social-Science Commentary on the Book of Acts*, 7.

On the one hand, the twelve are witnesses to the risen Lord in Judea and Samaria, territories of Israel. Paul, on the other hand, bears witness to the descendants of Israel living in non-Israelite territory, where Israelites are in the minority.[25] "All significant interactions take place within Israelite groups and are about Israelite groups."[26] Therefore, Malina and Pilch conclude that Luke-Acts is about the history of Israel. Paul is a missionary to Israel.

To summarize, since Jervell began to challenge the view that Acts is anti-Jewish, more and more scholars have begun to recognize the Jewish character of Acts and the importance of Paul's mission to Israel. Paul brings the good news to the Jews in the diaspora. He proclaims that Jesus is the fulfillment of God's promise to their ancestors. Luke is not anti-Jewish. Rather, he defends Paul's Jewish identity. From the beginning to the end of his ministry, Paul is a missionary to Israel in Acts.

II. PAUL'S MISSION TO ISRAEL IN ACTS

How does Luke portray Paul's mission in Acts as a whole? To answer this question several commentators approach the issue through narrative criticism; among them are Tannehill, Marguerat, and Flichy.[27] In this section, I will study the material about Paul's mission in Acts by using a narrative-critical method. In doing so, I will focus on Paul's preaching to Israel, especially the significance of his inaugural sermon for his missionary activity among his fellow Jews.

Although Luke presents Paul as a preacher to Jews and Gentiles in Acts, he narrates only three full-length sermons of Paul. They are Paul's sermon to the Jews and God-fearers in 13:16–41, to the Gentiles in Athens in 17:22–41, and to the Christian community leaders in 20:18–35. "These three speeches give us an impression of how Paul responded to three major aspects of his mission."[28]

Before Paul's inaugural sermon, Luke prepares for Paul's ministry by showing his conversion from a persecutor to a preacher of the risen Lord. In the immediate context of his mission to Israel, Luke uses two elements to prepare for Paul's inaugural sermon. They are the prayer

---

25. Ibid., 9.
26. Ibid., 7.
27. Tannehill, *Narrative Unity of Luke-Acts: Acts*; Daniel Marguerat, *La Première Histoire du Christianisme*; Flichy, *La Figure de Paul dans les Actes des Apôtres*.
28. Tannehill, *Narrative Unity of Luke-Acts: Acts*, 164.

and fasting of the Christian community in Antioch and the commission of the Spirit to send Paul on mission (13:2). These are similar to the preparation for Jesus and Peter prior to their inaugural sermons. Luke prepares Jesus' inaugural sermon with the prayer of Jesus and the coming of the Spirit upon him in his baptism (Luke 3:21–22). Peter prayed with the Christian community in Jerusalem and they were filled with the Spirit at Pentecost before Peter's deliverance of his inaugural sermon (Acts 1:13–14; 2:4).

As I have demonstrated in Chapter Four, although Paul preached to the Jews in Damascus, Jerusalem, Antioch, and Salamis, Luke never presents the full content of his preaching there. He gives only summaries or previews of Paul's preaching. In the narration of Paul's mission to the Jews, he creates expectations for readers to know the full content of Paul's preaching. Paul's inaugural sermon is his only fully recorded sermon to Jews in Acts.

Both Jesus' and Peter's inaugural sermons serve as models of how they preach. Jesus' sermon serves as the model of how he preaches in the synagogues of Galilee. Peter's Pentecost sermon serves as a model of his apostolic preaching. In the same way, Paul's inaugural sermon functions as a model of his missionary proclamation to Jews in Acts.[29]

In Jesus' and Peter's inaugural sermons Luke introduces his main characters into the narration. Through Peter's inaugural sermon Luke presents Peter as the leading figure in the first half of Acts. In the same way, it is through this inaugural sermon that Paul becomes the leading character in the second half of Acts. Strauss writes, "Though Luke introduced Paul (Saul) into his narrative in 7.58; 8.1–2 and in the account of his conversion in 9.1–31, it is here that he brings him into the spotlight as the great diaspora missionary and the leading figure in Acts."[30] The three inaugural sermons serve to emphasize the key roles of the three main characters in Luke-Acts: Jesus, Peter, and Paul.[31]

Through this sermon (13:16–41), Paul becomes the key character of Acts and his missionary activity will become the dominant theme in the second half of Acts. This sermon lays the foundation for his preaching to Israel.

29. Barrett, *Acts of the Apostles,* 629; see also Buss, *Missionspredigt,* 17; Tannehill, *Narrative Unity of Luke-Acts: Acts,* 164.

30. Strauss, *Davidic Messiah in Luke-Acts,* 148.

31. Robert Irving Garrett, Jr., "The Inaugural Addresses of Luke-Acts" (Ph.D. diss., The Southern Baptist Theological Seminary, 1980) 267.

In this part, I will study Paul's mission to Israel during his three missionary journeys and his testimony as a prisoner in Jerusalem, Caesarea, and Rome.

A. Paul's Mission to Israel during His First Missionary Journey after His Inaugural Sermon (13:42–14:28)

The Jewish character of Paul's inaugural sermon is clear. This is a sermon delivered by a Jew to a Jewish audience in a Jewish synagogue on a Sabbath day during a Sabbath service. The main part of his sermon concerns the Israelites and God-fearers who are associated with them. After a brief review of the chosen people's history (13:16b–25), Paul focuses on David and the promise of a savior for his descendants (vv. 22–23). This promise is now fulfilled in Jesus' resurrection (vv. 32–33).

There are five characteristics to note in this speech. First, this is a well-crafted speech to Jews. Paul begins by relating himself to his audience. He calls his audience "brothers," noting that they have a common ancestor and history. Second, Paul uses the Scriptures, the written word of God, to achieve his rhetorical purpose. Third, the sermon shows the continuity between Israel and the church community. Fourth, Paul recalls that the God of Israel has promised Israel to set one of David's descendants to succeed him and establish his kingdom forever. God has raised Jesus from the dead and has fulfilled this promise to Israel in Jesus. Everyone who believes in him will find salvation, justification, and forgiveness of sins. Fifth, Paul argues that the Messiah had to suffer and be raised from the dead and that the Messiah is Jesus. What they need to do, therefore, is to have faith in Jesus Christ and open themselves to the grace of God.

1. Paul in Antioch of Pisidia on the Next Sabbath (13:42–52)

Paul's sermon to the Jews in Antioch of Pisidia is initially successful. The immediate reaction of the audience is to urge Paul and Barnabas to speak further on these matters the following Sabbath (13:42). Moreover, many Jews and worshipers who were converts to Judaism followed Paul and Barnabas, who continued speaking to them and urging them to remain faithful to the grace of God (13:42–43). Paul and Barnabas are invited to explain what they have said in greater detail. Luke uses "these subjects" (τὰ ῥήματα ταῦτα) to denote Paul's sermon.[32]

---

32. Bart J. Koet, "Paul and Barnabas in Pisidian Antioch: A Disagreement over the Interpretation of the Scriptures (Acts 13, 42–52)," in *Five Studies on Interpretation*

The present particle προσλαλοῦντες and the imperfect form ἔπειθον describe the continuing process of oral persuasion by Paul and Barnabas (13:43).[33] The content of the sermon is summarized as "the grace of God."[34] Paul has revealed God's grace and made it available to the Jews and the converts to Judaism who have faith in Jesus. "They have been shown both the blessings that flow from the message of grace (13:38, 39) and the dangerous consequences of rejecting it (13:40, 41). Now having received it, they must continue it."[35] They should hold fast to Paul's message about the fulfillment of the promise through the resurrection of Jesus and remain faithful in God's grace.[36]

The initial positive response soon turns to harsh opposition by the Jews, who become jealous when they see that almost the whole city (Gentiles included) gathered to hear the word of the Lord (13:44–45). In this context, "the word of the Lord" is synonymous with "what Paul just delivered" (13:45).

Luke uses the terms "the word of the Lord" and "the word of God" interchangeably (13:44, 46). The two terms refer to the kerygmatic preaching about Jesus the risen Lord, the Messiah (4:31; 6:2; 8:14, 25; 11:1; 13:5, 7, 44, 46, 48; 15:35, 36; 16:32; 18:11; 19:10). The early Christian community is the bearer of the word of God (4:31); the twelve are designated to preach the word of God (6:2); and Paul preaches the message of the savior, the risen Lord, the Messiah promised by God (13:5, 7, 44, 46, 48; 15:35, 36; 16:32; 18:11; 19:10). Luke uses these two terms to connect Paul's preaching with the preaching of the twelve and the Christian community.

Before Paul's inaugural sermon, Luke prepares his readers to hear the specific content of the word of God (13:5, 7). Paul's inaugural sermon is the model for how Paul preaches the word of God to Israel. After Paul's sermon in Antioch, Luke summarizes Paul's preaching as "these

---

of Scripture in Luke-Acts (Studiorum Novi Testamenti Auxilia 14; Leuven: Leuven University Press) 97–118, here 98.

33. Barrett, *Acts of the Apostles*, 654.

34. Tannehill, *Narrative Unity of Luke-Acts: Acts*, 164.

35. Barrettt, *Acts of the Apostles*, 654. Fitzmyer (*Acts*, 520) interprets "the grace of God" as a Pauline teaching. He writes, "The Lucan comment finally introduces a main element of Pauline teaching, the role of divine grace in the process of conversion and justification. Paul urges them to cooperate duly with such divine guidance and assistance."

36. Johnson, *Acts*, 240.

subjects" (τὰ ῥήματα ταῦτα) in 13:42, " the word of the Lord" and "the word of God" in 13:44, 46, or simply "what Paul said" in 13:45. Luke uses these summaries and phrases to recall Paul's sermon to Israel in Antioch. Plümacher notes, "Because Luke has already had Paul give a thorough presentation of the mission kerygma a few verses previously, and because from 13:42 the reader already knows that Paul will merely repeat what he said earlier, Luke has no need to present it again *verbaliter*; the simple reference suffices that Paul does indeed preach (τὰ ὑπὸ Παύλου λαλούμενα ["the words spoken by Paul"], v.45)."[37]

Paul's warning at the end of his sermon is fulfilled (13:41). Many in his audience do not accept his preaching and oppose what he said. Therefore, Paul says to them, "To you, first of all, the word of God had to be proclaimed. Since you reject it and thus judge yourself unworthy of eternal life, we now turn to the Gentiles" (13:46). Eternal life is equivalent to "salvation," and salvation is closely related to the acceptance of "the word of God" in faith. They should accept Paul's sermon about Jesus as the Messiah and have faith in Jesus so that they may have salvation in him. But they refuse.

Paul's announcement that "we now turn to the Gentiles" sounds like a change in his mission: he will turn from Jews to Gentiles. However, this announcement does not mean that Paul will cease preaching to Jews, for as soon as he comes to the next town he starts to preach to the Jews in the synagogue (14:1; 18:4–6, 19; 19:8). Indeed, he preaches to his fellow Jews until the end of his mission (28:31). Paul's announcement to turn to the Gentiles does not mean that his mission to the Gentiles is only an afterthought or a second choice; Paul has been called to preach to Gentiles, kings, and the children of Israel (9:15).

Preaching to the Gentiles is part of God's saving purpose announced in the Scriptures. Here Luke quotes Isa 49:6d and testifies that God has called the Israelites to be a light to bring salvation to all the nations, to the ends of the earth. The preaching of the gospel to the Gentiles is the fulfillment of OT prophecy. Nevertheless, there is a prescribed order in bringing this salvation to the ends of the earth, first to the Jews, then to the Gentiles.[38]

---

37. Eckhard Plümacher, "The Mission Speeches in Acts and Dionysius of Halicarnassus," in *Jesus and the Heritage of Israel*, 251–66, here 254.

38. Robert Tannehill, "Rejection by Jews and Turning to Gentiles: The Pattern of Paul's Mission in Acts" in *Luke-Acts and the Jewish People*, 83–101, here 83–84.

Why is it necessary to preach salvation to the Jews first? The sermon that Paul delivered to the Jews in Antioch provides some clues. The setting and content of the sermon show that this is a sermon given by a Jew to a Jewish audience with regard to God's promise to the Jewish people. In the first part of the sermon, this message was the fulfillment of Israel's history and prophecy.[39] It is the fulfillment of the promise to David that a savior would come from his descendents. This promise is for Israel (13: 23, 26, 31, 33).[40]

The meaning of this messianic promise to Israel (2 Samuel 7) is expressed by the quotation of Isa 55:3 in Acts 13:34. The plural pronoun ὑμῖν in δώσω ὑμῖν τὰ ὅσια Δαυὶδ τὰ πιστά shows that this promise is not a promise to the Messiah but to the Jewish people, the people of Paul's day. Luke affirms that God's promise to the Jewish people is found in Scripture. Tannehill writes, "If God sent the risen Messiah and his blessings to the Jews first, in fulfillment of promises to their ancestors, Paul must speak to the Jews first, as he indicated in 13:46."[41] Therefore, Paul follows the prescribed order. Tannehill writes:

> Paul's preaching reflects a view that characterizes Luke-Acts from its beginning, the view that Jesus is the Davidic Messiah who fulfills specific promises of God to the Jewish people. These promises are found in Scripture, which the narrator accepts as the revelation of God's saving purpose for Israel and the world. However, what happens if the Jews, or at least most of them, reject the gospel? Here we enter difficult terrain for the implied author, who has no clear and easy answers. If one believes in a powerless God, or one prone to easy changes of heart, one could assume that Jewish rejection is the last word and that God's saving purpose for them has no effect. God in Luke-Acts, however, relentlessly works for salvation even by means of human rejection, and Jesus' witnesses, including Paul, proclaim God as one who has chosen Israel and keeps promise with this people.[42]

---

39. Barrett, *Acts of the Apostles*, 656.

40. There is a strong motif of fulfillment of prophecy in Luke-Acts. See Charles H. Talbert, "Excursus A: The Fulfillment of Prophecy in Luke-Acts," in *Reading Luke: A Literary and Theological Commentary* (New York: Crossroad, 1984) 234–40; idem, "Promise and Fulfillment in Lucan Theology," in *Luke-Acts: New Perspective from the Biblical Literature Seminar* (ed. Charles H. Talbert; New York: Crossroad, 1984) 91–103.

41. Tannehill, "Rejection by Jews and Turning to Gentiles," 88.

42. Tannehill, *Narrative Unity of Luke-Acts: Acts*, 174–75.

After the sermon in Antioch, Paul continues to preach to Jews and to almost all the people of the city the next Sabbath day. Luke uses Paul's inaugural sermon as a model to present his preaching on the following Sabbath day. Some believed Paul's preaching, some refused to accept his message. In spite of human rejection, the word of the Lord continues to spread through the whole region. Paul continues to preach to Israel in Acts.

2. Paul's Ministry in Iconium, Lystra, Derbe, and the Rest of His First Missionary Journey (14:1-28)

After Paul and Barnabas were persecuted and expelled from the territory of Antioch, they came to Iconium (13:51). According to their custom, they entered the synagogue of the Jews there. Even though Paul announced that he would turn to the Gentiles (13:46), he continues to go to the synagogue and preach to the Jews during his first visit in Iconium.

The phrase κατὰ τὸ αὐτό is often regarded as having the same meaning as ἐπὶ τὸ αὐτό and is translated "together." There seems no good reason for Luke to stress that the two missionaries enter the synagogue together.[43] The phrase can also be translated "in the same way," i.e., as Barnabas and Paul did in Antioch, so now they do in Iconium.[44] Barrett notes, "It is better to understand Luke's point to be that they followed their custom (cf. 17.2). Their experience in the synagogue at Pisidian Antioch had been a lively one, but it did not lead to a change of policy or tactics."[45] They continue to go to the synagogue to preach to Jews. Luke is presumably thinking of the Sabbath service, when Paul and Barnabas are allowed to speak to a group of Jews.

Paul and Barnabas spoke in such a way that a good number of Jews and Greeks came to believe (17:1). Here οὕτως and ὥστε are used together. The adverb οὕτως means "in this manner, in this way, thus, so, in the same way, like this, with reference to what preceded."[46] The conjunction ὥστε expresses consequence or result. Barrett writes, "Luke no doubt intends his reader to think that, between them, Paul and Barnabas spoke on lines similar to those he ascribed to Paul in the synagogue at

---

43. Barrett, *Acts of the Apostles*, 667.
44. Fitzmyer, *Acts*, 527.
45. Barrett, *Acts of the Apostles*, 667.
46. BDAG, s.v. οὕτως.

Pisidian Antioch (13, 16–41), and with a similar result (13, 42f)."[47] Luke shows that the sermon that Paul delivered to the Jews in Antioch is a model for the sermon that he delivered to the Jews in Iconium. The result of his preaching in Iconium is also similar: an initial success leads to opposition. Yet there is a difference. The opposition in Iconium is from both Greeks and Jews (14:5). They attempted to stone and attack Paul and Barnabas. The city is divided after their preaching.

Paul and Barnabas continued to speak boldly on behalf of the Lord, who confirmed the word about his grace by granting signs and wonders through their hands. These signs confirm the authenticity of their message. This is similar to Peter's preaching and the signs and wonders done through his hand (4:29–30; 5:12).[48] They spoke boldly for the Lord (14:3). Fitzmyer notes that their message is about "the word of his (the Lord's) grace," i.e., "a message of how God's favor manifests itself in Christ and in the preaching about him toward those who are open to it."[49] This is also Luke's summary of the message that Paul delivered to the Jews in Antioch. He summarizes Paul's preaching as a message of "the grace of God" (13:43). Here Luke wants his reader to recall Paul's sermon on God's grace to the Jews in Antioch.

When Paul and Silas realize that they will be attacked by both Jews and Greeks, they flee to Lystra and Derbe and to the surrounding countryside to continue to proclaim the good news (14:6–7). Yet Luke does not mention any specific content of their preaching because he has already presented the specific message in the discourse that Paul delivered to the Jews in Antioch.

Paul's first missionary journey in Acts 13–14 foreshadows his missionary activity in the following chapters. Thus, Luke presents Paul's first missionary journey as a paradigm for his future missions. Many themes noted here will appear again in Paul's future missions. Among them is Paul's missionary strategy of going to the synagogues of the Jews first. After being persecuted by the local communities he flees to another place to continue preaching with boldness. The sermon that he preaches to the Jews in Antioch serves as a model for his preaching to the Jews in the rest of Acts.[50]

---

47. Barrett, *Acts of the Apostles*, 667–68.

48. Susan Marie Praeder, "Jesus-Paul, Peter-Paul, and Jesus-Peter Parallelisms in Luke-Acts: A History of Reader Response," in *Society of Biblical Literature 1984 Seminar Papers* (ed. Kent Harold Richards; Chico, CA: Scholars Press, 1984) 23–39, here 34.

49. Fitzmyer, *Acts*, 527.

50. Edwin Nelson, "Paul's First Missionary Journey as Paradigm: A Literary-Critical

B. Paul's Ministry to Israel during His Second and Third Missionary Journeys (15:40–20:38)

During the Jerusalem council narrated in Acts 15, Paul's and Barnabas's proclamation of the good news was officially approved by the church at Jerusalem. Some days after the council, Paul proposes to Barnabas that they revisit the Christian communities to which they had preached the word of the Lord during their first missionary journey. The towns evangelized during the first missionary journey were Salamis and Paphos in Cyprus (13:4–6), Perga in Pamphylia (13:13; 14:25), Antioch of Pisidia (13:14), Iconium (13:51; 14:1), Lystra (14:6, 8), and Derbe (14:20). At the end of their first missionary journey, they return to Syrian Antioch (14:26).

There is a disagreement between Paul and Barnabas whether or not to bring John Mark with them. Accordingly, Paul and Barnabas separate. Paul chooses new co-workers. First he selects Silas, a leading man of the Jerusalem church (15:22), and Timothy from Lystra, the son of a Jewish mother and a Greek father from one of the communities he visited during his first missionary journey. According to Tannehill, Silas represents support for Paul's mission from Jerusalem and Timothy from the churches founded by Paul and Barnabas, with their mixed Jewish and Gentile membership (14:1).[51]

The second missionary journey resembles the first one. It begins in Syrian Antioch with the support of the local church community. Paul and Silas are commended by the brothers to the grace of the Lord (15:40). This recalls 13:3 and 14:26 which note that Paul's first missionary journey was initiated by the Spirit. In Troas Paul was instructed through a vision to preach to Macedonia (16:10). Thus his mission is to bear witness to the eastern Mediterranean world and bring the good news beyond Asia to Europe.

Paul wanted to bring Timothy with him as a co-worker, but "on account of the Jews of that region, Paul had him circumcised" (16:3). It is surprising to learn that Paul had Timothy circumcised immediately after the decision of the Jerusalem council. But this is not a conflict from Luke's point of view. The reader is expected to take Paul's action as "motivated by prudential considerations."[52] The action is intended to assure

---

Assessment of Acts 13–14" (Ph.D. diss., Boston University, 1982) 70–71, 101–2.

51. Tannehill, *Narrative Unity of Luke-Acts: Acts*, 195.
52. Johnson, *Acts*, 284.

acceptability among the Jews with whom (together with Paul) Timothy will work.⁵³ Fitzmyer further notes that the main reason that Paul circumcised Timothy was so that "Paul would gain in having a circumcised Jewish Christian collaborator when he would be dealing with Jews of the area. Paul is obviously not contravening the decision of the 'Council' (15:10–12)."⁵⁴ The local Jews knew that Timothy was legally a Jew by descent, yet since his Gentile father had probably been dead, the local Jews would wonder whether Timothy had been circumcised on the eighth day. It would cause some trouble if Paul treated him or

presented him as a Jew and Timothy was not circumcised.⁵⁵ This also shows that Paul is not against the Law, or Jewish customs, which prepares for his defense speeches later in the narrative. Accordingly, he accommodates himself to the Jewish customs. Jervell concludes that in Acts, "the main theme is Paul the Jew, the Jewish-Christian Paul. Luke presents him as the Pharisee Paul who remains a Pharisee after his conversion and never becomes an ex-Pharisee."⁵⁶

1. Paul in Philippi (16:11–40)

In Philippi, on the Sabbath, Paul and his companions again look for his fellow Jews. They go outside the city gate along the river where they thought there would be a προσευχή. This word usually means "prayer" in the NT, but it is also used for a "place of prayer." It can sometimes denote a synagogue building. Sometimes it is used as a technical term for a place where Jews gathered to pray (3 Macc 7:20), especially where there were only a few Jews in a city. It is not stated whether the place of prayer in Philippi was a synagogue building. Most probably, it was not a synagogue, for Luke frequently uses συναγωγή for "building" and his choice of προσευχή here may be deliberate.⁵⁷ Here it most likely means a place of prayer.

The reason that Paul and his companions sought a place of prayer on the Sabbath was to find a Jewish community in Philippi in order to

---

53. Ibid.
54. Fitzmyer, *Acts*, 576.
55. Barrett, *Acts of the Apostles*, 761–62.
56. Jacob Jervell, "Paul in the Acts of the Apostles: Tradition, History, Theology," in *The Unknown Paul: Essays on Luke-Acts and Early Christian History* (Minneapolis: Augsburg, 1984) 68–76, here 71.
57. Barrett, *Acts of the Apostles*, 781.

evangelize them. They sat down and engaged in conversation with some women who had gathered there to pray (16:13). Fitzmyer writes, "Some of these women would have been Jewish, or at least sympathizers with Judaism."[58] Luke does not make clear whether it was a synagogue service or not, since only women participated. Luke may want to emphasize the prominent role of women in diaspora synagogue meetings. For Johnson, this story is "a separate encounter on the way to the synagogue (see 16:16), in which Paul takes advantage of a crowd of women on the beach to preach."[59] In any case, Luke shows that Paul tries to preach to the Jews in Philippi as he preached to them in Antioch, Iconium, and other places before. Jervell writes, "Wie auch immer das zu verstehen ist: Es geht auch in Philippi um eine Verkündigung für Juden, also eine Parallele zu den gewöhnlichen Synagogenpredigten der Apg."[60]

Lydia is described as a worshiper of God (σεβομένη τὸν θεόν). The present participle of σέβω is often used as a substantive to denote Gentiles who sympathized with the Jewish religion (10:2; 13:43, 50). Because Lydia was a Jewish sympathizer (God-fearer), she comes to the place of prayer on the Sabbath day. The Lord opens her heart to follow what Paul was saying (16:14). Lydia puts her faith in the gospel preached by Paul.[61] Yet the specific content of Paul's preaching is not mentioned. Here Luke wants to present Paul's preaching as a parallel to his preaching to the Jews and God-fearers in the synagogue of Antioch. Luke has already presented the model speech and his reader can fill in the specific content of Paul's proclamation to the women in Philippi. After Paul and Silas are free from prison, they go to Lydia's house where they see and encourage the brothers (16:40).

2. Paul in Thessalonica (17:1-9)

After leaving Philippi, Paul and his companions go through Amphipolis and Apollonia and arrive in Thessalonica, where there is a Jewish synagogue. Following his usual custom, Paul joins the Jews there, and for three Sabbaths he enters into discussions with them from the Scriptures, expounding and demonstrating that the Messiah had to suffer and rise

---

58. Fitzmyer, *Acts*, 585.
59. Johnson, *Acts*, 292.
60. Jervell, *Apostelgeschichte*, 421.
61. Fitzmyer, *Acts*, 586.

from the dead, and he proclaims, "This is the Messiah, Jesus whom I proclaim to you" (17:1-3).

Acts 17:1 reads ὅπου ἦν συναγωγὴ τῶν Ἰουδαίων. According to Zerwick, ὅπου has a causal sense. Therefore, he concludes that it is because there was no synagogue at Amphipolis or Apollonia that Paul did not stop at those places.[62] This suggests that Paul first goes to the synagogues to preach. Then he moves to other places. Malina and Pilch argue that Paul is not interested in non-Israelites.[63] Rather, he focuses on his mission to Israel in the diaspora. According to Paul's usual practice, he goes to the service of the Jews in Thessalonica (κατὰ δὲ τὸ εἰωθὸς τῷ Παύλῳ εἰσῆλθεν πρὸς αὐτούς). Wherever he goes, Paul goes to the synagogue first. This is his regular practice (13:14, 44; 14:1; 16:13, 16), and he continues to follow it in Beroea (17:10), Athens (17:17), Corinth (18:4), and Ephesus (18:19; 19:8). Luke does not want his reader to lose sight of Paul's preaching to Jews. Johnson recognizes that Luke wants to emphasize "Paul's fundamental commitment to spreading the good news among his own people."[64]

For three Sabbaths Paul conducts discussions with the Jews of Thessalonica about the Scriptures. The subject of his discussions (διελέγετο) concerns what Paul preaches to the Jews (17:17; 18:4, 19; 19:8, 9; 20:9; 24:25). The verb διελέξατο can refer to a philosophical discussion on the basis of the texts of the Torah.[65] Paul discusses the Scriptures. But Luke does not provide his readers with the scriptural passages that Paul used.[66]

In 17:3 Luke presents the gist of Paul's preaching to the Jews. Paul explains and demonstrates from the Scriptures that the Messiah had to (ἔδει) suffer and rise from the dead. As the risen Lord opened the minds of the two disciples on the way to Emmaus to understand the Scriptures that the Messiah would suffer and rise from the dead (Luke 24:45-46), so Paul expounds the meaning of the Scriptures so that the Jews can

---

62. Maximilian Zerwick, *Biblical Greek: Illustrated by Examples* (ed. Joseph Smith; Scripta Pontificii Instituti Biblici 114; Roma: Editrice Pontificio Instituto Biblico, 2001) 69.

63. Malina and Pilch, *Social-Science Commentary on the Book of Acts*, 122.

64. Johnson, *Acts*, 305.

65. Ibid.

66. According to Fitzmyer (*Acts*, 594), this is another instance that Luke presents general Christological interpretation of the OT in terms of Jesus as the Messiah.

understand and accept a Messiah who suffered and rose from the dead. Interpretation of the Scriptures plays a key role in Paul's preaching ministry to Israel (17:2, 11). This emphasis, together with the summary reference to the suffering and resurrection of the Messiah in 17:3, recalls the preaching of Paul in the synagogue of Antioch.[67]

The reader of Acts can suppose that the content of Paul's preaching in Thessalonica is the same or similar to his preaching in Antioch of Pisidia. No detailed speech is necessary in Thessalonica because Paul has already given an explicit demonstration from the Scriptures that Jesus is the Messiah. By his suffering and resurrection, Jesus has fulfilled the promise that God made to the ancestors of the Israelites.

As happened in Antioch of Pisidia, Paul's proclamation of Jesus as the Messiah convinces some of the Jews and a great number of Greeks to join Paul and Silas. The rest of the Jews become jealous and persecute them. Consequently, they are forced to move to Beroea.

3. Paul in Beroea (17:10–15)

As happened in Damascus (9:23–25), Jerusalem (9:30), Antioch of Pisidia (13:50–51), and Lystra (14:20), Paul is forced to make a rapid escape from Thessalonica because his preaching is rejected. When he arrives in Beroea, he and Silas enter the synagogue and proclaim the word of God to the Jews there. Here the Jews are more fair-minded than at Thessalonica, for they receive the word with great enthusiasm, and they accept Paul's preaching about Jesus the Messiah.

Luke uses "the word" (τὸν λόγον) to denote the Christian proclamation of Jesus as the Messiah (17:11). It means "the word of God" preached by Paul (17:13). The Jews there also read the Scriptures each day and examine the texts to see whether these things were so. Here the ταῦτα in εἰ ἔχοι ταῦτα οὕτως means "these things" or "these subjects," the instructions that Paul preached to the Jews there. This situation is similar to the situation in Antioch when Paul was invited to speak on "these subjects" (τὰ ῥήματα ταῦτα) the following Sabbath after he delivered his sermon to the Jews in Antioch (13:42).

The adverb οὕτως here means "so" or "true." It implies that Paul uses the Scriptures to prove that Jesus is the Messiah promised to their ancestors. Here we may suppose Paul employed the text of 2 Samuel 7 and other texts from his speech to the Jews in Antioch. Paul's listeners

---

67. Tannehill, *Narrative Unity of Luke-Acts: Acts*, 206.

The Significance of Paul's Inaugural Sermon 171

examine these texts to see whether they point to Jesus as the Messiah.⁶⁸ As a result, many of the Jews come to believe, as do many of the influential Greek women and not a few men.

"The many" of the Beroean Jews stands in contrast to "some" of the Jews from Thessalonica (17:4). This shows the success of Paul's sermon to the Jews in Beroea. It also shows that a fair-minded reading of the Scriptures will lead Jews to accept Jesus as the Messiah, just as many Jews in Beroea did. Although this alludes to Paul's sermon, Luke does not recount the content of the sermon. He only uses "the word of God" (17:13) to denote the whole Christian message of Jesus as the Messiah, which Paul delivered in full to the Jews in Antioch.

4. Paul in Athens (17:16–34)

Luke does not present any specific proclamation of Paul to the Jews in Athens. He narrates that Paul first goes to the synagogue and debates with the Jews and with the worshipers. He also discusses with whoever happened to be in the public square (17:17). His proclamation focuses on Jesus and his resurrection (17:18). The Lukan reader can suppose that Paul's preaching to the Jews and God-fearers in Athens is along the lines of his preaching to the Jews in Antioch.

In Athens, the capital of the Greek culture, Luke also has Paul deliver a sermon to the Gentiles. This sermon serves as a model for how Paul preaches to the Gentiles in a diaspora setting surrounded by Greek cultures. Although he quotes from Greek writers, he does not neglect to preach Jesus' resurrection (17:31). God has provided confirmation for all by raising Jesus from the dead. He cautions his audience that God has overlooked the time of ignorance, and he invites his audience to repent (17:30). Although Paul does not mention believing in the risen Lord for the forgiveness of sins, it is clear from his preaching in 13:39 that everyone who believes in the Lord is acquitted of sin. Accordingly, there is some connection between Paul's inaugural sermon to the Jews and his sermon to the Gentiles in Athens. Jesus' resurrection is the core of Paul's preaching.

5. Paul in Corinth (18:1–17)

After Athens, Paul travels to Corinth. There he finds Aquila and Priscilla. He stays with them, and later they will travel with him from Corinth to Ephesus (18:18) and play a prominent role in Ephesus when Paul is

---

68. Witherington, *Acts*, 505.

absent (18:26). Every Sabbath Paul enters into discussion in the synagogue, attempting to convince both Jews and Greeks (18:4). Since he is in the synagogue, the Greeks who attend the synagogue must be Jewish sympathizers (God-fearers). As in 17:17, the verb διαλέγομαι refers to Paul's reasoning and debating with his fellow Jews from the Scriptures in a synagogue setting.

In 18:5, when Silas and Timothy come down from Macedonia, Paul begins to occupy himself with preaching the word, testifying to Jews that the Messiah was Jesus. This explains the message of his synagogue discussions (18:4). Tannehill notes, "This summary recalls an important aspect of Paul's message in the Antioch synagogue."[69] His message would have been formulated as in his preaching to the Jews in Antioch, attempting to persuade them to believe that the Davidic Messiah is Jesus, the risen Lord.

The scene of 18:5–7 follows the pattern of events in Antioch, where Paul and Barnabas were reviled and announced that they would turn to the Gentiles (13:44–47). Corinth is the second such scene. The third will be Paul's preaching and turning from the Jews in Rome (28:28).

The second scene in Corinth is parallel to the first scene in Antioch: (1) The Jews reject and revile Paul's preaching; (2) Paul shakes his cloak to protest and announces that he is clear of responsibility for their unbelief. He will now go to the Gentiles. Paul does not neglect to proclaim the good news to his fellow Jews. Because of their unbelief, Paul repeats what he said to the Jews in Antioch: he will go to the Gentiles. Johnson writes that this has the "double function of legitimating the Gentile mission but also asserting God's fidelity to his people; thus this narrative tension which remains unresolved till the end."[70] Paul continues to preach to Israel first in the following narration.

After the announcement to the Jews in Corinth, Paul moves to the house of Titus Justus, a Gentile worshiper of God. The change of location indicates that Paul has shifted his mission from a predominantly synagogue-based mission to the Jews and Gentile God-worshipers to a mission to all the people in the city at large. He settles in Corinth for a year and half and teaches the word of God among them. Luke does not mention what Paul teaches in Corinth. But the reader can suppose that Paul must have preached something similar to his preaching in Antioch.

69. Tannehill, *Narrative Unity of Luke-Acts: Acts*, 222.
70. Johnson, *Acts*, 323.

Next Paul comes to Ephesus. Once again he enters the synagogues and holds discussions with the Jews in 18:19, even though he had announced that he would go to the Gentiles in 18:6. As in Corinth, Paul holds discussions with the Jews in Ephesus, yet no specific content of his discussion is necessary, because Luke has presented a model sermon at the beginning of Paul's first missionary journey in Antioch. Paul finally returns to his missionary base in Syrian Antioch and ends his second missionary journey.

6. Paul in Ephesus (19:1–41)

While Paul is away from Ephesus, a Jew named Apollos arrives there. He is an authority on the Scriptures. Yet he knows only the baptism of John (18:25). He speaks boldly in the synagogue. After being further instructed by Priscilla and Aquila, he vigorously refutes the Jews in public, establishing from the Scriptures that the Messiah is Jesus. For Luke, this shows that the proclamation that the Messiah is Jesus is based on the Scriptures. Besides Paul, then, another authority on the Scriptures bears witness that Jesus is the Messiah.

Paul starts his third missionary journey and arrives in Ephesus. He is informed that the people there received only the baptism of John. Paul instructs them that "John baptized with a baptism of repentance, telling the people to believe in the one who was to come after him, that is, in Jesus" (19:14). This recalls Paul's preaching to the Jews in the synagogue of Antioch. There he preaches, "John heralded his coming by proclaiming a baptism of repentance to all the people of Israel; and as John was completing his course, he would say, 'What do you suppose that I am? I am not he. Behold, one is coming after me; I am not worthy to unfasten the sandals of his feet'" (13:24–25). The baptism of John is mentioned in 1:22 and 10:37. In the cases of Apollos's further instruction and Paul's explanation of John's baptism, Luke is concerned to incorporate such disciples of John into the mainstream Christian fold.[71]

According to his custom, Paul enters the synagogues (9:20; 13:5, 14; 14:1; 17:1, 17; 18:4, 19; 19:8) and boldly debates with persuasive arguments with his fellow Jews. The topic of his preaching in Ephesus is the kingdom of God (19:8), which shows that Paul's proclamation is in continuity with that of Jesus (Luke 4:43; 8:1) and in obedience to Jesus' command to the twelve (Luke 9:2). This theme runs throughout

---

71. Fitzmyer, *Acts*, 637.

Acts. This is the theme concerning which the risen Lord instructed his disciples in Acts 1:3. Paul preaches the kingdom of God in 14:22, 19:8, 20:25, and 28:23. He proclaims the kingdom and teaches about the Lord Jesus Christ (28:31).[72]

The topic of the kingdom of God is one that would appeal to Paul's Jewish audience. In the OT, God is called king. The kingship of God expresses God's spiritual dominion over the whole human being. Fitzmyer writes, "In the NT, it expresses the new way the kingship of God has entered into human experience through Jesus' ministry, passion, death, and resurrection."[73] Jesus the Nazorean plays a key role in the kingdom of God. In the context of Paul's preaching in Ephesus, Paul reveals his preaching about the kingdom of God as "the Way" (19:9). This "Way" is the preaching about Jesus Christ and the kingdom of God. For Luke, as Fitzmyer notes, "the kingdom of God is closely tied to the person of Jesus, especially as the risen Christ, and that is why he depicts Paul so preaching."[74]

In Paul's preaching to the Jews in Antioch, Paul proclaims that God is in full control of Israel's history. God brought up David to Israel as their king on his behalf. Yet the whole of Israel's history moves toward Jesus, for God will give Jesus the benefits that he assured to David in Jesus' resurrection. Thus Jesus is the savior in whom everyone who believes is justified.[75] Jesus, the promised Messiah, has a central role in the kingdom of God.[76]

Luke presents Paul's ministry in Ephesus as the climax of his mission. Paul is able to preach in the synagogue for three months. Later he moves to the lecture hall of Tyrannus and is able to preach for two years, with the result that all the inhabitants of the province of Asia hear

---

72. Charles B. Puskas, *The Conclusion of Luke-Acts: The Significance of Acts 28:16–31* (Eugene, OR: Pickwick Publications, 2009) 112.

73. Fitzmyer, *Acts*, 203.

74. Ibid., 647–48.

75. Hermie C. van Zyl, "The Soteriology of Acts: Restoration to Life," in *Salvation in the New Testament: Perspective on Soteriology* (Supplements to Novum Testamentum 121; ed. Jan G. van der Watt; Leiden/Boston: Brill, 2005) 133–60.

76. I. Howard Marshall, "'Israel' and the Story of Salvation: One Theme in Two Parts," in *Jesus and the Heritage of Israel*, 340–57, here 353. He thinks that the theme of Luke-Acts is the kingdom of God and the risen Lord, the Messiah. The Messiah functions as savior and the kingdom of God as the powerful action of God to save people and establish a community of the saved.

the word of the Lord, Jews and Greeks alike. The detailed content of his preaching is not provided, for the reader already knows it as the kind of proclamation Paul preached in Antioch.

After the riot of silversmiths, Paul encourages the disciples there and sets out on his journey to Macedonia (20:1). As he travels throughout those regions, he provides many words of encouragement for the people there (20:2). This recalls the request of the leaders of the synagogue in Antioch. "My brothers, if one of you has a word of encouragement for the people, please speak." Paul delivers his word of encouragement to the Jews there, and this preaching in Ephesus leads many Jews and Greeks to convert (19:17–18).

To summarize, Luke frequently mentions Paul's teaching in synagogues (9:20; 13:5, 14; 14:1; 17:1–3, 10, 17; 18:4, 19, 26; 19:8) describing it as his normal pattern of evangelism (17:1–2). For Luke the sermon that Paul delivered to the Jews in Antioch of Pisidia represents a model for the message Paul brings to the synagogues of the diaspora.[77]

7. Paul in Miletus (20:18–38)

After leaving Ephesus, Paul and his companions sail to Troas and stay there for a week. In Paul's farewell speech to the presbyters of Ephesus in Miletus (20:18–35), Paul recalls his ministry and foresees his forthcoming imprisonment and hardships. At the same time, he encourages the presbyters to follow his example to be good shepherds to the people who have been entrusted to them.

The term πρεσβύτερος appears in 4:4, 8, 23; 6:12; 23:14; 24:1; 25:15. It refers to the authority figures in the Jewish community. Now it designates the leaders of the Christian community. It is used in this sense in 14:23; 15:2, 4, 6, 22, 23; 16:4; 21:18.[78] How the institution of elders started in the Christian community is unknown. According to Jervell, the first Christian communities probably tried to imitate the institutional system of the Jewish community.[79]

In this speech, Luke presents a review of Paul's mission in Ephesus and a preview of what will happen to him and the Christian community there. In this review of his mission (20:18–21) and situation to his audience (20:22–27), Paul recalls his missionary preaching. He describes it

---

77. Strauss, *Davidic Messiah in Luke-Acts*, 149.
78. Fitzmyer, *Acts*, 482–83.
79. Jervell, *Apostelgeschichte*, 509.

in several ways. He bears witness to "repentance to God and faith in our Lord Jesus" (20:21). He bears witness to "the gospel of the grace of God" (20:24) and he proclaims "the kingdom of God" (20:25). He announces "the whole plan of God" (20:27). Finally, he refers to his preaching as "the word of God's grace" (20:32).

In 20:21 Haenchen says that Luke "presents with extreme condensation the content of the Christian proclamation to the Gentiles and the Jews: Paul has witnessed to the conversion to God in μετάνοια and belief in the κύριος Ἰησοῦς."[80] This is an excellent summary of the topics of Paul's preaching in general: the content of Paul's preaching, according to Zerwick, is to proclaim "conversion to God and faith in Christ, but under one article, so that one may almost understand 'conversion to God by faith in Christ.'"[81] Bock notes that conversion to God "entails faith in Jesus, so that the turning results in one placing trust in what God did through Jesus as one embraces his person and work."[82] Wallace writes that "Luke envisions repentance as the inceptive act of which the entirety may be called πίστις. Thus, for Luke, conversion is not a two-step process, but one step, faith—but the kind of faith that *includes* repentance."[83]

In Paul's missionary speeches to the Jews and the Gentiles, repentance is called for because they do not believe that Jesus is the Messiah who has been raised from the dead. Faith is summed up in acceptance of Jesus' resurrection.[84] This recalls Paul's speech in Antioch (13:16–41). Paul proclaims forgiveness of sins through Jesus Christ. In him everyone who believes is justified (13:39), for it is God who raised Jesus. At the end of the speech in Antioch, Paul warns his audience to have faith in Jesus Christ lest the oracle of the prophet be fulfilled because of their unbelief. Faith in Jesus Christ requires them to turn to God to accept the risen Lord as Messiah. Paul calls for faith in Jesus from the jailer and his household for their salvation (16:31). He invites the Athenians to repent, for God will judge the world through justice through the man that he raised from the dead (17:30–31).

Paul summarizes his preaching as "the gospel of the grace of God" (20:24). This is the only instance in Acts where Luke says that

80. Haenchen, *Acts*, 591.
81. Zerwick, *Biblical Greek*, 60.
82. Bock, *Acts*, 627.
83. Wallace, *Greek Grammar beyond the Basics*, 289.
84. Barrett, *Acts of the Apostle*, 969.

Paul proclaims the "gospel." Fitzmyer holds that the gospel sums up "the Christian message about Jesus Christ, especially as announced to Gentiles."[85] In 15:7, the "word of the gospel" characterizes Peter's preaching to Cornelius. In 15:11, Peter concludes, "We believe that we are saved through the grace of the Lord Jesus, in the same way as they." The "word of the gospel" is a message announcing that "the grace of the Lord Jesus" provides a way for both Jews and Gentiles to share in God's salvation on the same basis.[86] According to Barrett, τῆς χάριτος τοῦ θεοῦ must be taken as a genitive of content. The good news is this: God is gracious to human beings and bestows his unmerited favor upon them.[87]

Paul's proclamation is a gospel of God's grace. This is good news for both Jews and Gentiles, for they are all saved by God's grace through faith in Jesus Christ, for through him there is forgiveness of sins. All believers, Jews and Gentiles, are justified in Jesus Christ by God's grace. Paul calls those who follow him to remain faithful to the grace of God (13:43). Fitzmyer recognizes that Paul's farewell speech here has some allusions to Paul's own letters. He writes, "Luke might well have derived from his Pauline source" to compose this speech. He concludes that Luke "was not wholly unfamiliar with Pauline phraseology."[88]

Jesus' announcement of the good news for the poor and the oppressed is a "gospel of grace" in Luke 4. His message provides the foundation for Paul's preaching of the gospel of grace. The gospel of grace presented in Luke 4:18–19 is also the gospel of God's kingdom in 4:43–44, where Jesus speaks of "preaching the good news of God's kingdom." Jesus brings the good news of God's forgiveness of sins to human beings. This is the good news of the kingdom of God.

Paul does not shrink from announcing the whole plan of God. This plan refers to the saving purpose of God for all the human beings.[89] It is an understanding of God's purpose for world wide salvation. God's whole plan moves into the whole world seeking all. The emphasis is on

85. Fitzmyer, *Acts*, 547.
86. Tannehill, *Narrative Unity of Luke-Acts: Acts*, 256.
87. Barrett, *Acts of the Apostles*, 972.
88. Fitzmyer, *Acts*, 675.
89. Charles H. Talbert, "Once Again: The Gentile Mission in Luke-Acts," in *Reading Luke-Acts in Its Mediterranean Milieu* (Supplements to Novum Testamentum 107; Leiden/Boston: Brill, 2003) 161–73, here 161–65. See also John T. Squires, "The Plan of God in Luke Acts" (Ph.D. diss., Yale University, 1987); Robert Tannehill, "Israel in Luke-Acts," *JBL* 104 (1985) 69–85.

the inclusive scope of Paul's mission. He says, "I earnestly bore witness for both Jews and Greek to repentance before God and to faith in our Lord Jesus" (20:21). It is understandable that there are some Jewish Christian leaders among the presbyters who are present among Paul's audience. Luke presents Paul as a model to the Ephesian presbyters.[90] This is the way in which Luke wants Paul to be remembered, not only by the presbyters, but also by all—Jewish and Gentile Christians.[91]

C. Paul the Prisoner as a Missionary to Israel in Jerusalem, Caesarea, and Rome (21:1–28:31)

Paul has fulfilled his call to carry the name of the Lord to Gentiles and Israelites. Now he needs to preach it to kings as well. Therefore, Paul moves from synagogues to courtrooms to bear witness to the risen Lord.

1. Paul the Prisoner in Jerusalem (21:1–23:22)

When Paul arrives in Jerusalem, he greets James and all the presbyters there. He informs them of what God has accomplished among the Gentiles through his ministry (21:19). He has taught the diaspora Jews among the Gentiles (21:21). The Jerusalemite Jews understand Paul's ministry as a ministry to Jews in the diaspora, which is evident from the accusation against him, which is not about his ministry to Gentiles but to Jews. Clearly, his ministry to the Gentiles is not an issue any more since it has been solved by Peter and the leaders of the Jerusalem Council.

The accusations against him are that "you teach all the Jews among the Gentiles apostasy from Moses, telling them not to circumcise their children or observe their customary practices" (21:21). This is the first time that Paul is informed of charges against him in Jerusalem.

Paul listens to the suggestions of James and the presbyters in Jerusalem. He takes the four men who have taken a vow, purifies himself, and pays their expenses for the shaving of their heads (21:23–24). By doing this, Paul shows that he is a loyal Jew. When seven days are nearly completed, he is charged by the Jews from the province of Asia that he taught everywhere against the people and the law and this place (21:28).

---

90. Charles K. Barrett, "Paul's Address to the Ephesian Elders," in *God's Christ and His People: Studies in Honor of Nils Alstrup Dahl* (ed. Jacob Jervell and Wayne A. Meeks; Oslo-Bergen-Tromsö: Universitetsforlaget, 1977) 107–21, here 119.

91. Fitzmyer, *Acts*, 675.

The Significance of Paul's Inaugural Sermon   179

In short, as Tannehill notes, Paul is accused of being "anti-Jewish, attacking the very foundations of Judaism, the special role of the chosen people, called to live by the law and worship in the Jerusalem temple. The charge refers to Paul's teaching."[92]

In his defense before the Jerusalem Jews, Paul defends his Jewish identity and loyalty.[93] Here there is a parallel between the arrest and trials of Jesus and Paul.[94] This parallel provides an "irresistible apology for Paul." "Paul did not deviate from the life and teachings of Christ, but was in harmony with them."[95] He addresses the assembly in Hebrew as "my brothers and fathers."

Here, Paul deals with the issue of the relationship between loyal Christians and loyal Jews. His hearing before the Sanhedrin in 22:30–23:10 continues to focus on his Jewish identity. He addresses the chief priests and the whole Sanhedrin as "my brothers" (22:30–23:1). He quotes the Scriptures by saying, "For it is written, 'You shall not curse a ruler of your people'" (23:5). In 23:6, Paul is able to clarify the main issue of the accusation against him: he is on trial for his hope in the resurrection of the dead. It has nothing to do with Roman law. Rather, it is a dispute concerning Jewish religion (25:18–19, 25; 26:31–32). Through this redefinition of the real issue of the trial, Paul's personal defense becomes a witness to the risen Lord.

Paul's intension is not apparent here, for he does not speak of Jesus' resurrection but of the hope of the Pharisees: the general resurrection

---

92. Robert C. Tannehill, *The Shape of Luke's Story: Essays on Luke-Acts* (Eugene, OR: Cascade Books, 2005) 241.

93. He was born a Jew and received a strict Jewish education in the law and was zealous for God. Because of his zeal for God, he persecuted the Christians in Damascus. On the journey there, the risen Lord appeared to him, and he was sent to a mission. Ananias, a devout observer of the law and highly spoken of by all the Jews who lived there, came and healed him. It was in the Temple that Paul was commissioned to the mission. Tyson ("Wrestling with and for Paul," in *Contemporary Studies in Acts* [ed. Thomas E. Phillips; Macon, GA: Mercer University Press, 2009] 13–28, here 27) writes, "The characterization of Paul in Acts is internally consistent. He is a loyal Jew, obedient to Torah and faithful to Jewish practices. His message is that Jesus fulfills the words of the Hebrew Prophets: he is the Messiah of Israel."

94. Puskas (*Conclusion of Luke-Acts*, 117) writes, "By comparing the Jewish portrait of Paul with that of Jesus we see that Paul like Jesus: lived according to the law from his youth, preached in synagogues, affirmed the Pharisaic doctrine of resurrection, and used the Jewish Scriptures to explain the necessity of Christ's suffering, death, and resurrection."

95. Ibid., 132.

of the dead (ἀναστάσεως νεκρῶν).⁹⁶ He refers to "hope in the resurrection of the dead" in Acts 23 and 24, using the plural for the "dead." Paul's strategy is to build a basis for common ground with the Pharisees before speaking of Jesus' resurrection.⁹⁷ Fitzmyer writes, "He does this because he has been preaching Christ raised from the dead by the Father (13:30-34; cf. 26:23) and is shrewd enough to realize that he cannot put it just that way. So he makes his claim more generic."⁹⁸ Yet for Luke the resurrection of the dead is not a special doctrine of the Pharisees or an optional element in Judaism. It represents the fulfillment of a promise that is central to Jewish existence and to being the chosen people of God.⁹⁹ Belief in a general resurrection is the link between genuine Judaism and Christianity.¹⁰⁰

2. Paul the Prisoner in Caesarea (23:23-26:32)

Before Felix, Paul's defense (24:9-21) returns to the issue of hope and resurrection. He does not attempt to quote scriptural passages to prove that Jesus is the Messiah. Yet he insists that he serves the God of his ancestors and believes what is written in the law and the prophets, "I have the same hope in God as they themselves have that there will be a resurrection of the righteous and the unrighteous" (24:15). This statement combines the emphasis on Paul's authentic Jewishness with the theme of hope and resurrection.¹⁰¹ Luke shows that there is no contradiction between Judaism and the Christianity that Paul espouses. Both have the same God, the same Scriptures, and the same hope of resurrection.¹⁰² At the end of the defense, Paul recapitulates his argument that he is on trial for his hope in the resurrection of the dead (24:21). He concludes his defense by emphasizing this topic.

The climax of his defense is once again the affirmation of his Pharisaic belief in the resurrection of the dead. He does not mention

---

96. Tannehill, *Shape of Luke's Story*, 244.
97. Ibid., 245.
98. Fitzmyer, *Acts*, 718.
99. Robert J. Kepple, "The Hope of Israel, the Resurrection of the Dead, and Jesus: A Study of Their Relationship in Acts with Particular Regard to the Understanding of Paul's Trial Defense," *JETS* 20 (1977) 231-41, here 240-41.
100. Conzelmann, *Acts*, 192.
101. Tannehill, *Shape of Luke's Story*, 247.
102. Larry D. McCormick, "Paul's Address to Jewish Audiences in the Acts of the Apostles: Luke's Model Witness and his Calling to Testify to 'the Hope of Israel'" (Ph.D. diss., Fordham University, 1996) 270.

specifically the resurrection of Jesus. Yet the reader of Acts understands that "he means the resurrection of Christ, the Lord."[103]

Several days after Paul's defense, Felix has Paul summoned and listens to him speak about faith in Christ Jesus (24:24). Here, Paul's witness shifts his focus from the hope of general resurrection to faith in Christ Jesus, the risen One.

In his recounting to King Agrippa with regard to Paul's case, Festus concludes that the dispute against Paul is about "a certain Jesus who had died but whom Paul claimed was alive" (25:19). Although Luke does not have Paul preach Jesus or his resurrection, now Festus cites that Jesus' resurrection is the core of the accusation against Paul by his fellow Jews.[104] It is understood by the reader that Paul must have preached Jesus' resurrection in his defense speeches. Yet the specific proclamation of Paul's testimony to Jesus' resurrection is not recorded, because Paul has already given a full presentation of the fulfillment of God's promise in the resurrection of Jesus the Messiah in his speech to the Jews in Antioch (13:16–41).

After all of these defenses, Paul stands before King Agrippa to defend his missionary activities and to bear witness to the risen Lord. Paul acknowledges that King Agrippa is an expert in all the Jewish customs and controversies (26:3). Paul states that he is on trial because of his hope in the promise of the resurrection of the dead made by God to their ancestors. The noun and verbal form of hope occurs three times in 26:6–8. Such an emphasis on hope in the resurrection of the dead is not found anywhere in the trials of Paul even in the whole of Luke-Acts. This hope is not only the hope of Paul but also the hope of their ancestors and all the twelve tribes. This is the hope of all Israel.[105]

In 26:22–23 Paul continues that this promise has been fulfilled in the resurrection of the Messiah, who is the first one to be raised from the dead. Fitzmyer notes that, for the most part, Paul recapitulates in his

---

103. Fitzmyer, *Acts*, 732. Kepple ("The Hope of Israel, the Resurrection of the Dead, and Jesus," 240) understands that the resurrection of Jesus is seen as bound up with the general resurrection of the dead. "It probably was obvious to Luke and to those for whom he wrote."

104. McCormick, "Paul's Address to Jewish Audiences in the Acts of the Apostles," 283.

105. Robert F. O'Toole, *Acts 26: The Christological Climax of Paul's Defense (Ac 22:1–26:32)* (AnBib 78; Rome: Biblical Institute, 1978) 89.

defense speeches what Acts has already reported.[106] In Paul's inaugural sermon, he uses the Scriptures to establish that by Jesus' resurrection God has fulfilled his promise to their ancestors.[107]

The passages of 26:6-8, 22-23 are particularly related to 13:32-37. In 13:32-37 the promise to their ancestors is fulfilled in the resurrection of Jesus, whereas in 26:6-8 the promise finds its fulfillment in the resurrection of the dead. The two promises are one and the same, for in 26:23 Paul proclaims the resurrection of the Messiah.[108] Tannehill writes:

> In this Paul's last major reported speech, he is developing a theme from his first major reported speech, the speech in the synagogue of Pisidian Antioch. The theme of the promise to the Jewish people was central in that speech (13:23, 32-33). The promise concerns the Davidic Messiah, but this promise is tied to resurrection because Jesus is established as ruling Messiah through resurrection and his rule is characterized by resurrection of life.[109]

In 13:33 Paul proclaimed that God fulfilled this promise to us, the children of their ancestors, by raising Jesus from the dead.[110] There is a connection between the resurrection of Jesus and their resurrection. In Jesus' resurrection, God has fulfilled his promise made to their ancestors and to them. The Messiah's eternal reign is a result of his resurrection, and others will be freed from corruption to share the benefits of his eternal rule, for the Messiah is the "first of the resurrection of the dead." Tannehill writes, "Thus the hope and promise of which Paul speaks before King Agrippa is not merely a hope for individual life after death but a hope for the Messiah's rule with all its benefits for the Jewish people. This hope is realized through resurrection."[111]

---

106. Fitzmyer, *Acts*, 732.

107. Kepple, "The Hope of Israel, the Resurrection of the Dead, and Jesus," 235.

108. O'Toole, *Acts 26*, 86.

109. Tannehill, *Shape of Luke's Story*, 250.

110. Fitzmyer ("The Use of the Old Testament in Luke-Acts," in *To Advance the Gospel: New Testament Studies* [2nd ed.; The Biblical Resource Series; Grand Rapids, MI: Eerdmans, 1998] 295-313, here 310) writes, "Acts itself turns out to be an account of how Jesus the Messiah fulfills that promise, of how God brings about in a new way that salvation of his people. Luke shows how God has been faithful to his promise, and Jesus becomes the proof incarnate of God's fidelity to the promise made through Moses and the prophets of old."

111. Tannehill, *Shape of Luke's Story*, 250. Kepple ("The Hope of Israel, the Resurrection of the Dead, and Jesus," 240) explains the connections among Paul's

The connection between Paul's first and last major speeches is supported by the repetitions of a complex phrase. Both speeches refer to "the promise made to the fathers" (13:22; 26:6), with both using the verb γίνομαι in the same word order. It is the same promise. Paul's synagogue speech in 13:16–41 makes it clear that it concerns the Davidic Messiah who will bring to the Jewish people all the benefits of his rule. Thus the intense hope that Paul describes in 26:7 is not confined to an individualistic hope for life after death. It is a hope for the Messiah's promised rule, which is established through resurrection and characterized by resurrection life corporately shared. That is why it is so important to Israel.[112]

The proper response to the risen Messiah is to have faith in him (26:18) so that the believers can obtain forgiveness of sins and receive the benefits from the Messiah, the resurrection. Paul concludes his defense by a missionary sermon and invitation in 26:27. He expresses his desire that not only King Agrippa but his whole audiences might share his Christian faith. Tannehill concludes, "The final and climactic defense scene shows Paul continuing his witness to a Jew on the basis of the prophetic promise to the Jewish people, a witness most fully expressed in the synagogue speech in Pisidian Antioch."[113]

3. Paul the Prisoner in Rome (27:1–28:31)

In Paul's defense speeches, he shows that he is a loyal Jew who is innocent as judged by any human authority. He uses the opportunity of his defense to bear witness to the risen Lord to his fellow Jews, Roman rulers, and the Jewish King Agrippa. He testifies that in Jesus' resurrection God has fulfilled his promise to the ancestors. He preaches that Jesus is the first who has been raised from the dead. God is faithful. He will fulfill his promise to all who hope for the resurrection from the dead. During the sea voyage, Paul's deliverance is due to God's divine plan that Paul should go to Rome to bear witness to the Jews there. That he is not

---

preaching about the hope of Israel, the resurrection of Jesus, and general resurrection in his defense speeches. He concludes that there are four beliefs for Jews in Acts. They are: (1) The hope of Israel is closely bound up with the resurrection of the dead; (2) the resurrection of Jesus is prophesied in the law and the prophets and is part of the key messianic promise upon which Israel's hope is based; (3) the resurrection of Jesus is the key fulfillment of the promise; and (4) the resurrection of Jesus is inextricably bound up with the resurrection of the dead.

112. Tannehill, *Shape of Luke's Story*, 250–51.
113. Ibid., 251.

harmed by a snakebite and that his prayers are answered shows that he is deemed not guilty by God (27:1–28:10).[114]

When Paul arrives in Rome, he invites the Jewish leaders and talks with them. This shows his constant strategy of going to the Jews first. His statement in 28:17–20 is a summary of his defense speeches in Acts 22–26. He makes clear that he is innocent of anything worthy of death. The most important point is that he is not hostile toward his own people or against their ancestral customs. It is because of the hope of Israel that he wears these chains (28:20). According to Tannehill, this statement summarizes that "Paul's mission and imprisonment are acts of loyalty to Israel."[115] Luke presents his readers with the scene of Paul's preaching to his fellow Jews in Rome as the final, lasting preaching of Paul. This shows that it is very important for Luke that Paul the prisoner still bears witness to the word of God to the Jews in Rome.

The hope of Israel is explained in 23:6 as hope in "the resurrection of the dead," which Paul regards as the fulfillment of the promise made to their ancestors, now realized in Jesus (24:15; 26:6–7). This reference to the resurrection is central to Jewish existence. According to Luke, this is the essence of Jewish belief. Barrett writes, "This belief is guaranteed and anticipated by the resurrection of Jesus, but the hope is wider than the personal resurrection of the crucified Messiah."[116]

After their initial meetings with Paul, the Jewish leaders arrange for a second meeting. From morning till evening, Paul lays his case before them and keeps bearing witness. His explanation is his last opportunity to bear witness to the risen Lord. Paul's mission is to bear witness, as he carries out the commission of the risen Christ (1:8; 9:19). He keeps bearing witness about the kingdom of God and about the Lord Jesus Christ (28:31). This is a Lukan summary of Paul's witness in Rome.

The kingdom of God is the constant content of the preaching of Jesus (Luke 6:20; 7:28; 8:1; 9:11; 11:20; 12:31–32; 16:16; 17:20–21; 18:29; 19:11; 21:31; 22:30; 23:42; Acts 1:3) and his prophetic representatives (Luke 9:2; 10:9–11; Acts 8:12; 14:22; 19:8; 20:25).[117] Fitzmyer notes, "At this point in Luke's story, the gospel message about the kingdom of God

---

114. Charles H. Talbert and J. H. Hayes, "A Theology of Sea Storms in Luke-Acts," in *Jesus and the Heritage of Israel*, 267–83, here 283.

115. Tannehill, *Shape of Luke's Story*, 345.

116. Barrett, *Acts of the Apostles*, 1240.

117. Johnson, *Acts*, 470.

connotes the good news about the reign and dominion of God over humans beings that is achieved through Jesus Christ (cf. 8:12; 19:8; 20:25)."[118] This understanding is a significant part of several speeches throughout Acts (2:17-36; 3:12-26; 13:32-39).[119]

Paul tries to persuade the Jews in Rome concerning Jesus. Luke uses the verb πείθω (13:43; 18:4; 19:8, 26) to describe Paul's efforts to convince a Jewish audience of the truth of the gospel.[120] In 28:24 he tries to convince the Jews about Jesus. The name "Jesus" is used as a summary term for the life, ministry, passion, death, resurrection, and exaltation of Jesus and his salvation for humanity.[121] Jesus has fulfilled the promises of the Law and the Prophets.[122] Paul tries to persuade his Jewish brothers about Jesus by appealing to their common sacred Scripture. Their Scriptures include the Law of Moses and the Prophets. As he did in 17:2-3; 18:5; 26:22-23 and in his detailed presentation from the Scriptures in his inaugural speech to the Jews in Antioch (13:16-41), here Paul tries to "show the connection of Christianity with Judaism of old. His christological argument is based on Scripture."[123] He testifies that Jesus is the fulfillment of Jewish hope.

After Paul's preaching, the Jewish assembly is divided. The unbelief of some of the audience has been foreseen in Scripture itself (Isa 6:9-10 in Acts 28:26-27). Luke has demonstrated in 28:24 that at least some of the great number of the Jews who came to hear Paul's preaching were attracted to Paul's teaching. In 28:30-31, Luke narrates that Paul's two years of ministry in imprisonment is open to all. Paul continues to preach "the kingdom of God" and "the things concerning the Lord Jesus Christ" as he preached to the Jews according to 28:23.[124] Tannehill concludes, "Paul in Rome continues to preach the themes which he had addressed the Jews, suggesting that Jews are at least included in his audience."[125]

Paul's preaching about "the kingdom of God" and "the Lord Jesus Christ" demonstrates the original Jewish setting of his mission. "The

118. Fitzmyer, *Acts*, 794.
119. Bock, *Acts*, 754.
120. McCormick, "Paul's Address to Jewish Audiences in the Acts of the Apostles," 161.
121. Fitzmyer, *Acts*, 794.
122. Barrett, *Acts of the Apostles*, 1243.
123. Fitzmyer, *Acts*, 794.
124. McCormick, "Paul's Address to Jewish Audiences in the Acts of the Apostles," 184.
125. Tannehill, *Narrative Unity of Luke-Acts: Acts*, 351.

kingdom of God" is a central theme of Jesus' preaching in its Jewish context. In Acts it is also the theme that he primarily addressed to the Jews or to Christian communities (Acts 1:3, 6; 14:22; 19:8; 20:25; 28:23). This is connected with Jesus as the Davidic Messiah. Jesus is presented as the successor to David's throne in Paul's speech to the Jews in Antioch (13:22-23; 32-37). The message of the kingdom of God is connected to the message of Jesus as the Messiah (8:12; 28:23, 31). Here Paul is not preaching about two separate things. He is preaching about the realization of God's kingdom through the enthronement of Jesus at God's right hand as the royal Messiah.[126]

As Hermann Hauser has noted, Paul's preaching about the "kingdom of God" in 28:31 forms an inclusion with 1:3. The topic of "the Lord Jesus Christ" in 28:31 also forms an inclusion with the climax of the Pentecost speech in 2:36 that God has made Jesus both Lord and Messiah.[127] This is the summary of Peter's Pentecost speech. Paul's inaugural speech to the Jews in Antioch (13:16-41) also proclaims that Jesus is the Messiah. Both Dupont and Flichy recognize the similarity between Paul's preaching in Rome (28:23-28) and his preaching in Antioch of Pisidia and afterwards (13:16-49). Flichy writes:

> Les circonstances de cette nouvelle rencontre avec la communauté juive de Rome confirment au lecteur la pertinence du rapprochement avec l'épisode d'Antioche de Pisidie dans deux cas, rendez-vous est pries, pour le sabbat suivant ou au « jour fixé » ; dans les deux cas, les juifs viennent en plus grand nombre; l'unité de lieu suggérée dans le cas de las synagogue d'Antioche, est explicitement rappelée ici. Le parallè le ainsi souligné entre les deux épisodes accentue pour le lecteur le caractère crucial de cette rencontre : il peut annoncer soit la répétition soit le renversement du scénario connu du lecteur.[128]

Dupont thinks that Paul's sermon in the Antioch synagogue gives an idea of the content of Paul's preaching to the Roman Jews at the end of Acts, which is briefly summarized in 28:23. He writes, "Le long discourse de 13, 16-39 donne une idée de ce que Luc peut avoir dans la tête

---

126. Ibid., 351-52.

127. Hermann Hauser, *Strukturen der Abschlusserzählung der Apostelgeschichte (Apg 28, 16-31)* (AnBib 86; Rome: Biblical Institute, 1979) 118.

128. Flichy, *La Figure de Paul dans les Actes des Apôtres*, 308.

quand, en 28, 23, il résume en deux mots le contenu d'une prédication qui a duré « depuis le matin jusqu'au soir »."[129]

At the end of Acts, Paul is presented as a faithful preacher to the Jews about Jesus the Messiah. He faithfully bears witness to Jews and Gentiles about what the risen Lord commissioned him to do (9:15; 22:15; 26:16–18).

In Acts 28:23 Paul bears witness and tries to convince the Roman Jews concerning the Messiah "from early morning till evening." Puskas notes that this phrase underscores "the remarkable persistency of Paul's witness to the Roman Jews." Paul preaches to the Jews from the Law of Moses and the prophets. This latter phrase, according to Puskas, emphasizes, "the thoroughness of Paul's witness to the Roman Jews." He further notes that in 28:31, the term μετὰ πάσης παρρησίας is "linked with the hapaxlegomenon ἀκωλύτως to qualify the manner and extent of Paul's witness at Rome: boldly and unhindered."[130] He concludes that this conveys the final triumph of the good news of Jesus Christ "over various religious, racial, and political obstacles."[131]

To summarize, after Paul delivers his inaugural sermon to the Jews in Antioch, he continues to bear witness to the risen Lord during his first, second, and third missionary journeys. Wherever he goes he seeks the Jews first and preaches the good news to them. His inaugural sermon serves as a model speech for his preaching to diaspora Jews. After Paul's missionary journeys, Paul goes to Jerusalem, where he is accused of not being a loyal Jew in his preaching to the Jews. Paul then starts his defense speeches here. His audience is made up of Jews, Jewish leaders, the Jewish King Agrippa, and Roman leaders. His defense speeches become opportunities for Paul to preach to his fellow Jews. He testifies that he is a faithful Jew who recognizes God's fulfillment of his promise to their ancestors in Jesus' resurrection and argues that he suffers for the hope of Israel: the resurrection of the dead. Paul continues on to Rome. Finally he reaches Rome and from morning to evening he bears witness to the risen Lord to the Roman Jews from the Scriptures.

---

129. Dupont, "La Conclusion des Actes, " 487.

130. Puskas, *Conclusion of Luke-Acts,* 111. See further studies by Dupont ("La Conclusion des Actes et Son Rapport à L'Ensemble de L'Ouvrage de Luc," in *Nouvelles Etudes sur les Actes des Apôtres,* 457–511); Daniel Marguerat, "The Enigma of the Silent Closing of Acts (28:16–31)," in *Jesus and the Heritage of Israel,* 284–304.

131. Ibid., 113.

III. CONCLUSION

Paul is often regarded as a rival of Peter and as the great apostle to the Gentiles. Many commentators interpret Paul's mission as announcing a rejection of the Jews and the bringing of the good news to the Gentiles. Consequently, Paul is considered anti-Jewish. In this chapter, I have tried to show that this is a misunderstanding of Paul and his ministry in Acts.

I have employed a narrative-critical method to focus on the study of the significance of Paul's inaugural sermon to the Jews in Antioch in order to understand his mission to Israel in Acts. It is clear that in Acts Luke provides a model sermon of Paul for his preaching to Israel. This sermon serves as a model of how Paul preached to the Jews before his preaching to the Jews in Antioch and how he will continue to preach to the Jews after this inaugural speech. After this sermon is presented, Paul goes to synagogues to preach to Jews, yet no full discourses are recorded. Luke only narrates summaries and phrases of Paul's preaching to Jews.

Through Paul's inaugural sermon, Luke brings his main character in the second half of Acts into the spotlight. Paul becomes the central figure in Acts. This keynote speech identifies the character of Paul and his mission. That is, he proclaims that God has brought fulfillment for them the promises he made to their ancestors by raising Jesus from the dead (13:32–33). Luke places this sermon at the outset of Paul's first missionary journey. He does this to show that Paul's mission to his fellow Jews plays a significant role in his mission.

Paul's inaugural sermon demonstrates that he has become a keen interpreter of Scripture and proclaims the fulfillment of the promises made to the ancestors in Jesus' resurrection from the Scriptures. This sermon presents the main themes that Paul will preach in his mission to Israel in the rest of Acts.

Paul's inaugural sermon and the narrative around it provide the model of his ministry: he first goes to the synagogue to seek out his fellow Jews and Gentile sympathizers. Then he preaches to them. After Luke presents Paul's inaugural sermon to the Jews, he does not present the full content of his preaching in detail. He only presents summaries or brief phrases of Paul's preaching. It is not necessary to present the full content of his preaching any more, for Paul's inaugural sermon serves as a model of his preaching to the Jews. After his preaching to the Jews, the audience is divided. Some believe in his preaching and some reject it. Those who reject Paul's message persecute him, but he escapes from one place and moves to another. Still he goes first to synagogues to Jews to persuade them from the Scriptures that Jesus is the Messiah, who comes to fulfill God's promise in his resurrection.

Luke wants to emphasize that from the beginning Paul is a missionary to his fellow Jews in Damascus, Jerusalem, Antioch of Pisidia, and Salamis. The place where he first preaches is a synagogue or place of prayer of diaspora Jews. During Paul's three missionary journeys, he preached to his fellow Jews in Antioch, Iconium, Lystra, Derbe, Philippi, Thessalonica, Beroea, Athens, Corinth, and Ephesus. Even in the Greek cultural center Athens, Luke never loses his emphasis on Paul's mission to Israel, for Paul first preaches to the Jews in the synagogue in Athens. Furthermore, in his preaching to the Gentiles there, Paul emphasizes the Jewish concept of the resurrection of the Messiah. In Miletus Paul delivers his farewell speech to Christian leaders. Surely some in his audience are Jewish Christian leaders. He summarizes his preaching in Jewish concepts, like the gospel of the grace of God and the kingdom of God.

In his preaching Paul argues from the Scriptures that Jesus is the fulfillment of the promises that God made to their ancestors. He is the promised Messiah, the Lord and savior. His preaching is Jewish in nature. Paul's mission is to persuade his fellow Jews that Jesus is the Davidic Messiah.

As a result of being a missionary to the Jews among the Gentiles, Paul's mission to the Gentiles is not a problem for his fellow Jews. Rather, he is accused of not being a loyal Jew. In his defense speeches, Paul argues that he is a loyal Jew who preaches faithfully to his fellow Jews. He emphasizes that he proclaims the fulfillment of the promise God made to their ancestors in Jesus' resurrection.

Paul's defense speeches are his opportunity to bear witness to his fellow Jews. He bears witness to the risen Lord before the Jerusalem Jews (22:3–21), the Sanhedrin (23:1, 3, 5–6), and Jewish King Agrippa (26:2–23, 25–27, 29). Finally, as a prisoner he continues to bear witness to the risen Lord in Rome (28:17–20, 23). Luke presents his reader with a last image of Paul preaching to all, Jews and Gentiles alike, in Rome (28:30–31).

Although Paul announces in Antioch of Pisidia, Corinth, and Rome that he will turn from his fellow Jews to go to Gentiles, he continues to go to Jewish synagogues first to preach to his fellow Jews. In Paul's missionary activities, he faithfully fulfills the mission that the risen Lord gave him:

to be his chosen vessel to carry his name to the Gentiles, kings, and the children of Israel. Paul is a missionary to Israel as well as to Gentiles.

6

Conclusion

INTRODUCTION

THIS DISSERTATION WAS DESIGNED to investigate the significance of Paul's inaugural sermon to the Jews in Antioch of Pisidia (Acts 13:14–41) in order to understand the literary function of this sermon and his ministry among Jews according to the Acts of the Apostles. I have argued that Paul's inaugural speech functions as a model for the kind of speech that he would have regularly delivered to Jews. Consequently, this speech provides an important clue for understanding Paul's ministry among his fellow Jews in Acts. Based on my research, I have concluded that Luke portrays Paul as a missionary to Jews as well as to Gentiles.

In this conclusion, I will first summarize how I developed my dissertation. Next, I will summarize Paul's ministry to Israel in Acts. Finally, I will highlight the contributions and implications of this study.

I. GENERAL CONCLUSION

I developed my research in the following way. In the first chapter, I began with a brief history of research on Acts, the speeches in Acts, and Paul's speech in Acts 13:14–41. I concluded that although some commentators hold that the speeches have a historical basis today, since the seminal studies of Dibelius more and more scholars think that the speeches were composed by Luke who used some stories or legends about the preaching of Peter and Paul. Luke was the final redactor and consequently the speeches express his theological and missionary aims. The historicity of the speeches in Acts, therefore, has been called into question by recent scholarship.

Dibelius recognized the literary function of the speeches, and he thought that they were used to illustrate the significance of the events in the narrative. Following a similar line, Soards concluded that the speeches had the literary function of unifying the diverse and incoherent narratives in Acts.

Most exegetes have focused on the literary unity of Paul's speech to the Jews in Antioch, or they have compared this speech with Stephen's speech or Peter's speech at Pentecost. However, there has not been a thorough and comprehensive narrative study of this speech in relation to Paul's missionary activity among Jews, according to Acts. Consequently, there was need to investigate further the literary function of this speech with regard to the narrative of Paul's mission to Israel in Acts and how this speech unifies his missionary activities in Acts.

Paul's speech to the Jews in Antioch is his inaugural speech. In addition to this speech, there are two other inaugural speeches in Luke-Acts. They are Jesus' inaugural speech in Luke 4:16–30 and Peter's inaugural speech in Acts 2:14–40. In order to understand the literary function of Paul's inaugural speech in relation to his missionary activity in Acts, I studied the literary functions of Jesus' and Peter's inaugural speeches to learn if they shed any light on the literary function of Paul's inaugural sermon for understanding his missionary activity in Acts.

In the second chapter, I studied Jesus' inaugural sermon. I concluded that this sermon has a significant literary function in Luke-Acts. Luke uses Jesus' sermon to introduce Jesus, his ministry, and his message. This sermon serves as a keynote speech to set the program for Jesus' ministry in the Gospel. Luke unfolds the program detailed in this speech in the rest of the narrative. This sermon also serves as a model for Jesus' teaching in the Jewish synagogues in Galilee and throughout Judea. Furthermore, this sermon announces many of the themes that Luke will explore further in Luke-Acts. Luke sets Jesus' inaugural sermon at the outset of his ministry as an interpretive key to guide his reader through the rest of the narrative.

Employing a similar method, in the third chapter I studied Peter's inaugural sermon to the Jews in Jerusalem at Pentecost. I concluded that this inaugural sermon has a significant literary function in Acts. Through this sermon, Luke introduces Peter, the main character of the first half of Acts. Luke presents Peter as a keen interpreter of Scripture. He proclaims from the Scriptures that Jesus is Lord and Messiah. His

Conclusion 193

mission is to bear witness to the risen Lord, to proclaim repentance for the forgiveness of sins, and faith in the name of the Lord. This sermon serves as a model for apostolic preaching to Jews. It is programmatic for Peter's mission in Acts and serves as a preview of the main themes that Luke will develop later.

At the end of the third chapter, I drew a brief conclusion about the literary function of Jesus' and Peter's inaugural speeches. I found that both speeches have a parallel literary function. Both introduce Jesus and Peter in Luke-Acts. Both foreshadow the ministries of Jesus and Peter, and both announce the main themes that Luke will explore in the rest of Luke-Acts. Since there is a parallel between Jesus' and Peter's inaugural sermons with regard to their literary functions for understanding Jesus' and Peter's ministries in Luke-Acts, I concluded that Paul's inaugural sermon may have a similar literary function for understanding his ministry in Acts.

In the fourth chapter, I exegeted Paul's inaugural sermon to the Jews in Antioch. The literary context of the sermon prepares for the sermon. Luke narrates how the risen Lord transformed Saul the persecutor to Paul the preacher of the risen Lord. After being called to be a chosen vessel by the Lord, Paul begins to preach in Damascus, Jerusalem, and Salamis, but the full content of his preaching is not yet presented. I noted that Luke reserves the presentation of the full content of Paul's preaching for his inaugural speech to the Jews in Antioch of Pisidia.

With Paul's inaugural sermon, Luke brings Paul to center stage. Paul proclaims that God fulfilled his promise to David by raising Jesus from the dead. He emphasizes the motif of fulfillment and proclaims that by his resurrection Jesus brings salvation to all who believe in him.

In the fifth chapter, I studied the literary function of Paul's inaugural sermon and its significance for understanding his ministry to Israel in Acts. In light of my study of the literary function of Jesus' and Peter's inaugural sermons, I found that there is a close relationship between Paul's inaugural speech and the narration of his ministry to Jews in Acts. Luke places Paul's inaugural sermon at the outset of his first missionary journey to show that this sermon plays a significant role in Paul's ministry to Jews. He uses this sermon to emphasize the character of Paul's mission among Jews in Acts, that is, Paul is called to proclaim the fulfillment of the promise that God made to Israel's ancestors through the resurrection of Jesus. Paul's inaugural speech also serves as a model for his preaching to Jews in Acts.

After Paul's inaugural sermon at Antioch, he continues to preach to Jews in synagogues in the rest of the narrative. However, the full content of Paul's preaching to Jews is never again presented since Luke understands Paul's inaugural sermon as the model for how Paul regularly preaches to Jews in Acts. However, Luke does use some phrases, terms, and summaries in order to recall Paul's inaugural sermon to the Jews in Antioch. This sermon functions as the golden thread that connects the different narratives of Paul's ministry among Jews.

To summarize, Paul's inaugural sermon is programmatic for his ministry in Acts. It presents a model of how Paul regularly preaches the theme of fulfillment from the Scriptures to Jews. This theme of fulfillment runs throughout the narrative of Paul's mission to Jews in Acts.

II. SPECIFIC CONCLUSIONS

Paul's inaugural sermon to the Jews in Antioch is significant for understanding his ministry in Acts since this is a model speech of how he preaches to Jews according to Acts. Luke shows that Paul's ministry to his fellow Jews is a significant part of Acts: Paul is a missionary to his fellow Jews as well as to Gentiles.

The beginning of Acts presents Paul as a zealous Jew. He consents to Stephen's death. He wants to expand the persecution of Christians to communities beyond Jerusalem. His persecution of the Christians shows his zeal as a loyal and orthodox Jew.

After the risen Lord appears to Paul on the road to Damascus and calls him to bear witness to him, Paul begins to proclaim Jesus to Jews in the synagogues of Damascus. He grows all the stronger and confounds the Jews there, proving that Jesus is the Messiah. In Luke's view, from the very beginning of his ministry Paul is a missionary to his fellow Jews.

Paul first preaches to Jews in Damascus and Jerusalem. Yet the full content of his preaching is not specified, and he remains a minor figure in the narrative. The whole narrative of Paul's preaching among Jews prepares for his inaugural sermon to the Jews in Antioch. Up to this point, the reader has been wondering about the full content of what Paul preached to Jews in Damascus and Jerusalem. Luke thereby creates an expectation among his readers who wait to hear the full content of Paul's preaching. Paul delivers a complete sermon to Jews in a synagogue setting at the outset of his first public missionary journey. This sermon provides readers with a fuller insight to the content of the sermons that Paul delivered in Damascus and Jerusalem.

Through this inaugural sermon, Paul becomes the main character of the second half of Acts. Like Peter he becomes a keen interpreter of Scripture. By this inaugural speech, Paul helps his fellow Israelites to understand their history and argues from the Scriptures that God has fulfilled his promise by raising Jesus from the dead.

After Paul's inaugural speech, he regularly goes to synagogues first and preaches to his fellow Jews since the synagogue is the place where Paul can find a Jewish audience. He preaches to Jews in Antioch, Iconium, Lystra, Derbe, Philippi, Thessalonica, Beroea, Athens, Corinth, and Ephesus. His inaugural sermon serves as the model for how he preached to the Jews in those places. According to Acts, Paul did not neglect his mission to the Jews.

In this inaugural speech, Paul announces that his ministry to Jews is to proclaim from the Scriptures the fulfillment of God's promise to Israel in Jesus' resurrection (13:32–33). Later, Luke narrates that Paul proclaims from the Scriptures that Jesus is the Messiah. He talks to his fellow Jews about the Messiah, expounding from the Scriptures and demonstrating that Jesus is the Messiah. At Rome, he tries to persuade the Jews about Jesus from the Law of Moses and the Prophets. The Scriptural passages quoted in Paul's inaugural sermon serve as the foundation for how he regularly argues from the Scriptures that Jesus is the Messiah. Throughout the narrative, Luke demonstrates how Paul fulfills his ministry, which was announced in his inaugural speech (13:32-33).

Paul's inaugural sermon forms the pattern of his ministry to Israel in Acts. His usual custom is to go to a synagogue or a place of prayer first in order to seek out his fellow Jews. He then preaches to them from the Scriptures, arguing that Jesus is the Messiah who has fulfilled the promise that God made to their ancestors. After his preaching, the audience is often divided over his preaching. Some Jews and Gentiles believe in his preaching. Others, however, are jealous and persecute Paul and his companions. Paul and his companions are then forced to move to another place. Despite this opposition, they go to synagogues and preach to Jews. This pattern runs throughout the narrative of Paul's mission among Jews in Acts.

Although the main focus of Paul's ministry is to his fellow Jews, he also preaches to God-fearers in synagogue settings. The God-fearers were Gentiles who were sympathetic to Judaism. It was among this group that Paul had his greatest success. These God-fearers probably formed the bridge group between Judaism and Gentiles.

Even in the Greek cultural center of Athens, Paul follows his usual custom of first preaching to his fellow Jews. Next he moves to a public place and then preaches to the Gentiles at the Areopagus. Paul focuses on Jesus and his resurrection in his preaching there. The theme of Jesus' resurrection is the main theme of Paul's preaching to Jews and Gentiles. This theme is closely related to Paul's inaugural speech in Antioch. After Paul's preaching to the Gentiles at the Areopagus, the audience is divided over his preaching. Some reject his preaching, and some accept it. This pattern is similar to what happens when Paul preaches to Jewish audiences.

Paul delivers his farewell speech to the presbyters of the church at Miletus. Some of them were probably Jewish Christians. He summarizes his preaching in Jewish terms such as "the kingdom of God" and "the word of God's grace." He emphasizes that he has announced the whole plan of God, for he has earnestly born witness to both Jews and Greeks. He has faithfully preached God's message to all. He has not forgotten his fellow Jews in his ministry.

In his defense speeches, Paul the zealous Jew, a persecutor of the Christian community in the beginning of the narrative, is persecuted for not being a loyal Jew. His defense speeches become opportunities for him to bear witness to the risen Lord. Paul proclaims that Jesus is the first to have been raised from the dead. Consequently, Jesus' resurrection is the hope of Israel, for the general resurrection of the dead has already begun in the resurrection of Israel's Messiah. Accordingly, Paul testifies to this hope of Israel, the resurrection of the dead. He does not quote any specific Scriptural passages in these speeches. But the idea is that the reader understands that Paul must have quoted Scriptural passages similar to those in his inaugural speech in order to persuade the Jewish leaders, King Agrippa, and the Jewish audience to believe in Jesus as the Messiah who fulfilled the promises to David when he was raised from the dead. In him Israel finds its hope in the general resurrection of the dead.

Conclusion

In the narrative of Acts, Paul begins his ministry to his fellow Jews in the synagogue of Damascus, after his call by the Lord. He remains a Jew and proclaims to his fellow Jews the fulfillment of God's promise to their ancestors in Jesus' resurrection. This promise is to the Jewish people, and Jesus' resurrection is the fulfillment of Israel's Scripture. Accordingly, Paul preaches that Jesus is Israel's promised Messiah, Lord, and Savior. The content of Paul's preaching is thoroughly Jewish in nature. This is why it is Paul's usual custom to go to synagogues or places of prayer to seek out his fellow Jews first and to preach to them. Paul faithfully preaches to his fellow Jews until the end of Acts.

In the narrative of Acts, however, Paul announces that he will turn from his fellow Jews to Gentiles (13:46; 18:6; 28:28) three times. These announcements serve two purposes.

The first purpose of the announcement is that Paul, as a prophet to Israel, warns his fellow Israelites to heed his message about Jesus the Messiah. Therefore, they should listen to his preaching, repent, and believe in the name of the Lord. These announcements do not mean, however, that Paul will abandon his fellow Jews; for as soon as Paul announces at Antioch (13:46) that he will go to Gentiles, he continues to go to the synagogue in Iconium and preach to Jews and Greeks (God-fearers) there (14:1), since he has a responsibility to preach to his fellow Israelites (18:6). When he recalls his ministry, he concludes that he has preached the whole plan of God to both Jews and Gentiles (20:26–27).

The second purpose of the announcement is to explain the phenomenon of Paul's universal mission among Jews and Gentiles. In the narrative of Acts, there is a movement of Paul's mission from a mission directed solely to his fellow Jews in the synagogues to his preaching to all, Jews and Gentiles alike. After Paul's inaugural speech, he preaches to the whole city of Antioch on the following Sabbath (13:44). In Athens, after preaching to Jews, he preaches to all in the public square (17:16–17). After leaving the synagogue in Corinth, Paul moves to the home of Titus Justus next to the synagogue (18:7). In Ephesus, after preaching in the synagogue, he moves to the lecture hall of Tyrannus and holds discussions with all. As a result of this, all of the inhabitants of the province of Asia hear the word of the Lord, Jews and Greeks alike. At the end of Acts, Paul preaches to the Jews in Rome and later to all who come to him (28:30–31). According to Acts, Paul is a missionary to his fellow Jews.

He does not abandon them. Rather, he chooses them as the first group to whom he brings God's salvation.

To summarize, in Luke's view Paul is a missionary to his fellow Jews as well as to Gentiles. There is a prescribed order in Paul's ministry. He is a Jew who bears witness to his fellow Jews about the fulfillment of God's promise to David in Jesus' resurrection. At the same time, he understands the universal aspect of the salvation brought by the risen Lord. He also preaches to Gentiles. Yet, according to Acts, his primary audience is composed of Jews and Gentile sympathizers of Judaism (God-fearers). Cornelius is the model of a Gentile sympathizer in Peter's ministry. Similarly, Luke mentions several God-fearers in Paul's ministry, e.g., Lydia in Philippi (16:14), Titus Justus in Corinth (18:7). It seems that Paul had some success with this group of God-fearers. He does not show favoritism to Gentiles according to Acts. They too could become divided over Paul's preaching. Luke depicts Paul as a chosen vessel of the Lord who is a missionary to his fellow Jews as well as to Gentiles.

III. CONTRIBUTIONS AND IMPLICATIONS

My research contributes to Lukan scholarship in two ways. First, I have presented a comprehensive study of the relationship between Paul's inaugural sermon and his ministry among Jews in Acts from a narrative-critical point of view. In doing so, I have shown the literary function of Paul's inaugural speech in relation to his missionary activity among Jews according to Acts: how Paul's inaugural sermon functions as a model speech that he preached to the Jews in synagogues, how his sermon functions as an introduction to Paul and his ministry, how his sermon illustrates the characteristics of his ministry among Jews, how it functions as an interpretative key to guide the reader through the narrative of Paul's missionary activity among his fellow Jews, and how this sermon unifies the different narratives of Paul's missionary career among Jews according to Acts.

Second, this study contributes to our understanding of the relationship of Paul and Judaism. Ever since the tendency-criticism of the Tübingen School, Lukan scholarship has been influenced by the thesis that Paul is a rival of Peter. Accordingly, Paul has been seen as an apostle solely to Gentiles in Acts. According to this thesis, he rejects his fellow Jews and preaches to Gentiles. Jacob Jervell has challenged this thesis, and I have tried to demonstrate that Paul is not anti-Jewish. He remains a faithful Jew who proclaims from the Scriptures to his fellow Jews the fulfillment of God's promise to David in Jesus' resurrection. If this is so, Acts is not an anti-Jewish document.

This study has two implications for the study of Acts. First, this presentation of Paul as a missionary to Jews as well as to Gentiles suggests that Acts may be of more historical value than is often thought. Luke presents Paul as a loyal Jew who is zealous for Judaism. After being commissioned by the Spirit, he delivers his inaugural sermon. He then goes to Asia Minor and Greece to bear witness to the Lord. Since he is a Jew, his message is about the Jewish Messiah. He goes to synagogues and places of prayer to seek out fellow Jews and preach to them. Accordingly, Luke presents Paul as a Jewish missionary. The narrative of Acts, then, gives an irenic presentation of how Paul lives his life as a faithful Jew and missionary to Jews and Gentiles. He faithfully carries out the mission for which the risen Lord commissioned him.

Luke presents a consistent portrait of a Jewish Paul. This presentation of Paul in Acts may also shed some light on what Jacob Jervell calls the "unknown Paul" of the Pauline letters.

When exegetes try to organize a chronology of Paul's life, they claim that the Pauline letters are their primary source and Acts their secondary source. But it is necessary to remember that the Pauline letters are occasional writings for the purpose of answering specific questions for specific communities in specific situations. According to Jervell, they present a polemical, fragmentary, and inconsistent portrait of Paul and his theology. Because of the nature of the letters of Paul, it is difficult to pin down a consistent historical Paul. Consequently, there is an "unknown Paul" hidden in his letters.

Luke, however, presents a portrait of Paul in Acts that complements what is in the shadows of the Pauline letters: Paul is a law-observant Jew who is called to preach to his fellow Jews and Gentiles. He lives his life as a Jewish Christian, and he fulfills his call to be a missionary to Jews and Gentiles alike (9:15). Sometimes there are some informational notes about Paul in the Pauline letters that are in the marginal notes or in the shadows. Luke gives them more light and presents them in a clearer way in Acts. In 1 Cor 9:9–11, for example, Paul writes that he lived as a pious Jew. In Acts, where Paul is presented as a loyal Jew, this aspect is given more light. The main purpose of Paul's defense speeches is to show that he lived as a pious Jew. In Romans 9–11, Paul presents a reflection on the role of Jews in Israel's history. He concludes that Israel has a special role in salvation history. God has not abandoned Israel. In Acts, Luke presents Paul as a missionary who brings salvation to his fellow Israelites first. He goes from synagogue to synagogue to preach to them. The information about Paul's life and ministry in Acts and his letters suggests that Acts may have more historical value than some exegetes realize. The historical value of Acts needs to be studied further.

Second, this study has implications for understanding Gentiles in Acts. There is no favoritism toward Gentiles in Acts. Paul preaches to both Jews and Gentiles. Yet he preaches mostly to Gentile sympathizers. According to Acts, Paul has his greatest success when preaching to Gentile sympathizers (God-fearers). In his inaugural sermon, he preaches to Jews and God-fearers. He continues to preach to these two groups throughout his missionary career. It is likely that these God-fearers formed a bridge between the Jews and the non-God-fearing Gentiles.

The scope of Paul's mission in Acts is universal in Luke's view, and Paul's speech at the Areopagus serves as a model speech for how he regularly preached to Gentiles. According to Acts, Paul first preaches to his fellow Jews and God-fearers, then to all, which includes Gentiles. The significance and literary function of these God-fearers in Acts needs further study.

The Gentile mission is not a problem in the second half of Acts. This issue has been solved in the Jerusalem Council. Rather, Paul is accused by his fellow Jews of not being a loyal Jew. He is accused of teaching Jews to abandon Moses, circumcision, and their customary practices (21:21). This accusation suggests that there were significant Jewish concerns in the Lukan Christian community. These Christians want to make sure that they are the faithful heirs of Judaism who understand the fulfillment of God's promise in Jesus' resurrection. Their concern about being faithful to Judaism implies that some Christians may have relapsed to Judaism because they thought that Christianity betrayed Judaism or some Christians were accused by some non-Christian Jews of not being loyal to Judaism. The accusation against Paul for not being faithful to Judaism suggests that the Jewish influence on Christians probably became stronger in the development of Christianity, at least in the Lukan Christian community.

To summarize, in this dissertation I have investigated the relationship of Paul's inaugural sermon and his ministry among the Jews in the

Acts of the Apostles from a narrative-critical point of view. I have concluded that Paul's inaugural sermon has a significant literary function for understanding his ministry among Jews. This is the model speech that he preached to his fellow Jews wherever he preached to them. It unifies the different narratives of Paul's ministry among Jews in Acts. Through this inaugural sermon and its related narratives, Luke demonstrates that Paul is a missionary to both Jews and Gentiles in the Acts of the Apostles.

Bibliography

Achtemeier, Paul J. "An Elusive Unity: Paul, Acts, and the Early Church." *CBQ* 48 (1986) 1-26.

Alexander, Loveday A. *Acts in Its Ancient Literary Context: A Classicist Looks at the Acts of the Apostles*. Edited by John M. G. Barclay. Library of New Testament Studies 298. New York / London: T & T Clark, 2005.

———. "Fact, Fiction and Genres of Acts." *NTS* 44 (1998) 380-99.

———. "The Preface to Acts and the Historians." In *History, Literature, and Society in the Book of Acts*, edited by Ben Witherington III, 73-103. Cambridge: Cambridge University Press, 1996.

Anderson, Hugh. "Broadening Horizons: The Rejection at Nazareth Pericope of Luke 4:16-30 in Light of Recent Critical Trends." *Int* 18 (1964) 259-75.

Anderson, Kevin L. *"But God Raised Him from the Dead": The Theology of Jesus' Resurrection in Luke-Acts*. Paternoster Biblical Monographs. Grand Rapids: Paternoster, 2006.

Aletti, Jean-Noël. "Jésus à Nazareth (Lc 4, 16-30): Prophétie Écriture et Typologie." In *À Cause de L'Évangile: Études sur Synoptiques et les Actes Offertes au P. Jacques Dupont, O. S. B. à l'Occasion de son 70e Anniversaire*, 431-51. LD 123. Paris: Publications de Saint-André, Cerf, 1985.

———. *Il Racconto come Teologia: Studio Narrativo nel terzo Vangelo e del Libro degli Atti degli Apostoli*. Collana Biblica. Rome: Editions Dehoniane, 1996.

———. *Quand Luc Raconte: Le Récit comme Théologie*. Lire la Bible 114. Paris: Cerf, 1998.

Arnold, Bill T. "Luke's Characterizing Use of the Old Testament in the Book of Acts." In *History, Literature, and Society in the Book of Acts*, edited by Ben Witherington III, 300-23. Cambridge: Cambridge University Press, 1996.

Atkinson, Kenneth. "On Further Defining the First-Century CE Synagogue: Fact or Fiction?" *NTS* 43 (1997) 491-502.

Baarlink, Heinrich. "Die Bedeutung der Prophetenzitate in Lk 4,18-19 und Apg 2,17-21 für das Doppelwerk des Lukas." In *The Unity of Luke-Acts*, edited by J. Verheyden, 483-91. BETL 142. Leuven: Leuven University Press, 1999.

Bachmann, Michael. "Die Stephanusepisode (Apg 6,1-8,3): Ihre Bedeutung für dieLukanische Sicht des Jerusalemischen Tempels und des Judentums." In *The Unity of Luke-Acts*, edited by J. Verheyden, 545-62. BETL 142. Leuven: Leuven University Press, 1999.

Bajard, Jean. "La Structure de la Péricope de Nazareth en Lc IV, 16-30." *ETL* 45 (1969) 165-71.

Baker, Murray. "Paul and the Salvation of Israel: Paul's Ministry, the Motif of Jealousy,and Israel's Yes." *CBQ* 67 (2005) 469-84.

Barbi, Augusto. "The Use and Meaning of (Hoi) Ioudaioi in Acts." In *Luke and Acts*, edited by Gerald O'Collins and Gilberto Marconi, translated by Matthew J. O'Connell, 32–47. Mahwah, NJ: Paulist, 1993.

Barclay, John M. G. "Paul among Diaspora Jews: Anomaly or Apostate?" *JSNT* 60 (1995) 89–120.

Barr, Beth Allison, et al., eds. *The Acts of the Apostles: Four Centuries of Baptist Interpretation*. Waco, TX: Baylor University Press, 2009.

Barrett, Charles K. *The Acts of the Apostles. A Shorter Commentary*. Edinburgh/New York: T&T Clark, 2002.

———. *A Critical and Exegetical Commentary on the Acts of the Apostles*. ICC. 2 vols. New York: T & T Clark, 1994.

———. *The New Testament Background: Selected Documents*. London: SPCK, 1987.

———. "Paul's Address to the Ephesian Elders." In *God's Christ and His People: Studies in Honour of Nils Alstrup Dahl*, edited by Jacob Jervell and Wayne A. Meeks, 107–21. Oslo-Bergen-Tromsö: Universitetsforlaget, 1977.

———. "Old Testament History According to Stephen and Paul." In *Studien zum Text und zur Ethik des Neun Testaments: Festschrift zum 80. Geburtstag von Heinrich Greeven*, edited by Wolfgang Schrage, 57–69. BZNW 47. Berlin: Walter de Gruyter, 1986.

Bassler, Jouette M. "Luke and Paul on Impartiality." *Bib* 66 (1985) 546–52.

Bauckham, Richard. "Kerygmatic Summaries in the Speeches of Acts." In *History, Literature, and Society in the Book of Acts*, edited by Ben Witherington III, 185–217. Cambridge: Cambridge University Press, 1996.

———, ed. *The Book of Acts in Its Palestinian Setting*. Vol. 4 of BAFCS. Grand Rapids: Eerdmans, 1995.

Béchard, Dean P. "The Disputed Case Against Paul: A Redaction-Critical Analysis of Acts 21:27—22:29." *CBQ* 65 (2001) 84–101.

———. *Paul outside the Walls: A Study of Luke's Socio-Geographical Universalism in Acts 14:8-20*. AnBib143. Rome: Editrice Pontificio Istituto Biblico, 2000.

Benéitez, M. *"Esta salvación de Dios" (Hech 28,28). Análisis narrativo estructuralista de "Hechos."* Publicaciones de la Universidad Pontificia Comillas de Madrid. Estudios 35. Madrid: UPCM, 1986.

Berder, Michel, ed. *Les Actes des Apôtres : Histoire, Récit, Théologie XXe Congrès de L'Association Catholique Française pour L'É tude de la Bibble (Angers, 2003)*. ACFEB. LD 199. Paris: Cerf, 2005.

Betz, Otto. "The Kerygma of Luke." *Int* 22 (1968) 131–46.

Beuken, W. A. M. "Isa. 55, 3–5: The Reinterpretation of David." *Bijdr* 35 (1975) 49–64.

Billerbeck, Paul. "Ein Synagogengottesdienst in Jesu Tagen." *ZNW* 55 (1965) 143–61.

Blomberg, Craig L. "The Christian and the Law of Moses." In *Witness to the Gospel: The Theology of Acts*, edited by I. Howard Marshall and David Peterson, 397–416. Grand Rapids: Eerdmans. 1998.

———. "The Law in Luke–Acts." *JSNT* 22 (1984) 53–80.

Bock, Darrell L. *Acts*. BECNT. Grand Rapids: Baker, 2007.

———. "Jesus as Lord in Acts and in the Gospel Message." *BSac* 143 (1986) 146–54.

———. *Luke 1:1—9:50*. ECNT 3A. Grand Rapids: Baker, 1994.

———. *Proclamation from Prophecy and Pattern: Lucan Old Testament Christology*. JSNTSup 12. Sheffield: Sheffield Academic, 1987.

Boismard, M.-É., and A. Lamouille. *Les Actes des Deux Apôtres*. 3 vols. EBid 12–14. Paris: Gabalda, 1990.
Bossuyt, Philippe. *L'Esprit en Actes: Lire les Actes des Apôtres*. Le Livre et le Rouleau 3. Bruxelles: Éditions Lessius, 1998.
Bottini, G. C., *Introduzione all'Opera di Luca: Aspetti Teologici*. Studium Biblicum Franciscanum Analecta 35. Jerusalem: Franciscan Printing Press, 1992.
Bovon, François. *Luke 1: A Commentary on the Gospel of Luke 1:1—9:50*. Hermeneia. Translated by Christine M. Thomas. Minneapolis: Fortress, 2002.
———. *Luke the Theologian: Fifty-five Years of Research (1950-2005)*. 2d rev. ed. Waco, TX: Baylor University Press, 2006.
———. *L'Oeuvre de Luc: Études d'Exégèse et de Théologie*. LD 130. Paris: Cerf, 1987.
———. "Studies in Luke–Acts: Retrospect and Prospect." *HTR* 85 (1992) 175–96.
Bowker, Jan W. "Speeches in Acts: A Study in Proem and Yelammedenu Form." *NTS* 14 (1967) 96–111.
Brawley, Robert L. *Centering on God: Method and Message in Luke–Acts*. Literary Currents in Biblical Interpretation. Louisville: Westminster/Knox, 1990.
———. "Ethical Borderlines between Rejection and Hope: Interpreting the Jews in Luke–Acts." *CTM* 6 (2000) 415–23.
———. "The God of Promises and the Jews in Luke–Acts." In *Literary Studies in Luke–Acts*, edited by Richard P. Thompson and Thomas E. Phillips, 279–96. Macon, GA: Mercer University Press, 1998.
———. "The Identity of Jesus in Luke 4:16–30 and the Program of Luke–Acts." In *Luke–Acts and the Jews: Conflict, Apology, and Conciliation*, 6–27. SBLMS 33. Atlanta: Scholars Press, 1987.
———. *Luke–Acts and the Jews: Conflict, Apology, and Conciliation*. SBLMS 33. Atlanta: Scholars Press, 1987.
———. "Paul in Acts: Lucan Apology and Conciliation." In *Luke–Acts: New Perspective from the Biblical Literature Seminar*, edited by Charles H. Talbert, 129–47. New York: Crossroad, 1984.
———. *Text to Text Pours Forth Speech: Voices of Scripture in Luke–Acts*. Bloomington: Indiana University Press, 1995.
Brown, Raymond E. *The Churches the Apostles Left Behind*. Mahwah, NJ: Paulist, 1984.
———. "Not Jewish Christianity and Gentile Christianity but Types of Jewish/Gentile Christianity." *CBQ* 45 (1985) 74–79.
Bruce, Fredrick F. *The Acts of the Apostles: the Greek Text with Introduction and Commentary*. 3d ed. Grand Rapids: Eerdmans, 1990.
———. *The Book of the Acts*. NICNT. Rev. ed. Grand Rapids: Eerdmans, 1988.
Bultmann, Rudolf. ἀφίημι, *TDNT* 1 510–11.
Bunine, Alexis. "Paul: «Apôtre des Gentils» ou . . . «des Juifs d'abord, puis des Grecs»?" *ETL* 82 (2006) 35–68
———. "Paul, Jacques, Félix, Festus et les Autres: Pour une Revision de la Chronologie des Derniers Procurateurs de Palestine." *RB* 111 (2004) 387–408.
———. *Une Légende Tenace: Le Retour de Paul à Antioche après sa Mission en Macédoine et en Grèce (Actes 18,18—19,1)*. Cahiers de la Revue Biblique 52. Paris: Gabalda, 2002.
Buss, Matthäus F. J. *Die Missionspredigt des Apostels Paulus im Pisidischen Antiochien:Analyse von Apg 13,16–41 im Hinblick auf die literarische und thematische Einheit der Paulusrede*. FB 38. Stuttgart: Katholisches Bibelwerk, 1980.

Busse, Ulrich. *Das Nazareth-Manifest Jesu: Eine Einführung in das lukanische Jesusbild nach Lk 4,16-30*. SBS 91. Stuttgart: Katholisches Bibelwerk, 1977.
Cadbury, Henry J. *The Making of Luke-Acts*. London: SPCK, 1958.
———. *The Book of Acts in History*. New York: Harpers, 1955.
Campbell, Douglas. "Paul in Pamphylia (Acts 13.13-14a; 14.24b-26): A Critical Note." *NTS* 46 (2000) 595-602.
Caquot, André. "Les «Graces de David»: A Propos d'Isaie 55/3b." *Sem* 35 (1965) 45-59.
Carras, G. P. "Observant Jews in the Story of Luke and Acts: Paul, Jesus, and Other Jews." In *The Unity of Luke-Acts*, edited by J. Verheyden, 693-708. BETL 142. Leuven: Leuven University Press, 1999.
Carroll, John T. "Luke's Portrayal of the Pharisees." *CBQ* 50 (1988) 604-21.
———. *Response to the End of History: Eschatology and Situation in Luke-Acts*. SBLDS 92. Atlanta: Scholars Press, 1988.
Cazeaux, Jacques. *Les Actes des Apôtres: L'Église entre le Martyre d'Étienne et la Mission de Paul*. LD. Paris: Cerf, 2008.
Chance, J. Bradley. *Jerusalem, the Temple, and the New Age in Luke-Acts*. Macon, GA: Mercer University Press, 1988.
Cifrak, M. *Die Beziehung zwischen Jesus und Gott nach den Petrusreden der Apostelgeschichte. Ein exegetischer Beitrag zur Christologie der Apostelgeschichte*. FB 101. Würzburg: Echter, 2003.
Clark, A. C. *Parallel Lives: The Relation of Paul to the Apostles in the Lucan Perspective*. Paternoster Biblical and Theological Monographs. Carlisle, UK: Paternoster, 2001.
Combrink, H. J. B. "The Structure and Significance of Luke 4:16-30." *Neot* 7 (1973) 24-48.
Conroy, Charles. "Methodological Reflections on Recent Studies of the Naaman Pericope (2 Kings 5): Some Background to Luke 4:27." In *Luke and Acts*, translated by Matthew J. O'Connell, edited by Gerald O'Collins and Gilberto Marconi, 32-47. Mahwah, NJ: Paulist. 1993
Conzelmann, Hans. *Acts of the Apostles: A Commentary on the Acts of the Apostles*. Translated by James Limburg, A. Thomas Kraabel and Donald H. Juel. Hermenia. Philadelphia: Fortress, 1987.
———. *Theology of St. Luke*. Translated by Geoffrey Buswell. Philadelphia: Fortress, 1982.
Cook, Michael J. "The Mission to the Jews in Acts: Unraveling Luke's 'Myth of the Myriad.'" In *Luke-Acts and the Jewish People: Eight Critical Perspectives*, edited by Joseph B. Tyson, 102-23. Minneapolis: Augsburg, 1988.
De Boer, Martinus C. "God-fearers in Luke-Acts." In *Luke's Literary Achievement: Collected Essays*, edited by Christopher M. Tuckett, 50-71. JSNTSup 116. Sheffield: Sheffield Academic Press, 1995.
Culy, Martin M., and M. C. Parsons. *Acts: A Handbook on the Greek Text*. Waco, TX: Baylor University Press, 2003.
Dahl, Nils Alstrup. *Jesus in the Memory of the Early Church: Essays by Nils Alstrup Dahl*. Minneapolis: Augsburg, 1976.
Darr, John A. *On Character Building: The Reader and the Rhetoric of Characterization in Luke-Acts*. Literary Currents in Biblical Interpretation. Louisville: Westminster/ Knox, 1992.
Davies, Alan, ed. *Antisemitism and the Foundations of Christianity*. New York / Ramsey / Toronto: Paulist, 1979.

Del Agua, Agustín. "The Lucan Narrative of the 'Evangelization of the Kingdom of God': A Contribution to the Unity of Luke-Acts." In *The Unity of Luke-Acts*, edited by J. Verheyden, 639-61. BETL 142. Leuven: Leuven University Press, 1999.

Denova, Rebecca I. *The Things Accomplished among Us: Prophetic Tradition in the Structural Pattern of Luke-Acts*. JSNTSup 141. Sheffield: Sheffield Academic Press, 1997.

Deutschmann, Anton. *Synagoge und Gemeindebildung: Christliche Gemeinde und Israel am Beispiel von Apg 13, 42-52*. Biblische Untersuchungen 30. Regensburg:Friedrich Pustet, 2001.

DeSilva, David A. "Paul's Sermon in Antioch of Pisidia." *BSac* 151 (1994) 32-49.

Dibelius, Martin. *The Book of Acts: Form, Style, and Theology*. Edited by K. C. Hanson. Minneapolis: Fortress, 2004.

———. "Stilkritsches zur Apostelgeschichte." In *Aufsätze zur Apostelgeschichte*, edited by Heinrich Greeven, 9-28. Göttingen: Vandenhoeck & Reprecht, 1968.

Dillon, Richard J. "Acts of the Apostles." In NJBC, edited by Raymond E. Brown et al., 722-67. Englewood Cliffs, NJ: Prentice Hall, 1990.

———. *From Eye-Witnesses to Ministers of the Word: Tradition and Composition in Luke 24*. Rome: Biblical Institute, 1978.

———. "The Prophecy of Christ and His Witnesses According to the Discourses of Acts." *NTS* 32 (1986) 544-56.

Dionne, Christian. *La Bonne Nouvelle de Dieu: Une Analyse de la Figure Narrative deDieu dans les Discours Pétriniens d'Évangélisation des Actes des Apôtres*. LD 195. Paris: Cerf, 2004.

Dodd, Charles H. *The Apostolic Preaching and its Development*. New York: Harper & Brothers, 1962.

Doeve, Jan W. *Jewish Hermeneutics in the Synoptic Gospels and Acts*. Assen: Van Gorcum, 1953.

Downs, David J. "Freedom from the Law in Luke-Acts." *JSNT* 26 (1986) 49-52.

Dumais, Marcel. "Les Actes des Apôtres: Bilan et Orientations." In *«De Bien des Manière», La Rechercher Biblique aux Abords du XXIe Siècle*, edited by Michel Gourgues et Léo Laberge. LD 163. 307-64. Montréal-Paris: Fides/Cerf 1995.

———. *Communauté et Mission: Une Lecture des Actes des Apôtres*. Montreal: Bellarmin, 2000.

———. *Le Langage de l'évangélisation: L'Annonce Missionaire en milieu juif (Actes 13, 16-41)*. Tournai/Paris: Desclée; Montréal: Bellarmin, 1976.

Dunn, James D. G. *The Acts of the Apostles*. Valley Forge: Trinity International, 1996.

Dupont, Jacques. "La Conclusion des Actes et Son Rapport à L'Ensemble de L'Ouvrage de Luc." In *Nouvelles Etudes sur les Actes des Apôtres*, 457-511. LD 118. Paris: Cerf, 1984.

———. "Les Discours Missionnaires des Actes des Apôtres: d'après un ouvrage récent." In *Études sur les Actes des Apôtres*, 133-55. Paris: Cerf, 1967.

———. "The First Christian Pentecost." In *The Salvation of the Gentiles*, translated by John R. Keating, 35-59. New York: Paulist, 1979.

———. "La Portée Christologique de L'Évangélisation des Nations." In *Nouvelles Études sur Les Actes des Apôtres*, 37-57. LD 118. Paris: Cerf, 1984.

———. "Repentir et Conversion d'après les Actes des Apôtres." In *Études sur les Actes des Apôtres*, 421-57. LD 45. Paris: Cerf, 1967.

———. "The Salvation of the Gentiles and the Theological Significance of Acts." In *The Salvation of the Gentiles*, translated by John R. Keating, 11–33. New York / Ramsey / Toronto: Paulist, 1979.

———. "ΤΑ ΌΣΙΑ ΔΑΥΙΔ ΤΑ ΠΙΣΤΑ." In *Études sur les Actes des Apôtres*, 337–65. LD 45. Paris: Cerf, 1967.

———. *Teologia della Chiesa negli Atti degli Apostoli*. Studi biblici 10. Bologna: Dehoniane, 1984.

Eckey, Wilfried. *Die Apostelgeschichte: Der Weg des Evangeliums von Jerusalem nach Rom*. 2 vols. Neukirchen-Vluyn: Neukirchener, 2000.

Eisen, Ute E. Rainer Riesner and Daneil Marguerat. "Wie historisch ist die Apostelgeschichte? Rainer Riesner vs. Daniel Marguerat. " *ZNW* 18 (2006) 37–51.

Elbert, Paul. "An Observation on Luke's Composition and Narrative Style of Questions." *CBQ* 66 (2004) 98–109.

Ellul, Danielle. "Antioche de Pisidie: Une Prédication... trois Credos? (Actes 13,13–43)." *FilolNT* 5 (1992) 3–14.

Epp, Eldon J. "Anti-Judaic Tendency in the D-Text of Acts: Forty Years of Conversion." In *The Book of Acts as Church History*, edited by Tobias Nicklas and Michael Tilly, 111–46. BZNW 120. Berlin: Walter de Gruyter, 2003.

———. "The 'Ignorance Motif' in Acts and Anti-Judaic Tendencies in Codex Bezae." *HTR* 55 (1962) 51–62.

Evans, Craig A. "The Twelve Thrones of Israel: Scripture and Politics in Luke 22:24–30." In *Luke and Scripture: The Function of Sacred Tradition in Luke-Acts*, edited by Craig A. Evans and James A. Sanders, 154–70. Minneapolis: Fortress, 1993.

Fearghail, Fearghus. "Rejection in Nazareth: LK 4:22." *ZNW* 75 (1984) 60–72.

Finn, Thomas M. "The God-fearers Reconsidered." *CBQ* 47 (1985) 75–84.

Fitzmyer, Joseph A. *The Acts of the Apostles: A New Translation with Introduction and Commentary*. AB 31. New York: Doubleday, 1998.

———. "David, 'Being Therefore a Prophet...' (Acts 2:30)." *CBQ* 34 (1972) 332–39.

———. *The Gospel According to Luke I-IX: Introduction, Translation, and Notes*. AB 28. New York: Doubleday, 1981.

———. *The Gospel According to Luke X-XXIV: Introduction, Translation, and Notes*. AB 28A. New York: Doubleday, 1985.

———. "Jesus in the Early Church through the Eyes of Luke-Acts." *ScrB* 17 (1987) 26–35.

———. *Luke the Theologian: Aspects of His Teaching*. Mahwah, NJ: Paulist, 1989.

———. *The One Who is to Come*. Grand Rapids: Eerdmans, 2007.

———. *Paul and His Theology: A Brief Sketch*. 2d ed. Englewood Cliffs, NJ: Prentice Hall, 1989.

———. "The Role of the Spirit in Luke-Acts." In *The Unity of Luke-Acts*, edited by J. Verheyden, 165–83. BETL 142. Leuven: Leuven University Press, 1999.

———. "The Use of the Old Testament in Luke-Acts." In *To Advance the Gospel: New Testament Studies*, 295–313. 2d ed. The Biblical Resource Series. Grand Rapids: Eerdmans, 1998.

Flichy, Odile. *La Figure de Paul dans les Actes des Apôtres: Un Phénomène de Réception de la Tradition Paulinienne à la Fin du 1er Siècle*. LD 214. Paris: Cerf, 2007.

———. *L'Oeuvre de Luc: L'Évangile et les Actes des Apôtres*. Cahiers Evangile 114. Paris: Cerf, 2000.

———, et al. *Relectures des Actes des Apôtres*. Cahiers Évangile 128. Paris: Cerf, 2004.

Franklin, Eric. *Luke: Interpreter of Paul, Critic of Matthew*. JSNTSup 92. Sheffield: Sheffield Academic, 1994.
García, N. Esaú. "El Discurso de Antioquía de Pisidia en los Hechos de los Apóstoles." *May* 33 (2007) 109–69.
Garrett, Robert Irving, Jr. "The Inaugural Addresses of Luke–Acts." PhD diss., Southern Baptist Theological Seminary, 1980.
Gasque, W. Ward. *A History of the Interpretation of the Acts of the Apostles*. Peabody, MA: Hendrickson, 1989.
———. "The Speeches of Acts: Dibelius Reconsidered." In *New Dimensions in New Testament Study*, edited by R. N. Longenecker and M. C. Tenney, 232–50. Grand Rapids: Zondervan, 1974.
Gaventa, Beverly Roberts. *The Acts of the Apostles*. Abingdon New Testament Commentaries. Nashville: Abingdon, 2003.
———. "Toward a Theology of Acts: Reading and Rereading." *Int* (1988) 146–57.
George, Augustin. "Israël dans l'oeuvre de Luc." *RB* 75 (1968) 481–525.
Gill, David H. "The Structure of Acts 9." *Bib* 55 (1974) 546–48.
Gill, David W. J. "Paul's Travel through Cyprus (Acts 13:4–12)." *TynBul* 46 (1995) 219–28.
Gill, David W. J., and Conrad H. Gempf, eds. *The Book of Acts in Its Graeco-Roman Setting*. Vol. 2 of *Book of Acts in Its First Century Setting*. Grand Rapids: Eerdmans, 1994.
Glombitza, Otto. "Akta XIII. 15–41: Analyse einer lukanischen Predigt vor Juden." *NTS* 5 (1959) 306–17.
Goldsmith, Dale "Acts 13,33–37: A Pesher on II Samuel 7." *JBL* 87 (1968) 321–24.
Gourgres, Michel. *L'Évangile aux Païens (Actes des Apôtres 13–28)*. Cahiers Évangile 67. Paris: Cerf, 1989.
———. *Mission et Communauté (Actes des Apôtres 1–12)*. Cahiers Évangile 60. Paris: Cerf, 1987.
Green, Joel B. "Internal Repetition in Luke–Acts: Contemporary Narratology and Lucan Historiography. " In *History, Literature, and Society in the Book of Acts*, edited by Ben Witherington III, 283–99.Cambridge: Cambridge University Press, 1996.
Green, Joel B., and Michael C. McKeever. *Luke–Acts and New Testament Historiography*. IBR Bibliographies 8. Grand Rapids: Baker, 1994.
Grundmann, Walter. "δεκτός." *TDNT* 2: 59.
———. "δύναμαι." *TDNT* 2: 284–317.
Guillaume, Paul-Marie. "Les Actes des Apôtres: De La Résurrection a la Mission." *Liturgie* 136 (2007) 82–101.
Haenchen, Ernst. *The Acts of the Apostles: A Commentary*. Philadelphia: Westminster, 1971.
Hansen, G. Walter. "The Preaching and Defence of Paul." In *Witness to the Gospel: The Theology of Acts*, edited by I. Howard Marshall and David Peterson, 295–324. Grand Rapids: Eerdmans, 1998.
Hauser, Hermann. *Strukturen der Abschlusserzählung der Apostelgeschichte (Apg 28, 16–31)*. AnBib 86. Rome: Biblical Institute, 1979.
Haya-Prats, Conzalo. *L'Esprit Force de L'Église: Sa Nature et son Activité d'après les Actes des Apôtre*. Translated by José J. Romero and Hubert Faes. LD 81. Paris: Cerf, 1975.

Hedrick, Charles. "Paul's Conversion/Call: A Comparative Analysis of the Three Reports in Acts." *JBL* 100 (1981) 415–32.
Hellholm, David., et al., eds. *Mighty Minorities?: Minorities in Early Christianity—Positions and Strategies: Essays in Honour of Jacob Jervell on His 70th Birthday, 21 May 1995*. Oslo/Boston: Scandinavian University Press, 1995.
Hengel, Martin. *Between Jesus and Paul: Studies in the Earliest History of Christianity*. Translated by John Bowden. Minneapolis: Fortress, 1983.
Horsley, G. H. R. "Speeches and Dialogue in Acts." *NTS* 32 (1986) 609–14.
Hur, Ju. *A Dynamic Reading of the Holy Spirit in Luke–Acts*. JSNTSup 211. Sheffield: Sheffield Academic, 2001.
Jeremias, Joachim. *Jesus' Promise to the Nations*. Translated by S. H. Hooke. London: SCM, 1958.
Jervell, Jacob. *Die Apostelgeschichte*. KEK 3. Göttingen: Vandenhoeck & Ruprecht, 1998.
———. "The Church of Jews and Godfearers." In *Luke–Acts and the Jewish People: Eight Critical Perspectives*, edited by Joseph B. Tyson, 11–20. Minneapolis: Augsburg, 1988.
———. "The Divided People of God: The Restoration of Israel and Salvation for the Gentiles." In *Luke and the People of God: A New Look at Luke–Acts*, 41–74. Minneapolis: Augsburg, 1972.
———. "The Future of the Past: Luke's Vision of Salvation History and Its Bearing on His Writing of History." In *History, Literature, and Society in the Book of Acts*, edited by Ben Witherington III, 104–26. Cambridge: Cambridge University Press, 1996.
———. "God's Faithfulness to the Faithless People: Trends in Interpretation of Luke–Acts." *Word & World* 12 (1992) 29–36.
———. "Paul: The Teacher of Israel, The Apologetic Speeches of Paul in Acts." In *Luke and the People of God: A New Look at Luke–Acts*, 153–83. Minneapolis: Augsburg, 1972.
———. "Retrospect and Prospect in Luke–Acts Interpretation." In *SBLSP* 1991, edited by Eugene H. Lovering Jr., 383–404. Atlanta: Scholars Press, 1991.
———. *The Theology of the Acts of the Apostles*. NTT. Cambridge: Cambridge University Press, 1996.
———. "The Twelve on Israel's Thrones: Luke's Understanding of the Apostolate." In *Luke and the People of God: A New Look at Luke–Acts*. Minneapolis: Augsburg, 1972.
———. *The Unknown Paul: Essays on Luke–Acts and Early Christian History*. Minneapolis: Augsburg, 1984.
Jervell, Jacob, and Wayne A. Meeks, eds. *God's Christ and His People: Studies in Honour of Nils Alstrup Dahl*. Oslo-Bergen-Tromsö: Universitetsforlaget, 1977.
Jeska, Joachim. *Die Geschichte Israels in der Sicht des Lukas*. FRLANT 195. Göttingen: Vandenhoeck & Reprecht, 2001.
Jipp, Joshua W. "Luke's Scriptural Suffering Messiah: A Search for Precedent, a Search for Identity." *CBQ* 72 (2010) 255–74.
Johnson, Luke T. *The Acts of the Apostles*. Sacra Pagina 5. Collegeville, MN: Liturgical Press, 1992.
———. *The Gospel of Luke*. Sacra Pagina 3. Collegeville, MN: Liturgical Press, 1991.
———. "Literary Criticism of Luke–Acts: Is Reception-History Pertinent?" *JSNT* 28 (2005) 159–62.
———. *The Literary Function of Possessions in Luke–Acts*. SBLDS 39. Missoula: Scholars Press, 1977.

Jolivet, Ira J., Jr. "The Lukan Account of Paul's Conversion and Hermagorean Stasis Theory." In *The Rhetorical Interpretation of Scripture: Essays from the 1996 Malibu Conference*, edited by Stanley E. Porter and Dennis L. Stamps, 210–20. JSNTSup 180. Sheffield: Sheffield Academic, 1999.

Juel, Donald. "Social Dimensions of Exegesis: The Use of Psalm 16 in Acts 2." *CBQ* 43 (1981) 543–56.

Kaiser, Walter C., Jr. "The Promise to David in Psalm 16 and Its Application in Acts 2:25–33 and 13:32–37." *JETS* 23 (1980) 219–29.

———. "The Unfailing Kindness Promised to David: Isaiah 55.3." *JSOT* 45 (1989) 91–98.

Kaumba-Mufwata, Albert. *«Jusqu'aux Extrémités de la Terre»: La Référence aux Prophètes comme Fondement de l'Ouverture Universaliste aux Chapitres 2 et 13 des Actes des Apôtres*. CahRB 67. Paris: Gabalda, 2006.

Keck, Leander E., and J. Louis Martyn, eds. *Studies in Luke–Acts*. Philadelphia: Fortress, 1980.

Kee, Howard C. "Defining the First-Century CE Synagogue: Problems and Progress." *NTS* 41(1995) 481–500.

———. "The Jews in Acts." In *Diaspora Jews and Judaism: Essays in Honor of and in Dialogue with, A. Thomas Kraabel*, edited by J. Andrew Overman and Robert S. MacLennan, 183–95. South Florida Studies in the History of Judaism. Atlanta: Scholars Press, 1992.

———. "The Transformation of the Synagogue after 70 CE: Its Import for Early Christianity." *NTS* 36 (1990) 1–24.

Kepple, Robert J. "The Hope of Israel, the Resurrection of the Dead, and Jesus: A Study of Their Relationship in Acts with Particular Regard to the Understanding of Paul's Trial Defense." *JETS* 20 (1977) 231–41.

Kerrigan, Alexander. "The 'Sensus Plenior' of Joel, III, 1–5 in Act., II, 14–36." In *Sacra Pagina: Miscellanea Biblica Congressus Internationalis Catholici de Re Biblica*, edited by J. Coppens et al., 295–313. BETL 12–13. Gembloux: J. Duculot, 1959.

Kilgallen, John J. "Acts 13,38–39: Culmination of Paul's Speech in Pisidia." *Bib* 69 (1988) 480–506.

———. "Hostility to Paul in Pisidian Antioch (Acts 13,45)—Why?" *Bib* 84 (2003) 1–15.

———. "Paul Before Agrippa (Acts 26,2–23): Some Considerations." *Bib* 69 (1988) 170–95.

———. "Provocation in Luke 4,23–24." *Bib* 70 (1989) 511–16.

———. "'With many other words' (Acts 2,40): Theological Assumption in Peter's Pentecost Speech." *Bib* 83 (2002) 70–87.

Kilpatrick, George D. "An Eclectic Study of the Text of Acts." In *Biblical and Patristic Studies in Memory of Robert Pierce Casey*, edited by J. Neville Birdsall and Robert W. Thomson. Freiberg: Herder, 1963.

Kingsbury, Jack D. *Conflict in Luke: Jesus, Authorities, Disciples*. Minneapolis: Fortress, 1991.

Klinghardt, M., *Gesetz und Volk Gottes: Das lukanische Verständnis des Gesetzes nach Herkunft, Funktion und seinem Ort in der Geschichte des Urchristentums*. WUNT 2. Reihe 32. Tübingen: Mohr, 1988.

Kodell, Jerome. "Luke's Gospel in Nutshell (Lk 4:16–30)." *BTB* 13 (1983) 16–18.

Koenig, Jean. *L'Herméneutique Analogique du Judaïsme Antique d'après les Témoins Textuels d'Isaïe*. VTSup 33. Leiden: Brill, 1982.

Koet, Bart J. "Paul and Barnabas in Pisidian Antioch: A Disagreement over the Interpretation of the Scriptures (Acts 13, 42–52)." In *Five Studies on Interpretation of Scripture in Luke–Acts*, 97–118. Studiorum Novi Testamenti Auxilia 14. Leuven: Leuven University Press, 1989.

———. "Today This Scripture Has Been Fulfilled in Your Ears: Jesus' Explanation of Scripture in Luke 4,16–30." In *Five Studies on Interpretation of Scripture in Luke–Acts*, 24–55. Studiorum Novi Testamenti Auxilia 14. Leuven: Leuven University Press, 1989.

Korn, Manfred. "Jesu Antrittspredigt in Nazareth als Programm des lukanischen Doppelwerks." In *Die Geschichte Jesu in Veränderter Zeit: Studien zur Bleibenden Bedeutung Jesu im Lukanishen Doppelwerk*, 56–85. WUNT 2. Reihe 51. Tübingen: Mohr, 1993.

Kraabel, Thomas "The God-Fearers–A Literary and Theological Invention." *BAR* 12(1986) 46–53.

Kremer, Jacob, ed. *Les Actes des Apôtres: Traditions, Rédaction, Théologie*. BETL 48. Leuven: Leuven University Press, 1979,

Krodel, G. A. *Acts*. ACNT. Minneapolis: Augsburg, 1986.

Kurth, C. "*Die Stimmen der Propheten erfüllt.*" *Jesu Geschick und "die" Juden nach der Darstellung des Lukas*. BWA(N)T 148. Stuttgart/Berlin/Cologne: Kohlhammer, 2000.

Kurz, William S. "Hellenistic Rhetoric in the Christological Proof of Luke–Acts." *CBQ* 42 (1980) 171–95.

———. "Luke 3:23–38 and Greco-Roman and Biblical Genealogies." In *Luke–Acts: New Perspectives from the Society of Biblical Literature Seminar*, edited by Charles H. Talbert, 169–87. New York: Crossroad, 1983.

———. "Narrative Approaches to Luke–Acts." *Bib* 68 (1987) *CBQ* 195–220.

———. *Reading Luke–Acts: Dynamics of Biblical Narratives*. Louisville: Westminster John Knox, 1993.

Lane, T. J. *Luke and the Gentile Mission: Gospel Anticipates Acts*. European University Studies, Series 23: Theology 571. Frankfurt/Berlin/Bern: Lang, 1996.

Lentz, John C. Jr. *Luke's Portrait of Paul*. SNTSMS 77. Cambridge: Cambridge University Press, 1993.

Leonardi, G. *Atti degli Apostoli: Traduzione Strutturata, Analisi Aarrativa e Retorica*. 2 vols. Sussidi Biblici 61–61b. Reggio Emilia: Edizioni San Lorenzo, 1998.

Levine, Lee I. "The Nature and Origin of the Palestinian Synagogue Reconsidered." *JBL* 115 (1996) 425–48.

Levinskaya, Irina. *The Book of Acts in Its Diaspora Setting*. BAFCS 5. Grand Rapids: Eerdmans, 1996.

Levinsohn, Stephen H. *Textual Connections in Acts*, SBLMS 31. Atlanta: Scholars Press, 1987.

Liefeld, W. L. *Interpreting the Book of Acts*. Guides to New Testament Exegesis 4. Grand Rapids: Baker, 1995.

Lin, S. C. *Wundertaten und Mission: Dramatische Episoden in Apg 13–14*. Europäische Hochschulschriften, Reihe 23: Theologie 623. Frankfurt/Berlin/Bern: Lang, 1998.

Litwak, Kenneth D. *Echoes of Scripture in Luke–Acts: Telling the History of God's People Intertextually*. JSNTSup 282. London: T & T Clark International, 2005.

Lohfink, Gerhard. *Die Sammlung Israels. Eine Untersuchung zur lukanischen Ekklesiologie*. StANT 34. München: Kösel-Verlag, 1975.

Lövestam, Evald. *Son and Savior: A Study of Acts 13, 32–37 with an Appendix: 'Son of God' in the Synoptic Gospels.* Translated by Michael J. Petry. ConNT 18. Lund: Gleerup; Copenhagen: Ejnar Munksgaard, 1961.

Lüdemann, Gerd. *The Acts of the Apostles: What Really Happened in the Earliest Days of the Church.* Amherst, NY: Prometheus, 2005.

———. *Early Christianity according to the Traditions in Acts: A Commentary.* Translated by J. Bowden. Minneapolis: Fortress, 1989.

Maddox, Robert. *The Purpose of Luke–Acts.* FRLANT 126. Göttingen: Vandenhoeck & Ruprecht, 1982.

Mainville, O. *L'Esprit dans l'Oeuvre de Luc.* Héritage et Projet 45. Montreal: Fides, 1991.

Malina, Bruce J. *Windows on the World of Jesus: Time Travel to Ancient Judea.* Louisville: Westminster John Knox, 1993.

Malina, Bruce J., and John J. Pilch. *Social-Science Commentary on the Book of Acts.* Minneapolis: Fortress, 2008.

Malina, Bruce J., and Jerome H. Neyrey. *Portraits of Paul.* Louisville: Westminster John Knox, 1996.

Marguerat, Daniel. "The Enigma of the Silent Closing of Acts (28:16–31)." In *Jesus and the Heritage of Israel: Luke's Narrative Claim upon Israel's Legacy. Luke the Interpreter of Israel*, edited by David P. Moessner, 284–304. Vol. 1. Harrisburg, PA: Trinity International, 1999.

———. *The First Christian Historian: Writing the "Acts of the Apostles."* Translated by Ken McKinney et al. SNTSMS 121. Cambridge: Cambridge University Press, 2002.

———. *La Première Histoire du Christianisme: Les Actes des Apôtres.* LD 180. 2d ed. Paris: Cerf, 2003.

———. "Saul's Conversion (Acts 9, 22, 26) and the Multiplication of Narrative in Acts." In *Luke's Literary Achievement: Collected Essays*, edited by Christopher M. Tuckett, 127–55. JSNTSup 116. Sheffield: Sheffield Academic, 1995.

Marshall, I. Howard. *The Acts.* TynNTC. Grand Rapids: Eerdmans, 1994.

———. *The Acts of the Apostles.* NTG. Sheffield: JSOT Press, 1992.

———. *The Gospel of Luke: A Commentary on the Greek Text.* NIGTC. Grand Rapids: Eerdmans, 1978.

———. "'Israel' and the Story of Salvation: One Theme in Two Parts." In *Jesus and the Heritage of Israel: Luke's Narrative Claim upon Israel's Legacy*, 340–57. Vol.1 of *Luke the Interpreter of Israel*, edited by David P. Moessner. Harrisburg, PA: Trinity International, 1999.

———. *Luke: Historian and Theologian.* Enl. ed. Grand Rapids: Zondervan, 1989. Reprint, New Testament Profiles, Downers Grove, IL: InterVarsity, 1998.

Marshall, I. Howard, and David Peterson, eds. *Witness to the Gospel: The Theology of Acts.* Grand Rapids: Eerdmans. 1998.

Matera, Frank J. "Jesus' Journey to Jerusalem (Luke 9:51—19:46): A Conflict with Israel." *JSNT* 51 (1993) 57–77.

———. *New Testament Christology.* Louisville: Westminster John Knox, 1999.

———. *New Testament Theology: Exploring Diversity and Unity.* Louisville: Westminster John Knox, 2007.

———. "Responsibility for the Death of Jesus according to the Acts of the Apostles." *JSNT* 39 (1990) 77–93.

Mealand, David L. "The Close of Acts and Its Hellenistic Vocabulary." *NTS* 36 (1990) 583–97.

Meier, John. "From Elijah-like Prophet to Royal Davidic Messiah." In *Jesus: A Colloquium in the Holy Land*, edited by Doris Donnelly, 145–83. New York: Continuum, 2001.

Menzies, Robert P. *The Development of Early Christian Pneumatology with Special reference to Luke–Acts*. JSNTSup 54. Sheffield: JSOT, 1991.

———. *Empowered for Witness: The Spirit in Luke–Acts*. Journal of Pentecostal Theology Supplement Series 6. Sheffield: Sheffield Academic, 1994.

———. "Spirit and Power in Luke–Acts: A Response to Max Turner." *JSNT* 49 (1993) 11–20.

Metzger, Bruce M. *A Textual Commentary on the Greek New Testament*. 2d ed. Stuttgart: German Bible Society, 1994.

McCormick, Larry D. "Paul's Address to Jewish Audiences in the Acts of the Apostles: Luke's Model Witness and his Calling to Testify to 'the Hope of Israel.'" PhD diss., Fordham University, 1996.

Michaels, J. Ramsey. "Paul and John the Baptist: An Odd Couple?" *NTS* 34 (1988) 96–104.

Michel, Otto. *Der Brief an die Hebräer*. KEK 13. Göttingen: Vandenhoeck & Ruprecht, 1966.

Moessner, David P. "Paul in Acts: Preacher of Eschatological Repentance to Israel." *NTS* 34 (1988) 96–104.

———. "The 'Script' of the Scriptures in Acts: Suffering as God's Plan (βουλή) for the 'Release of Sins.'" In *History, Literature, and Society in the Book of Acts*, edited by Ben Witherington III, 218–50. Cambridge: Cambridge University Press, 1996.

———. "Two Lords 'at the Right Hand'? The Psalms and an Intertextual Reading of Peter's Pentecost Speech (Acts 2:14–36)." In *Literary Studies in Luke–Acts: Essays in Honor of Joseph B. Tyson*, edited by Richard P. Thompson and Thomas E. Philips, 215–32. Macon, GA: Mercer University Press, 1998.

———, ed. *Jesus and the Heritage of Israel: Luke's Narrative Claim upon Israel's Legacy*. Vol. 1 of *Luke the Interpreter of Israel*. Harrisburg, PA: Trinity International, 1999.

Moule, C. F. D. "Jesus, Judaism, and Paul." In *Tradition and Interpretation in the New Testament: Essays in Honor of E. Earle Ellis for his 60th Birthday*, edited by Gerald F. Hawthorne and Otto Betz, 43–52. Grand Rapids: Eerdmans, 1987.

Mount, C. *Pauline Christianity: Luke–Acts and the Legacy of Paul*. Supplements to Novum Testamentum 104. Leiden/Boston/Cologne: Brill, 2002.

Muhlack, Gudrun. *Die Parallelen von Lukas-Evangelium und Apostelgeschichte*. Theologice und Wirklichkeit 8. Frankfurt am Main: Peter Lang, 1979.

Müller, Mogens. "The Reception of the Old Testament in Matthew and Luke–Acts: From Interpretation to Proof from Scripture." *NovT* 43 (2001) 315–30.

Murphy-O'Connor, Jerome. "Lots of God-Fearers? Thosebeis in the Aphrodisias Inscription." *RB* 99 (1992) 418–24.

Nave, G. D. *The Role and Function of Repentance in Luke–Acts*. SBL Academia Biblica 4. Atlanta: Society of Biblical Literature, 2002.

Neirynck, Frans. "Le Livre des Actes dans les Récents Commentaires." *ETL* 59 (1983) 338–49.

Neirynck, Frans, and Frans van Segbroeck. "Le Texte des Actes des Apôtres et les Caractéristiques Stylistiques Lucaniennes." *ETL* 61 (1985) 304–39.

Neyrey, Jerome H. "The Forensic Defense Speech and Paul's Trial Speeches in Acts 22–26: Form and Function." In *Luke–Acts: New Perspective from the Biblical Literature Seminar*, edited by Charles H. Talbert, 210–24. New York: Crossroad, 1984.

———. "Luke's Social Location of Paul: Cultural Anthropology and the Status of Paul in Acts." In *History, Literature, and Society in the Book of Acts*, edited by Ben Witherington III, 251–79. Cambridge: Cambridge University Press, 1996.

Nelson, Edwin. "Paul's First Missionary Journey as Paradigm: A Literary-Critical Assessment of Acts 13–14." PhD diss., Boston University, 1982.

Nolland, John. *Luke 1–9:20*. WBC 35A. Dallas: Word, 1989.

Noth, Martin. *The Deuteronomistic History*. Translated by David J. A. Clines et al. Tübingen: Niemeyer, 1957; 2d ed., JSOTSup 15, Sheffield: JSOT, 1981.

Noorda, S. J. "'Cure Yourself Doctor!' (Luke 4,23). Classical Parallels to an Alleged Saying of Jesus." In *Logia: Les Paroles de Jésus: The Saying of Jesus*, edited by Joël Delobel, 459–67. BETL 59. Louvain: Louvain University Press, 1982.

O'Neil, J. C. "The Connection between Baptism and the Gift of the Spirit in Acts." *JSNT* 63 (1996) 87–103.

O'Reilly, L. *Word and Sign in the Acts of the Apostles: A Study in Lucan Theology*. Analecta Gregoriana 243. Rome: Pontificia Università Gregoriana, 1987.

Oster, Rechard E. "Supposed Anachronism in Luke–Acts' Use of συναγωγή: A Rejoinder to H. C. Kee." *NTS* 39 (1993) 178–208.

O'Toole, Robert F. "Activity of the Risen Jesus in Luke–Acts." *Bib* 62 (1981) 471–98.

———. *Acts 26: The Christological Climax of Paul's Defense (Ac 22:1—26:32)*. AnBib 78. Rome: Biblical Institute, 1978.

———. "Christ's Resurrection in Acts 13, 13–52." *Bib* 60 (1979) 361–72.

———. "The Christian Mission and the Jews at the End of Acts of the Apostles." In *Biblical Exegesis in Progress: Old and New Testament Essays*, edited by Jean-Noël Aletti and Jean Louis Ska, 371–96. AnBib 176. Roma: Editrice Istituto Biblico, 2009.

———. "Parallels between Jesus and His Disciples in Luke–Acts: A Further Study." *BZ* 27 (1983) 195–212.

———. "Reflections on Luke's Treatment of the Jews in Luke–Acts." *Bib* 74 (1993) 529–55.

———. *The Unity of Luke's Theology: An Analysis of Luke–Acts*. Good News Studies 9. Wilmington, DE: Michael Glazier, 1984.

Overman, J. Andrew. "The God-Fearers: Some Neglected Features." *JSNT* 32 (1988) 17–26.

Parsons, Mikeal C. *Acts*. Paideia Commentaries on the New Testament. Grand Rapids: Baker Academic, 2008.

Parsons, Mikeal C., and Joseph B. Tyson, eds. *Cadbury, Knox, and Talbert: American Contributions to the Study of Acts*. SBLBSNA. Atlanta: Scholars Press, 1992.

Penner, Todd, and Caroline V. Stichele, eds. *Contextualizing Acts: Lukan Narratives and Greco-Roman Discourse*. SBLSymS 20. Atlanta: Society of Biblical Literature, 2003.

Pervo, Richard I. *Acts: A Commentary*. Hermeneia. Minneapolis: Fortress, 2009.

———. "Direct Speech in Acts and the Question of Genre." *JSNT* 28 (2006) 285–307.

———. *The Mystery of Acts: Unraveling Its Story*. Santa Rosa, CA: Polebridge, 2008.

———. *Profit with Delight: The Literary Genre of the Acts of the Apostles*. Philadelphia: Fortress, 1987.

Pesch, Rudolf. *Die Apostelgeschichte: Apg 13–28*. Vol. 2. EKK 5. Neukirches-Vluyn: Neukirchner Verlag, 1986.

Peterson, David G. *The Acts of the Apostles*. Grand Rapids: Eerdmans, 2009.

———. "The Motif of Fulfillment and the Purpose of Luke–Acts." In *The Book of Acts in Its Ancient Literary Setting*, edited by Bruce W. Winter and Andrew D. Clarke, 83–104. Vol. 1 of BAFCS. Grand Rapids: Eerdmans, 1994.

Phillips, Thomas E. "Subtlety as Literary Technique in Luke's Characterization of Jews and Judaism." In *Literary Studies in Luke–Acts*, edited by Richard P. Thompson and Thomas E. Phillips, 313–26. Macon, GA: Mercer University Press, 1998.

———, ed. *Contemporary Studies in Acts*. Macon, GA: Mercer University Press. 2009.

Pillai, Christie A. Joachim. *Apostolic Interpretation of History: A Commentary on Acts 13:16–41*. Hicksville, NY: Exposition, 1980.

———. *Early Missionary Preaching: A Study of Luke's Report in Acts 13*. Hicksville, NY: Exposition, 1979.

Pichler, Josef. *Paulusrezeption in der Apostelgeschichte: Untersuchungen zur Rede im pisidischen Antiochien*. Innsbruck: Tyrolia-Verlag, 1997.

———. "Das theologische Anliegen der Paulusrezeption im lukanischen Werk." In *The Unity of Luke–Acts*, edited by J. Verheyden, 731–43. BETL 142. Leuven: Leuven University Press, 1999.

Plümacher, Eckhard. "Lukas als griechischer Historiker." *PWSup* 14 (1974) 235–64.

———. "The Mission Speeches in Acts and Dionysius of Halicarnassus." In *Jesus and the Heritage of Israel: Luke's Narrative Claim upon Israel's Legacy*, edited by David P. Moessner, 251–66. Vol. 1 of *Luke the Interpreter of Israel*. Harrisburg, PA: Trinity International, 1999.

Poirier, John C. "Jesus as an Elijianic Figure in Luke 4:16–30." *CBQ* 71 (2009) 349–63.

Porter, Stanley E. "The Messiah in Luke and Acts: Forgiveness for the Captives." In *The Messiah in the Old and New Testament*, edited by Stanley E. Porter, 144–64. Grand Rapids: Eerdmans, 2007.

———. *The Paul of Acts: Essays in Literary Criticism, Rhetoric, and Theology*. WUNT 115. Tübingen: Mohr, 1999.

———. "Thucydides 1.22.1 and Speeches in Acts: Is There a Thucydidean View?" *NovT* 32 (1990) 121–42.

Praeder, Susan Marie. "Acts 27:1—28:16: Sea Voyage in Ancient Literature and the Theology of Luke–Acts." *CBQ* 46 (1984) 683–706.

———. "Jesus-Paul, Peter-Paul, and Jesus-Peter Parallelisms in Luke–Acts: A History of Reader Response." In *SBLSP 1984*, edited by Kent Harold Richards, 23–39. Chico, CA: Scholars Press, 1984.

Prieur, Alexander. *Die Verkündigung der Gottesherrschaft: Exegetische Studien zum lukanischen Verständnis von basilei,a tou/ qeou/*. WUNT 2. Reihe 89. Tübingen: Mohr, 1996.

Puskas, Charles B. *The Conclusion of Luke–Acts: The Significance of Acts 28:16–31*. Eugene, OR: Pickwick, 2009.

Quesnel, Michel "Paul Prédicateur dans les Actes des Apôtres." *NTS* 47 (2001) 469–81.

———. *Baptisés dans l'Esprit: Baptême et Esprit Saint dans les Actes des Apôtres*. LD 120. Paris: Cerf, 1985.

Radl, Walter. *Paulus und Jesus im lukanischen Doppelwerk: Untersuchungen zu Parallelmotiven im Lukasevangelium und in der Apostelgeschichte*. Europäische Hochschulschriften Reihe 23. Theologie 49. Bern: Herbert Lang; Frankfurt: Peter Lang, 1975.

Rau, E. *Von Jesus zu Paulus: Entwicklung und Rezeption der antiochenischen Theologie im Urchristentum*. Stuttgart/Berlin/Cologne: Kohlhammer, 1994.

Ravens, David. *Luke and the Restoration of Israel*. Edited by Stanley E. Porter. JSNTSup 119. Sheffield: Sheffield Academic, 1995.

Ray, Jerry L. *Narrative Irony in Luke-Acts: The Paradoxical Interaction of Prophetic Fulfillment and Jewish Rejection*. Mellen Biblical Press Series 28. Lampeter, UK: Mellen Biblical, 1996.

Reasoner, Mark. "The Theme of Acts: Institutional History or Drive Necessity in History?" *JBL* 118 (1999) 635–59.

Rese, Martin. "The Jews in Luke-Acts: Some Second Thought." In *The Unity of Luke-Acts*, edited by J. Verheyden, 185–201. BETL 142. Leuven: Leuven University Press, 1999.

Richard, Earl. "The Divine Purpose: The Jews and the Gentile Mission (Acts 15)." In *Luke-Acts: New Perspective from the Biblical Literature Seminar*, edited by Charles H. Talbert, 188–209. New York: Crossroad, 1984.

———. "The Old Testament in Acts: Wilcox's Semitisms in Retrospect." *CBQ* 42 (1980) 330–41.

———. "Pentecost as a Recurrent Theme in Luke-Acts." In *New Views on Luke-Acts*, edited by Earl Richard, 133–49. Collegeville, MN: Liturgical Press, 1990.

———, ed. *New Views on Luke and Acts*. Collegeville, MN: Liturgical Press, 1990.

Riesner, Rainer. "Synagogue in Jerusalem." In *The Book of Acts in Its Palestinian Setting*, edited by Richard Bauckham, 179–210. Vol. 4 of BAFCS. Grand Rapids: Eerdmans, 1995.

Robinson, John A. T. "Most Primitive Christology of All." *JTS* 7 (1956) 177–89.

Rosenblatt, Marie-Eloise. *Paul the Accused: His Portrait in the Acts of the Apostles*. Zacchaeus Studies: New Testament. Collegeville, MN: Liturgical Press, 1995.

Rosner, Brian S. "Acts and Biblical History." In *The Book of Acts in Its Ancient Literature Setting*, edited by Bruce W. Winter and Andrew D. Clarke, 65–82. Vol. 1 of BAFCS. Grand Rapids: Eerdmans, 1993.

———. "The Progress of the Word." In *Witness to the Gospel: The Theology of Acts*, edited by I. Howard Marshall and David Peterson, 215–33. Grand Rapids: Eerdmans. 1998.

Roth, Samuel J. *The Blind, the Lame, and the Poor: Character Types in Luke-Acts*. Edited by Stanley E. Porter. JSNTSup 144. Sheffield: Sheffield Academic, 1997.

Rothschild, Clare K. *Luke-Acts and the Rhetoric of History: An Investigation of Early Christian Historiography*. WUNT 2. Reihe 175. Tübingen: Mohr, 2004.

Rowe, C. Kavin. "Acts 2.36 and the Continuity of Lukan Christology" *NTS* 53 (2007) 37–56.

———. "History, Hermeneutics and the Unity of Luke-Acts." *JSNT* 28 (2005) 131–57.

———. *World Upside Down: Reading Acts in the Graeco-Roman Age*. New York: Oxford University Press, 2009.

Salmon, Marilyn. "Insider or Outsider? Luke's Relationship with Judaism." In *Luke-Acts and the Jewish People: Eight Critical Perspectives*, edited by Joseph B. Tyson, 76–82. Minneapolis: Augsburg, 1988.

Salo, Kalervo. *Luke's Treatment of the Law: A Redaction-Critical Investigation*. Annales Academiae Scientiarum Fennicae, Dissertationes Humanarum Litterarum 57. Helsinki: Suomalainen Tiedeakatemia, 1991.

Sanders, Jack T. "The Jewish People in Luke-Acts." In *Luke-Acts and the Jewish People: Eight Critical Perspectives*, edited by Joseph B. Tyson, 51–75. Minneapolis: Augsburg, 1988.
———. *The Jews in Luke-Acts*. Philadelphia: Fortress, 1987.
———. "The Parable of the Pounds and Lucan Anti-Semitism." *TS* 42 (1981) 660–68.
———. "The Salvation of the Jews in Luke-Acts." In *Luke-Acts: New Perspective from the Biblical Literature Seminar*, edited by Charles H. Talbert, 104–28. New York: Crossroad, 1984.
———. "Who Is a Jew and Who Is a Gentile in the Book of Acts?" *NTS* 37 (1991) 434–55.
Sanders, James A. "From Isaiah 61 to Luke 4." In *Christianity, Judaism, and Other Greco-Roman Cults: Studies for Morton Smith at Sixty*, edited by Jacob Neusner, 75–106. SJLA 12. Leiden: Brill, 1975.
———. "Isaiah in Luke." In *Luke and Scripture: The Function of Sacred Tradition in Luke-Acts*, edited by Craig A. Evans and James A. Sanders. Minneapolis: Fortress, 1993.
Schmidt, Karl Matthias. "Abkehr von der Rueckkehr: Aufbau und Theologie der Apostelgeschichte im Kontext des Lukanishcen Diaspoaverständnissss." *NTS* 53 (2007) 406–24.
Schmidt, Daryl D. "Rhetorical Influences and Genre: Luke's Preface and the Rhetoric of the Hellenistic Historiography." In *Jesus and the Heritage of Israel: Luke's Narrative Claim upon Israel's Legacy*, edited by David P. Moessner, 27–60. Vol. 1 of *Luke the Interpreter of Israel*. Harrisburg, PA: Trinity International, 1999.
Schreck, Christopher J. "The Nazareth Pericope: Luke 4,16–30 in Recent Study." In *L'Evangile de Luc: The Gospel of Luke*, edited by Frans Neirynck, 399–471. BETL 32. Leuven: Leuven University Press, 1989.
Schweizer, Eduard. "The Concept of the Davidic 'Son of God 'in Acts and Its Old Testament Background." In *Studies in Luke-Acts*, edited by Leander Keck and J. Louis Martyn. Philadelphia: Fortress, 1980.
———. "Concerning the Speeches in Acts." In *Studies in Luke-Acts*, edited by Leander Keck and J. Louis Martyn, 208–16. Nashville: Abingdon, 1966.
Seccombe, David. "The New People of God." In *Witness to the Gospel: The Theology of Acts*, edited by I. Howard Marshall and David Peterson, 349–72. Grand Rapids: Eerdmans. 1998.
Sheeley, Stephen. *Narrative Asides in Luke-Acts*. JSNTSup 72. Sheffield: JSOT, 1992.
Shelton, James B. *Mighty in Word and Deed: The Role of the Holy Spirit in Luke-Acts*. Peabody, MA: Hendrickson, 1991.
Shepherd, Willaim H., Jr. *The Narrative Function of the Holy Spirit as a Character in Luke-Acts*. SBLDS 147. Atlanta: Scholars Press, 1994.
Sieber, John H. "The Spirit as the 'Promise of My Father' in Luke 24:49." In *Sin, Salvation, and the Spirit: Commemorating the Fiftieth Year of the Liturgical Press*, edited by Daniel Durken, 271–78. Collegeville, MN: Liturgical Press, 1979.
Siker, Jeffrey S. "'First to the Gentiles': A Literary Analysis of Luke 4:16–30." *JBL* 111 (1992) 73–90.
Skinner, Matthew L. *Locating Paul: Places of Custody as Narrative Settings in Acts 21–28*. SBL Academia Biblica 13. Atlanta: Society of Biblical Literature, 2003.
Smith, David E. *The Canonical Function of Acts: A Comparative Analysis*. Collegeville, MN: Liturgical Press, 2002.

Soards, Marion L. *The Passion According to Luke: The Special Material of Luke 22*. JSNTSup 14. Sheffield: JSOT, 1987.

———. *The Speeches in Acts: Their Content, Context, and Concerns*. Louisville: Westminster John Knox, 1994.

———. "The Speeches in Acts in Relation to Other Pertinent Ancient Literature." *ETL* 70 (1994) 65–90.

Spencer, Franklin S. *Acts*. Sheffield: Sheffield Academic, 1997.

———. "Acts and Modern Literary Approaches." In *The Book of Acts in Its Ancient Literary Setting*, edited by Bruce W. Winter and Andrew D. Clarke, 381–414. Vol. 1 of BAFCS. Grand Rapids: Eerdmans, 1994.

———. *The Gospel of Luke and Acts of the Apostles*. Nashville: Abingdon, 2008.

———. *Journeying through Acts: A Literary-Cultural Reading*. Peabody, MA: Hendrickson, 2004.

———. *The Portrait of Philip in Acts: A Study of Roles and Relations*. JSNTSup 67. Sheffield: JSOT, 1992.

Squires, John T. "The Function of Acts 8.4–12.25." *NTS* 44 (1998) 608–17.

———. *The Plan of God in Luke-Acts*. SNTSMS 76. Cambridge: Cambridge University Press, 1993.

———. "The Plan of God in the Acts of the Apostles." In *Witness to the Gospel: The Theology of Acts*, edited by I. Howard Marshall and David Peterson, 19–39. Grand Rapids: Eerdmans 1998.

———. "The Plan of God in Luke Acts." PhD diss., Yale University, 1987.

Standley, Christopher S. "'Neither Jew nor Greek': Ethnic Conflict in Graeco-Roman Society." *JSNT* 64 (1996) 101–24.

Stanton, Graham N. *The Gospels and Jesus*. Oxford: Oxford University Press, 1989.

Stenschke, Christoph W. *Luke's Portrait of Gentiles Prior to Their Coming to Faith*. WUNT 2. Reihe 108. Tübingen: Mohr, 1999.

Steyn, Gert J. *Septuagint Quotations in the Context of the Petrine and Pauline Speeches of the Acta Apostolorum*. Contributions to Biblical Exegesis and Theology 12. Kampen: Kok Pharos, 1995.

Stolle, Volker *Der Zeuge als Angeklagter: Untersuchungen zum Paulus-Bild des Lukas*. BWA(N)T 102. Stuttgart: Kohlhammer, 1973.

Stoll, John R. W. *The Message of Acts*. Leicester: InterVarsity, 1990.

Storm, Hans-Martin. *Die Paulusberufung nach Lukas und das Erbe der Propheten. Berufen zu Gottes Dienst*. ANTJ 10. Frankfurt/Berlin/Bern: Lang, 1995.

Stowers, Stanley Kent. "Social Status, Public Speaking and Private Teaching: The Circumstances of Paul's Teaching Activity." *NovT* 26 (1984) 59–82.

Strauss, Mark L. *The Davidic Messiah in Luke–Acts: The Promise and Its Fulfillment in Lukan Christology*. JSNTSup 110. Sheffield: Sheffield Academic, 1995.

Strelan, Rick, *Strange Acts: Studies in the Cultural World of the Acts of the Apostles*. Beihefte zur Zeitschrift für die neutestamentliche Wissenschaft und die Kunde der älteren Kirche 126. Berlin: Walter de Gruyter, 2004.

———. "We Hear Them Telling in Our Own Tongues: The Mighty Works of God (Acts 2:11)." *Neot* 40 (2006) 295–319.

Stuhlmueller, Carroll. "Deutero-Isaiah and Trito-Isaiah." In *NJBC*, edited by Raymond E. Brown et al., 329–48. Englewood Cliffs, NJ: Prentice Hall, 1990.

Swanson, Reuben J, ed. *New Testament Greek Manuscripts: Variant Readings Arranged in Horizontal Lines Against Codex Vaticanus. The Acts of the Apostles.* Sheffield: Sheffield Academic. 1998.

Talbert, Charles H. "Excursus A: The Fulfillment of Prophecy in Luke-Acts." In *Reading Luke: A Literary and Theological Commentary*, 234-40. New York: Crossroad, 1984.

———. *Literary Patterns, Theological Themes and the Genre of Luke-Acts.* SBLMS 20. Missoula: Scholars Press, 1974.

———. "Once Again: The Gentile Mission in Luke-Acts." In *Reading Luke-Acts in Its Mediterranean Milieu*, 161-73. Supplements to Novum Testamentum 107. Leiden/Boston: Brill, 2003.

———. "Promise and Fulfillment in Lucan Theology." In *Luke-Acts: New Perspective from the Biblical Literature Seminar*, edited by Charles H. Talbert, 91-103. New York: Crossroad, 1984.

———. *Reading Acts: A Literary and Theological Commentary on the Acts of the Apostles.* Reading the New Testament. New York: Crossroad, 1997.

———. *Reading Luke-Acts in Its Mediterranean Milieu.* Supplements to Novum Testamentum 107. Leiden/Boston: Brill, 2003.

———. *Reading Luke: A Literary and Theological Commentary on the Third Gospel.* Rev. ed. Macon, GA: Smyth & Helwys, 2002.

———, ed. *Perspectives on Luke-Acts.* Danville, VA: Association of Baptist Professors of Religion, 1978.

Talbert, Charles H., and J. H. Hayes. "A Theology of Sea Storms in Luke-Acts." In *Jesus and the Heritage of Israel: Luke's Narrative Claim upon Israel's Legacy*, edited by David P. Moessner, 267-83. Vol. 1 of *Luke the Interpreter of Israel*. Harrisburg, PA: Trinity International, 1999.

Tannehill, Robert C. "Freedom and Responsibility in Scripture Interpretation, with Application to Luke." In *Literary Studies in Luke-Acts*, edited by Richard P. Thompson and Thomas E. Phillips, 265-78. Macon, GA: Mercer University Press, 1998.

———. "The Functions of Peter's Mission Speeches in the Narrative of Acts." In *The Shape of Luke's Story: Essays on Luke-Acts*, 169-84. Eugene, OR: Cascade, 2005.

———. "Israel in Luke-Acts." *JBL* 104 (1985) 69-85.

———. *The Narrative Unity of Luke-Acts: A Literary Interpretation.* 2 vols. Philadelphia: Fortress, 1986.

———. "Rejection by Jews and Turning to Gentiles: The Pattern of Paul's Mission in Acts." In *Luke-Acts and the Jewish People: Eight Critical Perspectives*, edited by Joseph B. Tyson, 83-101. Minneapolis: Augsburg, 1988.

———. *The Shape of Luke's Story: Essays on Luke-Acts.* Eugene, OR: Cascade, 2005.

———. "The Story of Israel within the Lukan Narrative." In *Jesus and the Heritage of Israel: Luke's Narrative Claim upon Israel's Legacy*, edited by David P. Moessner, 325-39. Vol. 1 of *Luke the Interpreter of Israel*. Harrisburg, PA: Trinity International, 1999.

Tiede, David L. "Acts 2:1-47." *Int* 33 (1979) 62-67.

———. "'Glory to Thy People Israel': Luke-Acts and the Jews." *Luke-Acts and the Jewish People: Eight Critical Perspectives*, edited by Joseph B. Tyson, 21-34. Minneapolis: Augsburg, 1988.

———. *Luke.* ACNT. Minneapolis: Augsburg, 1988.

———. *Prophecy and History in Luke-Acts.* Philadelphia: Fortress, 1980.

Tosco, Lorenzo. *Pietro e Paolo Ministri del Giudizio di Dio: Studio del Genere Letterario e della Funzione di At 5,1–11 e 13,4–12*. Supplementi alla Rivista Biblica 19. Bologna: Dehoniane, 1989.
Trobisch, David. "Die narrative Welt der Apostelgeschichte." *ZNW* 18 (2006) 9–14
Trull, Gregory V. "An Exegeis of Psalm 16:10." *BSac* 161 (2004) 304–21.
———. "Peter's Interpretation of Psalm 16:8–11 in Acts 2:25–32." *BSac* 161 (2004) 432–48.
———. "Views on Peter's Use of Psalm 16:8–11 in Acts 2:25–32." *BSac* 161 (2004) 194–214.
Tucker, J. Brian. "God-Fearers: Literary Foil or Historical Reality in the Book of Acts." *JBS* 5 (2005) 21–39.
Tuckett, Charistopher M., ed. *Luke's Literary Achievement: Collected Essays*. JSNTSup 116. Sheffield: Sheffield Academic, 1995.
Tyson, Joseph B. "The Gentile Mission and the Authority of Scriptures in Acts." *NTS* 33 (1987) 619–31.
———. *Images of Judaism in Luke–Acts*. Columbia, SC: University of South Carolina Press, 1992.
———. "The Jewish Public in Luke–Acts." *NTS* 30 (1984) 574–83.
———. "Jews and Judaism in Luke–Acts: Reading as a Godfearer." *NTS* 41 (1995) 19–38.
———. *Luke, Judaism, and the Scholars: Critical Approaches to Luke–Acts*. Columbia, SC: University of South Carolina Press, 1999.
———. "The Problem of Jewish Rejection in Acts." In *Luke–Acts and the Jewish People: Eight Critical Perspectives*, edited by Joseph B. Tyson, 124–37. Minneapolis: Augsburg, 1988.
———. "Wrestling with and for Paul." In *Contemporary Studies in Acts*, edited by Thomas E. Phillips, 13–28. Macon, GA: Mercer University Press, 2009.
Van de Sandt, Huub. "Acts 28,28: No Salvation for the People of Israel? An Answer in the Perspective of the LXX." *ETL* 70 (1994) 341–58.
———. "An Explanation of Acts 15.6–21 in the Light of Deuteronomy 4.29–35 (LXX)." *JSNT* 46 (1992) 73–97.
———. "The Fate of the Gentiles in Joel and Acts 2: An Intertextual Study." *ETL* 66 (1990) 56–77.
———. "The Quotations in Acts 13: 32–52 as a Reflection of Luke's LXX Interpretation." *Bib* 75 (1994) 26–58.
Vanhoye, Albert. "L'Intérêt de Luc pour la Prophétie en Lc 1,76; 4, 16–30 et 22,60–65." In *The Four Gospels 1992: Festschrift Frans Neirynck*, edited by F. Van Segbroeck et al., 1529–48. BETL 100. Leuven: Leuven University Press, 1992.
———. "Les Juifs selon les Actes des Apôtres et les Épîtres du Nouveau Testament." *Bib* 72 (1991) 70–89.
Viviano, Benedict T., and Justin Taylor. "Sadducees, Angels, and Resurrection (23:8–9)." *JBL* 111 (1992) 496–98.
Van Minnen, Peter. "Paul the Roman Citizen." *JSNT* 56 (1994) 43–52.
Van Zyl, Hermie C. "The Soteriology of Acts: Restoration to Life." In *Salvation in the New Testament: Perspective on Soteriology*, edited by Jan G. van der Watt, 133–60. Supplements to Novum Testamentum 121. Leiden/Boston: Brill, 2005.

Wall, Robert W. "The Acts of the Apostles: Introduction, Commentary, and Reflections." In *The New Interpreter's Bible*, edited by Leander E. Keck. Vol. 10. Nashville: Abingdon, 2002.

———. "The Function of LXX Habakkuk 1:5 in the Book of Acts." *BBR* 10 (2000) 247–58.

———. "Israel and the Gentile Mission in Acts and Paul: A Canonical Approach." In *Witness to the Gospel: The Theology of Acts*, edited by I. Howard Marshall and David Peterson, 437–57. Grand Rapids: Eerdmans. 1998.

Walker, William O. "Acts and the Pauline Corpus Reconsidered." *JSNT* 24 (1985) 3–23.

Wallace, Daniel B. *Greek Grammar beyond the Basics: An Exegetical Syntax of the New Testament*. Grand Rapids: Zondervan, 1996.

Wander, Bernd *Gottesfürchtige und Sympathisanten*. WUNT 104. Tübingen: Mohr Siececk, 1998.

Wasserberg, Günter. *Aus Israels Mitte—Heil für die Welt. Eine narrativ-exegetische Studie zur Theologie des Lukas*. Beihefte zur Zeitschrift für die neutestamentliche Wissenschaft und die Kunde der älteren Kirche 92. Berlin / New York: Walter de Gruyter, 1998.

Weatherly, J. A. *Jewish Responsibility for the Death of Jesus in Luke–Acts*. JSNTSup 106. Sheffield: Sheffield Academic, 1994.

Wedderburn, Alexander J. M. "Paul and Jesus: Similarity and Continuity." *NTS* 34 (1988) 161–82.

———. "Traditions and Redaction in Acts 2.1–13." *JSNT* 55 (1994) 27–54.

———. "Paul and Barnabas: The Anatomy and Chronology of a Parting of the Ways." In *Fair Paly: Diversity and Conflicts in Early Christianity: Essays in Honour of Heikki Raïsänen*, edited by Ismo Dunderberg et al., 291–310. NovTSup 103. Leiden/Boston/Köln: Brill, 2002.

Wilcox, Max. "The 'God-fearers' in Acts: A Reconsideration." *JSNT* 13 (1981) 102–22.

Wilckens, Ulrich. *Die Missionsreden der Apostelgeschichte: Form- und traditionsgeschichtliche Untersuchungen*. 3d ed. WMANT 5. Neukirchen-Vluyn: Neukirchener Verlag, 1974.

Wills, Lawrence M. "The Depiction of Jews in Acts." *JBL* 110 (1991) 631–54.

Winter, V., and A. D. Clarke, eds. *The Book of Acts in Its Ancient Literary Setting*. BAFCS 1. Grand Rapids: Eerdmans, 1993.

Williamson, H. G. M. "'The Sure Mercies of David': Subjective or Objective Genitive?" *JSS* 23 (1978) 31–49.

Witherington, Ben, III. *The Acts of the Apostles: A Socio-Rhetorical Commentary*. Grand Rapids: Eerdmans, 1998.

———, ed. *History, Literature, and Society in the Book of Acts*. Cambridge: Cambridge University Press, 1996.

Witherup, Ronald D. "Cornelius Over and Over and Over Again: 'Functional Redundancy' in the Acts of the Apostles." *JSNT* 49 (1993) 45–66.

———. "Functional Redundancy in the Acts of the Apostles: A Case Study." *JSNT* 48 (1992) 67–86.

Wolfgang, Fenske. "Aspekte Biblischer Theologie dargestellt an der Verwendung von Ps 16 in Apostelgeschichte 2 und 13." *Bib* 83 (2002) 54–70.

Wong, Foon Yee (黄凤仪). 《宗徒大事录：早期教会一系列福传故事研读》香港: 论尽神学出版社有限公司, 2007.

Woodall, David L. "Israel in the Book of Acts: The Foundation of Lukan Ecclesiology." PhD diss., Trinity Evangelical Divinity School, 1998.
Wuellner, Wilhelm. "Where is Rhetorical Criticism Taking Us?" *CBQ* 49 (1987) 448–63.
Yadin, Y. *The Temple Scroll 2.* Jerusalem: Israel Exploration Society, 1983.
Zedda, S. *Teologia della Salvezza negli Atti degli Apostoli: Studi sulla Terminologia.* Studi biblici 20. Bologna: Dehoniane, 1994.
Zehnle, Richard F. *Peter's Pentecost Discourse: Tradition and Lukan Reinterpretation in Peter's Speeches of Acts 2 and 3.* Edited by Robert A. Kraft. SBLMS 15. Nashville: Abingdon, 1971.
Zerwick, Maximilian. *Biblical Greek: Illustrated by Examples.* Edited by Joseph Smith. Scripta Pontificii Instituti Biblici 114. Roma: Editrice Pontificio Istituto Biblico, 2001.

Scripture Index

OLD TESTAMENT

Genesis

6:2	117n39
15:13	131
32:29	85
37:5	83n56
41:8	83n56

Exodus

1:20	129
4:8	100
4:9	100
4:15–16	59
4:17	100
4:22	117n39
4:28	100
4:30	100
6	128n81
6:1	129
6:6	129
6:8	129
7:3	100
7:9	100
8	129
10:1	100
10:2	100
11:9–10	100
12:51	129
15:6	88
19–20	74n36
19:16	74, 74n36, 113
19:18	74n36
19:18–19	74
24:18	67
34:28	67

Leviticus

25:8–17	45
25:10	49

Numbers

6:24–26	42n36
14:33–34	130, 131
24:4	83n56
24:16	83n56

Deuteronomy

1	128n81
1:31	130, 130n86
4:34	129
4:37	129
5:15	129
6:4–9	42n36
6:13	106n115
6:16	106n115
7	128n81
7:1	130
7:7	129
8:3	106n115
9:26	129
10:15	129
11:13–21	42n36
13:1–5	83n56

Deuteronomy–continued

18:15–18	59
26:5–9	20
29:18	145, 146n141
32:5	93
34:9	70n20
34:10–12	85n64

Joshua

14–17	128n81

Judges

2:4	78
2:16	131
2:18	131
2:19	131
3:9	134
3:10	46
3:15	134
9:7	78
11:19	46
21:2	78

Ruth

1:1	131
1:9	78
1:14	78

1 Samuel

3:1	83n56
3:20	131
7–10	128n81
7:15	131
8:6	131
8:7–8	131
9:1–2	131
10:1	132
10:5–13	46
10:19	134
10:20–21	132
10:24	132
11:15	132
12:1–25	131
13–14	132–33
13:1	132
15–16	128n81
16:11–13	132
28:15	83n56

2 Samuel

7	16, 17, 128n81, 163, 170
7:5–16	146
7:6–16	133n99
7:10b–14a	16
7:11–16	16
7:12	133, 134, 143
7:12–16	87
7:12b–14a	16
7:14	117, 117n39, 143, 143n130
7:14–16	143
7:15–16	146
7:16	143
7:17	83n56
13–16	146
13:36	78
22	128n81
22:15	113
22:51	133

1 Kings

17:8–16	59
17:23	59
19:8	67

2 Kings

2:1	71n
2:9	71n
2:10	71n
2:12	71n
2:14	70n20

2:19	88
6:18	114n24

1 Chronicles

6:39	88
17:10	131
17:13	117n39

Nehemiah

8:4	88

Job

1:6	117n39
2:1	117n39

Psalms

1	143n129
2	24, 36, 143n129, 144
2:1–2	143
2:7	26, 117, 118, 141, 142, 142n128, 143
2:7b	23, 24
8:8–11	86
15:10	26, 141, 147
16	90, 96
16:8–11	84, 86, 86n67, 87, 94, 97
16:10	24, 87
16:11b	88
16:11c	86n68
17:4	146
17:14	113
17:21–34	133
17:35	88
19:1	117n39
25:10	88
32:12	129
43:3	88
47:10	88
59:5	88
76:18	113
77	128n81
77:8	93
88:21	132
89:4–5	87, 145
89:19	83n56
89:30	146
89:34–36	146
96:4	113
97:1	88
107:20	136
109	89, 96
109:1	86n68, 88, 89, 94, 118
110	90
110:1	92n82
117:16	88
122:3–5	72n27
132:10	87
132:11	87, 145
136:11–12	129
137:7	88
143:6	113

Isaiah

1:1	83n56
6:9	115
6:9–10	185
9:1–7	145
11:1–2	46
13:1	83n56
19:1	83n56
42:1–4	36
44:28	133
45:1	133n95
45:15	134
45:21	134
45:23–25	24
49:6	23, 27
49:6b	23
49:6d	162
49:8	49n72
53:9	139n115
55:3	26, 141, 144, 146, 147, 163
55:3b	144, 144n134

Isaiah–continued

55:3c	23, 24
55:7d	24
55:11	24
55:14–15	146n144
57:19	104
58	45n49, 61
58:6	41, 43, 44, 49n72, 49n73
58:6d	43
61	45n49, 47, 50, 61
61:1	49n73
61:1–2	41, 43, 45
61:1–2a	44
61:1–11	45
61:1a	43
61:1b	43
61:1c	43
61:1d	43
61:2a	43
61:2b	43, 44

Jeremiah

1:9–10	115
14:14	83n56
28:25–32	83n56
28:36	83n56
30:9	133

Lamentations

2:9	83n56

Ezekiel

1:1	83n56
1:4	113
1:7	113
1:13	113
2:3–4	115
8:3	83n56
37:24–25	133
40:2	83n56

Daniel

1:17	83n56
2:1	83n56
3:25	117n39
4:2	83n56
4:20	83n56
7:9–27	72n27
8:1	83n56
9:25	133
10:6	113

Hosea

3:5	133
12:10	83n56

Joel

2:17	27
3:1	80
3:1–5	69
3:1–5a	79, 80, 81, 84, 93, 97, 105
3:1–5a	96
3:1a	80
3:2	99

Obadiah

1:1	83n56

Micah

3:6	83n56

Nahum

1:1	83n56

Habakkuk

1:1–11	24
1:5	23, 24, 150
2:2–3	83n56

Zechariah

10:2	83n56

NEW TESTAMENT

Matthew

26:28	49n73

Mark

1:4	49n73
1:4–15	50
1:14–15	57
5:22	125n60
6:1–6	38

Luke

1:5–2:52	47
1:5–3:1	71
1:9–11	35n4
1:24	40
1:32	92n82, 143
1:32–33	87
1:35	58
1:41	75n39
1:67	75n39
1:77	48, 49n73
1:78–79	49
2:4	40, 53
2:11	50n77, 134
2:30–32	49
2:32	23, 28, 47
2:34	54
2:34b	28
2:35	47
2:37–38	35n4
2:39	40
2:49	92n82
2:51	40
3:1–20	135
3:1–4:13	35
3:3	91
3:3–24:51	71
3:7–16	91
3:8	136, 136n109
3:15–16	135
3:15–17	35
3:16	69, 74n36, 75, 94
3:21	35, 105, 106
3:21–22	35, 47, 106n114, 108, 159
3:21–38	37
3:21–4:13	35
3:22	35, 36, 45, 46n55, 47, 69, 75n38, 105, 106, 143
3:23	36, 73
3:23–37	35, 105, 106
3:23–38	36
3:38	35, 37
4	58, 59, 59n109, 177
4:1	35, 36, 69
4:1–13	35, 37, 105, 106n115
4:3	35
4:9	35
4:13	38
4:14	40, 58, 69, 107
4:14–15	38, 51n82, 57, 107, 152
4:14–9:50	35
4:15	38, 40, 41
4:16	38, 124
4:16–22	39
4:16–27	95n87
4:16–30	28, 29, 32, 34–64, 105–6, 107, 109, 110, 124, 125n62, 192
4:16ab	39, 40
4:16b–20	39
4:16c	39, 41
4:16c–20	39, 41–49
4:16c–20a	39, 41–49
4:17	53
4:17a	39, 41
4:17b	39, 41
4:18	36, 43, 47, 48, 49n72, 49n73, 58, 69

Scripture Index

Luke–continued

4:18–19	39, 41, 43, 44, 47n63, 58, 60, 62, 63, 177
4:19	43, 44, 53
4:20–22	55n96
4:20a	39, 42
4:20b	39, 42
4:20c	39, 42
4:20d	39, 49
4:21	40, 50, 62
4:21–22	40, 50–52
4:22	38, 40, 50–52, 54, 55, 57, 152
4:23	40, 44, 50, 51, 52–53, 54, 55
4:23–27	40, 52–55, 55, 63
4:23–29	40, 52–56
4:23–30	39, 55n96
4:24	38, 40, 41, 53–54, 53n91, 54
4:25–26	40, 54–55
4:25–27	54, 55, 59
4:27	40, 53, 54–55
4:28	54
4:28–29	40, 55–56
4:28–30	55
4:30	40, 56–57
4:31	41, 56, 57, 152
4:31–37	38, 60
4:31–41	100
4:32	57, 59, 152
4:32–36	51n82
4:33	41
4:38–39	38
4:38–41	47
4:40–41	38
4:41	47
4:42–44	38
4:43	44n44, 59, 60, 68, 173
4:43–44	47, 59–60, 177
4:44	41
5:1	59
5:3	57
5:12–16	61
5:17	57
5:17–26	100
5:20	61
5:22	52
5:24	61
5:26	50n77
5:27–32	61
5:29–30	60
5:30	61
5:32	61
6:6	41, 58, 152
6:8	52
6:11	63
6:13	72, 115
6:20	184
6:20b–22	48
7:1–10	61, 64
7:2–53	62
7:11–17	61
7:16	59
7:22	62
7:28	184
7:31–35	63
7:39–40	52
7:47	48
7:48	60
8:1	60, 173, 184
8:26–39	61, 64
9:1–19	3
9:2	173, 184
9:6	60
9:8	59
9:11	184
9:19	59
9:22	67, 74n34, 132
9:31	74n34
9:35	59, 143
9:41	63, 93
9:44	67, 74n34
9:47	52
9:51	28, 66, 74, 74n34
9:51–19:27	35, 73
10:9–11	184
10:9–16	3

Scripture Index 231

11:5–17	3	23:14	138
11:13	69n12, 94	23:22	138
11:17	52	23:23–25	138
11:20	68n7, 184	23:26	55
11:29	93	23:42	184
11:29–37	64	23:43	50n77
12:28	50n77	23:50—Acts 1:26	71n23
12:31–32	184	23:53	139, 139n114
13:10	41, 58, 152	23:56b–24:53	35
13:10–17	60, 61	24	66, 66n2, 67, 67n5
13:14	125n60	24:1	68
13:32–33	50n77	24:1–49	66
13:33	59	24:5	67
15:1–2	60	24:6	132
15:10	61	24:13	68
15:32	61	24:18	67
16:16	73, 184	24:19	59, 67
17:11–19	61	24:24–30	72n27
17:20–21	184	24:26–27	66, 73, 139
17:25	67	24:28	68
18:29	184	24:30	67
18:31	62	24:32	73
18:31–33	67	24:36	68
19:1–10	61	24:36–48	67
19:5	50n77	24:38	67
19:9	50n77	24:41–42	87n70
19:10	61	24:44	62, 87n70, 102, 138
19:11	184	24:44–45	73, 94
19:28–21:38	35	24:44–53	67
19:35–43	61	24:45–46	169
20:1	60	24:46	62, 94, 102n
20:41–44	92n82	24:47	48, 61, 67, 70, 91, 102, 149
21:31	184	24:47–48	94
22:1–23:56	35	24:48	67, 88, 140
22:3–16	3	24:49	58, 68, 69, 70, 73, 74, 75, 78, 79, 92n82, 94
22:15–20	30	24:50	68
22:29–30	72	24:51	71
22:30	184	24:52—Acts 1:3–28:31	71
22:34	50n77	26:2–18	3
22:37	62, 67, 139		
22:47–23:25	28		
22:56	49		
22:61	50n77		
23:4	138		

John

19:38–42	139n114
20:22–23	75n37

Acts

1:1–2	67
1:1–12	67, 105
1:1–26	66
1:1–8:4	66
1:2	69, 69n11, 71, 71n, 75, 115
1:2–3	94
1:3	67, 68, 88, 139, 174, 184, 186
1:4	69, 74, 78, 94
1:4–5	69
1:5	68, 69n11, 70, 73, 74, 78
1:6	186
1:7–8	70
1:8	23, 26, 27, 35, 68, 69n11, 70, 73, 74, 78, 88, 94, 99, 115, 116, 132, 140, 184
1:9	71
1:9–10	71n
1:10	49
1:10–11	71n
1:11	71n
1:12	72
1:13–14	72, 105, 106, 159
1:14	108
1:15–26	66, 78, 105, 106n115
1:16	69n11, 73, 87n70, 102
1:20	87n70
1:21	28, 68, 73, 102
1:21–22	67
1:22	71n, 88, 140, 173
1:24	115
1:26	78
1:32	117
1:35	117
2	11, 74n36, 95, 147
2–5	101
2–13	14, 15, 15n52, 32
2:1	73
2:1–4	73, 105, 106
2:1–12	98n93
2:1–13	73, 78, 79, 84
2:1–8:4	66, 140
2:2–4	108
2:3	78
2:3–4	73
2:4	69n11, 73, 75, 78, 94, 107, 159
2:5	65, 75, 104
2:5–13	73, 75, 105
2:7	150
2:9–11	106
2:9–11a	75
2:11	76, 82, 95, 99, 104
2:11b	75
2:14	76, 77, 78–79, 79n49, 90, 91
2:14–16	13
2:14–21	77, 78–84
2:14–36	76n43
2:14–39	14
2:14–40	32, 34, 65–107, 108, 110, 192
2:14–41	29
2:14b–35	30
2:15–16	77, 79, 96
2:16–22	69
2:17	69n11, 80, 81, 82, 84, 92, 99, 104
2:17–18	82, 85, 88
2:17–21	77, 80–84, 97, 104
2:17–36	185
2:17–40	75n39
2:18	69n11, 81, 82, 99
2:19	99
2:19–20	82, 83
2:20–21	81
2:21	23, 76, 82, 83, 83n57, 89, 93, 101
2:22	12, 70, 76, 85, 96, 100, 126

2:22–24	77, 84, 85–86, 94, 97, 99, 136, 137	2:46	41
2:22–36	77, 84–90	2:47	93
2:23	85, 86n66, 94	3	11
2:23–24	90	3:1	41
2:23a	86n66	3:1–10	100
2:23b	86n66	3:4	49
2:23c	86n66	3:6	101
2:24	85, 86n66	3:12	13, 49, 70, 126, 150
2:24a	86n66	3:12–26	14, 62, 185
2:24b	86n66	3:13	12
2:24c	86n66	3:13–15	137
2:25	85, 86	3:14	138
2:25–28	77, 84, 86–87, 88, 97	3:15	102, 132, 140, 140n117
2:26–27	86	3:16	101
2:28	49n73	3:17	138
2:29	76, 84, 99, 119	3:17–18	102
2:29–31	77, 87, 88	3:19	91, 103
2:30	87, 143	3:22	117, 142n124
2:31	96	3:22–23	150
2:32	99, 140, 140n117	3:23	74n36
2:32–33	77, 88	3:24	131n90
2:33	58, 69, 69n11, 88, 92, 129	4:1	41
2:34	88, 89n75	4:1–3	100
2:34–35	77, 88–89	4:1–22	66
2:34b	86n68	4:3	117
2:36	72, 76, 76n43, 77, 79, 84, 86, 89–90, 96, 99, 104, 186	4:4	175
		4:7	70, 101
		4:8	69n11, 75n39, 99, 175
		4:9	117
2:36b	90	4:9–12	14
2:37	76, 77, 90, 91	4:10	79n49, 101, 132
2:37–40	77, 90–93	4:10–11	102
2:37–41	76, 76n43	4:11–12	150
2:37–42	76n43	4:12	101
2:38	48, 61, 69n11, 89, 91, 91, 95, 103, 149	4:13	119, 150
		4:17	101
2:38–39	77, 91–92	4:18	97, 101
2:38a	78, 91–92	4:20	97
2:38b–39	78, 92	4:21	100
2:39	104	4:23	101, 175
2:40	76, 77, 78, 89n76, 92–93, 103	4:24	101
		4:25	69n11, 87n70
2:41	76	4:25–28	143
2:43	100	4:26–27	46n55

Acts–continued

4:28	102
4:28–31	98n93
4:29	97, 119
4:29–30	165
4:29–31	99
4:30	100, 101
4:31	69n11, 75n39, 97, 98, 119, 161
4:32	101
4:33	70, 96, 97
4:35	111
4:36	100
4:36–37	111n
4:37	111
4:38	100
4:40	101
4:41	117
5	11
5:1	111
5:3	69n11
5:9	69n11
5:12	41, 100, 165
5:14	96
5:17–42	66
5:20	78, 136
5:21	97
5:25	97
5:28	97, 101
5:29	13, 102
5:30	102, 132
5:30–31	137
5:30–32	14, 97
5:31	48, 49n73, 61, 91, 103, 129, 134, 149
5:32	69n11, 140, 140n117
5:35	126
5:36–37	9n
5:38	24
5:40	101
5:41	101
5:42	41, 96
6:2	136, 161
6:4	115
6:5	69n11
6:7	97, 136
6:8	70, 100
6:9	111n5
6:9–11	120
6:9–14	119
6:10	99
6:12	175
6:13	120
6:15	49
7:1–53	55
7:2	136
7:2–50	128n78
7:4–8:4	66
7:6	131
7:23	131
7:30	131
7:31	83, 150
7:36	99, 131
7:37	59, 142n124
7:39–43	130
7:39–45	130
7:42	131
7:45	130
7:51	69n11, 103
7:51–52	112
7:51–53	128n78
7:52	112
7:55	49, 69n11, 98
7:55–56	83
7:58	110, 112, 159
8:1–2	159
8:3	111, 111n5, 112
8:4	97, 120
8:5	96, 97, 104
8:5–40	66, 140
8:12	60, 68, 97, 101, 184, 185, 186
8:13	70
8:14	97, 161
8:14–24	120
8:15	69n11, 98n93
8:16	101
8:16–17	98

Scripture Index 235

8:17–19	69n11	9:28–30	119
8:22	91	9:28b	119
8:25	97, 161	9:28b–29a	119
8:29	69n11, 98n93	9:29	120
8:34	138	9:30	120, 170
8:35	97	9:31	69, 69n11, 120
8:37	117	9:34	102n107
8:39	69n11, 98n93	9:35	91
8:40	97	9:42	96
9	111, 112	10	11, 29, 116n36
9:1	112	10:1ff.	155
9:1–12:25	140	10:2	168
9:1–15:35	66	10:2–6	35n4
9:1–19a	112–16	10:3	83
9:1–31	159	10:4	49
9:3–10	83	10:9–16	35n4
9:4	112	10:17	83
9:11–12	35n4	10:19	69n11, 83, 98n93
9:12	83	10:22	126, 155
9:13–14	118	10:25	21
9:14	101	10:34f.	155
9:15	28, 101, 104, 114, 115, 121, 162, 187, 199	10:34–35	13
		10:34–43	14
9:15–16	115, 116, 118	10:35	104, 126
9:15–18	114n24	10:36	59
9:16	101, 116	10:37	73, 173
9:17	69n11, 98	10:37–41	137
9:17–20	99	10:38	40, 46, 69n11, 70, 100
9:19	132, 184	10:39	140, 140n117
9:19b	119	10:39–40	102
9:19b–25	116	10:40	132
9:20	116, 118, 122, 151, 173, 175	10:41	140
		10:42	150
9:20–22	119	10:43	27, 48, 49n73, 61, 101, 149
9:20–25	119		
9:21	101	10:44	69n11, 98n93
9:22	151	10:44–46	98
9:23–25	170	10:45	69n11
9:25–31	118–21	10:45–48	104
9:26	114, 118	10:47	69n11
9:27	101, 111n, 118	10:48	101
9:27–28	119	11:1	161
9:27–29	119	11:5	83
9:28	101, 119, 122, 151	11:6	49

Acts—continued

11:12	69n11, 98n93
11:13	78
11:15	69n11, 98
11:16	69n11, 73
11:18	103
11:19	120
11:20–21	96
11:21	91
11:22–26	120
11:23–24	99
11:24	69n11
11:25	120
11:25–26	120
11:26	122, 151
11:28	69n11
12:25	120
13	11, 13, 15, 16, 18, 115
13–14	165
13:1–14:28	66, 121–22
13:1–28:28	110
13:1–28:31	66
13:2	24, 35n4, 69n11, 98, 98n93, 121, 150, 159
13:3	166
13:4	69n11, 98n93
13:4–6	166
13:5	41, 115, 117, 122, 124, 151, 161, 173, 175
13:7	121, 127, 161
13:9	49, 69n11, 75n39, 121, 121n50, 132
13:12	127
13:13	121, 127n71, 166
13:13–16	117
13:13–52	17
13:14	41, 124, 166, 169, 173, 175
13:14–41	191
13:14–43	122
13:14–52	28
13:15	42, 42n36, 124, 125, 125n62, 127n71
13:15–41	115
13:16	22, 122, 123n54, \ 126, 127
13:16–22	12
13:16–23	15, 20
13:16–25	22, 123n54, 135
13:16–39	186
13:16–41	1, 5, 11–31, 32, 33, 34, 65, 110–51, 153, 158, 159, 165, 176, 181, 183, 185, 186
13:16–49	186
13:16–52	28
13:16a–22	21
13:16b	123, 126–27
13:16b–23	20
13:16b–25	17, 25, 123, 125–36, 160
13:16b–41	25, 30, 125
13:17	127n71, 128, 129, 134, 136, 141
13:17–20	123, 128–31
13:17–20a	20
13:17–22	17, 18, 19, 23, 125n64
13:17–23	18, 26, 123, 128–34, 133n99
13:17–25	125n64
13:17b–23	22
13:18	129, 130, 131
13:18–20a	130
13:19	130
13:19–20a	130
13:20	131
13:21	128, 131
13:21–23	123, 131–36
13:22	132, 133, 134, 183
13:22–23	143, 160, 186
13:23	18, 20, 21, 26, 126, 127n71, 128, 129, 134, 136, 137, 138, 140, 142, 146, 147, 163, 182
13:23–25	12
13:24	18, 127n71, 128
13:24–25	18, 19, 22, 73, 123, 134–36, 173

Scripture Index

13:24–26	20	13:34–35	141, 144
13:25	18, 135	13:34–36	147
13:26	20, 22, 122, 123, 123n54, 126, 127n71, 129, 136, 136n109, 137, 140, 142, 163	13:34–37	144
		13:34a	24
		13:34b	24
		13:35	145, 147
13:26–31	22	13:35–37	24
13:26–37	17, 22, 25, 26, 123, 123n54, 136–47, 142, 143	13:36	26, 102, 129
		13:36–37	123, 147
		13:37	128, 132
13:26b–31a	18	13:38	17, 18, 21, 22, 24, 48, 49n73, 61, 79n49, 122, 123n54, 127n71, 134, 161
13:27	137, 138, 139, 140, 141		
13:27–28	137		
13:27–29	139		
13:27–31	20, 123, 137–40	13:38f.	21
13:27–33	24	13:38–39	17, 21, 22, 24, 124, 135, 146, 147, 148–49
13:28–30	102		
13:29	139, 141		
13:30	128, 132, 134, 139	13:38–41	12, 19, 20, 22, 25, 123, 123n54, 147–50
13:30–34	180		
13:30–37	17		
13:31	12, 26, 127n71, 128, 140, 140n117, 163	13:38–51	17
		13:38a	123, 148
13:31b	18	13:39	18, 27, 104, 127, 148, 161, 171, 176
13:31b–37	19		
13:32	18, 21, 127n71, 129, 134, 140, 141	13:40	18, 21, 161
		13:40–41	22, 103, 124, 150
13:32–33	17, 127n71, 160, 182, 188, 195	13:41	18, 24, 122, 127n71, 138, 150, 161, 162
13:32–35	123, 138, 140–47	13:42	125, 160, 162, 170
13:32–37	20, 22, 139, 182, 186	13:42f.	165
13:32–39	185	13:42–43	160
13:32–41	23	13:42–52	160–64
13:32–52	23	13:42–14:28	160–65
13:32b–33a	140	13:43	122, 127, 161, 165, 168, 177, 185
13:33	17, 21, 128, 129, 134, 141, 143, 144, 146, 163, 182		
		13:43–14:28	153
13:33–34	117	13:44	161, 162, 169, 197
13:33–35	143	13:44–45	161
13:33–36	87n70	13:44–47	172
13:33–37	18	13:45	161, 162
13:33b	24, 141	13:46	15n54, 17, 21, 119, 124, 161, 162, 163, 164, 197
13:34	127n71, 142, 143, 144, 146, 147, 163		

Acts–continued

Reference	Pages
13:46–47	25
13:47	23, 27, 104, 136, 136n109
13:48	15n54, 17, 21, 161
13:50	126, 168
13:50–51	170
13:51	164, 166
13:52	69n11
14	15n52
14–17	15, 32
14:1	41, 117, 162, 166, 169, 173, 175, 197
14:1–7	115
14:1–28	164–65
14:3	100, 119, 165
14:5	165
14:6	166
14:6–7	165
14:8	166
14:8–20	115
14:9	49
14:14–18	155
14:15	91
14:20	166, 170
14:22	60, 68, 174, 184, 186
14:23	175
14:25	166
14:26	24, 121, 166
14:27	104
15	28, 64, 140n117
15:2	175
15:3	91, 115
15:4	175
15:6	175
15:7	115, 177
15:7–11	149
15:7–12	66
15:8	69n11
15:10–12	167
15:11	96, 149, 177
15:12	100
15:16	72n26
15:19	91
15:22	115, 166, 175
15:23	175
15:25	115
15:26	101
15:28	69n11, 98
15:35	161
15:36	161
15:36–22:21	66
15:38	24
15:40	166
15:40–20:38	153, 166–78
16:3	166
16:4	175
16:6	69n11, 98n93
16:6f.	98
16:7	69n11, 98n93
16:9–10	83
16:10	166
16:11–40	167–68
16:13	117, 168, 169
16:14	126, 168, 198
16:16	117, 168, 169
16:18	101
16:31	176
16:32	136, 161
16:35–39	138
16:40	168
17	15n52
17:1	117, 164, 169, 173
17:1–3	175
17:1–2	175
17:1–3	115, 169
17:1–9	168–70
17:2	41, 124, 164, 170
17:2–3	185
17:3	169, 170
17:4	126, 171
17:10	41, 169, 175
17:10–11	115, 138
17:10–15	170–71
17:11	170
17:13	170, 171
17:16	155
17:16–17	115, 197
17:16–34	171

Scripture Index   239

17:17	126, 169, 171, 172, 173, 175
17:18	171
17:22	78
17:22–31	115
17:22–41	158
17:22b–31	30
17:30	103, 171
17:30–31	150, 176
17:31	74n36, 171
18:1–17	171–73
18:4	41, 117, 169, 172, 173, 175, 185
18:4–5	115
18:4–6	162
18:5	172, 185
18:5–7	172
18:6	173, 197
18:7	126, 197, 198
18:8	96, 125n60
18:9	83
18:11	161
18:13	126
18:14–16	138
18:17	125n60
18:18	21, 171
18:18–19	115
18:19	162, 169, 173, 175
18:25	73, 173
18:26	41, 119, 172, 175
19:1	98n93
19:1–41	173–75
19:2	69n11
19:3–4	73
19:5	101
19:6	69n11, 98n93
19:8	41, 60, 68, 115, 117, 119, 162, 169, 173, 174, 175, 184, 185, 186
19:9	169, 174
19:10	136, 161
19:11	70
19:13	101
19:14	173
19:17	101
19:17–18	175
19:21	28, 98, 102
19:26	185
19:27	126
19:31	138
19:37	138
20:1	175
20:2	175
20:9	169
20:18–21	175
20:18–35	158, 175
20:18–38	175–78
20:18b–35	30
20:21	96, 103, 176, 178
20:22	98n93
20:22f.	98
20:22–27	175
20:23	69n11
20:24	176
20:25	60, 68, 174, 176, 184, 185, 186
20:26–27	197
20:27	102, 176
20:28	69n11
20:32	176
21–28	157
21:1–23:22	178–80
21:1–28:31	153, 178–87
21:4	69n11, 98
21:11	69n11, 98
21:13	101
21:18	175
21:19	178
21:21	178, 200
21:23–24	178
21:26	41
21:27–26:32	28
21:28	120, 126, 156, 178
22	112, 112n13
22–26	184
22:3–21	189
22:15	115, 187
22:16	101

Acts–continued

22:17–21	35n4
22:20	111
22:22–28:31	66
22:30–23:1	179
22:30–23:10	179
22:70	117
23	180
23:1	49, 189
23:3	189
23:5	179
23:5–6	189
23:6	179, 184
23:11	102
23:14	175
23:23–26:32	180–83
23:29	138
24	180
24:1	175
24:9–21	180
24:13–16	156
24:15	180, 184
24:21	180
24:24	181
24:25	169
24:44	139
25:14–19	138
25:15	175
25:18	78
25:18–19	179
25:19	181
25:23–26:29	115
25:25	179
26	112, 112n13
26:2–23	189
26:3	138, 181
26:6	183
26:6–7	72, 184
26:6–8	181, 182
26:9	101
26:16–18	187
26:17	116
26:18	48, 49, 49n73, 61, 91, 149, 183
26:20	91
26:22	156
26:22–23	102n107, 181, 182, 185
26:23	23, 49, 180, 182
26:23b	27
26:25–27	189
26:26	119
26:27	183
26:29	189
26:31–32	179
27:1–28:10	184
27:1–28:31	183–87
27:21	78
27:23	83
28:17	156
28:17–20	184, 189
28:17–29	115
28:20	184
28:23	27, 60, 68, 174, 185, 186, 187, 189
28:23–28	115, 186
28:24	185
28:25	69n11
28:25–27	103
28:26–27	185
28:28	79n49, 137, 172, 197
28:30–31	116, 185, 189, 197
28:31	60, 68, 104, 119, 162, 174, 184, 186, 187

Romans

1:3–4	117
9–11	199
11:1	132

1 Corinthians

9:9–11	199
15	14
15:3–8	14
15:45	75n37

Galatians

1:17b	2
2	28

Philippians

3:5	132

Colossians

1:18	49n73

1 Thessalonians

1:9–10	10
1:10	117

Hebrews

1:5	142n128
5:5	142n128
5:11–6:2	10
10:18	49n73
13:22	125, 125n61, 125n62

APOCRYPHA AND SEPTUAGINT

1 Esdras

4:29	88
9:43	88

2 Esdras

19	9

1 Maccabees

2:57	146

3 Maccabees

7:20	167

Sirach

4:10	117n39

Wisdom of Solomon

11:23	91
12:19	91

OLD TESTAMENT PSEUDEPIGRAPHA

Book of Jubilees

6:17–21	74

PHILO

On the Decalogue

33	74n36

THUCYDIDES

1.22.1	6

Subject/Name Index

Absicht und literarischer Charakter der Apostelgeschichte (Weiss), 3
Acts
    accounts of Peter and Paul in, incompleteness of, 2
    apologetic tone in, 9–10
    beginning to proclaim good news to the Gentiles, 23
    distinctive content of speeches in, 9
    functions of speeches in, 7, 11, 26, 96n91
    interpreting speeches in, as a whole, 25
    literary unity of, 17
    Luke as source of speeches in, 5–6
    main character of, 3
    modern critical study of, beginnings of, 2
    portrayal of Jesus' resurrection in, 17
    purpose of, 3
    reliability of, 2
    repetition in speeches of, 10–14, 25
    sources of speeches in, 3–6
    speeches related to Greco-Roman historiography, 6
    speeches related to narrative settings, 96–97
    speeches resembling Deuteronomistic History speeches, 9
    thematic unity of, 17
    traditional view of, in 17th and 18th centuries, 1
    turning point of, as sermon in Pisidia, 15
Aletti, Jean-Noël, 63–64n129
anti-Jewish tendency, in Luke-Acts interpretation, 153–55
apologetic speeches, 4
apostles' mission, character of, as theme in Peter's inaugural sermon, 99–100
apostrophes, dividing text into three parts in three successive moments, 22
Athens, as scene for Paul's speech to the Gentiles, reasons for, 13

Bajard, Jean, 53n91
baptism, associated with repentance and forgiveness, 91–92
Barrett, Charles K., 126–27, 75n38, 83n58, 133n95, 137n112, 164–65, 177
Baur, Ferdinand C., 2–3
Billerbeck, Paul, 42n36
Bock, Darrell L., 47, 75n39, 176
Bossuyt, Philippe, 121n49
Bovon, François, 36
Brawley, Robert L., 29, 59n109, 74n36, 155, 156
Bruce, Frederick F., 125n60, 131n87, 139n114, 142
Bultmann, Rudolf, 49
Buss, Mattäus J., 19–21, 32, 133, 136n109, 144n133
Busse, Ulrich, 39

Cadbury, Henry J., 6–7
Capernaum, Jesus' compatriots' jealousy of, 52–53
chiastic structure, 39–42
Christian message
    communicated to the Jews, in the early church, 16–17
    universal dimension of, 27

244 Subject/Name Index

conversion, as one-step process, 176
Conzelmann, Hans, 10, 50n77, 144n134
covenantal promise, 146
creed, three types of, in Paul's speech, 22

David
   connection with Jesus emphasized, 133–35
   prophesying Jesus' resurrection, 96
   prophetic foreknowledge of the Messiah, 87
Delebecque, Éduoard, 43–44n40
Denova, Rebecca I., 114n24
de Sandt, Huub van, 23–25
Desilva, David A., 23
de Wette, Wilhelm M. L., 5
Dibelius, Martin, 4, 7, 8–13, 20, 25, 31–32, 135, 191–92
Dillon, Richard J., 67nn3, 4
Dodd, Charles H., 10
Doeve, Jan W., 16
dreams, as prophetic modes, 82–83
Dumais, Marcel, 16–17, 125n62
Dupont, Jacques, 14, 67n5, 74n36, 145, 186–87

Eichhorn, Johann G., 5, 10
elders, emergence of, in Christian community, 175
Ellul, Danielle, 22, 123n54
eschatological prophet, anointing of, 46–47
evangelizing speeches, uniform elements in, 10n34
exegetical inquiry, into speech in Antioch of Pisidia, variations of, 18–19

faith, summed up in acceptance of Jesus' resurrection, 176
Fearghail, Fearghus, 51n81
fire, metaphorical meanings of, 74n36
Fitzymer, Joseph A., 10, 11, 46, 48n66, 54, 55n96, 68n7, 71, 72n30, 74n36, 76n34, 79n51, 87n70, 91–92nn80–81, 111, 116n36, 117n39, 118, 121n50, 126, 131, 133n95, 139n114, 139n116, 145n135, 148, 161n35, 165, 167, 169n66, 174, 177, 180, 181–82, 184–85
Flichy, Odile, 113–14n22, 129n84, 133n99, 186
forgiveness, 21, 24
form criticism, 4–11
fulfillment, as central theme in Luke-Acts, 32, 62

Garcia, N. Esaú, 30–31
Gasque, W. Ward, 2, 8n27
Gaventa, Beverly Roberts, 139n116
Gentiles
   history of, as history of idolatry, 155
   preaching to, as part of God's saving purpose, 162
   understanding, in Acts, 200
gezerah shavah, 44, 61, 145
Glombitza, Otto, 19, 125n62
God
   authority of, 26
   in control of Israel's history, 174
   foreknowledge in Jesus, as theme Peter's inaugural sermon, 101–2
   fulfillment of plan of, 26
   grace of, 161, 177
   graciousness and promise to Israel, 128–31
   making Jesus Lord and Messiah, 89–90
   plan of, as theme in Peter's inaugural sermon, 101–2
   promising Israel a savior, 133–34
   right hand of, significance of, 88–89
   saving purpose of, for all human beings, 177–78
   as sole actor in Israel's history, 130–31
God-fearers, 127
Goldsmith, Dale, 16
grace, gospel of, 176–77
Grotius, Hugo, 1
Grundmann, Walter, 49n72
Gunkel, Hermann, 4

Subject/Name Index 245

Haenchen, Ernst, 3, 10, 112, 148, 176
Hauser, Hermann, 186
historians, methodology of, for recording speeches, 6–7
Holtz, Traugott, 43n39
Holy Spirit
  active in the infancy narrative, 69–70
  as driving force in Acts, 69
  linked with OT prophecy, 69
  power of, 70
  as source of prophecy, 99
  theme of, in Peter's inaugural sermon, 97–98
  as theme in Luke-Acts, 58

ignorance, motif of, 138
Israel
  calling for a king, 131–33
  creed of, literary scheme of, 17
  God's election of and graciousness toward, 128–31
  history of, 15, 174
  messianic promise to, meaning of, 163
  Paul's selective history of, 128
  repentant, reestablishment of, 103

Jeremias, Joachim, 51
Jerusalem, emphasis on and significance of, 68–69
Jervell, Jacob, 117, 153–56, 158, 167, 175, 199
Jesus. *See also* Jesus, inaugural sermon of
  announcing Jubilee Year, 49
  ascension of, 71–72
  baptism of, 35–36, 37, 45–46
  as center of Scripture, 66–67
  character of his ministry, as theme in Luke-Acts, 60–61
  completing his mission, 56
  connection with David emphasized, 133–35
  death of, contrast formula in relation to, 85–86
  forty-day instruction of, 68n6, 69
  fulfilling OT prophecies, 62, 88, 96, 147
  as fulfillment of the promise, scriptural proof of, 140–47
  genealogy of, 36–37
  habitually going to the synagogue, 41
  identifying himself as a prophet, 53–55
  identity of, 37
  incorruptibility of, 146–47
  innocence of, emphasized, 138
  manifesting God's power, 85
  as a messianic prophet, as theme in Luke-Acts, 59
  ministry of, compared with ministries of Elijah and Elisha, 46–47
  mission of, four groups of people as objects, 47–49
  proclaimed as the Messiah, 70, 96
  recognized as the Messiah, 137–38
  rejection of, after his inaugural sermon, 55–56
  resurrection of, fulfilling the promises to the ancestors, 140–47, 182
  Spirit coming upon, 36, 45–46
  temptation of, 37–38
Jesus, inaugural sermon of
  announcing main themes in Luke-Acts, 58–64
  interpreting Isaiah's prophecies and audience's response, 50–52
  Jesus leaving Nazareth after, 56–57
  Jesus responding to audience's response, 52–56
  literary context of, 35–38
  literary function of, 57–64, 107–9
  as model for later preaching, 57–58, 152–53, 159
  parallel literary context with Peter's inaugural sermon, 105–6
  presented in Nazareth, 40–41
  reading from Isaiah and audience's response, 41–49
  repeated words and grammatical forms in, 45
  structure of, 38–40

Subject/Name Index

Jews
    four beliefs for, in Acts, 183n
    positive attitude toward, in Acts, 155
John the Baptist, bearing witness, 134–36
Johnson, Luke Timothy, 46, 59n110, 70n20, 74n36, 75n37, 76n34, 83n56, 85n64, 98n93, 100, 106n114, 111, 131n90, 137n111, 169, 172
Jubilee Year, 49
Juel, Donald, 155
Jülicher, Adolf, 6
justification, 21, 24

Kepple, Robert J., 181
kerygma, christological, 137–40
Kilgallen, John J., 21, 60n114, 89–90n75, 92n82, 147
Kilpatrick, George D., 80–81
kingdom of God, 68, 173–74
Koenig, Jean, 44n43
Koet, Bart J., 39, 50n79, 51n82
Korn, Manfred, 51n82
Kurz, William, 36

Lentz, John, Jr., 157
Lichler, Josef, 27–29
Lightfoot, John, 1
Lövestam, Evald, 145–46
Lüdemann, Gerd, 111
Lukan scholarship, 198–99
Luke
    following literary technique of ancient historiography, 8–9
    inventing the missionary speech, 8, 13–14
    linking beginning of Acts with the end of his Gospel, 67–68
    literary creativity of, 20
    narrating Jesus' ascension twice, 71
    preparing for Jesus' inaugural sermon, 159
    preparing for Paul's inaugural sermon, 158–59
    preparing for Peter's inaugural sermon, 159
    prophetic role of Moses and Elijah in, 70–71n20
    sources of, 4
    using geography to structure and advance his narrative, 35

Maddox, Robert, 156–57
Malina, Bruce J., 79n48, 127n76, 157–58
Marshall, I. Howard, 44n44, 174
Matera, Frank, 59n112, 89n75, 149n150
Meier, John, 46
Messiah, source and meaning of title, 118n42
methodology, historical research in, 27–29
Metzger, Bruce M., 129–30n85, 140n117
midrash
    establishing analogies with other scriptural texts, 31
    homiletic, Acts speech as, 16–17
Miletus address, 4, 175–78
missionary speeches, 4
    Luke's invention of, 8, 13–14
    uniform elements in, 10, 12
mission to the Gentiles, as theme in Luke-Acts, 63–64
Moessner, David P., 101–2n104, 155
Mosaic Law, risen Lord replacing, 148–49

narrative-critical method, 158, 188
Nathan oracle, interpretative tradition of, 16
Neyrey, Jerome, 157
Nolland, John, 46
Noorda, S.J., 52n86
Noth, Martin, 25

O'Toole, Robert F., 17

Paley, William, 1–2
Paul. *See also* Paul, inaugural sermon to the Jews
    affirming belief in resurrection of the dead, 180–81
    in Athens, 171
    attacked after preaching, 165
    becoming key character in Acts, 122, 159

Subject/Name Index 247

in Beroea, 170–71
changed role for, in proclaiming the
  good news, 122
choosing new coworkers, 166
comparing, between Acts and the
  Pauline epistles, 1–2
in Corinth, 171–73
dealing with relationship between
  loyal Christians and loyal Jews,
  179–80
defending his Jewish identity and
  loyalty, 179
distinguishing diaspora Jews from
  those in Jerusalem, 138
emphasizing connection between
  David and Jesus, 133–35
encounter with Christ, Luke
  describing three times, 112
in Ephesus, 173–75
first and last speeches of,
  thematically connected, 183
first missionary journey of, as
  paradigm for future missions,
  164–65
first use of name, 121
going to the synagogue first, 164–65,
  169
life of, paralleling Jesus' life, 30
linking Judaism and Christianity,
  180, 185–87
in Miletus, 4, 175–78
ministry to Israel, during second
  and third missionary journeys,
  166–87
organizing a chronology of his life,
  199–200
in Philippi, 167–68
portrayal of, approached through
  sociological method, 157
postconversion career of, divided
  into three periods, 156–57
preaching to the Gentiles, 171
preparation of, 122
presented as defending his
  Jewishness and as a missionary
  to Israel, 156
as prisoner and missionary, 178–87

recalling his missionary preaching,
  175–77
reception and description of, in Acts,
  28–29
sermon to the Jews, on the
  subsequent Sabbath in Antioch
  of Pisidia, 160–64
shifting focus from general
  resurrection to faith in Christ
  Jesus, 181–82
shifting mission of, 172
speeches of, synoptic analysis of, 30
summarizing his preaching as the
  gospel of the grace of God,
  176–77
in Thessalonica, 168–70
three aspects of his ministry in Acts,
  153
three full-length sermons of, in Acts,
  158
Paul, inaugural sermon to the Jews
  addressing his audience, 148
  audience for, 126–27
  building connections with his
    audience, 129
  as core of evangelization realized by
    Antioch missionaries, 30–31
  five notable characteristics, 160
  four themes in, 25–27
  immediate context for, 121–22
  as inaugural sermon, 32–33, 34
  inaugurating evangelization of Asia
    Minor, 30
  Jewish character of, 160
  as the last call to the Jews, 32
  literary context of, 110–22
  as model for his preaching, 159,
    161–62
  parallel to Peter's speech, 29
  salvation message in, 136–47
  serving as model for Paul's later
    preaching, 153
  significance of location, 124
  structure of, 122–24
  variations of exegetical inquire in,
    18–19

Subject/Name Index

Paul—continued
   warning his listeners not to scoff at God's message, 150
Pentecost, 73–76
   significance of, relative to the prophet Joel, 79–84
   three types of, 79n51
Pervo, Richard I., 68n9, 83n59, 149n151
Peter. *See also* Peter, inaugural sermon of
   proclaiming Jesus as Lord and Messiah, 96
   as prototype for preaching the gospel to the Gentiles, 29
Peter, inaugural sermon of
   announcing Acts' main themes, 97–105
   call to repentance and promise of salvation, 90–93
   Christological argument in, 84–90
   as foundation for the missionary sermons in Acts, 95–97
   immediate literary context of, 73–76
   laying foundation for his missionary sermons, 152–53
   literary context of, 66–76
   literary function of, 94–105, 107–9
   as model for apostles' response to Jesus' instruction and commission after resurrection, 94–95
   as model for his preaching, 159
   opening address, 78–79
   parallel literary context with Jesus' inaugural sermon, 105–6
   presenting significance of Pentecost from the prophet Joel, 79–84
   structure of, 76–78
Peterson, David G., 139n115, 141n120
Pilch, John J., 79n48, 127n76, 157–58
Pillai, Christie A. Joachim, 18–19, 32, 125n64
place of prayer, 167–68
Plümacher, Eckhard, 8–9, 162
Poirier, John C., 56n98
Porter, Stanley E., 8n27
Portraits of Paul (Malina and Neyrey), 157

postapostolic time, 28
proclaiming the good news, as theme in Luke-Acts, 59–60
promise, as central theme, 32
prophecy, as theme in Luke-Acts, 62
prophets, rejection of, 53–55
Puskas, Charles B., 179n94, 187

Quesnel, Michel, 30

Ravens, David, 47
redaction-criticism method, 19–20
redemptive history, 19
rejection, as theme in Luke-Acts, 62–63
repentance
   call to, 90–91
   connected with forgiveness, 91
   as theme in Peter's inaugural sermon, 102–3
repetition, as feature of speeches in Acts, 10–14, 25
resurrection
   bearing witness to, importance of, 70
   belief in, as link between Judaism and Christianity, 180
   as enthronement ritual, 143
   fulfilling the OT promise, 20–21, 31, 88, 96, 136, 139–47, 182
   as mystery of salvation, 30
   OT proof for, 86–87
   as part of God's plan, 86
   portrayal of, in Acts, 17
   proper response to, 183
   scriptural proof text of, 24
   significance of, 24
revelational history, 19
Roth, Samuel, J., 47n63

sacred history, process of, 19
salvation, 21
   apostolic witnesses of, two stages in, 14–15
   as central theme in Acts, 103
   equivalent to eternal life, 162
   healing linked with, 101
   meaning of, 147–50

message of, in Paul's inaugural
    sermon to the Jews,
    portrayal of, in Acts, 17
    preaching first to the Jews, 162–63
    promise of, 92–93
    as theme in Peter's inaugural sermon,
        100–101
    universal, as theme in Peter's
        inaugural sermon, 104–5
    worldwide, 177–78
salvation history, 15
    division of, 71–72
    programmatic understanding of, 20
Sanders, Jack T., 154
Sanders, James A., 45n49, 62n122
Saul. *See also* Paul
    as the arch-persecutor, 111
    assuming role of the martyr Stephen,
        120
    call of, 112–16
    at the martyrdom of Stephen, 110–12
    new relationship of, with the apostles
        and other disciples, 119
    preaching in Damascus, 116–18
    as transitional figure in Israel's
        history, 132
    visiting Jerusalem, 118–21
Schneckenburger, Matthias, 5–6
Schwanbeck, Eugen A., 2
Schweizer, Eduard, 10
Septugint, speeches in Acts related to,
    9–10
Sieber, John H., 71n23
signs and wonders, 99–100
sins
    acquittal of, 171
    forgiveness of, 61, 148
Soards, Marion L., 6, 8–10, 11, 25–27,
    102n107, 128n81, 132n91
*Social-Science Commentary on the Book
    of Acts* (Malina and Pilch), 157
Son of God, title of, 118
source criticism, 2, 3–4
speeches
    apologetic, 4
    comparing, with different bodies of
        literature, 8–9

evangelizing, 10n34
literary function of, in Acts, 7
missionary, 4, 8, 10, 12–14
purpose of, in historical literature, 7
Stanton, Graham N., 58n106, 58–59n108
Stephen, martyrdom of, 110–11
Steyn, Gert J., 86n66, 142
Strauss, Mark L., 142
synagogue
    description of services in, 42–43
    Jesus habitually going to, 41
    significance of, for Paul's inaugural
        sermon, 124
    Paul going first to, 164–65, 169

Talbert, Charles H., 68n6, 69n13, 72n27
Tannehill, Robert, 36, 45, 46, 69n14,
    96n91, 114, 115, 119, 155, 156,
    163, 166, 172, 179, 182, 184, 185
tendency criticism, 2–3, 153
Thucydides, 6, 7
Tiede, David L., 39, 47, 95n87, 103n110,
    155
Timothy, circumcision of, 166–67
tradition-historical analysis, 8
Trull, Gregory V., 86n67
Tübingen School, 2–3, 153
Twelve, restoration of, 72
two-period theory, 32
Tyson, Joseph B., 153, 179n93

Vanhoye, Albert, 51–52n84, 52n87
vision, as prophetic mode, 82–83

Wallace, Daniel B., 141n122, 176
Weiss, Johannes, 3
Wilckens, Ulrich, 8–9, 10–11, 13–15, 31,
    32, 153
Witherington, Ben, III, 89n75, 130n86,
    148
witness, 26
women, role of, in diaspora synagogue
    meetings, 168
Woodall, David L., 127

Zerwick, Maximilian, 176

www.ingramcontent.com/pod-product-compliance
Lightning Source LLC
Chambersburg PA
CBHW051105230426
43667CB00013B/2444